KANT'S DIALECTIC

KANT'S DIALECTIC

BY

JONATHAN BENNETT

PROFESSOR OF PHILOSOPHY AT THE
UNIVERSITY OF BRITISH COLUMBIA

CAMBRIDGE UNIVERSITY PRESS

Published by the Syndics of the Cambridge University Press
Bentley House, 200 Euston Road, London NW1 2DB
American Branch: 32 East 57th Street, New York, N.Y. 10022

© Cambridge University Press 1974

Library of Congress Catalogue Card Number: 73-89762

ISBNS: 0 521 20420 8 hard covers
0 521 09849 1 paperback

First published 1974

Printed in Great Britain
at the University Printing House, Cambridge
(Brooke Crutchley, University Printer)

CONTENTS

Preface   *page* viii

System of References   x

I INTRODUCTION
   1. Locating the subject-matter   1
   2. The main topics   3
   3. Background materials   5

2 CONCEPTS AND INTUITIONS
   4. The sensory/intellectual continuum   9
   5. Trouble from the continuum   12
   6. Kant's breakthrough   16
   7. Content *v.* activity   20
   8. Concepts and judgments   23
   9. Concept-empiricism   26
  10. The theory of categories   30
  11. Categories and 'innate ideas'   35

3 SUBSTANCES AND REALITY
  12. Substances and aggregates   40
  13. Cartesian substances   42
  14. Leibniz on substances and reality   44
  15. Leibniz on relations and reality   46
  16. Kant on reality   49
  17. Things in themselves   52
  18. Imposition and things in themselves   54
  19. Substances as sempiternal   56
  20. The balance principle   59
  21. Existence-changes and quantifiers   62

4 THE SUBSTANTIALITY OF THE SOUL
  22. The Cartesian basis   66
  23. The search for the thinking subject   69
  24. The soul as substance   72
  25. Inflating the first paralogism   76
  26. My death   78

CONTENTS

5 THE SIMPLICITY OF THE SOUL   *page*
    27. The soul as simple   82
    28. Mental fission   85
    29. Mental disunity   87
    30. Simplicity and immateriality   90

6 THE IDENTITY OF THE SOUL
    31. The third paralogism: blind alleys   93
    32. Locating the third paralogism   94
    33. Quasi-memory   97
    34. Kant's observer   100
    35. Identity and substrata   103
    36. Substrata: two sources   105
    37. Substrata: four consequences   108
    38. Strawson on the paralogisms   111

7 INFINITY
    39. The antinomies chapter   114
    40. The limits of the world   117
    41. Infinite tasks   121
    42. The futurizing move   123
    43. Infinite number   125
    44. Numbers and natural numbers   129
    45. The weakening move   132
    46. Infinite and indefinite   137

8 LIMITS
    47. Leibniz on space   143
    48. Leibniz on vacuum   146
    49. Why the world is not finite   151
    50. Other arguments   155
    51. Why the world did not begin   159

9 DIVISIBILITY
    52. Simple substances   163
    53. The divisibility of the extended   164
    54. Real divisibility   167
    55. Kant against atomism   170
    56. Substance and substances   174
    57. The supposed infinity problem   177
    58. The divisibility of space   180

CONTENTS

10 FREEDOM   *page*
    59. The third antinomy   184
    60. From cosmology to humanity   187
    61. The skeleton of a theory   189
    62. A reconciliation?   193
    63. Hume and Schlick   195
    64. Restricting determinism   199
    65. When does freedom occur?   201
    66. Reactive attitudes   204
    67. Kant and reactivity   209
    68. Agency   211
    69. Self-prediction   214
    70. Kant and agency   218
    71. Excuses for Kant's theory   223

11 GOD
    72. The Kant–Frege view   228
    73. Existence and necessary existence   232
    74. Why Malcolm's argument fails   234
    75. Aquinas's third way   237
    76. The fourth antinomy   240
    77. The cosmological argument   243
    78. The second step   247
    79. Kant's attack   250
    80. The radical criticism   253
    81. The argument from design   255

12 REASON
    82. Inferences of reason   258
    83. Ascending reason   260
    84. Conditions   264
    85. The source of dialectical error   267
    86. Regulative principles   270
    87. Are there any regulative principles?   274
    88. Regulative and constitutive   275
    89. The architectonic of the Dialectic   280
    90. Reason and cosmology   284

Index   289

PREFACE

This book is a sequel to my *Kant's Analytic*, but it does not presuppose knowledge of the earlier work. It is the only English book-length commentary on the Dialectic in Kant's *Critique of Pure Reason*. It may be suggested that one is one too many – that my book fills a welcome gap in the literature – but I would dispute that. I have found that the Dialectic, together with relevant materials from earlier philosophers, especially Descartes and Leibniz, provides the basis for a satisfactory course of fifty-odd classroom hours for graduate students and able undergraduates. Such a course covers a useful amount of 'history of philosophy', guided throughout by an interest in a varied but not too scattered set of philosophical problems. *Kant's Dialectic* might be a help, but what I am confidently recommending is a different work – Kant's Dialectic.

I continue to be, in the words of an unhappy reviewer of my earlier work, 'one of those commentators who are more interested in what Kant ought to have thought than in what he actually did think'. Still, I try to describe the Dialectic accurately and in some detail. This part of Kant's work is at once knottier and more interesting than is commonly supposed, but the interest is lost if the knots are left tied, and so my philosophical aims have driven me to endeavours which may count as scholarly.

The Dialectic is full of mistakes and inadequacies, or so I shall contend, and *of course* this is consistent with its being a valuable contribution to philosophy. Still, there are doubtless fewer mistakes than I allege: my charge-list has gradually shortened as I have gained in understanding of the work, and presumably it could be reduced further. But I have worked for as long as I am prepared to, and I now offer what now seems to me to be true. Anyway, when there is evidence of error the truth is better served by an open accusation than by a respectful averting of one's eyes, even in cases where the charge of error can eventually be refuted.

Throughout, I use existing translations of non-English works, modifying them where accuracy demands it. I follow Kemp Smith's translation of the *Critique* except for a few changes in the interests of clarity and a larger number of corrections of mistranslations which are philosophically significant. The most serious of the latter are noted as

viii

they arise. For help with the German – my knowledge of which is very limited – I am indebted to Lewis White Beck, Petra von Morstein and Margaret Jackson.

Kant's Dialectic grew out of teaching, scattered through a decade, at several universities. My largest block of indebtedness is to students at the University of British Columbia, where I have taught courses on the Dialectic in 1971–3. A few of them are named in the text, in acknowledgment of particular contributions; but to many others – far more than I could appropriately name in a Preface – I owe stimulation, encouragement, criticism and guidance of a high order.

I have been glad of the help of Michael Beebe, who served as my research assistant and gave me, among other things, most of what grasp I have of the issue about absolute space. I am also grateful for help with various parts of the book from my colleagues D. G. Brown, Howard Jackson, Peter Remnant, Richard E. Robinson, Steven Savitt and John Stewart; from J. J. MacIntosh; and especially from M. J. Scott-Taggart.

Secretarial and other expenses were met by research grants – here gratefully acknowledged – from the Canada Council and the University of British Columbia.

Vancouver, B.C. J.F.B.
July 1973

SYSTEM OF REFERENCES

To keep down the number of footnotes, some references are given in the text. Also, sometimes references which could occupy several footnotes are gathered into one. Each composite footnote refers forwards, and never beyond the end of the paragraph.

Numerals occurring alone refer to page-numbers in the second edition ('B') of the *Critique of Pure Reason*. Numerals immediately preceded by 'A' refer to pages in the first edition, and concern material omitted from B. The following abbreviations are also used:

*Bounds of Sense	P. F. Strawson, *The Bounds of Sense* (London, 1966).
*Commentary	N. Kemp Smith, *A Commentary to Kant's Critique of Pure Reason* (London, 1918).
Essay	Locke, *An Essay Concerning Human Understanding*.
Gerhardt	C. I. Gerhardt (ed.), *Die philosophischen Schriften von G.W. Leibniz* (Berlin, 1875–90).
Haldane & Ross	E. S. Haldane and G. R. T. Ross (eds.), *Philosophical Works of Descartes* (Cambridge, 1911–12), Vol. II.
Kant's Analytic	J. Bennett, *Kant's Analytic* (Cambridge, 1966).
Kant's Arguments	S. J. Al-Azm, *The Origins of Kant's Arguments in the Antinomies* (Oxford, 1972).
*Leibniz–Arnauld	H. T. Mason (ed.), *The Leibniz–Arnauld Correspondence* (Manchester, 1967).
*Leibniz–Clarke	G. H. Alexander (ed.), *The Leibniz–Clarke Correspondence* (Manchester, 1956). For references to this work in Chapter 8, see that chapter's first footnote
Locke, Berkeley, Hume	J. Bennett, *Locke, Berkeley, Hume: Central Themes* (Oxford, 1971).
Loemker	L. E. Loemker (ed.), *G. W. Leibniz: Philosophical Papers and Letters*, 2nd edn (Dordrecht, 1969).

*Metaphysical Foundations	Kant, *Metaphysical Foundations of Natural Science* (trans. J. Ellington, Indianapolis, 1970).
New Essays	Leibniz, *New Essays Concerning Human Understanding*.
*Practical Reason	L. W. Beck, *A Commentary on Kant's Critique of Practical Reason* (Chicago, 1960).
Prolegomena	Kant, *Prolegomena to any Future Metaphysic that will be able to present itself as a Science* (trans. P. G. Lucas, Manchester, 1953).

* I offer as a Select Bibliography of the most important readily available writings on matters treated in this book: the *Critique of Pure Reason*, Descartes' *Meditations*, and the starred items in the above list.

1

INTRODUCTION

§ 1. Locating the subject-matter

The *Critique of Pure Reason* is arranged in a hierarchy of Parts and Books
and Divisions and Chapters and so on downwards. This arrangement
distorts more than it reflects the real bones and sinews in Kant's work.
Let us face this matter squarely right away, and get it behind us.

On the surface, the *Critique*'s main division is into a long portion
about 'Elements' and a shorter one about 'Method'. The work's claim
to greatness lies wholly in the five-sixths of it which Kant calls 'Transcendental Doctrine of Elements', and our present concerns are restricted
to that. Its surface structure is this:

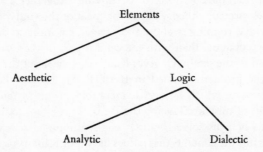

Like many writers on Kant, I prefer to split the work into two roughly
equal parts, one containing the Aesthetic and Analytic, and the other
containing the Dialectic. The Aesthetic/Logic line is supposed to follow
a line between senses and intellect, but really does not. As for the division within the Logic, Kant sees the Analytic as concerned with one
intellectual faculty (understanding) and the Dialectic with another
(reason), and also sees the Analytic as concerned with satisfactory intellectual operations and the Dialectic with a certain kind of malfunction.
(He apparently uses 'dialectic(al)' to mean 'pertaining to error or
illusion', giving the word this unusual sense for a reason which seems
to be a joke.[1]) Both of those rationales for the Analytic/Dialectic division rest on Kant's theory that the problems treated in the Dialectic

---

[1] 85–6; see also *Commentary*, p. 441.

result from malpractice by the faculty of reason; and in my last chapter I shall argue for the rejection of that theory.

Kant also has a better picture of the situation: the Aesthetic and Analytic jointly *present and defend* a philosophical position which the Dialectic then *applies* to certain difficulties and disputes. In fact, what is applied is not minute doctrine but only a broad stream of thought, and even that is disturbed by cross-currents; but still this second picture of the *Critique*'s structure has merits, including that of drawing the main line in the right place. That placing is endorsed by anyone who writes a book just on the Aesthetic and Analytic. I now endorse it in a less usual manner, by writing one just on the Dialectic.

On the surface, the Dialectic has four parts: an Introduction, two Books, and an Appendix. Really, though, it is a sandwich, with a thick slice of meat enclosed between two wafers of bread. The meat is the bulk of Book II, comprising several hundred pages of nourishing philosophy which are my main topic. The Introduction, Book I and the first three paragraphs of Book II, occupying altogether about fifty of Kant's pages, present a theory about the meat of the sandwich; and the final Appendix, running to about sixty pages, has more to do with that introductory material than with the central part of the Dialectic.

The bread of the sandwich gives Kant's theory about the nature and origin of the problems treated in Book II. He blames them on our faculty of *reason*, which he says is incurably prone to tempt us into certain kinds of mistake. Tracing the Book II problems to this source is supposed to help us solve them. It is also supposed to explain why Book II has just the contents that it does have; for Kant, typically, claims to have a theoretical basis for listing all the reason-induced errors:

I have found a way of guarding against all those errors which have hitherto set reason, in its non-empirical employment, at variance with itself. I have not evaded its questions by pleading the insufficiency of human reason. On the contrary, I have specified these questions exhaustively, according to principles; and after locating the point at which, through misunderstanding, reason comes into conflict with itself, I have solved them to its complete satisfaction.[2]

The boast is made even more resounding by Kant's view that all metaphysical problems are generated by reason-induced error, so that 'There is not a single metaphysical problem which has not been solved, or for the solution of which the key at least has not been supplied' in the Dialectic.

[2] A xii–xiii. Next quotation: A xiii.

These extravagant claims are hollow. Kant's theory of reason, as well as being false, has little bearing on the real contents of Book II and is often positively inconsistent with them; and so it cannot help to solve the problems in Book II. Nor does it seriously explain why there are just such and such metaphysical problems: that is just Kant's undignified attempt to derive his choice of topics from the structure of human reason rather than the philosophical preoccupations then current in the German universities.[3]

In a remark I have quoted, Kant speaks of troubles that beset reason 'in its non-empirical employment'. In the title *Critique of Pure Reason*, the word 'pure' means 'non-empirically employed', and so his title means 'a critique of. . .the faculty of reason in general, in respect of all knowledge after which it may strive *independently of all experience*' (A xii). This reflects one aspect of the theory of reason, namely the view that the Dialectic's problems are supposed to arise from reason's having somehow cut itself loose from sense-experience. The troubles which Kant treats in the Dialectic do indeed arise partly from a failure to root one's thoughts in ~~one~~'s *sensory* experience; but this has nothing to do with reason, and so I cannot take seriously the title of Kant's great masterpiece. Considered as a critique of pure reason, the *Critique of Pure Reason* is negligible.[4]

I postpone discussing Kant's theory of reason until my last chapter, but really there is no satisfactory placing for it. Because some of the terminology of the theory of reason occurs in Book II of the Dialectic, readers who are new to the work might find it helpful to read §§ 82–5 in my Reason chapter before moving into Chapter 7 and subsequent chapters of this book. Only the final two sections really need to be left until everything else has been read.

§ 2. The main topics

Book II of the Dialectic has three chapters. Their topics are, respectively, (1) the self or soul or thinking subject, (2) the cosmos, or the world in space and time, and (3) God. Kant pretends that he can also

---

[3] See W. H. Walsh, 'Kant', in P. Edwards (ed.), *The Encyclopedia of Philosophy* (New York and London, 1967); F. C. Copleston, *A History of Philosophy* (London, 1960), Vol. 6, p. 106.

[4] Kant also wrote a *Critique of Practical Reason*, but he has no pure/practical contrast. In those two titles, 'pure' is short for 'pure theoretical', and 'practical' includes 'pure practical', and so theoretical questions about what is the case are being contrasted with practical questions about what ought to be done. See *Practical Reason*, pp. 9–10, n. 21.

I-2

associate them, respectively, with three forms of proposition with which reason may be busy when it goes astray: (1) subject–predicate, (2) if–then, (3) either–or. Anticipating my final two sections, I should say right away that Kant does not integrally connect conditionality with the cosmos, or disjunction with the divine!

The chapter about the soul – about the I of the Cartesian 'I think' – is called 'The Paralogisms of Pure Reason'. A paralogism is a certain kind of invalid argument – a kind which Kant thinks is the typical outcome of reason's going astray when thinking about the soul. This claim is not helpfully true, and Kant fortunately does not press it very hard. He does set up as targets some brief arguments which are perhaps paralogisms, but they are quite inadequate to express the material which Kant really wants to discuss and criticize. I shall use the word 'paralogisms' to refer to the lines of thought – the dense tangles of confusion and error – which are Kant's real topic in this chapter, and not to the jejune syllogisms which purport to embody them.

The Paralogisms chapter is the only part of the Dialectic that Kant thoroughly rewrote for the second edition (B). I shall attend mostly to the version in the first edition (A), which divides the material into four – a division which gets only a passing nod in B. Although this four-way split is not a total success, it is worth more attention than it usually gets. The fourth paralogism, incidentally, is not directly about the soul; but its presence in this chapter will be explained.

The chapter about the cosmos is called 'The Antinomy of Pure Reason'. In Kant's usage, an 'antinomy' is a pair of conflicting propositions each of which is supported by seemingly conclusive arguments. In this chapter he treats four of them, which are supposed to embody the four ways in which pure reason can be 'set at variance with itself' in thinking about the cosmos. That is theory-of-reason stuff; as is Kant's view that there is something inherently antinomal about the cosmological problems he discusses in this chapter (433). In fact, although those problems can be forced into an antinomal form, there is no necessity about this; it is just a matter of expository convenience or, sometimes, inconvenience.

The first two antinomies are genuinely cosmological, in that they have to do with the contents of space and time. The third is about freedom: can there be an action or event which is 'free' in the sense of not being caused by a prior event? This hardly seems to belong to cosmology, whose subject-matter is supposed to be 'the world-whole' (434). Kant tries to connect it up, by arguing that if freedom is possible then that might be how the world began; but he really cares about freedom's bearing not on the beginning of the world but on the human condition *now*. So the third antinomy is an interloper. Still, it is an interesting one, and I shall give it a chapter.

The fourth antinomy is cosmological, all right; but it heavily overlaps with Kant's theology chapter, and so I shall postpone discussion of it until I reach the latter. This overlap, incidentally, illustrates something one must simply become accustomed to, namely Kant's irresponsibility about the *real* shape, or shapelessness, of his work. This may be partly explained by his obsession with *apparent* shape, his stubborn insistence on having everything labelled and pigeon-holed and numbered, usually in three-by-four formations.

The third chapter is called 'The Ideal of Pure Reason'. Although its subject matter is also supposed to arise from a malfunction of the faculty of reason, the word 'ideal', unlike 'paralogism' and 'antinomy', does not itself stand for any sort of reason-induced error or difficulty. In Kant's technical usage, an 'ideal' is a special sort of concept, of which the concept of God is an example (596). In this chapter, Kant attacks three famous arguments for the existence of God.

Observe that we have an '-ology' for each chapter: psychology, cosmology, theology.

§3. Background materials

Kant wrote the Dialectic with certain predecessors and contemporaries in mind, ranging from such great philosophers as Descartes and Leibniz down to minor figures like Baumgarten and Mendelssohn. I am not equipped to handle the minor figures, and I am prepared to miss the subtleties in Kant's work that reflects them, referring the reader to Beck's admirable account of them.[5] On the other hand, I shall say a good deal about Descartes (psychology and theology) and Leibniz (cosmology). I emphasize Leibniz not just because he is important in the Dialectic's background, but also because I want to make amends for my earlier book on Kant in which I wrongly neglected Leibniz in favour of Hume.

One recent writer, Al-Azm, makes Leibniz even more dominant in the background of the Dialectic than I do, contending that all four of the antinomies, which make up Kant's cosmology chapter, are best

---

[5] L. W. Beck, *Early German Philosophy* (Cambridge, Mass., 1969). See also T. D. Weldon, *Kant's Critique of Pure Reason*, 2nd edn (Oxford, 1958), Part I, Ch. 2.

understood as commentaries upon Leibniz's correspondence with Clarke.[6] The Leibniz–Clarke correspondence is indeed crucial to the first antinomy (see Chapter 8 below), but Al-Azm has not persuaded me of his stronger thesis.

Kant's exposure to Leibnizian thought was largely second-hand, through the work of Christian Wolff. One gathers that Wolff had a second-rate mind, and it is a matter for regret that he came to be interposed, as a distorting glass or a muffling pillow, between the two great geniuses of German philosophy. I am unable to explore Wolff's yard-long shelf of philosophy, in which Leibniz's views are developed inaccurately and in infinite detail. I shall mainly ignore Wolff and write as though Kant's only Leibnizian source were Leibniz. I think that no harm will come of this.

My reason for introducing philosophers other than Kant is philosophical, not historical. If some view of Kant's is high-lighted or clarified by being played off against some view of an earlier thinker, then it is worthwhile so to present it. I do not much care whether Kant actually had that thinker in mind; for what I am doing is not history with a special subject-matter, but philosophy with a special technique.

By far the most important material in the Dialectic's background is by Kant himself. I refer to the general philosophical position which is developed in the Aesthetic and Analytic and then applied to certain problems in the Dialectic.

As I have already remarked, Kant himself sees the Dialectic as applying the doctrines of the Aesthetic and Analytic; but he also sees these two parts of the Critique as related in a different way.

It involves a special view of Kant's about the problems treated in Book II of the Dialectic. Those problems, he thinks, arise from the endeavour of 'pure reason' to prove certain propositions. The proofs are supposed to be 'a priori', i.e. to have no empirical input, to appeal to no special facts about sense-experience; and so the conclusions should also count as a priori propositions, meaning simply propositions which can be known independently of all empirical facts (and therefore known as necessarily true, or true-come-what-may). But these conclusions are supposed to be 'synthetic', i.e. their truth is supposed not to stem purely from the meanings of the words or structure of the concepts that are involved. Combining the two points, 'Metaphysics consists, at least *in intention*, entirely of *a priori* synthetic propositions.'[7] From this Kant infers that 'The proper problem of pure reason is contained

---

[6] Al-Azm, *Kant's Arguments*.   [7] 18. Next quotations: 19; 56.

in the question: How are *a priori* synthetic judgments possible?' Kant believes that such judgments are possible: he undertakes to show this for one kind of synthetic a priori judgment in the Aesthetic, and for a second kind in the Analytic. There is, however, a vital difference between these propositions to which Kant accords a synthetic and a priori status and the ones for which 'pure reason' claims that status. Propositions of the latter kind are supposed to express truths about reality, considered just 'in itself' and absolutely apart from any question of how we might experience it; whereas the former kind, which Kant defends as synthetic and a priori in the Aesthetic and Analytic, are propositions about how reality must be experienced. In Kant's slightly unhappy terminology, 'These *a priori* sources of knowledge...apply to objects only...viewed as appearances, and do not present things as they are in themselves.'

Summing up, then: pure reason purports to establish a priori various results about reality 'in itself', never mind how we might experience it; and Kant maintains that genuine synthetic a priori truths always concern what experience must be like, or what the world must be experienced as being like. The Aesthetic and Analytic establish the legitimate sorts of synthetic and a priori propositions, while the Dialectic cuts down the illegitimate sort.

That gloss on the situation, though truthful in its bearing on the Aesthetic and Analytic, is misleading about the content of the Dialectic. The latter is indeed essentially negative, though Kant says that in ruling out knowledge or valid argument on certain topics he has 'made room for faith';[8] but its negations have little to do with synthetic and a priori propositions as such. When a thesis is attacked in the Dialectic, it is attacked on its own demerits rather than as a false claimant to the title 'synthetic and a priori'. So we cannot take too seriously Kant's remark about 'the proper problem of pure reason', or the account of the *Critique*'s structure which goes with it. Significantly, this account, in which primacy is given to the notion of synthetic and a priori propositions, was first offered by Kant in the *Prolegomena*, a semi-popular work based upon A, and only in B did it find its way into the *Critique* itself.

However, as I said before, the Dialectic connects with the Aesthetic and the Analytic in other and more substantial ways than that. In my next two chapters I shall introduce some of the background material –

[8] See xxv–xxxv. Final reference in this paragraph is to Kant's *Prolegomena*; see especially §§ 5, 31.

Kantian and other – referred to in the present section. Some of the material in these chapters is distilled from – and some implicitly quarrels with – fuller treatments of the same topics in my *Kant's Analytic*. It will usually be clear where the earlier work is relevant, and I shall not give detailed references to it.

2

CONCEPTS AND INTUITIONS

§4. The sensory/intellectual continuum

Two philosophical traditions – the rationalist and the empiricist – came together in Kant's philosophy, not in an inconsistent jumble but in a coherent synthesis of truths drawn from each. Underlying this positive achievement is a crucial negative one, namely Kant's avoiding of a certain error which was common to the empiricists and the rationalists. I shall chart this error in the present section and the next, and Kant's correction of it in §§6–8. Topics related to this will occupy the rest of the chapter.

The error is that of assimilating the sensory to the intellectual aspects of the human condition. No one would fail to distinguish seeing a man from thinking about men, hearing a whistle from understanding a lecture about whistles, feeling running water from drawing a conclusion; but the philosophers I am concerned with put all these matters on a continuum, representing as a difference of degree what is really one ✓ of kind.

A common vehicle for this mistake is the word 'idea'. Some philosophers have said that 'ideas' are what one has or is confronted with in ordinary sense-experience, in hallucinations, in some kinds of imagining and so on, and that they are also involved in thinking and understanding – so that having a meaning for a word is associating it with an 'idea', and thinking through a problem is mentally manipulating 'ideas'. Descartes clearly commits himself to using 'idea' as widely as that. He takes the term 'idea' to stand for 'whatever the mind directly perceives',[1] and he says explicitly that 'perception' covers 'sense-perception, imagining, and even conceiving things that are purely intelligible'. Descartes' detailed procedures also show him allowing 'idea' to sprawl across the whole realm of the mental. On the sensory side, for example, he says: 'If I now hear some sound, if I see the sun, or feel heat,... I can perhaps persuade myself that these ideas are adventitious', where 'these ideas' are clearly items of sensory intake that occur in

---

[1] Reply to Third Objections, Haldane & Ross, pp. 67–8. Next three quotations: *Principles of Philosophy*, Part I, § 32; *Third Meditation*, about one fifth of the way through; *ibid.*, a little past the mid-point.

hearing, seeing etc. But there is nothing sensory about Descartes' 'idea' of God, when he asks what there is 'in that idea', and bases his answer on the fact that 'By the name God I mean a substance that is infinite, eternal, immutable, independent, omniscient, omnipotent. . .'. In this passage, an idea of God is a meaning for the word 'God', and there is nothing sensory about that. There is indeed nothing sensory about any meaning, e.g. the meaning of the word 'red'; but where the word in question is 'God' it is more obvious – though no more true – that having a meaning for it is not like being in a sensory state.

The double use of 'idea', and the sensory/intellectual assimilation it embodies, are even more prevalent in Locke's writings. The *Essay Concerning Human Understanding* abounds with evidence that Lockean 'ideas' are sometimes sense-data. For example: 'The idea of *solidity* we receive by our touch. . .There is no idea which we receive more constantly from sensation than solidity.'[2] But 'ideas' also flourish as the raw materials of 'thinking', not in the Cartesian sense in which 'thinking' covers the whole range of the mental, but in a more normal sense in which thinking is a strictly intellectual, ratiocinative activity: 'Thinking, in the propriety of the English tongue, signifies that sort of operation in the mind about its ideas, wherein the mind is active.' Also on the intellectual side, Lockean 'ideas' are meanings. For someone to have real language and not just parrot-chatter, Locke says, he must 'be able to use these sounds. . .as marks for the ideas within his own mind, whereby they might be made known to others'. Also: 'So far as words are of use and signification, so far is there a constant connexion between the sound and the idea.'

Berkeley also mainly accepted the Lockean theory of meaning, I think, but the point is controversial. He certainly regarded thinking as a mental involvement with 'ideas' which are also something like sense-data. This was his basis for a notorious attempt to prove that nothing could exist when not perceived. Try to think of something existing when not perceived: to succeed you must think of something, i.e. conceive it, i.e. have an idea of it, i.e. perceive it; and so you must fail. It follows that the existence of an object when unperceived cannot be thought, and so is inconceivable, and so is impossible.[3] This is not the place to dissect this argument minutely; but clearly something has gone wrong, and Berkeley's use of 'idea' has helped it to do so.

None of these philosophers fails to distinguish the sensory from the

[2] *Essay* II. iv. 1. Next three quotations: II. ix. 1; III. i. 2; III. ii. 7.
[3] *Principles of Human Knowledge* § 23.

intellectual, but they make the distinction in the wrong way: specifically, they regard the sensory and the intellectual as differing only in degree, as constituting two ends of a single continuum. In Descartes' view, the 'ideas' of sense are always less clear than intellectual ones, whereas for Locke sensory 'ideas' are less abstract – more dense with detail – than those which constitute meanings and the raw materials of thought. Berkeley attacked Locke's theory about the abstractness of certain ideas, and instead marked off the sensory realm as involving ideas which are more forceful and in respect of which we are passive, or not the masters of the situation. This last difference is not one of degree, but nor does it even approximate to correctly locating the sensory/intellectual line.

Hume does not use 'idea' as broadly as the others. He tries to reserve it for the intellectual sphere, using 'impression' for the sensory:

> Those perceptions, which enter with most force and violence, we may name *impressions*; and under this name I comprehend all our sensations, passions and emotions, as they make their first appearance in the soul. By *ideas* I mean the faint images of these in thinking and reasoning.[4]

Hume insistently reiterates that impressions differ from ideas only in their greater 'force' or 'vivacity'. So he too thinks there is a sensory/intellectual continuum, with the ends differing in degree but not in kind.

Leibniz predates Hume, but did not influence him, so we can safely take him last.[5] Although the textual evidence is spotty, Leibniz does belong here. In one passage he uses a single term to spread across the whole mental range, from items which are 'produced by each sense' to ones which 'belong to the understanding'; but that passage raises distracting problems, so I shall not explore it.[6] Elsewhere, he associates the sensory with the confused, and the intellectual with the distinct, as in a remark distinguishing 'distinct ideas' from 'confused ideas, or rather images or...impressions'. Furthermore, Leibniz clearly regards the difference between distinctness and confusedness as one of degree: for example, he says that our idea of colour is 'not as distinct or as intelligible' as our idea of shape.

[4] *Treatise*, p. 1.

[5] Regarding Hume on Leibniz, see A. Flew, *Hume's Philosophy of Belief* (London, 1961), p. 69.

[6] It is in a letter to the Queen of Prussia, Loemker, p. 549. Next two quotations: *New Essays* IV. xvii. 13; 'On Locke's Examination of Malebranche', Gerhardt, Vol. VI, p. 577.

Whether Leibniz wishes actually to define the sensory/intellectual difference in terms of confusedness and distinctness, I am not sure; but I cannot find that he offers any other account of what is involved. The opening paragraphs of his 'Meditations on Knowledge, Truth, and Ideas' are dominated by the distinct/confused approach to the intellectual/sensory.[7] They also make rather obvious a mistake of Leibniz's which helps him – and probably others too – to accept the sensory/intellectual continuum. This is the mistake of just overlooking the difference between sense-data and thoughts about sense-data, e.g. between being in a state as though one were seeing something green and, on the other hand, thinking about being in such a state. With that chasm bridged by a sheer failure to notice it, Leibniz can then put the thought of seeming to see something green on a continuum with less directly sense-linked thoughts such as the thought of an active force, or a rational number, or space, or God; and so he can believe that he has an account of mental items ranging from thoughts about non-empirical items like God and numbers, at one end, right across to items of sensory intake at the other end. But that is just a mistake; for at best the continuum stretches from the *thought* of God to the *thought* of seeming to see something green; but what this latter is the thought *of*, namely the visual state or sense-datum or item of sensory intake involved in seeming to see something green, is not on that continuum at all. I agree with this:

On the basis of Leibniz's philosophy it is easy to show that perception and conception have important features in common, but it is difficult to show precisely how they differ. The difficulty is especially great when, for example, we try to distinguish the perception of a green thing from the conception of greenness.

§5. Trouble from the continuum

The sensory/intellectual continuum figures in the work of some philosophers as more than just an item of false doctrine: it leads them into further errors. Some of these are merely infelicities of wording. For example, against Descartes' view that the notion of 'empty space' is logically defective, Locke contends that 'we have the clear idea of space without solidity'.[8] He uses that wording because for him all questions about consistency and logical propriety do concern 'ideas'.

[7] In Loemker, pp. 291–2. The final quotation in this paragraph is from R. M. Yost, Jr., *Leibniz and Philosophical Analysis* (Berkeley, 1954), pp. 193–4.
[8] *Essay* II. iv. 3.

But he does not handle the question as though it concerned the having of a certain kind of sense-datum or sensory type of image; rather, he treats it as a conceptual question requiring conceptual arguments. So the infection from the sensory/intellectual continuum is, in this case, only word-deep. Sometimes, though, it is subcutaneous, generating arguments which presuppose the continuum not just for their wording but for their real structure. One example of this is Berkeley's argument about things' existing when not perceived. I now offer three more.

The first concerns Hume – who could supply many examples, just because he was so resolutely faithful to the sensory/intellectual continuum. Hume argues that space could have indivisible parts, and he starts with a fact about images:

The *idea*, which we form of any finite quality [*sic*], is not infinitely divisible... When you tell me of the thousandth and ten thousandth part of a grain of sand, I have a distinct idea of these numbers...; but the images, which I form in my mind to represent the things themselves, are nothing different from each other, nor inferior to that image, by which I represent the grain of sand itself, which is suppos'd so vastly to exceed them.[9]

Hume here thinks of an image as having a size, and as being capable of division or shrinkage, just like a physical surface; and his point is that we have extended ideas (images) which are not divisible – 'In the division of its ideas...the imagination reaches a *minimum*.' Now, in Hume's view as in Locke's, something is logically possible just so long as we can form an idea of it, and so he can argue:

'Tis certain we have an idea of extension...'Tis likewise certain, that this idea, as conceiv'd by the imagination, tho' divisible into parts or inferior ideas, is not infinitely divisible...Here then is an idea of extension, which consists of parts or inferior ideas, that are perfectly indivisible: consequently this idea implies no contradiction: consequently 'tis possible for extension really to exist conformable to it.

The argument goes: I have an extended indivisible idea, so I have the idea of something extended and indivisible, so there could be something extended and indivisible. That is a case of subcutaneous infection.

The second example is an extraordinary passage in which Descartes gives reasons for the conclusion, not explicitly drawn here, that 'reasoning' is more reliable than 'the senses' as a source of information about the physical world:

I find two completely diverse ideas of the sun in my mind: the one derives from the senses, and...according to it the sun seems to me extremely small; but the

---

9 *Treatise*, p. 27. Next two quotations: *ibid.*; *ibid.* p. 32.

other is derived from astronomical reasonings...; in accordance with it the sun appears to be several times greater than the earth. These two ideas cannot, indeed, both resemble the same sun, and reason makes me believe that the one which comes immediately from the appearance of the sun is the one which is the more dissimilar to it.[10]

What, in plain language, are these two 'ideas'? The one from 'the senses' is presumably a (kind of) sense-datum, an item of sensory intake; while the one 'derived from astronomical reasonings' must be a theory or belief about the sun or, perhaps, the concept of 'the sun' which is used in a certain theory or belief. Neither of these can properly be said to 'resemble' a physical object. If one wrongly regards the sensory 'idea' as a kind of internal picture which has shape and size, then one may think it can be compared with the sun and found to be smaller than it. But not even that philosophical mistake gives a basis for speaking of a resemblance between the sun and the astronomer's concept of or theory about the sun. Descartes was probably helped to overlook this difference by his confident double use of the term 'idea'.

Descartes might revise his position, backing off from the use of 'resemble' and 'dissimilar' and saying, more cautiously, that he has a sense-based 'idea' which represents the sun as small, and an astronomy-based 'idea' which represents it as very large; or that the sun is small according to one 'idea' and large according to the other. There is now no difficulty on the astronomer's side: we can say that the astronomer's 'idea' represents the sun as large because the so-called 'idea' is a theory – a set of propositions of which one is the proposition that the sun is many times the size of the earth. The notion of representation which is involved here is just that of any proposition's 'representation' of its subject-matter. But now the difficulty reappears in connexion with the sense-based 'idea': for that is just a sense-datum, a sensory episode, a state that one is in when seeing the sun; but that does not 'represent' the sun in the way a proposition does. Unlike the astronomical so-called 'idea', the sense-based idea is not a belief or proposition at all, and so we cannot directly hook it into the propositional form '...that the sun is small'. Nor would it help if we treated the sense-datum as a sort of inner picture, for pictures are no more propositional than sensory states are.

To get a real conflict, we must adduce two beliefs or theories or propositions; and there is indeed a pair of beliefs which I think Descartes noticed but then mis-handled. We might speak of the untutored

[10] *Third Meditation*, about one quarter of the way through.

belief that the sun is smaller than Luxembourg, and the tutored belief that it is larger than the earth. The former belief might be reached by someone who goes by little more than what happens when he sees the sun: because he ignores other astronomical data, he does not suspect that the sun is much further from him than terrestrial objects which he sees; and so his belief about its size reflects his perhaps unconscious assumption that the sun is not more than a few miles away. The astronomer's belief, on the other hand, is based upon far more empirical evidence, and a more elaborate theoretical structure for interrelating it. But now see what has happened to Descartes' contrast! Instead of a false result based on the senses and a true one based on reasoning, we have a false result derived from scanty reasoning about a small set of empirical data, and a true one derived from thorough reasoning about a rich set of empirical data. Rather than reason triumphant over the senses, we have thoroughness triumphant over unthoroughness.

The third example will be presented only briefly. One sort of vulnerability to error can be avoided by saying things which are not synthetic but analytic, true by virtue only of meanings; and one can avoid the risk of error of another sort by talking not about the objective realm of physical things, other people, etc. but only about one's own inner or mental states. These two sorts of safety are quite different, but each is a retreat from a sort of vulnerability. Now, in the pre-Kantian language of 'ideas', a statement whose truth stems purely from meanings or from concepts is based simply on the speaker's 'ideas'; and a statement about the speaker's inner states has his 'ideas' as its subject-matter. Someone who uses 'ideas' in both these ways, and is not conscious of the split or ambiguity which that use involves, might actually conflate the two sorts of safety, treating them as on a par because each involves playing safe by restricting oneself to what can be said on the basis of one's own 'ideas'. Hume made this impressive mistake, in a manner too complex to be described here. So did Descartes, for example when he compiled this list: 'Each of us can see by intuition that he exists, that he thinks, that the triangle is bounded by three sides only . . . and the like.'[11] Locke is also guilty of using 'intuition' to cover knowledge of analytic truths ('That *white* is not *black*, that a *circle* is not a *triangle*, that *three* are more than *two* . . . the mind perceives . . . by bare intuition'), and also to cover knowledge of one's inner states ('There can be nothing more certain than that the idea we receive from an external object is in our minds: this is intuitive

---

[11] *Rules for the Direction of the Mind* III. Next two quotations: *Essay* IV. ii. 1 and 14. See also *Locke, Berkeley, Hume* § 52.

knowledge'). This horrendous conflation has its roots in the double use of the term 'idea'.

§6. Kant's breakthrough

Kant's mature thought, embodied in the *Critique of Pure Reason*, breaks radically with the tradition I have been describing. Kant does away with the sliding scale from sensory through to intellectual, with its borderline region occupied by fairly distinct ideas (Leibniz) or rather undetailed ones (Locke) or somewhat faded impressions (Hume); replacing it by an account in which the notion of a sensory/intellectual *borderline* is just nonsense. This account certainly first gained prominence in Kant's writings, and Beck says it was 'wholly Kant's own work'. I agree with Beck's judgment that the account – which he calls a 'theory of the radical diversity of two sources of knowledge' – represents 'the most important strategic move Kant made in his philosophical development'.[12]

As a start towards getting the Kantian picture, consider this: 'There are two stems of human knowledge, namely, *sensibility* and *understanding*...Through the former, objects are given to us; through the latter, they are thought' (29). In this, 'objects' does not mean only objective particulars – outer things which can exist unperceived etc. – but particular things and events of any kind whatsoever. 'Through sensibility objects are given to us' – this primarily means that sensibility is the source of all our data, our brute facts, our raw material, so that sensibility is the basis for our beliefs about what there is. Understanding, on the other hand, does not *provide* data, but rather operates on them. The data which sensibility gives us are brought under intellectual control by the understanding.

Here Kant says it again, introducing two more technical terms: 'Objects are *given* to us by means of sensibility, and it alone yields us *intuitions*; they are *thought* through the understanding, and from the understanding arise *concepts*' (33). The word 'intuition' translates *Anschauung*, which literally means 'view'. The translation is unhappy, but so was Kant's original choice of term. He uses the word to cover sense–data, or Humean 'impressions', or items of sensory intake. Concepts are, so to speak, Kant's substitute for Leibniz's distinct ideas, Locke's abstract ideas, Hume's ideas, and so on. They replace the

---

[12] L. W. Beck, *Early German Philosophy* (Cambridge, Mass., 1969), p. 458 and n.; see also *ibid.* pp. 268–9.

mythical 'ideas' at the intellectual end of the mythical sensory/intellectual continuum.

I still have not said what concepts *are*, in Kant's theory. The essential fact about the understanding is what it does, namely that it is the data-handling faculty; and the main thing it does in bringing data under intellectual control is to make judgments about them. My present visual field, as of seeing something red, is just a datum given to me by my sensibility; but my understanding is involved if I make any judgment at all about it – e.g. if I think that I see a sunset, or that I see something red, or merely that I have a visual field as of seeing something red (Kant distinguishes being in a sensory state from thinking that one is in it). In Kant's theory, any *concept* corresponds to some *kind of judgment* or of proposition.

Thinking of concepts as human possessions ('Does he *have* the concept of...?'), we can identify each concept with the ability to make, fairly competently, judgments of a given kind. Someone has the concept of cause, or of humanity, or of neurosis, if he is pretty much in command of causal judgments or judgments about humans or about neurotics. On this account, a concept is an ability or skill, and is therefore a kind of disposition. A borderline between intuitions and concepts would thus be a borderline between episodes and dispositions – as it were between pains and allergies, or between a sneeze and a proneness to hay fever. Clearly, there can be no such borderline.

Concepts can be peeled off people. They can be regarded as items to be analysed, and as constituents not of judgments that people make but rather of impersonal propositions. On that view, they are not human possessions, not something that people 'have', at all. That doesn't harm the basic correspondence between concepts and judgment-kinds, and – the main point – it puts concepts further than ever from being on a continuum with intuitions.

To make a judgment about an intuition always involves classifying it together with other intuitions. Even to judge that I am in pain, I must classify my present state with other past states which I have taken to be pains; and if I take my pain as evidence for the stronger and more contentful judgment that I am about to see blood, then I must be relating my present state to other past states in several ways at once. Kant puts this by saying that the understanding's fundamental business is *synthesis*, which is 'the act of putting different representations together, and of grasping what is manifold in them in one [act of] knowledge' (103). The word 'grasp' there translates *begreifen*, and Kant's standard word for 'concept' is *Begriff*. Kant himself notes that a concept in German is etymologically a *grasp* (A 103); and so his very terminology reminds us of his theory that in making a synthetic judgment or applying a concept one is always synthesizing or holding together a number of disparate data.

Two flaws in Kant's handling of his theory are both present in this:

Whereas all intuitions, as sensible, rest on affections, concepts rest on functions. By 'function' I mean the unity of the act of bringing various representations under one common representation. Concepts are based on the spontaneity of thought, sensible intuitions on the receptivity of impressions.[13]

The term 'representation', which occurs in the middle sentence of this, is a blanket term which Kant uses to cover intuitions and concepts. It permits him certain pseudo-neat formulations, as in the above passage in which 'bringing various representations under one common representation' has to mean 'bringing various intuitions under one concept'. Although it does little if any honest service, this use of 'representation' seems not to do serious harm either. It could encourage the view that intuitions and concepts do after all lie on a continuum of representations; but mercifully it does not actually do so, except perhaps once.

The first sentence in the quoted passage confirms my general account of Kant's theory as based on a radical distinction between (a) sensory states and (b) intellectual processings. But, unfortunately, Kant is also using 'affection' and 'function' to mark the contrast between (a) how the mind is passively *affected* and (b) what the mind actively *does*. So we have two dichotomies at once: state/happening, and passive/active. That is the force of the quoted contrast between 'receptivity' and 'spontaneity', as also here:

Our knowledge springs from two fundamental sources of the mind; the first is the capacity of receiving representations (receptivity for impresssions), the second is the power of knowing an object through these representations (spontaneity of concepts). Through the first an object is *given* to us, through the second the object is *thought*. (74)

The active/passive contrast lies also behind Kant's use of 'sensible intuition' in the former quoted passage. He uses 'sensible' to mean 'passive', so that a sensible intuition is one which occurs in someone not through his own will. Kant thinks that all human intuitions are sensible, which is why our data-presenting faculty is a sensibility.

[13] 93. The last remark in this paragraph refers to 176–8.

Many philosophers have thought we are passive in respect of our sensory intake and active in respect of our intellectual goings-on.[14] There may be a truth lurking behind this view, but the view itself is false. On the sensory side, I can actively give myself intuitions by the sort of imagining which involves inducing in myself, deliberately, a seeing in the mind's eye or hearing in the mind's ear. (Perhaps I also do so when I observe my own voluntary movements, but it might be objected that in that case I actively move and passively sense – a wrong objection, I think, but a plausible one.) The view I am challenging also fails on the intellectual side, for there I am not always active: I do not voluntarily perform all my intellectual operations, and some of them even occur against my will. The challenged view could be cut back to the claim that we are partly passive in respect of our intuitions and partly active in respect of our intellectual processing of them; but then no contrast at all is being marked.[15]

Kant develops the challenged thesis into a full-scale catastrophe. He speculates on whether some non-human creatures might have intuitions actively rather than passively; and these speculations, since they presuppose a falsehood about what humans can do, are at best quite empty. But they become worse than that. Because he uses 'sensible' to mean 'passive', Kant takes himself to be speculating about whether there might be creatures who have 'non-sensible intuitions'; and then he goes on to equate that with the having of 'intellectual intuitions', which he treats as though it somehow involved a single faculty which was both the data-giver and the operator on data.[16] I can attach no clear sense to this last notion, and Kant's route to it – in which he equivocates with 'non-sensible', using it first to mean 'active' and then to mean 'intellectual' in a more ordinary sense – is perfectly invalid.

I shall ignore all this, including the assumption that we humans are always passive in our receipt of data and always active in our intellectual control of them. When I use phrases like 'activity of the understanding', I shall only be contrasting happenings with states, not activity with passivity.

14 Descartes, *Principles of Philosophy*, Part I, § 32; Spinoza, *Ethics*, Part III, proposition 1; Locke, *Essay* II. ix. 1; Berkeley, *Principles of Human Knowledge* § 29; perhaps Leibniz, given his silence on the matter in *New Essays* II. ix. 1. Not Hume, I think, because he tended to regard us as passive in every respect.
15 For more on the alleged senses–passivity link, see M. R. Ayers, 'Perception and Action', in G. N. E. Vesey (ed.), *Knowledge and Necessity* (London, 1970).
16 68, 75, 307.

§7. Content v. activity

Kant's theory makes proper room for the mind's activities as well as its contents: it caters not just for data but for what happens to them, not just for intuitions but for judgments about them. It is instructive to compare Kant in this regard with Hume. In developing this comparison I shall lean on an important paper by Robert Paul Wolff. His main thesis is this:

> Hume began the *Treatise* with the assumption that empirical knowledge could be explained by reference to the contents of the mind alone, and then made the profound discovery that it was the activity of the mind, rather than the nature of its contents, which accounted for all the puzzling features of empirical knowledge. This insight...was...brilliantly exploited by Kant, and has become today a focus of attention through the studies of disposition terms and language habits.[17]

I shall explore one way in which Hume's commitment to the primacy of mental content forced him to confuse and misrepresent one of his best discoveries.

Hume had the following epistemological insight: When we say that *a* caused *b*, our evidence for this consists solely in evidence that the *a–b* sequence is *generalizable*. By that I mean that there is a true generalization G such that: (1) given G and the occurrence of *a*, the occurrence of *b* could have been validly predicted; and (2)...some further constraint which is still a matter of controversy. For present purposes, we need only stipulate that (2) is to state empirically discoverable conditions, e.g. concerning G's scope and its relations with other true generalizations, and not to state anything like 'G expresses causal necessity'.

Hume's insight could be the key to an account of the meaning of '*a* caused *b*'. If the only backing we can have for any causal statement consists in evidence that the relevant sequence is generalizable, then it is plausible to suppose that '*a* caused *b*' *means* something like 'The *a–b* sequence is generalizable'. Because my account of 'generalizable' has a gap in it, this analysis of the concept of cause is incomplete; but still it looks promising.

At one stage, Hume does entertain such an account of the meaning of 'cause'. He suggests that 'a cause' might be defined as 'An object precedent and contiguous to another, and where all the objects resembling the former are plac'd in like relations of precedency and con-

---

[17] R. P. Wolff, 'Hume's Theory of Mental Activity', *The Philosophical Review* (1960), p. 289.

tiguity to those objects, that resemble the latter'.[18] He goes on to remark that this definition might be regarded as faulty because it is 'drawn from objects foreign to the cause', i.e. because it implies that when we say 'a caused b' we are really talking not just about a and b but also about 'all the objects resembling' either of them. This is a bad objection, even if a plausible one. Kant is well placed to see through it, for he holds that every judgment involves items other than the judgment's ostensible subject-matter: '[In a judgment] a *higher* representation, which comprises the immediate representation and various others, is used in knowing the object, and thereby much possible knowledge is collected into one.' This emphasis is a sheer strength in Kant's position.

There is another objection which Hume, on his own showing, *ought* to bring against the suggested definition. Remember that for him a word's meaning is a kind of 'idea', and thus a faded copy of a sensory 'impression'; and consider how one could square *that* with the suggestion that 'a caused b' means 'The a–b sequence is generalizable'. What can we adduce as the idea of cause? Underlying that, what is the kind of sensory state which typically accompanies observing a generalizable sequence? There can be no satisfactory answer to this. In short, the generalizability of the a–b sequence does not offer raw materials for a Humean 'idea of cause'.

Hume does not state this objection to the suggested definition; but he must have felt its force, for he also offers a different account of the meaning of 'cause' – a dreadful one whose most notable feature is that it does purport to associate the word 'cause' with an 'idea' which is copied from an 'impression'. This second definition rests upon Hume's view that someone who has observed many As to be followed by Bs cannot help expecting each new A to be followed by a B. That fact, Hume thinks, explains why we make the predictions which are the home territory of our 'idea of cause'. So far, perhaps, so good; but then Hume adds a wild and unsubstantiated claim. When one is compelled to predict the occurrence of a B, he says, one has a special sort of feeling or impression, and faded copies of *that* constitute our 'idea of cause'. As Wolff notes, Hume doesn't claim that the alleged feeling-of-compulsion can be discovered by introspection. Rather, he *postulates* it, on the grounds that if it did not exist there could be no idea of cause or of causal necessity:

Necessity is something, that exists in the mind, not in objects; nor is it possible for us ever to form the most distant idea of it, consider'd as a quality in bodies. Either

---

[18] *Treatise*, p. 170. Next quotation: 94.

we have no idea of necessity, or necessity is nothing but that determination of the thought to pass from causes to effects...according to their experienc'd union.[19]

This connexion, therefore, which we *feel* in the mind, this customary transition of the imagination from one object to its usual attendant, is the sentiment or impression from which we form the idea of power or necessary connexion. Nothing farther is in the case. Contemplate the subject on all sides; you will never find any other origin of that idea.

The assumption that meanings are 'ideas' is patently doing harm here. Without it, Hume could have offered not just as epistemology but as concept-analysis his insight that our evidence for '*a* caused *b*' is always something of the form 'The *a–b* sequence is generalizable'; and that would have spared him the need to postulate feelings of intellectual compulsion. *But would that have explained where the concept or idea came from? or what a cause was?*

Kant opposed Hume's account of causation from an obscure and unfortunate angle, which I cannot go into here. What matters now is that at the heart of Kant's own treatment of causation there lies the idea that '*a* caused *b*' means 'The *a–b* sequence is generalizable'; and although Kant does not accept that as it stands, his qualifications of it do not attempt to introduce a special kind of impression into the picture. Nearly all Kant's dealings with the concept of cause show that he has enough elbow-room to make proper use of Hume's basic insight. For instance, Kant says that the empirically usable concept of cause is just the concept of 'the succession of the manifold, in so far as that succession is subject to a rule'.[20] Also, the principle 'Everything that happens... presupposes something upon which it follows according to a rule' is replaced in B by 'All alterations take place in conformity with the law of the connection of cause and effect', with no suggestion that this is a change of doctrine. And Kant's defence of this principle is addressed directly to the A version of it, for it argues that every event must be linkable with some earlier event to form a generalizable sequence. There is also this:

Every cause presupposes a rule according to which certain appearances follow as effects; and every rule requires uniformity in the effects. This uniformity is, indeed, that upon which the concept of cause...is based.

[19] *Treatise*, pp. 165–6. Next quotation: *Enquiry Concerning Human Understanding*, Section VII, Part II.
[20] 183. Next pair of quotations: A 189; 232. Final quotation in this paragraph: 577.

§8. Concepts and judgments

If the sentence '*a* caused *b*' means that the *a–b* sequence is generalizable, the word 'caused' presumably means '...occurred in such a relation to...that together they constituted a generalizable pair'. That is clumsy, to say the least; and the Hume-based thesis about generalizability is best expressed as a thesis not about the meaning of 'cause' but about the meanings of causal *statements*. There are indeed many concepts which are best explained in terms of sample judgments employing them, which amounts to saying that there are many individual words whose meanings are best explained in terms of sample sentences in which they occur.

There is an explanation for this fact. It is that in certain ways judgments are more basic than concepts, and sentences more basic than words. This is a point which Kant got absolutely right, not as a consciously held article of doctrine, but as an automatic by-product of his basic theory of the understanding. It may be controversial to say, as I did earlier, that Kant identifies concepts with abilities to handle judgments of various kinds; but there is a weaker claim which can hardly be disputed, namely that Kant's theory explains what concepts are by explaining how they are employed in judgments.

So Kant is committed to saying that to have a given concept one must be able to use it in judgments. As for the converse thesis, that to make judgments of a given kind one must have the corresponding concept, Kant's doctrine neither entails this nor rules it out. If the doctrine makes judgments independent of concepts in a certain way, the independence has to do with explanation: we can explain what judging is without using any such term as 'concept', but we cannot explain what concepts are without referring to their use in judgments.

The analogous thesis about the primacy of sentence-meaning over word-meaning also concerns the order of explanation. What it says is not that one can understand a sentence without understanding its constituent words, but rather that one can explain what sentence-meaning is without appealing to word-meaning, whereas any cogent account of what it is for a word to have meaning must refer to the word's role in sentences.[21]

The Kantian doctrine that 'concept' is to be explained through 'judgment' has at least two important corollaries. One is that one way

[21] For some elaboration of this large topic, see P. Ziff, *Semantic Analysis* (Ithaca, 1960), Ch. II. There is a helpful brief statement of the position in R. M. Hare, *Practical Inferences* (London, 1971), p. 95.

to classify concepts, and perhaps the best way, is through classifying kinds of judgments. There is a striking application of this in Kant's work: he catalogues all the kinds of judgment that (he believes) the understanding cannot do without, and from that he reads off a list of supposedly indispensable concepts. Although, starting with a bad list of judgment-kinds, Kant ends with a bad list of concepts, his strategy of deriving the one from the other shows an important insight.[22]

The second corollary returns us to the main theme of this section. It is that the basic way to explain or analyse any given concept is to make clear how *it* is used in judgments. One can sometimes express such an analysis without explicitly referring to judgments, but there need be nothing wrong or abnormal about a situation in which the analysis cannot be given in that manner.

Consider the linguistic analogue of all this, namely the doctrine that one may explain the meaning of a word by explaining how it is used in sentences. Not only is this permissible, but sometimes it seems to be inevitable. How could one explain the meaning of the word 'the' except by explaining the meanings of sentences of the form 'The F is G'? Another example: Frege made a tremendous philosophical advance by explaining 'number' through an explanation of statements of the form 'There are n Fs' where n stands for a number-word (see §44 below). And the example from which all this started: the best way to elucidate 'cause' is by explaining the meanings of sentences of the form 'a caused b'.

I do not insist that 'cause' must be explained in that way, but merely that if that is how 'cause' must be explained, that is not a ground for suspicion that there is something peculiar about the concept of cause. It is one of Kant's great strengths that he is prepared to elucidate a given concept by saying how judgments employing it do their work. This is illustrated by some of the remarks I have quoted regarding the concept of cause. A more striking example, though, is his treatment of objectivity-concepts, especially when it is compared with Berkeley's handling of the same topic.

Each of these philosophers holds that statements about objective items such as roses and hurricanes are in principle expressible in terms of Kantian 'intuitions' or Berkeleian 'ideas'. Then their ways part.

Berkeley, assuming that his fundamental unit of analysis was the concept or the single word, thought he had to explain in the language

---

[22] See G. Ryle, 'Categories', in A. G. N. Flew (ed.), *Logic and Language*, 2nd series (Oxford, 1953).

of 'ideas' what 'table' means, or what a table is. So he said the only thing he could say, namely that 'table' means 'collection of ideas which...', or that a table is a collection of ideas which..., with the blanks filled in somehow; and from this he validly inferred such noxious consequences as that we eat and drink ideas, and that tables cannot exist when no one perceives them.

Kant could avoid all those results, because he did not undertake to complete 'A table is...', or 'The word "table" means...', in the language of 'intuitions'. He addressed his doctrine first and foremost to objectivity-*judgments*, thus:

> The object is viewed as that which prevents our modes of knowledge from being haphazard or arbitrary, and which determines them...in some definite fashion. For in so far as they are to relate to an object, they must necessarily agree with one another, that is, must possess that unity which constitutes the concept of an object.[23] *this can be translated into talk about meaning*

Our 'modes of knowledge' are our intuitions. Given intuitions 'relate to an object' if one can correctly bring them under objectivity-concepts, i.e. make judgments about them such as '[I am now in this visual state because] I am seeing a house'. So Kant's account centres on objectivity-judgments. He later describes 'the concept of body' as 'a rule for intuitions', and this again gives primacy to judgments, for it seems clear that the only way a concept can be a 'rule for intuitions' is for it to impose discipline upon some of our judgments about our intuitions.

In this spirit, Kant can avoid Berkeley's calamity by applying himself only to the completion of '"There is a table in my study" means...', or 'To say that there is a table in my study is to say...', in the language of 'intuitions'. There is no pressure on him to identify objects with collections of intuitions, or, therefore, to draw Berkeley's unattractive conclusions. Consider, for example, the Berkeleian theorem that no object can exist when not perceived by someone. Kant can equate 'There is a table in my study' with some truth-functional compound of statements of the form 'If...were done, then...would be had or experienced', the second blank being filled by a description of an intuition. That allows for unperceived objects; for even while no one has any relevant intuitions, it may still be true that if such and such *were* done then relevant intuitions *would* be had; and so, by the given equation, the table can exist while no one perceives it.

[23] A 104-5. Next quotation: A 106.

On the few occasions when Kant does raise the Berkeleian question of what an object is or what 'object' means, he throws away all his great gains and gives the Berkeleian answer, 'Objects are nothing but representations' (A 371).

§ 9. Concept-empiricism

As often as he emphasizes the radical diversity of understanding and sensibility, Kant also stresses their interdependence:

To neither of these powers may a preference be given over the other. Without sensibility no object would be given to us, without understanding no object would be thought. Thoughts without content are empty, intuitions without concepts are blind.[24]

The error of his predecessors, Kant says, was to assume that there could be sensory ideas without intellectual ones (the empiricist bias) or intellectual ideas without sensory ones (the rationalist bias), whereas in fact each is absolutely dependent upon the other:

Leibniz intellectualised appearances, just as Locke...sensualised all concepts of the understanding...Instead of seeking in understanding and sensibility two sources of representations which, while quite different, can supply objectively valid judgments of things only in *conjunction* with each other, each of these great men holds to one only of the two...The other faculty is then regarded as serving only to confuse or to order the representations which this selected faculty yields.

Kant insists that what clears the way for his thesis about the interdependence of concepts and intuitions is the recognition of how disparate they are:

It is...just as necessary to make our concepts sensible, that is, to add the object to them in intuition, as to make our intuitions intelligible, that is, to bring them under concepts. These two powers or capacities cannot exchange their functions. The understanding can intuit nothing, the senses can think nothing. Only through their union can knowledge arise. But that is no reason for confounding the contribution of either with that of the other; rather is it a strong reason for carefully separating and distinguishing the one from the other.

Kant seems to think that one could not defend the interdependence thesis except by first making clear the radical diversity of intuitions and concepts. To assess this, we must split the interdependence thesis into two: that intuitions need concepts, and that concepts need intuitions.

[24] 75. Next two quotations: 327; 75–6.

The thesis that concepts need intuitions is a form of concept-empiricism or meaning-empiricism. Kant holds that a statement's meaning is a function of what it implies for actual and possible experience, and that a statement which has no such implications, no empirical cash value, means nothing. When he says of sensibility and understanding that 'only through their union can *knowledge* arise', he is understating his position. He does indeed hold to a sort of knowledge-empiricism:

Understanding and *sensibility*, with us, can determine objects *only when they are employed in conjunction*. When we separate them, we have intuitions without concepts, or concepts without intuitions – in both cases, representations which we are not in a position to apply to any determinate object. (314)

To 'determine' an object is to state or discover details about what it is like. So this passage says, in effect, that our statements or beliefs about objects should be based on intuitions; and this is knowledge-empiricism. Underlying that – and often mixed up with it[25]– is the distinct thesis of concept-empiricism. This says that I cannot articulate a judgment at all, even to consider it as a possible candidate for acceptance, unless I know something about what intuitions of mine *would*, if they occurred, be relevant to its truth or falsity. In Kant's words: 'The understanding can employ its various principles and its various concepts solely in an empirical and never in a transcendental manner.' The term 'transcendental' usually means 'non-empirical'. A transcendental employment of a concept would be its use in a judgment which had no implications for possible experience, and Kant's concept-empiricism says that such judgments are impossible.

Kant would presumably agree that one can understand a given sentence only if one could make the judgment which that sentence expresses. That, together with concept-empiricism, entails meaning-empiricism – the thesis that one cannot understand a sentence of the statement-making sort unless one knows something about what kinds of intuitions would support or disconfirm it. Kant does not mention this implication, probably because he was like the rationalists and unlike the empiricists in having little interest in language. Still, I am sure that he would have agreed that any limit on the possibility of judgments generates a limit on the meaningfulness of sentences, and I shall sometimes find it convenient to equate Kant's concept-empiricism with this linguistic consequence of it.

[25] 194–5. The next quotation is from 297 – see the whole paragraph 297–9.

Kant's concept-empiricism springs straight from his theory about the disparateness of sensibility and understanding. For if that theory is to be described positively, and not just as a rejection of the sensory/intellectual continuum, then we must say that it is the theory that understanding is the faculty for bringing data under intellectual control; and that already goes most of the way towards concept-empiricism. If Kant allowed that we could use some concept (i.e. make some judgment) without implying anything about actual or possible intuitions, he would be deserting his basic account of what concepts and judgments *are*.

Locke and Hume also accepted thought-empiricism – this being my label for the general doctrine that the limits on what can be sensed imply limits on what can be thought or understood or on what can make sense. Kant's concept-empiricism is one version of this, but I hesitate to use '*concept*-empiricism' to name doctrines held by Locke and Hume.

In the hands of Locke and Hume, thought-empiricism was drained of nearly all its power. Because they accepted the sensory/intellectual continuum, they construed thought-empiricism as saying that items at one end of the continuum require corresponding items at the other end – that abstract ideas require detailed ones (Locke), or that faint ideas require lively impressions (Hume). One form of this kind of theory is particularly bad, namely that in which it says that if I now have a certain intellectual item in my mind I must *earlier* have had a corresponding sensory item – as when Hume says that simple ideas copy earlier impressions. This implies that the way to determine whether someone is now capable of a certain thought is by searching his past to discover whether he has had a corresponding kind of impression (Hume) or sensory idea (Locke).[26]

If Locke and Hume were to allow that present intelligibility depends upon present facts, what facts could these be? How could one test for meaningfulness or thinkability? All I can find is the *image-test*, which says that you cannot have a meaning for any general term unless you can image – or see in your mind's eye – something to which the term would paradigmatically apply. The image-test, which does figure in the work of Locke and of Hume, results from accepting the sensory/intellectual continuum and looking at it from the sensory end – seeing thought as modified sense-data rather than vice versa. It is a bad test, because it is much too narrow, as Spinoza pointed out:

If...we regard quantity...as it exists in the imagination, we find it to be finite, divisible, and composed of parts; but if we regard it as it exists in the intellect [then]

[26] For a fuller discussion of this point, see *Locke, Berkeley, Hume* § 48.

we find it to be infinite, one, and indivisible. This will be plain enough to all who know how to distinguish between the imagination and the intellect.[27]

Similarly, Leibniz says that we have a perfectly satisfactory 'idea' of eternity, even though we have no 'image' of it. Before congratulating Leibniz on this insight, however, we should consider whether he is really entitled to it. For, given what seems to be his account of the sensory/intellectual continuum, does it not amount to saying that we can sometimes form a distinct idea of something of which we cannot form a confused one? Leibniz might draw the sting from this apparent paradox by saying that the difference between distinctness and confusion merely accompanies, and does not explain or define or analyse, the difference between the intellectual and the sensory. But then he would owe us some other account of what the latter difference is, and I cannot find that he offers one.

Anyway, Leibniz's rejection of the image-test is badly motivated. He rejects it not as unduly narrow thought-empiricism, but simply as thought-empiricism. Like any other rationalist, Leibniz divorces questions about intelligibility from questions about what could be experienced, and so he would not wish to replace the image-test by something which is less restrictive but still empiricist in spirit.

Kant is in a stronger position here than either Locke or Leibniz. He thinks that the limits on what can be experienced or imagined do set limits to what can be understood or made sense of, but he does not think that the limits are as narrow as those set by the image-test (180). To put his position as a thesis about language: a general term makes sense only if it has a working role in sentences which have implications for experience. We have a sense for 'electron', for example, because we can use it in theories with empirical cash-value; we needn't be able to imagine an electron. So Kant has the best of both worlds: meanings are answerable to experience, but in looser and more complex ways than the image-test would allow.

I shall have to return to concept-empiricism. Much of the Dialectic consists in Kant's attempts to show how this doctrine of his solves problems which had defeated the rationalists.

[27] *Ethics*, Part I, proposition 15, scholium. For the following Leibniz discussion, see *New Essays* II. xxix. 16. I do not cite Descartes because of the complexity of his view about thought and imagination – see for example *Rules for the Direction of the Mind* XII.

§ 10. The theory of categories

The second half of Kant's interdependence thesis says that intuitions in some way need concepts. As the passages quoted early in § 9 imply, concepts are required for 'judgments' and for 'knowledge'; but just that, in Kant's theory, makes the requirement wide and deep and stringent. One might be tempted to think this: 'Granted that I must employ concepts if I am to make judgments on the basis of my experience, I can intelligibly suppose that I might undergo and be aware of a stream of sensory states which I did not process in judgments at all.' Kant firmly rejects this. In his view, awareness of one's own states is awareness *that* one is in those states, and this involves the making of judgments. A vital role is played in Kant's philosophy by his doctrine that self-consciousness, because it is the ability to *judge that* one is in this or that inner state, requires the possession of concepts. Kant holds – though he seems not properly to defend – the view that sub-human animals do not have concepts and so are not self-conscious. His view seems to be that a dog can have a pain, and perhaps can even suffer pain, but cannot think that it is in pain.

According to Kant, then, any self-conscious creature must use concepts. Further, he has a list of twelve concepts – the so-called *categories* – which he claims must be used if any concepts are used. So the categories must be applicable to the data of any self-conscious creature. It follows that we can apply them a priori to our own data: there can be no question of our ever finding that our data do not fall under the categories; for if we could not apply the categories we could not make judgments, and so we should not be self-conscious, and so we could not 'find' anything about ourselves. There can be 'intuition without thought', Kant allows, but he says that this would be 'not knowledge; and consequently would be for us as good as nothing' (A111).

(That, incidentally, refutes the suggestion of Sellars that intuitions, rather than being 'nonconceptual' items which are merely 'the epistemically more important members of the sensation family', are themselves inherently conceptual – are indeed 'a special class of... conceptual representings'.[28] That cannot be right if there could be 'intuition without thought'. Anyway, Sellars is presumably trying to do justice to Kant's insistence that one can be aware of one's own intuitions only if they are brought under concepts; but Kant's reasons

---

[28] W. Sellars, 'Some Remarks on Kant's Theory of Experience', *The Journal of Philosophy* (1967), p. 636. Next quotation: 75–6.

for that view of his positively depend upon the fact that intuitions are inherently non-conceptual, and that knowledge consists in the application of concepts *to* intuitions. In his own words: 'The understanding can intuit nothing, the senses can think nothing...But that is no reason for confounding the contribution of either with that of the other; rather is it a strong reason for carefully separating and distinguishing the one from the other.' Hasn't Sellars failed to heed this warning?)

Kant based his list of categories on a list of judgment-kinds which he took complacently from some bad old logic-books. Also, his relating of self-consciousness to judgment-making and concept-using is not above criticism. Still his theory of categories probably contains a truth and certainly deserves a hearing. I have reconstructed and assessed Kant's defence of it elsewhere, and I shan't repeat that performance here.

I do wish to consider how Kant's doctrine of categories relates to the thought of his predecessors. Consider this remark of Strawson's:

[Kant] argues, on the one hand, that a certain minimum structure is essential to any conception of experience which we can make truly intelligible to ourselves; on the other, that the attempt to extend beyond the limits of experience the use of...concepts leads only to claims empty of meaning. Dogmatic rationalism exceeds the upper bound of sense, as classical empiricism falls short of the lower.[29]

Certainly, Kant's concept-empiricism sets an 'upper bound of sense' which the empiricists tried to respect and the rationalists simply flouted. Also, the theory of categories does set a 'lower bound', and this was not respected by the empiricists, who characteristically write as though one might be aware of a stream of impressions or ideas without bringing them under any intellectual control. But did the rationalists do any better in this regard? I think not. The theory of categories aligns Kant with the truth against rationalists as well as empiricists.

Strawson does not say otherwise; but the contrary view is suggested by his remarks, and is in any case plausible enough to be worth refuting. The rest of this section will not help in the understanding of Kant's Dialectic, but it should help to put Kant into a proper historico-philosophical perspective.

According to the Kantian theory of categories, I could be aware of a certain stream of experience E only if I brought E under the categories, employing those indispensable concepts in judgments about E. I could do that only if *I had* those concepts and E *conformed to them* – e.g. only if

[29] *Bounds of Sense*, pp. 11–12.

I had the concept of cause and E included instances of causation. Strawson seems to be thinking of the 'minimum structure' that E must have; but one could also speak of the 'minimum structure' that I must have – i.e. the minimum equipment of intellectual capacities which must, according to the theory of categories, be possessed and exercised by any self-conscious being. The question is: did the rationalists pay proper respect to either kind of minimum structure?

So far as I can discover, Descartes and Leibniz did not obey the 'lower bound of sense' to which Strawson refers, and did not flout it either; for in their work the question does not arise, even implicitly. Neither philosopher concerns himself with minimal experience or mental capacity. As a matter of history, that concern seems to have been a strictly empiricist one. Descartes' first two *Meditations* try to isolate and explore a certain minimum, but it is a minimum of assured belief rather than of possible experience or of mental capacity. The empiricist interest in how a world-view is built was foreshadowed by Descartes, because in trying to rebuild an edifice of belief on the basis of his assured minimum he had to adopt certain views about how various kinds of beliefs are interrelated; but since his foundation-stone was not an experiential one, this did not commit him to any views about the lower bound of supposable experience. Further, Descartes' programme did not touch the other part of the foundational inquiry, which explores the foundations of those intellectual capacities, skills, habits, etc. that are involved in the development of our world-view. Descartes thought hard about the bricks, but very little about the mortar.

Still, that does not complete the matter. Descartes or Leibniz might have anticipated Kant's insight that self-consciousness requires intellectual capacity, even if they had no occasion to draw any conclusions about minima or lower bounds. I shall argue, however, that they came nowhere near to doing so.

Descartes does not distinguish consciousness from self-consciousness. He equates the realm of the mental with 'everything which takes place in us so that we are conscious of it, in so far as it is an object of consciousness', or with 'everything which takes place in us so that we perceive it immediately'.[30] This and other evidence makes it clear that in Descartes' view the occurrence of any mental event automatically brings it within the reach of what Kant called self-consciousness. My ability to know or judge that I am in a certain mental state is, for

[30] *Principles of Philosophy*, Part I, § 9, Latin and French versions respectively.

Descartes, an inevitable consequence of the state's being a mental one, and does not require any special intellectual capacities on my part. Does he then allow that dogs may be self-conscious? On the contrary, he denies that they are conscious.[31] When Gassendi challenges Descartes to explain how 'you manifest yourself to yourself just by that operation which is called thought', Descartes replies testily that this passage of Gassendi's 'seems to me not to consist of objections so much as of carpings that require no answer'. In his *Passions of the Soul*, Descartes actually gives an answer. It is about knowledge of one's own desires, but I presume that Descartes would apply it to all knowledge of facts about one's own mind. What an implausible account it is! According to Descartes, the reason why 'we cannot want anything without perceiving by the same means that we want it' is that 'the perception and the wanting are in fact the same thing'.

Incidentally, Locke and Hume shared the Cartesian view that whatever happens in anyone's mind must be known to him; and they, like Descartes, assumed that my mental states automatically and inevitably declare themselves to me without my contributing anything to the transaction.[32]

Leibniz dissented sharply from the Cartesian view. He had special reasons for contending that there are many mental events ('perceptions') whose subjects do not know or judge that they are occurring:

It is well to make a distinction between perception, which is the inner state of the [mind] representing external things, and *apperception*, which is consciousness or the reflective knowledge of this inner state itself and which is not given to all souls or to any soul all the time. It is for lack of this distinction that the Cartesians have made the mistake of disregarding perceptions which are not themselves perceived, just as people commonly disregard imperceptible bodies.[33]

What Leibniz calls 'consciousness' and 'reflective knowledge' is what Kant calls 'self-consciousness'. This interpretation is confirmed by Russell: 'An unconscious perception [for Leibniz] *is* a state of consciousness, but is unconscious in the sense that we are not aware *of* it.'

In Leibniz's view, whether a given soul knows about one of its perceptions depends on the nature of the perception and not on the capa-

---

[31] *Discourse on Method*, Part V, last three pages. Next quotations: Fifth Objections and Descartes' Reply, Haldane & Ross, pp. 144 and 211; *Passions of the Soul*, Part I, § 19. For more on Descartes' tying of mentality to self-consciousness, see A. Kenny, *Descartes* (New York, 1968), p. 76.

[32] *Treatise*, p. 190; *Essay* I. i. 5 and II. i. 10.

[33] *Principles of Nature and of Grace* § 4, in Loemker, p. 637. Next quotation: B. Russell, *A Critical Exposition of the Philosophy of Leibniz* (London, 1949), p. 156.

cities of the soul. He speaks of 'perceptions that are little noticed' because they are 'minute and confused'.[34] Also, and more notably, he says that what makes us aware of any perceptions, rather than being in a perpetual stupor, is that we have perceptions which are 'distinctive', 'conspicuous', and 'more highly flavoured'. There is little room here for a theory of self-consciousness as requiring intellectual structure or capacity.

Kant connects self-consciousness with memory. It is essential to his defence of the theory of categories that the capacity for making judgments about one's past is a partly intellectual matter. This is our last chance to find in the rationalists some foreshadowing of Kant's view about the lower bound on supposable intellectual structure, and here again they fail.

Descartes says little about memory. In one work he mentions 'imagination, sense, and memory' and promises to 'examine these faculties in order'; but the promise is broken and memory remains undiscussed.[35] A passing reference to 'impressions that are preserved in the memory' mildly suggests an un-Kantian picture of memory as passive and unstructured. In a controversy with Gassendi, Descartes says that 'the mind remembers' its past states by 'turning and applying itself' to traces which those states have left in the brain. This could lead on to some Kantian theory, but in Descartes' hands it does not. In that same paragraph he explains why the thoughts of a child are so likely to be forgotten: not because children are incapable of the requisite 'turning and applying', but rather because their brains cannot receive the requisite traces. The door is slammed in Kant's face.

Leibniz does little better. Like Kant, he links self-consciousness with memory, but only by letting his non-intellectual account of the former spread over into the latter. The perceptions which are not 'distinct' enough to hoist themselves over the threshold into (self-)consciousness, it seems, are also not 'distinct enough to be remembered'.[36] He also refers to cases 'in which perception is more distinct and accompanied by memory', and describes 'deep and dreamless sleep' as 'a state in which we remember nothing and have no distinguishable perceptions'. Note also what happens when Leibniz has to confront Locke's blank, bland account of memory: 'The mind has a power...to revive percep-

---

[34] *New Essays* II. i. 11. Next quotation: *Monadology* § 24.
[35] *Rules for the Direction of the Mind* VIII. Next two quotations: *ibid.* XII; Reply to Fifth Objections, Haldane & Ross, pp. 210–11.
[36] *Principles of Nature and of Grace* § 4. Next two quotations: *Monadology* § 19; *ibid.* § 20.

tions which it has once had, with this additional perception annexed to them, that *it has had them before*.'[37] Leibniz uses this to start a quarrel about what 'ideas' are, but not to demur at Locke's account of what memory is. Leibniz clearly had no inkling of Kant's insight that memory depends upon intellectual capacities.

§ 11. Categories and 'innate ideas'

According to Kant's theory, the categories are 'prior' to experience in the sense that one cannot be aware of any experience to which one is not already applying the categories. This might seem to give them a status similar to that which Leibniz and others have claimed for 'innate ideas'. I shall examine this apparent similarity, though solely with refer-ence to the exchange on this topic between Locke and Leibniz. The present section is not needed for the understanding of the rest of the book.

Strictly, something is 'innate' if one is born with it; but Locke says that this is irrelevant, and that the vital question is not *when* but *whence* ideas enter men's minds.[38] Locke's answer is that all our ideas come 'from experience'. Leibniz also thought that 'Where do our ideas come from?' is a coherent question to which 'They come from experience' is a discussable answer. But this is an illusion. The 'ideas' in question are supposed to be intellectual items like Kantian concepts; and I contend that that makes them something like skills or abilities – e.g. the 'idea' or concept of cause is the ability to handle causal judgments. The question of where a given skill 'comes from' is just not well-formed: we cannot answer Yes or No to the question 'Does experience supply us with our ability to walk?', for example. But although Locke wanted his 'ideas' to serve as something like concepts, he thought of them as on a continuum with sense-data; and so he could regard 'Where do ideas come from?' as having the same kind of co-herence as, say, 'Where do pains come from?' The whole defect of his position and Leibniz's is captured in Locke's question as to whether experience 'supplies our understandings with all the materials of thinking'.[39] The very notion of *materials* of thinking is incoherent unless it refers to the things that we think *about*, and that is certainly not what Locke means.

Locke's ill-formed claim that all our 'ideas' enter the mind 'from experience' is, however, a vehicle for two intelligible doctrines.

[37] *Essay* II. x. 2. Leibniz's reply is in *New Essays* II. x. 2.
[38] *Essay* II. ix. 6. 'From experience': *ibid.* II. i. 2.
[39] *Ibid.*

2-2

One is thought-empiricism. In saying that ideas come from experience, Locke is partly trying to secure his doctrine that all our 'ideas' must be so linked to experience that our judgments have empirical cash-value. But the debate over innate ideas is not directly addressed to thought-empiricism; certainly Leibniz did not see it in that way. Furthermore, Kant sides with Locke on the issue of thought-empiricism. The special status of the Kantian 'categories', far from exempting them from concept-empiricism, actually rests upon 'the relation of the categories to possible experience' (187), and so implies that they are concepts for the handling of sensory data.

Locke's contention that all our ideas come 'from experience' also says something about the growth of knowledge and intellectual skill. Each human mind, he says, begins as an empty page on which 'ideas' and knowledge are inscribed by experience. Faithful to this ink-on-paper metaphor, Locke neglects the intellectual capacities – for classification, memory etc. – which are needed if the mind is to be 'inscribed' by experience. He knows better than this, for he does think of the acquisition of 'ideas' and knowledge as involving rational performance and not merely passive reception of sensory ink; but he does not follow through the implications of this view of his. He says: 'Men, barely by the use of their natural faculties, may attain to all the knowledge they have, without the help of any innate impressions.'[40] The phrase 'natural faculties' gestures towards the intellectual structures needed for any disciplined acquisition of mental content or skill; but Locke simply doesn't face up to this, e.g. by considering how the 'natural faculties' which he allows differ from the 'innate ideas' which he rejects. He can neglect that question because, thinking of 'ideas' as like sense-data, he can assume that of course an idea is not even remotely like a capacity or ability or skill. Hence the phrase 'innate impressions'. The trouble is that he *also* uses 'idea' where Kant would use 'concept' or where one might use 'skill' or 'capacity'.

Locke is in a tangle here, which Kant is well placed to correct. To that extent, Kant's theory of concepts ranges him against Locke on a matter connected with the debate over innate ideas.

But it does not thereby align him with Leibniz, for at no stage does Leibniz make the point that Locke envisages the acquisition of 'ideas' through procedures which pre-require intellectual skills. I once thought otherwise. Leibniz does say that the slogan 'There is nothing in the mind which was not first in the senses' should be qualified by '... except the mind itself'. That qualification, I once suggested, 'may perhaps be taken to mean "... except such concepts as are prerequisite for learning anything"'.[41] That was wrong and unwarrantable, as I shall now try to show. The mistake is worth correcting because it exemplifies a currently fashionable trend towards giving the rationalists more than their due.

The contested slogan expresses a sort of thought-empiricism, together perhaps with a certain picture of how one acquires 'ideas' or concepts. For present purposes, we can take it as saying that one cannot have a given concept unless one's experience contains ostensive samples or explanatory paradigms of it. Now, Leibniz reads this as the claim that every concept must be instantiated in our experience of the *outer* world, and he is merely remarking that the paradigm may be not outer but inner. If all our ideas had to 'come to us from without', Leibniz says:

> Then we should have to be outside ourselves; for intellectual ideas or ideas of reflection are derived from our own mind. [We could not] have the idea of being, if we were not Beings ourselves and thus could not find being within ourselves.[42]

Although Leibniz here speaks of 'intellectual ideas', and instances the 'idea of being', he also refers to 'ideas of reflection' or introspection, and could as well have instanced one's 'idea of anger'. The point is not about the need for intellectual structure, but merely about the need for inner as well as outer paradigms for some of our concepts. Furthermore, it is a point which Locke himself makes, as Leibniz admits.

So we should not credit Leibniz with any Kantian insight about the need for intellectual structure. Just to round out the discussion, I shall expound Locke's worst mistake about innate ideas and Leibniz's total failure to correct it.

Locke wanted to deal not just with the straw man who says that at birth (or before any learning) one actually has a functioning concept of identity and conscious knowledge of the principles of logic, but also with the real philosophers who say that at birth (or before learning) we dispositionally or potentially have certain ideas and knowledge. Locke thought he could destroy the latter view by reducing it to triviality. He equates

(1) x is dispositionally or potentially F

with

(2) x has the disposition or capacity to become F,

41 *Kant's Analytic*, p. 98.
42 *New Essays* I. i. 23. Reference at end of this paragraph: *ibid*. II. i. 2. For a good critical treatment of this matter, see A. Savile, 'Leibniz's Contribution to the Theory of Innate Ideas', *Philosophy* (1972), especially p. 115.

and this in turn he equates with

(3) x can, somehow, become F.

This makes it trivially true that we are born dispositionally possessed of every idea and item of knowledge which we ever acquire; and so the doctrine of innate ideas and knowledge, in this 'dispositional' form, completely fails in its appointed task of distinguishing some of our ideas and knowledge from the rest.[43]

That is quite unfair to the innatist. Granted that his position has the form of (2), he can decline to flatten it out into (3) and claim that really it has the form of

(4) If x ever becomes G, x will then become F.

That is, rather than merely saying (3) that *in some circumstances* x will become F, the innatist can *specify* certain circumstances and say (4) that if *they* ever obtain then x will become F. On this basis, then, he may contend that the value of G which verifies

If x becomes G, x will then know that grass is green

differs from the value of H which verifies

If x becomes H, x will then know that $(P \rightarrow \sim \sim P)$,

in such a way that $(P \rightarrow \sim \sim P)$ counts as unlearned or innate in some important way in which 'grass is green' is not. For example, being G might consist in having certain visual sensations whereas being H consists merely in reaching cerebral maturity. I do not defend any such innatist thesis. I merely remark that such theses look plausible, and that they occupy middle ground between the two extremes – one obviously false, the other trivial – which are all that Locke allows to the innatist.

Leibniz, like every other commentator on Locke that I have read, misses this point entirely. He does say that Locke's account of dispositions (or 'faculties') is too weak, but not in the way I have pointed out. According to Leibniz, if someone is dispositionally or potentially F then he must have some positive and non-dispositional feature by virtue of which he can become F: 'It is not...the mere possibility of [becoming F]; it is a disposition, an aptitude, a preformation, which determines our soul and makes it possible for [it to become F].'[44] Also: 'It may be said that the philosophers' *blank page* means that all that the soul naturally and originally possesses are bare faculties. But faculties with-

43 *Essay* I. i. 5.   44 *New Essays* I. i. 11. Next quotation: *ibid.* II. i. 2.

38

out some action . . . are mere fictions which do not occur in nature.' This, even if it is true, is not what mainly needs to be said against Locke in the dispute over ideas which are dispositionally possessed at birth or before learning.

Leibniz was drawn off-course by his own metaphysical system in which, strictly speaking, nothing causes any change in anything else. Leibniz was committed to saying that all my ideas and knowledge are 'innate' in the sense that the causes of them lie wholly within myself; so he was not well placed to rebut Locke's argument for the conclusion that either no mental possessions are innate or else all are.

3

SUBSTANCES AND REALITY

§ 12. Substances and aggregates

This chapter will attend first to the concept of *substance*, which is important in the Dialectic and in the thought of Kant's rationalist predecessors,
and will lead on from that to certain other matters which are prominent
in the philosophical or historical background of the Dialectic. I can
offer only fragments of rationalist thought; but in the hope of making
them a little more shapely and less like mere bleeding chunks, I shall
sometimes follow a topic through to a natural stopping place, even if
that goes a page or two beyond what a consideration of the Dialectic
strictly requires.

The basic rationalist notion of substance is clearly stated by Leibniz:
'When several predicates can be attributed to the same subject, and this
subject can no longer be attributed to any other, we call it an individual
substance.'[1] Kant aligns himself with this when he says that the rock-
bottom, minimal notion of substance is that of 'a something which can
be thought only as subject, never as a predicate of something else'
(186). I shall often give this a linguistic turn, replacing 'thought as
subject' by 'referred to by a substantive or noun-like expression'. Thus
transmuted, the rationalist view becomes this: If a complete account of
what there is would need some substantival expression referring to the
Fs, then the Fs are substances; but not otherwise.

Items which we do in fact handle substantivally, i.e. refer to through
nouns or noun-phrases, may fail in either of two ways to qualify as
substances.

Firstly, an item may fail to qualify as a substance because it is an
aggregate, an assemblage of smaller items which are its parts. A cloud
is an aggregate of water-particles, an army is an aggregate of men and
weapons etc. That aggregates are not substances follows from the
explanation I have given of 'substance', at least in the linguistic form
of it. We could state all the facts about an aggregate by referring substantivally not to it but only to its parts – capturing the whole truth
about a cloud, say, in a set of truths about the histories of individual

[1] *Discourse on Metaphysics* § 8.

40

water-particles, with no mention of the cloud as such. The water-particles may not be substances, but they are closer to being so than the cloud is.

Secondly, something may fail to be a substance because it is a quality or property or attribute or 'accident' (I do not distinguish amongst these). Something is an attribute if all the facts about it can be expressed in statements about items which are other than it and are not parts of it. So quarrels are attributes, and thus not substances, because the facts about them are facts about quarrelling people; and diseases are not substances because the facts about them are facts about malfunctioning organisms. If organisms are not substances, they are nearer to being so than diseases are, because diseases are adjectival *upon* organisms. There are no special problems for us here, and I now return to aggregates.

Here is an argument for the conclusion that *nothing which fills a region of space is a substance*. There are three premisses:

(1) *Every region of space has parts.* Any region of space can be described, relative to a system of coordinates, by a set of equations; and then it is a matter of mere arithmetic to construct equations which delineate a sub-region, a mere part of the former one.

(2) *Whatever fills a region of space which has parts must itself have parts.* If a given region has two parts, x and y, then something filling all of that region must have an x-filling part and a y-filling part.

(3) *Whatever has parts is not a substance.* This follows immediately from my account of why no aggregate is a substance.

These premisses do jointly entail that nothing which fills a region of space is a substance. I have tried to make the premisses look plausible, but are they all true? This question will be fully explored in Chapter 9 below, but I must say something about it now.

Consider how the notion of 'a substance' is being used to support premiss (3). We rightly deny the label 'a substance' to any collection, such as a cloud or an army. Perhaps we should also count molecules and pebbles etc. as collections. It would take a stronger wind to scatter a pebble than to scatter a cloud, but, one might argue, it would be a shallow metaphysic which took account of such a difference. So we shall count as aggregates, and not as substances, all physical things which are splittable – i.e. ones whose parts are physically capable *somehow* of being dispersed. If our concept of a substance is no more severe than that, however, then my three-premiss argument fails; for all we have in support of premisses (1) and (2) is that whatever occupies space is logically or conceptually divisible, i.e. can coherently be described in

41

the language of 'whole' and 'part'. No reason has been given to think that every such thing is physically splittable.

§ 13. Cartesian substances

Descartes would count as an aggregate only what is splittable, but then he thinks that anything which fills space *can* actually be split, if not by us then by God.[2] It follows that space-taking things like pear-trees and icebergs and coyotes are not substances and are not composed of substances either.

Descartes' usual route to this conclusion is a slightly different one. He says that a substance is 'a thing which so exists that it needs nothing else in order to exist';[3] and by this criterion a substance cannot be vulnerable to destruction by anything else, for if *x* could be destroyed by *y*, then *x* would 'need' *y*'s non-interference if it was to continue to exist. In this line of thought, a thing is denied the label of 'substance', whether or not it can be physically split, just so long as it can be destroyed somehow by something else. Since Descartes thinks that worldly things can all be destroyed by God, and so 'need' God in order to continue to exist, he denies that any such thing is a substance:

The concept of substance is just that of a thing which so exists that it needs nothing else in order to exist...Strictly speaking, God is the only such thing, and no created thing can exist for a moment without being sustained and conserved by his power. That is why the Schoolmen were right to say that the term 'substance' cannot be applied in the same sense both to God and to creatures.[4]

The suggestion is that we have a weakened sense in which the term 'substance' can be applied to creatures, and Descartes proceeds to explain what this weakened sense is: a created 'substance' is something which depends for its existence only upon God and not upon any created thing. That needs cautious handling, for Descartes is committed to the view that everything depends for its existence, always and totally and exclusively, upon continual divine support.[5] Still, we can take him to mean that a created 'substance' is something which cannot be annihilated by any natural process but only by an unruly miracle – this being consistent with the view that even natural processes are one kind of divine activity.

---

[2] *Principles of Philosophy*, Part II, §§ 20, 34.

[3] *Ibid.* Part I, § 51. See also Reply to Fourth Objections, Haldane & Ross, p. 101. On the relationship between the two criteria, see W. C. Kneale, 'The Notion of a Substance', *Proceedings of the Aristotelian Society* (1939–40).

[4] *Principles of Philosophy*, Part I, § 51.   [5] *Ibid.* § 21.

Descartes seems never to use this weaker sense of 'substance' for any serious philosophical or scientific purpose; and his view that every extended thing is naturally splittable suggests that there are no weakened-sense 'substances' in the spatial realm. Rather than facing up to this, and considering how to give a comprehensive account of the extended world without using the concept of a substance, Descartes slides away from the whole question.

He sometimes uses 'substance' in a manner which admits phrases like 'quantity of substance' but not ones like 'a substance' or 'number of substances'. That is, he uses it as a mass-noun like 'water' or 'sand', rather than as a count-noun like 'pond' or 'pebble'. In this use, which I shall explore in §56, the question of whether something qualifies as '*a* substance' does not arise. The only context where Descartes uses 'substance', as a count-noun, in formulating one of his own positive doctrines, is when he says that mind and body are 'distinct substances'.[6] But he is not here counting substances in any sense of 'substance' I have so far introduced; for if he were, he would be asserting that a human body is precisely one extended substance – and that is an impossible reading of him. What he is really saying is just that minds and bodies are of radically different *kinds*. In these contexts, then, 'a substance' is really a basic *kind of substance* (mass-noun), and nothing is implied about the counting of individual substances. That is surely what Descartes means when he says that 'body, regarded generally, is a substance, which is why it cannot perish'.

In contrast with Descartes' uncertainty about substances in the physical realm, Spinoza was clear and forthright. The problem did arise for him too, partly because he identified logical possibility with causal possibility, so that he could not allow that something might be logically but not causally divisible. For this and other reasons, Spinoza must deny that the occupants of space are substances strictly so-called, and he would have no patience with the idea that they might be 'substances' in some attenuated sense, even if such a sense could be defined.

From this, Spinoza concluded that the only extended substance is extended Nature – meaning the whole of space and its contents. Granted that he had grounds for saying that no extended item which is

---

[6] Replies to Second and Fourth Objections, Haldane & Ross, pp. 53, 59, 101. Quotation at end of paragraph: *Synopsis of the Meditations*. On this matter, I follow J. L. Watling's helpful chapter on Descartes in D. J. O'Connor (ed.), *Critical History of Western Philosophy* (New York and London, 1964).

less than Nature can qualify as a substance, why did he think that Nature does qualify as one? This can be answered in two parts, one for each of the two criteria for being 'a substance' – though Spinoza himself would not have admitted that the criteria are distinct. (1) Taking a substance to be something which is not destructible by anything outside itself, Spinoza can regard extended Nature as a substance. It is invulnerable to causal attack from the outside because only the physical can act on the physical (Spinoza believes), and *ex hypothesi* there is nothing physical outside extended Nature. (2) On the other criterion, a substance is something which is neither an attribute nor an aggregate. Clearly, extended Nature is not an attribute; but Spinoza says that it is not an aggregate either – implying that it is not even logically divisible, i.e. that no sense attaches to the idea of its having parts. He has a reason for this, but it is a mistaken one. He assumes that space is infinite, and wrongly thinks that something infinite cannot have even two parts: if the parts were both finite, then so must the whole be; but if at least one were infinite, then one infinite (the whole) would be greater than another (a part), which Spinoza finds absurd.[7] This argument is part of a larger one which Spinoza rejects; but he does seem to accept this part of it, and he endorses its vital mistake when he says that 'by a part of substance nothing else can be understood than finite substance'. This is wrong, and it is a further error to suppose that infinite wholes must be greater than their parts; but these matters came clear only in the nineteenth century, and Spinoza was not alone in getting them wrong. They will be discussed in Chapter 7 below.

§14. Leibniz on substances and reality

Leibniz also thought that nothing which occupies a region of space can be a substance, and he too based this on the three-premiss argument given in §12 above. Leibniz insisted upon using the notion of 'a substance' – with 'substance' as a count-noun – in his theory of reality, but his way of achieving this was the opposite of Spinoza's. Where Spinoza found molecules and pebbles and galaxies too small to be substances, Leibniz found them too large; where Spinoza said that substances must be infinite in extent, Leibniz said that they must have no extent at all. The ultimate components of extended things, according to Leibniz, are not extended, and have no parts, and are genuine substances. He called them 'monads'.

7 *Ethics*, Part I, proposition 15, scholium. Following quotation: *ibid.* proposition 13, scholium.

In Leibniz's view, the only result of physically dividing an extended thing will be smaller extended things. Similarly for logical division: the thought of 'what results from splitting x' is the thought of extended things which are smaller than x. Making the same point from the other end, so to speak: one cannot reach (the thought of) something extended by (logically) juxtaposing any finite number of monads; for a finite number, however large, of unextended items can constitute only an unextended aggregate.

So if pebbles have monads as parts, this must be in an unusual sense of 'part'. For 'the parts' of a thing, in this sense, do not result from taking it apart, and the thing does not result from its parts' being put together. It seems unlikely that Leibniz could offer any empirical examples of the part–whole relationship in this sense of 'part', nor could he give any empirical cash-value to his doctrine that extended things are made up of unextended substances.

This is not an attack on the very notion of a monad. Leibniz has some account of what monads are, in his claim that minds are monads. He seriously contends that monads which are not minds differ only in degree from ones which are, and he boldly applies mentalistic language to the whole of reality. For instance, he credits all monads with having 'perceptions', and whenever we would say that something has affected something else, Leibniz will say that what has really happened is that some monads have 'perceived' changes in other monads. This metaphysic is more viable than it seems, but I shan't assess it as a whole. I am neither endorsing nor rejecting Leibnizian monads as such.

My point is just that extended things cannot contain monads as *parts*, properly so-called. Leibniz says as much himself: 'Matter is not composed of [monads] but results from them.'[8] That, as it stands, is still unclear and confusing, for how can extended things 'result' from monads? Not, one would think, in the ordinary causal way in which a forest-fire results from lightning. Indeed not; and Leibniz's considered view about the relationship of matter to monad is that it is one of appearance to reality. He thinks that monads are real, whereas extended things are only appearances of monads; or that we perceive aggregates of monads *as* extended, though really they are not:

Accurately speaking..., matter is not composed of these constitutive unities but results from them, since matter or extended mass is nothing but a phenomenon grounded in things, like the rainbow or the mock-sun, and all reality belongs only to unities...Substantial unities are not parts but foundations of phenomena.

[8] Letter to De Volder, Loemker, p. 536. Next quotation: *ibid.*

When Leibniz says that extended things are 'phenomena' he means, at least, that the bedrock account of what there is will not mention anything spatial, and that in our perceiving reality *as* extended there is an element of illusion.

This conclusion is not a mere *pis-aller* which Leibniz has reached by this route: 'There must be some systematic relationship between monads and matter; it cannot be part/whole or cause/effect, and the only other viable candidate is reality/appearance.' On the contrary, Leibniz has positive grounds for this view of monads and matter. He is committed to saying that the basic inventory of reality is a list of substances, and that no extended thing either is a substance or has substances as 'parts' in any ordinary sense. But if neither x nor the parts of x appear in the basic inventory of items which compose reality, then x presumably does not belong to reality, and is therefore not real; which is what Leibniz says about the entire extended world.

Not only *substance*, but also *reality*, will be important later in this book. A proper grasp of the Dialectic requires some understanding of Leibniz's doctrine that the extended world is not ultimately real; so I shall stay with it for a while.

§ 15. Leibniz on relations and reality

Leibniz denied the reality of the extended world for another reason also, stemming from his overwhelmingly strong preference for monadic or one-place or non-relational predicates. Leibniz insisted that reality must be wholly describable in statements of the form 'S is P', with no use of the form 'S_1 has R to S_2', and this metaphysical view seems to arise from a deep but unargued prejudice in favour of a monadic logic.[9]

Let us explore this idea that every truth can be expressed in non-relational statements. (I could have said '...in monadic statements', but that is ambiguous: it could refer to subject–predicate statements, i.e. ones which use only monadic or one-place predicates, or to statements about Leibnizian monads. My immediate concern is with the former only.) Faced with apparent truths which are not of that form, Leibniz can either deny that they are truths or else claim that they can be dis-

---

[9] B. Russell, *A Critical Exposition of the Philosophy of Leibniz* (London, 1937), pp. 9ff. The order is reversed, and the logic subordinated to the metaphysics, by N. Rescher, *The Philosophy of Leibniz* (Englewood Cliffs, N.J., 1967), pp. 75–6.

pensed with in favour of subject–predicate statements. He adopted the latter alternative.[10]

Some relational statements can be replaced by subject–predicate statements which say all that they do and perhaps more. For instance, we can replace any comparative statement by a pair of monadic ones, e.g. replacing 'Joan is cleverer than Henry' by a statement about how clever Joan is and another about how clever Henry is. In fact, that is open to the objection that in saying how clever someone is, one *does* implicitly compare him with others in respect of cleverness; but perhaps we can allow Leibniz to pretend that he has at his disposal a language in which statements about how F things are, for various values of F, involve comparing things only with an absolute standard and not with one another. Even if we make that indulgence, many relational statements are still not replaceable by monadic ones. Consider the statement, 'Mary is married to John'. A really comprehensive subject–predicate biography of just Mary, and another of just John, could not jointly entail that Mary is married to John. One of them might entail 'At time t, Mary was married to the man on her right if there was one', and the other might entail 'At t, John was married to the woman on his left if there was one'; but to get the desired conclusion we must add that 'At t Mary was to the left of John', which is relational.

The example is not frivolous. I seriously contend that one would need some statement spatially relating Mary to John (or each of them to telephones or the like) at the crucial time. I conjecture that whenever an empirical relational statement cannot be replaced by monadic ones, it is because the replacement attempt reaches a bedrock of spatial relations; but even if that is wrong, spatial-relational statements are one kind of obstacle to Leibniz's programme for describing the whole of reality in subject–predicate terms.

It seems clear that statements about how things are spatially related to one another cannot be replaced by monadic statements. We might try to avoid this conclusion by seeking to replace 'x has spatial relation R to y' by a pair of monadic statements saying *where* x and y respectively are. But this is no use to Leibniz. He has a theory (to be expounded in §47 below) according to which a statement about where x is can be analysed into a statement about how x is spatially related to other things, and so for him the suggested solution would lead from the frying-pan right back into the frying-pan.

[10] See Rescher, *op. cit.* Ch. 6. A dissenting view of Leibniz's attitude to relations is defended in H. Ishiguro, *Leibniz's Philosophy of Logic and Language* (London, 1972). It is interesting and considerable, but I am entirely unconvinced by it.

So Leibniz has an acute problem. His doctrine of space implies that all spatial statements reduce to ones of the form $R(x_1, .., x_n)$ where R stands for an n-adic spatial relation, and his doctrine of relations requires that these latter statements be replaceable by monadic ones. Yet it is quite unclear how such replacements are to be effected.

Leibniz makes no suggestions, and simply evades the whole problem. If that seems incredible, remember that for him fundamental reality consists of non-extended monads, so that he envisages replacing statements about how extended items are spatially interrelated by statements which are 'monadic' in both senses – i.e. *non-relational* statements *about monads*. That implies that all such replacements operate across a boundary which is in any case mysterious, with ultimate reality on one side of it and the whole extended world on the other; and that might seem to explain why illustrative examples cannot be given. In those comfortable cases where we can illustrate the replacement – e.g. replacing 'x is hotter than y' by 'x is at 99° C and y is at 97° C', and just forgetting that really these too are implicitly relational – all the statements involved are empirical. Leibniz might plausibly say that *of course* he could not illustrate in that accessible way the replacement of relational statements by non-relational ones about monads. That presumably explains the passages, which would otherwise be astonishingly lax, where Leibniz just helps himself to the replacement of relational by monadic statements. For example, he says: 'My opinion about relations is that paternity in David is one thing, and sonship in Solomon another, but that the relation common to both is a merely mental thing whose basis is the modifications of the individuals'; and he leaves it at that.[11]

I showed in § 14 that Leibniz had a problem about how extended things could be made up of unextended ones, and that he 'solved' it by shifting from part/whole to reality/appearance. Now he has a difficulty about how spatial-relational statements can be replaced by monadic ones, and this too must be 'solved' by a tactical retreat into the doctrine that spatially related things are only appearances whereas the replacing statements would be about monads which are really real. So the doctrine of the unreality of the extended world has two similar roles, both discreditable.

<hr>

[11] Letter to Des Bosses, Loemker, p. 609.

§ 16. Kant on reality

Kant normally uses the word 'appearance' to mean something like 'objective item which could be perceived'. That usage implies that no weighty doctrine is expressed by Kant's claim that the physical world is an appearance; but the usage itself reflects the substantial Kantian doctrine, which we have already encountered, that statements about the extended world are equivalent to statements about possible intuitions.

This does not involve Kant in contrasting 'appearance' with 'reality'. From the premiss that we must handle the extended world in judgments about possible experience, what Kant infers is not that the extended world is not our ultimate topic but rather that we must handle our ultimate topic in judgments about possible experience. For what the fact is worth, the concept of reality is one of Kant's twelve categories, which clearly implies that it is an empirical concept. Kant says: 'Reality, in the pure concept of the understanding, is that which corresponds to a sensation in general';[12] and his later discussion of the concept is concerned with 'reality in the [field of] appearance', 'reality in perception', and 'the real in space'. So far from restricting 'reality' to the realm of the experientially inaccessible, Kant restricts it to the realm of what he not very felicitously calls 'appearance'.

Nor does Kant reserve 'substance' for non-empirical use. It too is a category, and Kant's argument for its categorial status depends upon his view that the concept of substance, like any other concept, is a tool for the management of sensory intake (224–32).

A curious situation arises. When Leibniz and Kant say that the extended world is phenomenal or is an appearance, they mean pretty much the same thing and yet they are moving in opposite directions. Kant is propounding concept-empiricism: if we are to make anything of the extended world, we must apply empirical concepts to it, in judgments which have some empirical cash-value. He is not contrasting the extended world as 'appearance' with some unextended and perhaps unperceivable 'reality'. Leibniz, on the other hand, is doing just that. He calls the extended world an 'appearance' as a way of denying that it is ultimately real. Kant refuses to identify 'appearance' with what 'merely *seems*' to be the case (69–70), but for Leibniz that identification is important and correct.

Compare the two philosophers' treatments of one's knowledge that there is an external world. Here is Leibniz at his most Kantian:

[12] 182. Next three quoted phrases: 210; 214; 215.

The most powerful criterion of the reality of phenomena, sufficient even by itself, is success in predicting future phenomena from past and present ones...Even if this whole life were said to be only a dream, and the visible world only a phantasm, I should call this dream or this phantasm real enough if we were never deceived by it when we make good use of reason.[13]

But Kant would not have sanctioned that phrase 'real enough', implying that there is something missing. Nor would he have added, as Leibniz does:

The criteria for real phenomena thus far offered, even when taken together, are not demonstrative, even though they have the greatest probability...By no argument can it be demonstrated absolutely that bodies exist.

Contrast that with Kant's inference from his 'doctrine that appearances are...representations only, not things in themselves':

Our doctrine...removes all difficulty in the way of accepting the existence of matter on the unaided testimony of our mere self-consciousness, or of declaring it to be thereby proved in the same manner as the existence of myself as a thinking being is proved...External objects...are mere appearances, and are therefore nothing but a species of my representations...Thus external things exist as well as I myself,...upon the immediate witness of my self-consciousness.

The Berkeleian formulation, which says that objects *are* representations, leads to an unduly simple answer to scepticism – namely that just by having a certain representation I can thereby know that I am in the presence of an object. Reformulate the underlying doctrine, so that instead of echoing Berkeley it says that the concept of an object is a rule for one's intuitions, and a better treatment of scepticism results: a single intuition does not 'immediately' guarantee that I am perceiving an object, but such a guarantee does result if I have further intuitions which relate to the first one in appropriate ways. This revised handling of scepticism is more Kantian than Kant's own; and it still contrasts sharply with Leibniz, for it flatly rejects Leibniz's claim that 'By no argument can it be demonstrated absolutely that bodies exist'.

In drawing that contrast, I have assumed that Leibniz construes the question of whether 'bodies exist' as asking whether the 'phenomena' we experience really do correspond to monads on the other side of the veil of perception. He certainly identifies the real existence of 'bodies'

[13] 'On the Method of Distinguishing Real from Imaginary Phenomena', Loemker, p. 364. Next quotation: *ibid.*; see also *New Essays* IV. xi. 10. Following Kant quotation: A 370–1.

with that of 'substances' on some occasions,[14] and if he is not doing so here the passage is merely peculiar.

Be that as it may, Leibniz does say that ordinary empirical things are 'well-founded phenomena'; and although he thinks that the coherence etc. of a set of phenomena is *evidence* of their being well-founded, what he *means* by calling them 'well-founded' is that they somehow represent monadic reality.[15] Leibniz admits that there can be no empirical evidence that any phenomenon is well-founded. When asked, point-blank, 'Why should there be any bodies or any "other monads"?', Leibniz draws his answer from moralizing theology: There are many monads because it is better that there should be.

Incidentally, Leibniz cannot join Locke in postulating 'real things' as causes for our 'ideas', for he denies that our 'ideas' or 'perceptions' are caused by anything outside ourselves. According to Leibniz, 'Monads have no windows': whatever happens to any monad is caused solely by that monad, and the appearance of interconnexion is God's work. God does not interfere, but he initially chose to create just such monads as would harmonize in their histories as though they were interconnected. Thus, for instance:

A number of spectators believe that they see the same thing and are in fact in agreement about it, although each one sees and speaks of it according to the measure of his own point of view. It is only God...who is the cause of the correspondence between their phenomena and who brings it about that what is peculiar to one is public to all; otherwise there would be no interconnection.[16]

Consequently, Leibniz cannot adduce a causal–hypothetical argument for the existence of other monads – i.e. of an external world and of other minds, these two being indistinguishable within Leibniz's metaphysics.

As for Leibniz's denial that monads can interact: I shall expound one reason for this in §20 below. Another has already been reported in these pages and was well understood by Kant (330–1). It is that the fundamental account of reality is supposed to be expressible entirely in statements applying non-relational predicates to individual monads. Such statements cannot report any 'real relations' between monads, though the histories which they assign to various monads may harmonize with one another so as to produce an illusion of causal connectedness.

14 'Eclaircissement du nouveau systeme de la communication des substances', § 9, Gerhardt, Vol. IV, p. 495.
15 N. Rescher, *The Philosophy of Leibniz* (Englewood Cliffs, N.J., 1967), p. 81, is especially helpful on this point. Reference at end of this paragraph: Leibniz, *loc. cit.*
16 *Discourse on Metaphysics* § 14.

§ 17. Things in themselves

Unfortunately, Kant's over-all position with regard to the empirical world's being an 'appearance' is darker and more complex than I have so far allowed. Without retracting the contrast I have drawn between Kant's position and Leibniz's, I confess that it is not the whole story. I have so far suppressed Kant's view that physical things etc. are appearances or representations *and not things in themselves*. This notion of a 'thing in itself' (and the associated notion of 'noumenon') will give trouble at several points in the Dialectic, and it should be confronted right away.

A thing in itself is, roughly, a thing considered independently of any facts about how it might impinge upon our experience. Kant also has an adverbial use of 'in itself', in which the statement that something *verb*s in itself – e.g. exists in itself, or is known in itself – means that it *v*'s independently of how it might impinge upon our experience. Kant has no business to be using any such notion. His own concept-empiricism implies that we can understand only statements which have implications for possible experience: the language of 'thing in itself' or of '*v* in itself' betrays this, and seems to take Kant towards Leibniz, for 'things in themselves' have a role not unlike that of monads.

Here is an example. Kant affirms his concept-empiricism when he says: 'Everything is real which stands in connection with a perception in accordance with the laws of empirical advance';[17] for this means that a thing's reality is secured by the truth of statements about what perceptions would be had if certain inquiries were conducted. Kant proceeds to apply this, remarking that inhabitants of the moon 'are therefore real if they stand in an empirical connection with my actual consciousness . . .' – then he throws it all away –'. . . although they are not for that reason real in themselves, that is, outside this advance of experience.' This is a betrayal, for Kant's basic position does not allow that any sense can be attached to 'real in themselves'. Our only concept of reality is an empirical one, so that for us 'real' has to mean 'related to our experience in such-and-such ways'. Kant has no right to make even agnostic or negative uses of 'real in itself', which means 'real, whatever its relation may be to our experience'. Just after that, Kant says that empirical objects are 'mere representations'. This slips back into the Berkeleian formulation; but my present concern is with another defect in the phrase, namely the apologetic 'mere', suggesting that there is something more which objects might be but fail to be,

---

[17] 521. Final quotation in this paragraph: A 379–80.

namely things in themselves. Kant also sounds ominously Leibnizian when he says: 'The *transcendental object* which underlies appearances [is not] matter..., but a ground (to us unknown) of the appearances which supply to us the empirical concept of [matter].' This 'transcendental object' seems to be the same as a 'thing in itself'.

Kant often uses the 'thing in itself' terminology in a manner which, though unfortunate, involves no downright error – namely as a reminder of his concept-empiricism. He speaks of 'the problematic thought which leaves open a place for [things in themselves]' (315), and what he means is that the truth that all our thinking must be experience-directed 'leaves open a place for' the notion of thinking which is *not* experience-directed. We cannot properly make sense of this notion; still less could there *be* thinking to which the notion applied; but the 'place' is there, all the same – a 'place' created by the grammatical fact that if 'All *F*s are *G*s' is in the language then '*F*s which are not *G*s' must be in it too. With something like that in the background, Kant sometimes says that the physical world is not a thing in itself, meaning merely that the only judgments we can formulate about it are ones concerning possible experience. In these contexts, he does not pretend to have a line-drawing concept of a thing in itself – a concept which is used negatively in 'The spatial world is not a thing in itself', but which could also have affirmative uses. He is merely pointing out that we have no concepts but sense-linked ones to apply to the spatial world. His way of saying this is misleading, but no worse than that.

In any case, even when he is being unduly tolerant of the notion of 'things in themselves', Kant steadily refuses to allow any doctrine or even speculations about them. 'The problematic thought which leaves open a place for them', he says, 'serves only, like an empty space, for the limitation of empirical principles, without itself containing or revealing any other object of knowledge beyond the sphere of those principles.'[18] Contrast this with Leibniz. Although each of us is a monad, there is no way in which (other) monads can be empirically given; and yet for Leibniz they are what metaphysics is all about. Nearly all Leibniz's intellectual energies are expended on monads, not on that 'rainbow or mock-sun' the extended world. For Kant, the only possible doctrines – or anyway the only ones worth having – concern the world of appearances. 'We shall never dream of seeking to inform ourselves about the objects of our senses as they are in themselves, that is,

[18] 315. Next quotation: A 380.

out of all relation to the senses.' The only significant exception to this will be explored at length in Chapter 10 below.

§18. Imposition and things in themselves

Kant's uses of 'thing in itself' and 'v in itself' are not, I have agreed, always innocent. Among the suspect uses, there is one sub-class which can be fully explained, understood and neutralized.

Regarding Kant's view that there is a certain minimum of structure which our experience must have: self-consciousness requires that our experience conform to the twelve 'categories', and also – I now add – Kant has other reasons for thinking that experience must be temporal and that any experienced outer or objective world must be spatial. I want to focus attention on an aspect of Kant's way of viewing this body of doctrine: he sometimes suggests that these inevitable features of our experience are imposed upon it by the mind – conformity to the categories being the work of the understanding, and spatio-temporality being imposed by the sensibility.

For reasons given elsewhere, I reject this 'imposition' version of the theory about necessary features of experience. Experience may have features which it could not lack, or be known to lack; but if this is so, it arises not from facts of the form 'Before any experience can reach us, the mind *makes* it F', but rather from ones of the form 'If experience were not F, the mind would not let it reach us'. In short, Kant's 'imposition' theory should give place to a 'selection' theory. Objection: 'So the experiences which humans have *happen* to be of just the sort which the human mind insists upon receiving although it makes no contribution to shaping the experience itself! How do you explain this remarkable coincidence?' I am not sure that I need to explain it; but, if I must, what is wrong with an analogue of the explanation of why the air on this planet 'happens' to be of just the sort human lungs insist upon having?

Now, sometimes when Kant says that we experience things 'as they appear' and not 'as they are in themselves', he is expressing this 'imposition' theory. His point is that the over-all nature of our experience reflects the spatio-temporalizing, categorizing impact of the mind upon our data. Somewhat analogously, if someone's view of the world is distorted by an astigmatism, he *does* see things as they appear and not as they are.

Although it is not unreasonable to express the imposition doctrine in

54

the language of 'as they appear, not as they are in themselves', neither item in this equation can help to rescue the other. The equation is defensible, indeed, partly because the two are bad in the same way. A major objection to the imposition theory is that it represents experience as arising from a transaction between the human mind and...what? Something non-empirical, anyway, since everything empirical arises from the transaction. Perhaps, then, it is a transaction between the human mind and things as they are in themselves!

So Kant sometimes uses the language of 'as they appear, not as they are in themselves' to stress the alleged contribution of the mind to our intuitions, and there are many places in the *Critique* where it is helpful to remember this. The most striking of these is Kant's remark that 'Leibniz took the appearances for things-in-themselves' (320). This is *prima facie* intolerably puzzling. It seems to accuse Leibniz of taking extended things ('appearances') to be monads ('things in themselves') or anyway to be empirically inaccessible as monads are, but that was not Leibniz's view at all. Kant goes on to say that Leibniz 'still gave [appearances] the name of phenomena' only 'on account of the confused character of our representations of them'. One wants to protest that Leibniz called extended things 'phenomena' not for that reason but because he believed that they were not ultimately real, and it seems hard to square that with the extraordinary assertion that he took them to be things in themselves.

This assertion can be explained, however, in terms of the imposition doctrine: Kant is simply asserting that Leibniz did not do justice to the interfering, imprinting, shaping effects of the human mind upon our data. And so a remark which seemed at first to be a precise reversal of the truth now turns out to be true, for it is true that Leibniz did not have the imposition theory.

That explanation is borrowed from Beck's illuminating treatment of Kant's seemingly even wilder statement that Hume took the objects of experience to be things in themselves.[19] Now, Hume said that the only objects of experience are *impressions*; and Kant seems to be making the preposterous claim that Hume somehow made these empirically unavailable, hiding them behind the veil of perception. Beck, however, argues convincingly that Kant's point is merely that Hume does not think that the human mind imprints certain inevitable features upon our impressions.

It is not always clear whether a use of 'things in themselves' etc. is

19 *Critique of Practical Reason*, Akademie edition, p. 53; Beck, *Practical Reason*, p. 181.

innocent or guilty or, so to speak, both at once. Consider, for example, Kant's strikingly anti-Leibnizian claims: 'Appearances...do not represent things in themselves' (332), and 'Space does not represent any property of things in themselves, nor does it represent them in their relation to one another' (42). We can construe these as saying that appearances do not truthfully reflect things in themselves, because the mind leaves its mark upon appearances. But Kant might instead be saying merely that we must think about appearances on their own terms, using only such concepts as have an empirical cash-value, rather than trying to speculate about their alleged relationship to items which are empirically inaccessible to us. On the former construction, Kant is saying that the relation between spatial appearances and things in themselves is not one of representation, whereas on the second interpretation he is saying that the spatial world should not be theorized about in terms of any alleged relationship to an underlying non-empirical reality. The difference between the two is that between Kant's worst and his best.

The important opposition between Kant and Leibniz, however, does not concern what they affirm about the extended world; and Kant's charge that Leibniz takes the world to be a thing in itself is a red herring. Where the two philosophers significantly differ is in their attitude to anything other than the extended world. When Leibniz says that the extended world is an appearance or phenomenon, he is *contrasting* it with that ultimate reality which is his preferred subject of investigation. When Kant says that the extended world is an appearance, he is not contrasting it with any possible subject of investigation or even of conjecture.

§ 19. Substances as sempiternal

The concept of substance, dropped in § 14, must now be picked up again. We have met the idea of a substance as something indestructible, but our considerations of the Dialectic will involve the stronger thesis that a substance cannot come into or go out of existence, or, as I shall say, cannot be originated or annihilated. By this criterion, a substance must be sempiternal, i.e. must exist at all times.

Some terms of art will be needed. An *alteration* of x is a happening in which x's state changes while x remains in existence. An *existence-change* of x is x's being originated or annihilated. I divide existence-changes into *dependent* and *absolute*. In a dependent existence-change, the existence-change of some item is the alteration of some other item: for instance, the origination of a blush is the alteration of a face, and the annihilation of a quarrel is the alteration of some people. An absolute existence-change is one which is not dependent, i.e. does not consist in something's alteration. Of course any existence-change *entails* some alterations and may *cause* others, for if something is originated or annihilated then other things will alter in respect of certain relational properties; but that is not to say that every existence-change *is* an alteration.

The existence-change of an attribute must be a dependent one. Just because a bout of influenza is adjectival upon a victim, its annihilation is the victim's recovering or dying, just as its origination is the victim's falling ill. Aggregates are *prima facie* capable of undergoing existence-changes of either kind. In the dependent kind, the aggregate is originated or annihilated by the mustering or dispersing of its parts, whereas in the absolute kind the aggregate's parts themselves sheerly come into existence or go out of existence. Items which are neither attributes nor aggregates are capable only of absolute existence-change; for if x's existence-change is not absolute, it must be identical with the alteration of $y_1, \ldots, y_n$; and so x must be either an aggregate whose parts are included in $y_1, \ldots, y_n$ or else an attribute of such an aggregate.

I can now interrelate our two main accounts of what 'substance' means. If something is a 'substance' in our original sense of being in no way adjectival upon anything else, then the only existence-change it can undergo is an absolute one. Now, many philosophers have thought that *absolute existence-changes cannot occur*. That entails that a radically non-adjectival item cannot undergo existence change at all, so that if it ever exists it always exists. According to this line of thought, then, whatever is a substance by our original 'non-adjectival' criterion is also one by the 'sempiternity' criterion.

Most philosophers have agreed that absolute origination is impossible. But we are now concerned with the stronger thesis, also widely held, that there cannot be absolute existence-change of either kind – that 'creating and annihilating' are 'miracles which none but God can work; they exceeding all natural powers'.[20] There seems to be no one explanation for this prevalent belief. Of various possible supports, I shall present two in this section and one each in §20 and §21.

My first offering is an argument by Kant's contemporary, Moses Mendelssohn. Kant's attack on it treats it as an argument about the soul,

---

[20] *Leibniz-Clarke*, Leibniz's fourth letter, § 44.

but really it argues against the possibility of any absolute existence-change (413–15). According to Mendelssohn:

(a) Time is 'dense' in the mathematical sense: between any two instants there is an intermediate instant which is distinct from both.

(b) All changes must therefore be absolutely gradual: if the world is in state S_1 at t_1 and in a different state S_3 at t_3, then it must be in an intermediate state S_2 at an intermediate time t_2.

(c) But there is nothing intermediate between existing and not existing; and this, together with (b), rules out all absolute existence-changes, because there is no way such a change can occur gradually. Dependent ones are all right: a quarrel can be gradually annihilated, because people can gradually cease to quarrel.

Premisses (a) and (c) are both disputable, but here I shall attend only to (b). Why must all changes be gradual? Mendelssohn's reason is this: x could change discontinuously from being F to being G only by being F at one instant and G *at the next*; but according to premiss (a) there is no 'next instant' after a given instant.

Mendelssohn's argument fails, because it is based on a wrong view about what non-gradual or discontinuous change would have to involve. An item x can change discontinuously from being F to being G just so long as there is an instant t such that Fx at t and Gx at *every instant after t*. There is no question of x's being G at the 'next instant': there is no 'next instant', for the set of instants-later-than-t has no earliest member. Yet the change from being F to being G will be as discontinuous or non-gradual as anybody could wish, with x remaining F up to and including t and being G thereafter. Analogously, we can cleanly cut the set of fractions into those which are $\leqslant \frac{2}{3}$ and those which are $> \frac{2}{3}$, the latter sub-set having no smallest member.

My second offering is by Kant himself. He accurately identified and distinguished the two main strands in traditional thinking about substance, starting with the notion of a substance as neither an attribute nor an aggregate, and then moving in a controlled and deliberate way from this to the notion of substances as sempiternal. This move is taken by two distinct routes, of which the first is a transparent trick – a device which Kant calls 'schematism'.[21] The general idea is that every concept must be made applicable to temporal items, and so the notion of temporality must be added to any concept which does not already have it – the result being the 'schema' of the concept. Thus the non-temporal concept of *conditionality* or of if–then-connectedness has as its

[21] 176–87 and 300–2. On 'permanence', see 183.

schema or temporally fattened-up version the concept of *cause* – or so Kant hopes. Similarly, the non-temporal concept of substance, i.e. of something irreducibly non-adjectival, has as its schema the concept of 'permanence' – by which Kant means 'sempiternity'. For this bold, convenient, implausible claim, no justification is offered.

Later in the *Critique*, Kant makes the move again, this time by arguing that there cannot be absolute existence-changes. One of his arguments for this is unintelligible to me and, apparently, to everyone else.[22] The other, though, is quite manageable. Its basis is epistemological: we can rule out the possibility of an absolute existence-change because such a happening 'can never be a possible perception'. Kant argues as follows. To know that something x was annihilated between t_1 and t_2, I must be able to have experiential evidence that it existed at t_1 and that it did not exist at t_2. There is no problem about t_1: all I need is an experience of perceiving x. But what is to be my basis for saying that by t_2 x no longer existed? An experience of not-x? That is nonsense. It seems that the answer must be something of the form: an experience of an x-less world, or of space filled with other things to the exclusion of x, or of a reality in which no item can be identified with x. But anything of this form amounts to saying that what I had at t_2 was an experience of the world, or space, or reality, as being in an x-less condition; and that treats x's non-existence as adjectival upon the world, or space, or whatever; which suggests that it may be reasonable after all to treat x's existence-change as an alteration. The argument can clearly be adapted to cover origination as well.

I now think that this argument has a good deal of force. I shall say more about it at the end of §21 below.

§ 20. The balance principle

My first two offerings concerned individual philosophers. The third is less localized. It is what I call the balance principle, which says that in any fully intelligible causal transaction *something gains what something else loses*. This obviously implies that absolute existence-change could not occur in a causally explainable way. I shall detour a little to say something about the balance principle itself.

I don't offer the principle as true. Indeed, I am sure it is false. But it is important in the history of ideas, for its acceptance helps to explain the rejection of absolute existence-changes and many other beliefs as well.

---

[22] 224–7. The other argument is on 231.

if x is type F and y causes x then y must be x
A scholastic principle: Man begats man.

For example, the view that minds act upon bodies gave trouble to the Cartesians: 'The properties of the two kinds of substance seem to place them in such diverse categories that it is impossible for them to interact.'[23] But why should diversity rule out causal interaction? The immediate answer is that Cartesians and others held to a 'causal likeness principle' which says that a cause must resemble its effect; but one would like, if possible, to explain why they believed *that*. I offer the explanation: the causal likeness principle was accepted because it is entailed by the balance principle. That fits Berkeley, at any rate: 'It is...extravagant to say, a thing which...is unperceiving, is the cause of our perceptions, without any regard either to consistency, or the old known axiom: *Nothing can give to another that which it hath not itself.*' This explicitly connects the difficulty about body–mind causation with something like the balance principle.

I have spoken of something's gaining what another loses. That can be construed in either of two ways. (1) It can mean merely that for some value of F, x becomes more F while y becomes less F, or that x becomes F while y ceases to be F. (2) It can mean that x acquires some or all of that very same Fness which y had. Although (2) is incoherent, I contend that the balance principle's power in the history of ideas has owed more to (2) than to (1). I shall try to explain.

According to a certain world-picture, nature must balance her books, and any causal commerce between two things can only be the transmission of properties from one to the other, as though it were the handing on of a parcel, say. Someone entertaining this picture will regard any such transmission as natural and inevitable, but he will see any other sort of causal transaction as mysterious and therefore as impossible. Descartes, in that frame of mind, wrote: 'It is manifest by the natural light that there must be at least as much reality in [a] cause as in its effect. For whence can the effect derive its reality if not from its cause? And how could this cause communicate this reality to it, unless it possessed it itself?'[24]

Locke wanted an experiential basis for what he called the 'idea of power', and it seems that paradigms of 'power' had to be causal trans-

[23] A. Kenny, *Descartes* (New York, 1968), p. 223. Next quoted phrase: R. A. Watson, *The Downfall of Cartesianism* (The Hague, 1966). Final quotation: Berkeley, *Three Dialogues Between Hylas and Philonous*, one quarter of the way through the third dialogue.

[24] *Third Meditation*, about one third of the way through. Descartes sometimes envisages the cause as not losing what the effect gains; but that is only when the cause is God, whose infiniteness presumably excuses him from the normal standards of ontological accountancy.

actions which do *not* stand to reason, are *not* such as a rationalist would be fully comfortable with. Accordingly, cases where nature's books are balanced will not serve as paradigms of 'power':

For, when the ball obeys the motion of a billiard-stick, it is not any action of the ball, but bare passion. Also when by impulse it sets another ball in motion that lay in its way, it only communicates the motion it had received from another, and loses in itself so much as the other received: which gives us but a very obscure idea of an *active* power of moving in body, whilst we observe it only to *transfer*, but not to *produce* any motion.[25]

Locke here accords a special status to phenomena which conform to the balance principle, and apparently does so because he thinks of them as involving literal transfer.

On this matter, Leibniz saw clearly. He said that monads cannot interact and that their histories are only pseudo-causally correlated with one another. Many philosophers today would rightly want to strike out that 'pseudo-' on the ground that contingent correlations or 'harmony' are all there is to 'causal connection', properly understood. Still, Leibniz's incorrect claim was a vehicle for something quite correct, namely a denial that there is causal interaction involving the literal transfer of properties:

There is no way of explaining how a monad could be altered...internally by any other creature...Monads have no windows through which anything could enter or leave. Accidents [properties] could not detach themselves and wander about outside substances, as the sensible species of the scholastics used to do.[26]

Locke, long after the passage I have quoted, changes his ground somewhat. Wanting to allow that minds can move bodies, he says that this is no worse than the moving of bodies by bodies – the latter being, he confesses, 'obscure and inconceivable'. He makes impact phenomena look 'inconceivable' by describing them in terms of literal transfer of motion – 'the passing of motion out of one body into another'. Leibniz pounces:

I am not surprised if you find insurmountable difficulties where you seem to assume something as inconceivable as the passing of an accident from one subject to another...It is not true that a body loses as much motion as it gives to another; which seems to be conceived as if motion were a substantial thing and resembled salt dissolved in water.

[25] *Essay* II. xxi. 4.
[26] *Monadology* § 7. Next quotations: *Essay* and *New Essays*, both II. xxiii. 28.

Leibniz here puts an unerring finger on a philosophical error which, I submit, helped to nourish acceptance of the balance principle; and the latter, I further suggest, may have increased philosophers' confidence that absolute existence-changes cannot occur.

Kant, incidentally, attended to the notion of the literal transfer of properties, not in the *Critique* but in two other works which appeared between the publication of A and that of B. In the *Metaphysical Foundations of Natural Science*, he criticises property-transfer in terms much like Leibniz's, and opposes to it the principle *Accidentia non migrant e substantiis in substantias* – accidents do not travel from substances to substances.[27] Property-transfer also makes a curious appearance in the *Prolegomena*, when Kant says: 'It is. . .inconceivable how the intuition of a thing that is present should make me know it as it is in itself, for its properties cannot migrate into my faculty of representation.' The idea here is that because literal transfer of properties is nonsense, all that can happen is that the properties of the thing I perceive should somehow *correspond* to my sensory state when I perceive it; and this, Kant apparently assumes, means that I can perceive the thing only 'as it appears' and not 'as it is in itself'. This echo of Leibniz hardly fits Kant's other remarks about knowing a thing 'as it is in itself', but there is an ironic justice in his connecting that unintelligible notion with the equally incoherent idea of the literal transfer of properties.

§21. Existence-changes and quantifiers

My fourth suggested basis for the rejection of absolute existence-changes is a conceptual pressure which I do not know how to resist. It arises from what I call 'the Kant–Frege view' about the concept of existence. This was first defended in detail by Kant, though others foreshadowed it; it first received solid logical foundations in the work of Frege; and I shall explore it in more detail in §72 below in connexion with a famous argument for the existence of God.

According to the Kant–Frege view, 'existent' is not a predicate, existence is not a property, existing is not something things *do* all the time. To assert the existence of something is not to pick it out and then assert, as a fact about it, that *it exists*, as one might pick it out and assert that it is green or square or soluble. According to the Kant–Frege view, the only legitimate way of asserting the existence of a non-adjectival

[27] *Metaphysical Foundations*, p. 113. Next quotation: *Prolegomena* § 9.

item is to find a description which fits it – F, say – and then to assert that *there is something which is F*, or that $(\exists x)Fx$.

It has not been widely noticed that the Kant–Frege view entails that there is no legitimate way of reporting the occurrence of an absolute existence-change.

Dependent existence-changes are all right. The birth of a blush, say, can be reported in the form ($\sim Fa$ at t_1 and Fa at t_2) – John was not blushing at t_1 and was blushing at t_2. Similarly with other attributes, and with their annihilation as well as origination. Aggregates are no more problematical; a cloud's death by dispersal can be reported in the form 'Certain moisture-particles were closely assembled at t_1 and were scattered at t_2', which goes easily into a Fregean formula.

But how can we state in Fregean form that a hydrogen atom, say, absolutely went out of existence between t_1 and t_2? Let Hx mean 'x is a hydrogen atom'. Then we might try this:

(1) $(\exists x)(Hx$ at t_1 & $\sim Hx$ at $t_2)$.

But that means only that something which was a hydrogen atom at t_1 was not a hydrogen atom at t_2; perhaps it was not annihilated but merely transformed into something else.

Let us try another tack. Perhaps there is some property which every hydrogen atom has, and which cannot be gained or lost except through absolute origination or annihilation. This is to suppose, with Leibniz, that 'there are some sorts or species to which an individual cannot (naturally, at least) cease to belong, when it has been of their number, whatever revolutions may happen in nature.'[28] Let L stand for such a property, reading Lx as 'x is located', meaning that x is somewhere in space. Then we can try this:

(2) $(\exists x)(Hx$ at t_1 & Lx at t_1 & $\sim Lx$ at $t_2)$

– a hydrogen atom which was located at t_1 was not located at t_2, which implies, given our assumption that locatedness is unlosable except through annihilation, that between t_1 and t_2 the atom was absolutely annihilated.

I once suggested that this approach treats hydrogen atoms as adjectival upon space: an atom's existing is equated with its being somewhere, and thus with space's containing it; and this makes the atom relate to space rather as a blush does to a face. But that objection, I can now see, is not good enough. It depends upon the special detail that Lx is read as

[28] *New Essays* III. vi. 1.

'x is located', and so does not touch versions of this general approach which invoke some other unlosable property – for example, the property of being-located-or-unlocated, which has been suggested. What I now think to be the chief difficulty about (2) applies to it no matter what the unlosable property L is supposed to be. The difficulty is as follows.

If (2) is to report the annihilation of a hydrogen atom, the report is incomplete unless we can *say that* L stands for an unlosable property, in the sense that any atom x of which Lx becomes false must have been absolutely annihilated. But how can we say this while respecting the Kant–Frege view? We might try:

$$(3) \qquad (x)(t)(Hx \text{ at } t \to Lx \text{ at } t),$$

which says that while anything is a hydrogen atom it is also L. But that is quite inadequate. When it is combined with (2), what follows is not that a hydrogen atom was absolutely annihilated, but only that a hydrogen atom ceased to be a hydrogen atom. We might try instead:

$$(4) \qquad (x)[(\exists t)(Hx \text{ at } t \ \& \ Lx \text{ at } t) \to (t)(Lx \text{ at } t)],$$

which means that a hydrogen atom which is L at some time is L at every time. But that is much too strong; for it is inconsistent with (2), which says that a hydrogen atom which was L at one time was not L at a later time.

We need some way of saying that a hydrogen atom is L at every time at which *it exists*. There's the rub: how, in Fregean form, are we to capture 'it exists'? I think it cannot be done, and so I do seriously regard the Kant–Frege view as constituting a logical objection to the notion of an absolute existence-change.

The Kant–Frege view does not imply the durability or uncreatability of your favourite candidate for the title of 'a substance'; for *any* existence-change can be reported as an alteration. For example, the annihilation of a hydrogen atom can be reported in the form: a certain region of space was affected with a spatio-temporally continuous thickening, and then it thinned out in a certain way. What the Kant–Frege view does imply is that any existence-change ought to be reported in a manner which represents it as an alteration. The colloquial ' . . . and then it went clean out of existence' may be tolerated, but according to the Kant–Frege view there is a gain in clarity, a firmer handling of the relevant concepts, if the facts are expressed in Fregean form as an alteration of space.

One can see the Kant–Frege view of existence as giving a logical reason for saying what Kant – in the argument reported at the end of §19 – gave an epistemological reason for saying, namely that if we are really concerned with conceptual clarity and rigour we ought to think of every existence-change as a kind of alteration.

Of the philosophers who thought there could not be absolute existence-changes, most did not think of the Kant–Frege view about existence, and would have rejected it if they had. Still, if the view is correct, then it truly describes the concept of existence which those philosophers possessed and used, even if they would not have described it correctly, as Kant and Frege did. So they may have been under pressure from this source to deny that there could be absolute existence-changes, even if they were not equipped to understand the pressure by identifying its source.

4

THE SUBSTANTIALITY OF THE SOUL

§ 22. The Cartesian basis

We now start on the Dialectic, beginning with Book II (see § 1 above). The first chapter of this, to which my next three chapters will be devoted, is called 'The Paralogisms of Pure Reason'. Its topic is the soul – i.e. one's mind when considered independently of any beliefs about anything else whatsoever. In this use of 'soul', the word has no religious connotations.

I shall use the phrase 'the Cartesian basis' to refer to the intellectual situation in which one attends to nothing but one's mind and its states. Descartes worked his way down to the Cartesian basis by 'feigning doubt' of everything which did not meet a certain standard of indubitability. That left him with an indubitable residue which he embodied in the statement '*Cogito*', which I take to stand for any first-person, present-tense statement about one's own mind. Descartes' standard of indubitability is unattractive, his reason for interest in it is even more so, and his reconstruction on the basis of '*Cogito*' is lax and self-indulgent. What makes his endeavour still interesting is its representing one's knowledge of one's own states of mind as the *foundation* for all one's other knowledge. Even if I cannot doubt that I have a body while not doubting that my mind is thus and so, still all my beliefs about bodies somehow *rest on* what I know about states of my mind. So I am sympathetic to the adoption of the Cartesian basis, i.e. to the position sometimes called 'methodological solipsism'.

The following evident truths, I submit, show that the Cartesian basis is basic:

(1) Any intellectual problem which I have must, for me, take the form 'What should I think about x?'

(2) The decision as to what I am to think about x must be taken by me.

(3) My decision as to what to think about x must be based upon data which I have.

(4) How I use my data in reaching my decision must depend upon the concepts, or the intellectual capacities and dispositions, which I have.

These are almost trivial, and yet taken together they imply that the Cartesian basis is the foundation of all knowledge.

Most philosophers these days reject this conclusion, often for reasons of this form: 'I cannot know anything about my own mind unless P is true, so the truth of P cannot be something I know through the Cartesian basis.' Let us consider some values of P, that is, some possible candidates for the title of 'necessary condition for my self-consciousness'. I choose three:

(a) I inhabit an objective realm (containing objects other than myself);

(b) I have a body which shares an objective realm with other objects;

(c) I share an objective realm with other (embodied) people.

I neglect 'There are disembodied other people' and 'The only objective item is my body', for neither of these looks even remotely plausible as a requirement for self-consciousness.

Relations amongst these three are simple. (b) *is stronger than* (a), because I might be a disembodied mind which is located in space and perceives surrounding objects, in which case (a) would be true and (b) false. That (c) *is stronger than* (a) is obvious. It might be thought that (c) is also stronger than (b), resulting from the sheer addition to (b) of other embodied people. But I construe (c) as requiring bodies for other people but not necessarily for myself, and so (b) *and* (c) *are independent of one another*. I construe (c) in that way to keep the door open for someone who thinks that my self-consciousness requires me to know about other people but not them to know about me – this being as plausible as most of the offerings in the literature.

In fact, (a) and (b) and (c) themselves are not quite what we want. Someone with an (a)-involving view about requirements for self-consciousness, for instance, should opt for something stronger or for something weaker than (a) itself. Stronger: to be self-conscious I must know, or have adequate grounds for believing, that I inhabit an objective realm. Weaker: to be self-conscious I must have the thought of occupying, or know what it would be like to occupy, an objective realm. Similarly with (b) and with (c). I can see no conceivable grounds for thinking that my self-consciousness requires the mere truth of (a) or (b) or (c) without requiring any corresponding belief or thought on my part.

So, corresponding to each of (a), (b) and (c) there is a strong 'knowlege' version and a weaker 'thought' version. The stronger one in each case requires me to have data which I bring under certain concepts, whereas the weaker requires me only to have the concepts – i.e. to be able to employ them if suitable data should occur. (No one would argue, I think, that self-consciousness requires certain data but not certain concepts.) So we have six possible theses about requirements for self-consciousness; and the possibility of combining (b) with (c) brings the total to eight. My classification may omit something, or deal too crudely with what it does cover, but most current theorizing about requirements for self-consciousness can usefully be viewed in the light of the schema I have presented.

The position for which Strawson has argued seems to be the stronger, 'knowledge' version of (b) and (c) together.[1] Sometimes, however, he seems to contend for a 'knowledge' version of (b) and a 'thought' version of (c).

Wittgenstein's attack on the idea of a private language is notoriously unclear and evasive.[2] The best one can make of it is to suppose that in Wittgenstein's view self-consciousness requires a 'knowledge' version of (c) and perhaps of (b) as well.

Wittgenstein's argument has 'suggested' to Kenny a much more persuasive one.[3] That Kenny arguably succeeds where Wittgenstein manifestly fails is due to Kenny's having a much weaker conclusion: what he contends for is no stronger than a 'knowledge' version of the disjunction of (a) and (b) and (c).

Kant said that inner experience is possible only on the assumption of outer experience, meaning that my self-consciousness requires me to have data which I can and do bring under objectivity-concepts.[4] Kant thus opts for the 'knowledge' version of (a), untainted by (b) and (c).

Now, let R be any plausible view of the form 'I cannot be self-conscious unless P'. The view that the Cartesian basis is the foundation of all knowledge need not conflict with R. What the former view implies is that one ought to start from the Cartesian basis *even in arguing for* R. When I defended Kant's view that inner experience requires outer experience, my argument began by considering what is needed for awareness of one's own states of mind, and concluded that one needs to know that one occupies an objective world.[5] But knowing this is having certain sorts of data and applying certain concepts to them,

---

[1] P. F. Strawson, *Individuals* (London, 1959), Ch. 3. See also *Bounds of Sense*, pp. 163–6, and § 38 below.
[2] L. Wittgenstein, *Philosophical Investigations* (Oxford, 1953), Part I, §§ 243ff.
[3] A. Kenny, *Descartes* (New York, 1968), pp. 77–8.
[4] 274–9 and note on xxxix–xli.   [5] *Kant's Analytic* § 51.

and that can be fully described in terms of the Cartesian basis. So there is no conflict.

Suppose that *R* says that my self-consciousness requires me to make judgments about *Fs*. Suppose also that we adopt an extreme form of the thesis of the primacy of the Cartesian basis, taking it to imply that judgments about *Fs* are mere short-hand for certain kinds of judgments about one's inner states. Even this extremism does not yield a contradiction. The two theses together imply merely that I could not make judgments about my own inner states unless I could embody some of them in a certain shorthand.

All of this, I believe, would have been sympathetically received by Kant. In a multitude of ways, the *Critique of Pure Reason* takes the Cartesian basis to be the foundation of all one's knowledge. This goes with its being an intensely first-person singular work, which indeed pays too little attention to the fact that humans have bodies. In his chapter on the soul, Kant undertakes to correct certain mistakes regarding the Cartesian basis; but the view that the Cartesian basis deserves attention and respect as the foundation of all our knowledge is not said to be a mistake.

§ 23. The search for the thinking subject

In the Cartesian basis, all data occur as mine. All facts are facts about me. This is what Wittgenstein meant when he wrote 'I am my world' and 'What solipsism *means* is quite correct...That the world is *my* world is shown by the fact that the limits of language (the only language I understand) are the limits of *my* world.'[6] So the concept of myself has a very peculiar role in the Cartesian basis. Kant's main message in the Paralogisms chapter is that if I note the peculiarities in the concept of myself, and don't attend properly to what their source is, I may accord them a significance they don't deserve and take them to prove things which don't really follow. More specifically: I may wrongly think that *I* must be a very special kind of item within my world, whereas in fact I am not *in* my world but am its boundary. Wittgenstein again: 'There is no such thing as the thinking, representing subject...The subject doesn't belong to the world, but is a limit of the world.'

Kant expresses this general point by saying that all my knowledge of myself as an object arises not from the special role of the concept of

[6] L. Wittgenstein, *Tractatus Logico-Philosophicus* (London, 1961), 5.62–3. Next quotation: *ibid.* 5.631–2.

myself in the Cartesian basis, but rather from what I find in detail when I attend to my various states:

> I do not know myself through being conscious of myself as thinking, but only when I am conscious of the intuition of myself as [being in various particular states]...The object is not the consciousness of the *determining* self, but only that of the *determinable* self, that is, of my inner intuition.[7]

The 'determining self' is, so to speak, the omnipresent 'I' which is the limit of my world – the 'I' who *makes all* my judgments; whereas the 'determinable self' is the 'I' whose various states can be a matter of introspective examination ('inner intuition'), the 'I' who *is the topic of some* of my judgments. Something similar is involved here:

> Consciousness is, indeed, that which alone makes all representations to be thoughts, and in it, therefore,...all our perceptions must be found; but beyond this logical meaning of the 'I', we have no knowledge of the subject in itself.

In all this, Kant takes himself to be opposing 'the rational doctrine of the soul', of which he says:

> [It seeks] to learn in regard to the soul [only what] can be inferred, independently of all experience (which determines me more specifically and *in concreto*), from this concept 'I', so far as it is present in all thought...If in this science the least empirical element of my thought, or any special perception of my inner state, were intermingled with the grounds of knowledge, it would no longer be a rational but an *empirical* doctrine of the soul. Thus we have here what professes to be a science built upon the single proposition '*I think*'.

What makes rational psychology objectionable is not that it claims certainty for its results. Kant could very well allow that empirical knowledge of the soul, gained through 'inner intuition', meets Cartesian standards of indubitability. What he objects to is the attempt to base claims about the soul not upon 'determining' data but upon the merely 'formal' role of the concept of oneself in the Cartesian basis. Indeed, Kant shies away from the notion of a *concept* of oneself: 'The judgment "I think"...is the vehicle of all concepts...It can have no special designation, because it serves only to introduce all our thought, as belonging to consciousness.'[8] He also says that rational psychology is based on 'the simple, and in itself completely empty, representation

---

7 406–7. Next two quotations: A 350; 400.
8 399–400. Next quotation: 404.

"*I*'", of which he remarks, 'We cannot even say that this is a concept, ~~3·404~~ but only that it is a bare consciousness which accompanies all concepts.'

(I have quoted Kant as saying that rational psychology is based upon 'I think'; yet earlier I took '*Cogito*' differently, as embodying the whole set of present-tense statements about one's mind, a set on which one could base 'empirical psychology'. I am following Kant in using the Latin '*Cogito*' for the set of empirical inner facts, and the modern 'I think' for the world-limiting use of 'I' in the Cartesian basis:

> The proposition, 'I think', is...here taken only problematically, not in so far as it may contain perception of an existent (the Cartesian *cogito, ergo sum*), but in respect of its mere possibility, in order to see what properties applicable to its subject... may follow from so simple a proposition. (405)

This is unhappily expressed, but the point is clear: Kant uses '*Cogito*' as a reservoir of empirical self-knowledge, and uses 'I think' to express the peculiar role of oneself as the boundary of one's world in the Cartesian basis. He does not always use these expressions in these ways, but he holds firmly to the distinction itself.)

Kant offers four paralogisms, each supposedly embodying a mistake which a rational psychologist might make. In each of the first three, it seems, Kant regards the conclusion as expressing a truth of a peculiarly empty and formal kind – a truth stemming solely from the formal role of the representation 'I' in the Cartesian basis – and the rational psychologist's mistake is just that he inflates this truth, taking it to have content which it really lacks (A 400). These three conclusions say, respectively, that the soul is a *substance*, that it is *simple*, and – mysteriously – that it is a *person*. I shall discuss these, in turn, in this and my next two chapters.

The fourth paralogism does not fit that general account. It gives Kant an excuse to offer, strangely late in the *Critique*, his fullest defence of his view that judgments about the objective realm are analysable into judgments about one's inner states, this being a very strong formulation of the concept-empiricism described in §9 above. Kant calls this view 'transcendental idealism', a label which covers not merely phenomenalism but also Kant's doctrine that we perceive things not 'as they are in themselves' but only 'as they appear', i.e. as they are shaped and modified by the mind (see §18 above). In the discussion of the fourth paralogism, this overlay of bad theory is irrelevant. Kant is there contesting the claim that outer things have 'a merely doubtful existence' (A 366), and so he needs only his phenomenalism and not all the trappings of 'not as they are in themselves but only as they appear'.

Should the fourth paralogism occur in a chapter whose proper topic is the soul? Kant may have had in mind an argument of Descartes' to this effect: My own existence is not doubtful, but the existence of physical things is doubtful; therefore I am not a physical thing.[9] But even if Kant's attack on 'The existence of physical things is doubtful' is motivated by its role as a premiss in that argument, the attack is still mislocated. For what it implies, with regard to Descartes' argument for the immateriality of the self, is that the argument rests upon a mistake about the nature of objectivity-judgments, not that it involves any underlying error about the soul. Elsewhere, Kant offers a quick list of mistakes about the soul which are embodied in the four paralogisms, and he associates the fourth with the view that 'thinking beings...are conscious of their existence as...distinct from matter' (409), which is a mistake about matter, not about thinking beings. Since the fourth paralogism is misplaced, I shall say no more about it.

In B, Kant rewrote most of the paralogisms chapter in the light of criticisms which had been made of A. The later version does not seriously try to distribute the material amongst the paralogisms, but rather lumps the first three of them together and ignores the fourth. The common message for the first three paralogisms is, approximately, that the soul cannot be known as an object, ordinary concepts cannot be applied to it, it is not something 'given'. My own view is that the treatment in A, where this general message is split into three parts or aspects, deserves attention. The details of the individual paralogisms, flawed as they are, provide a finger-hold on an otherwise slippery surface.

§ 24. The soul as substance

In the first paralogism, the 'rational psychologist' argues that the soul is a 'substance'. Although Kant calls the argument a 'paralogism', implying that it is 'formally invalid',[10] and although he tries to argue that the argument is invalidated by a vitiating ambiguity, that is not his most considered or his best view of the matter. What we must attend to is Kant's view that the so-called paralogism is acceptable as long as one does not – as the rational psychologist does – misunderstand and inflate its conclusion in a certain way. Before discussing the inflation, we must see what the basic argument is – the argument which really does establish that I am a substance, this being understood as an empty

---

[9] *Second Meditation*, one third of the way through.
[10] 399. The alleged ambiguity: note on 411–12.

or 'formal' truth which neither arises from nor leads to any empirical knowledge of myself such as inner intuition might reveal.

The argument is based on the notion of a substance as 'a something which can be thought only as subject, never as a predicate of something else'.[11] This appears in the first premiss of the paralogism as a definition of 'substance' as 'that, the representation of which is the absolute subject of our judgments and cannot therefore be employed as determination of another thing'. This is just the earlier definition with the adjective 'absolute' added – an addition which is explained by Kant's need for it in the second premiss of the paralogism.

The second premiss says: 'I, as a thinking being, am the *absolute subject* of all my possible judgments, and this representation of myself cannot be employed as predicate of any other thing.' From the two premisses together, the conclusion syllogistically follows. Clearly, it is the second premiss that needs attention.

I start with the premiss's second clause: 'This representation of myself cannot be employed as predicate of any other thing.' This, like the first premiss, reminds us that substances *must* be handled substantivally whereas non-substances *need not* be. This clearly and rightly implies that we sometimes have a choice – e.g. between speaking of 'the duration of *the fight*' or of 'how long the men fought'. Now, the following seems reasonable: 'My concept of myself cannot play an adjectival role, because the difference between the substantival and the adjectival handling of something is a difference between two ways in which *I* can handle my data. Within the Cartesian basis, any question about how anything is to be handled is a question about how I am to handle it, and so every such question has a substantival "I" as a kind of substratum or framework. Therefore I cannot escape giving my concept of myself a substantival role, and so I must regard myself as a substance.' Kant sees the rational psychologist as arguing in that manner, and that presumably explains the phrase 'absolute subject of all my possible judgments' – 'absolute' meaning 'irreducible' or 'inevitable'.

This interpretation of the paralogism is mildly confirmed when Kant says that all the paralogism really establishes is that 'in thinking my existence, I cannot employ myself, save as subject of the judgment' (412n.). The interpretation also fits Kant's general thesis that the paralogisms rest upon genuine insights into the formal structure of the Cartesian basis.

But there is something which the interpretation does not cover,

---

[11] 186. Next quotation: A 348; see also 407.

namely the clause in the second premiss which says that I am 'the absolute subject of all my possible judgments'. This is a strange clause anyway. Granted that I cannot represent myself adjectivally, must I always – in every possible judgment – represent myself substantivally? Why can I not make judgments which are simply not about myself in any way at all?

Here are three possible explanations for the clause in question – all of them bad.

(1) 'The clause is to be thought of as something I assert when I am restricting myself to the Cartesian basis and construing the latter solipsistically: since I do not admit the existence of anything but myself, I have no topic or subject-matter but myself.' That, as well as being boring, is hardly the sort of line a rational psychologist would take.

(2) 'The clause is something I assert on the assumption that I have thoroughly phenomenalized my language, expressing as much as possible in terms of actual and possible states of myself, so that "I" is the only term in my language which retains a substantival role.' That has the merit of seriously involving the notion of a substance as something which cannot be handled adjectivally, which gives it a point of contact with the other premiss-material which I have discussed. But Kant doesn't actually believe that I can get by with 'I' as my only substantive (275–6), nor presumably does any rational psychologist.

(3) 'The clause reflects Kant's doctrine about self-consciousness, namely that any judgment I make can be accompanied by an "I think...".' But the self-consciousness doctrine does not say that all my judgments *are* of the form 'I think...', as though my judgment *that P* were really an ellipsis for my judgment *that I judge that P*. The doctrine makes no such absurd claim, but merely implies that given any judgment (P) which I make there is a *correlated* true judgment with myself as its subject-matter (I judge that P). That falls far short of 'I am the subject of all my possible judgments'.

So we still have no tenable conjecture as to what Kant means by 'I am the absolute subject of all my possible judgments'. Notice that each of the suggested interpretations renders this puzzling clause idle within the argument as a whole. But then the clause just *is* idle. If it is omitted, the residue of the paralogism has the form: 'If the representation of *x* cannot be handled adjectivally, then *x* is a substance; the representation of myself cannot be handled adjectivally; so I am a substance.' That is valid as it stands; or, if not, it cannot be rescued by adding a clause about 'subject of all my possible judgments'.

74

That suggests that the troublesome clause is the locus of a mistake, and so indeed it is. What the clause means, I contend, is merely that all my judgments are *mine*: not that I am their topic or subject-matter, but just that they are states of myself or episodes in my history. That must be Kant's point when he re-words the second premiss thus: 'In all our thought the "I" is the subject, in which thoughts inhere only as determinations' (A349), meaning that the thoughts occur as states of or processes in oneself. Kant's mistake is that he conflates this with the different and false claim that all my judgments are *about* myself. He has been led astray by 'subject of a judgment', which mainly means (1) 'topic of a judgment' but can be stretched to mean (2) 'maker or bearer of a judgment'. To see the difference, consider the fact that although my intuitions and my pains also (2) 'inhere in me as determinations', they do not (1) have any topic or subject-matter.

The two senses of 'subject of judgment' and cognate expressions are richly jumbled together in Kant's text. In a remark quoted above, for example, the clause 'In all our thought the "I" is the subject...' surely belongs to (1); but the remaining clause '...in which thoughts inhere only as determinations' belongs to (2). As a clue to other instances of the mix-up, notice that (1) concerns concepts or representations, which are constituents of propositions or judgments, whereas (2) concerns items in the world. That throws light on a passage where Kant says of 'this I which thinks' that 'it is known only through the thoughts which are its predicates' (404). The point is that thoughts are not (1) predicates, which are logical or linguistic entities. Rather, they are (2) properties or determinations or states, these being items in the world.

The primal example of the mix-up, however, is the second premiss itself. Look at it again: 'I...am the absolute subject of all my possible judgments, and this representation...' – *what* representation? All the other premiss-material does concern the role within a judgment of a certain concept or representation; but the clause which has given us difficulty is not about my representation of myself – it is about *myself*.

Let us force the entire paralogism into the mould of our troublesome clause, pretending that the point of the paralogism is just that I am a substance because my judgments (and other 'determinations') inhere in me. The result is a blunt and fairly uninteresting argument, which Descartes actually used:

No thought can exist apart from a thing that thinks, and in general no activity or accident can be without a substance in which to exist...There are activities which

75

we call *intellectual*...The substance in which they reside we call a *thinking thing* or a *mind*.[12]

In contrast with this, the subtler argument, from the premiss that I cannot accord an adjectival role to my representation of myself, seems not to have been explicitly used by anybody. Perhaps Kant thought that some philosophers had been nudged towards viewing the soul as a substance by a subliminal awareness of the force of the subtler argument.

Anyway, we cannot hold him to the blunt interpretation as against the subtle one, for the latter becomes prominent when Kant begins to warn us against misunderstanding the paralogism's conclusion. I now turn to that warning.

§ 25. Inflating the first paralogism

In each of the first three paralogisms, Kant insists, the conclusion states only an empty or 'formal' truth which we must be careful not to inflate, taking it to have empirical content which it really lacks. Kant equates this possible mistake with thinking that the conclusion uses its main concept in an empirical way when really it does not.

In the case of the first paralogism it is not clear what we are being warned against. If we do inflate the conclusion, *what* will we be thereby believing? One answer is implied here: 'We can indeed perceive that this representation [of "I"] is invariably present in all thought, but not that it is an abiding and continuing intuition' (A 350). That reflects the position, which Kant sometimes takes, that the empirical concept of substance is the concept of that-which-is-always-perceptually-present, so that its experiential cash-value is 'an abiding and continuing intuition'. This is such a bad account of the concept of substance that we cannot be much interested in anything which presupposes it.

Here is a more promising indication:

The proposition, ' *The soul is substance*', may...be allowed to stand, if only it be recognized that [it] does not carry us a single step further, and so cannot yield us any of the usual deductions of the pseudo-rational doctrine of the soul, as, for instance, the everlasting duration of the human soul in all changes and even in death.[13]

The paralogism might seem to prove the immortality of the soul because substances are by definition sempiternal, so that if the soul is a

---

[12] Reply to Third Objections, Haldane & Ross, p. 64; see also *Principles of Philosophy*, Part I, § 11.   [13] A 350-1. Next quotation: A 349.

substance then its imperishability is guaranteed. Furthermore, although he there says 'for instance', he admits elsewhere that the soul's immortality is the only 'instance' of a contentful conclusion which one might wrongly infer from the first paralogism:

> But what use am I to make of this concept of a substance? That I, as a thinking being, *persist* for myself, and do not in any natural manner either *arise* or *perish*, can by no means be deduced from it. Yet there is no other use to which I can put the concept of the substantiality of my thinking subject.

I take Kant's word for it: what we must avoid is thinking that the first paralogism proves the immortality of the soul. (Let us forget that sempiternity also rules out origination.)

We are supposed to be faced here with a bit of rational psychology – an argument which could lead one, plausibly though mistakenly, from formal facts about the Cartesian basis to the conclusion that one is immortal. But really Kant has presented a jumble of points which no one philosopher would string together on a line. For one thing, the argument starts with substances as substantival and ends with them as sempiternal, without a word about how the rational psychologist is supposed to make the shift. Presumably it won't be with the aid of Kant's 'schematism' trick.

The most probable route, historically speaking, is through the view that there cannot be absolute existence-changes. So perhaps Kant's rational psychologist is arguing: 'There cannot be absolute existence-changes; an existence-change of the soul would have to be absolute; so the soul cannot be annihilated.' But anyone arguing like that would surely try to rule out the soul's being an aggregate. When Descartes sketches an argument for immortality, there is careful emphasis on the soul's being 'simple', i.e. not an aggregate; and obviously the argument needs that premiss.[14]

Now, consider the two interpretations we have found for the first paralogism. On the blunt interpretation which says 'My thoughts inhere in me, so I am a substance', the possibility that I am an aggregate is simply ignored. On the subtler interpretation which says 'In the Cartesian basis, my concept of myself is irreducibly substantival', there are the makings of an argument purporting to show that I am not an aggregate. But that argument does not explicitly occur in the first

---

[14] The argument is an obscure affair which does not occur in the *Meditations* but only in Descartes' *Synopsis* of them.

paralogism, and it *is* the second paralogism![15] Either way, then, the first paralogism fails to isolate a line of thought which might persuade someone that his soul is immortal.

It is not surprising, therefore, that Kant sometimes cannot keep the first and second paralogisms apart from one another. He links them in the remark: 'With the objective reality of the concept of substance, the allied concept of simplicity likewise vanishes.'[16] In the following, they are not merely linked but fused:

[There is no] possibility of proving *a priori* that all thinking beings are in themselves simple substances, and that consequently (as follows from this same mode
of proof) personality is inseparable from them, and that they are conscious of their
existence as...distinct from all matter.

Kant there gives a clause each to the third and fourth paralogisms, but he rams the first two together in the phrase 'simple substances'. Especially in B, where he makes little of the separate identity of the paralogisms, but also sometimes even in A, Kant tends to use 'sub-stance' not as a specialized concept with roots in the notion of the irre-ducibly substantival and branches reaching up to sempiternity, but rather as meaning something like 'object'. That is, he tends to use 'simple substance' to mean merely 'simple object' or 'item which is "simple" in an ordinary empirical sense'. That allows the first para-logism to sprawl across territory which is officially divided between the first three: instead of a specific point about the concept of substance in application to the soul, we have just the general point that the soul's function as the limit of one's world should not be mistaken for any special facts about it considered as an item within one's world.

§ 26. My death

The first paralogism could embody a simpler argument than any can-vassed so far, one which goes straight from the role of 'I' in the Carte-sian basis to a conclusion about immortality, with no intermediate lemma about 'substance'. It is this: 'In the Cartesian basis, every possi-bility is the possibility of my knowing that such and such; so I can exclude from the realm of possibility anything which does not include my existence; and so I must always exist.' This, simple-minded as it

[15] Cf. *Prolegomena* § 48n.

[16] 413. Next quotation: 409. For a peculiar further example of the combination of 'simple' and 'substance', see 403. The four paralogisms are kept grammatically separate in the sentence on A 401–2.

seems to be, must be what Goethe had in mind when he said: 'It is entirely impossible for a thinking being to think of its own non-existence...To this extent everybody carries within himself...the proof of his own immortality.'[17]

With all respect to Goethe, the argument is no good. It moves, in effect, from 'I shall never have reason to think that I do not exist' to 'I shall always be assured that I do exist', and the move is clearly invalid. Furthermore, people clearly *do* think of their own non-existence, and even take precautions with respect to it – e.g. making wills and planting acorns. Yet there is an oddity, all the same, in the notion of one's own non-existence. It shows in the fact that although I may deplore my mortality I cannot be fearful at the prospect of my coming non-existence – for there is for me no such prospect. It also appears when one thinks from the standpoint of the Cartesian basis, as presumably Goethe did.

One aspect of this oddity seems not to have been properly noticed by Kant. He is given to saying that the crucial mistake in each paralogism is that of thinking that one can apply ordinary concepts to the soul:

> The unity of consciousness, which underlies the categories, is here mistaken for an intuition of the subject as object, and the category of substance is then applied to it. But this unity is only unity in *thought*, by which alone no object is given, and to which, therefore, the category of substance, which always presupposes a given *intuition*, cannot be applied. Consequently, this subject cannot be known.[18]

In the same vein, Kant says that the first paralogism does not prove anything in which 'the concept of *substance* [is] applied in a manner that is empirically serviceable', and that the conclusion, properly understood, uses that concept in a form 'of which I can make no use (empirically) *in concreto*'. If we do wrongly inflate the first paralogism, Kant says, 'We are thus making an empirical, but in this case inadmissible, employment of the category [of substance].' In remarks like these, he clearly implies that the judgment 'I shall last for ever' *does* use the concept of substance in a manner that is empirically serviceable. Arguably it does not.

The concept of everlastingness, as such, has a non-empirical aspect, for no finite amount of experience can directly and conclusively establish anything's sempiternity. But that is not my point. Experience can establish some facts about things' durations – x is not sempiternal,

---

[17] Quoted in P. Edwards, 'My Death', in P. Edwards (ed.), *The Encyclopedia of Philosophy* (New York and London, 1967). Throughout that article, Edwards is briskly common-sensical about the thinkability of one's own death.

[18] 421–2. Next three quotations: A 349; A 356; A 403.

y lasted for only five minutes, z will endure for at least three years – whereas there is a difficulty about bringing my experience to bear upon any statement about how long I shall last. The difficulty connects with the fact that statements about how long I shall last, uniquely amongst synthetic statements about myself, are not *experience-dividing* – i.e. they have no direct implications of the form 'I shall experience C rather than D'. They must have such implications indirectly, for otherwise I could not have good reason to believe that I am mortal. But it is instructive to see what such a belief has to be based upon.

If, *per impossibile*, someone knew about nothing but his own inner states, he could have no reason for any belief about his own duration, or about periods of unconsciousness within his life-span. Any such belief would require him to distinguish *what happens* from *what I am aware of*, and he has nothing on which to feed such a distinction.

Now move up a level: suppose we have someone who is aware of an objective realm but not of his own body or of any other people. He can give content to the idea of coma, or of interrupted consciousness; for the hypothesis 'I was unconscious between t_1 and t_2' might explain his experiencing a sequence A–E rather than the predicted sequence A–B–C–D–E. Notice that although evidence for interruptions of one's consciousness requires knowledge of an objective realm or at least an orderly one, it does not require knowledge of other conscious beings.

Could the person last described have grounds for *predicting* his comas? Only if he could explain past ones; and that, I suggest, would require him to know about his own body. Given a body, he might be able to explain past comas and predict future ones by associating his mental states with his bodily states, and applying his physics to the latter.

Given that much, he could have evidence of his coming annihilation in a certain peculiar sense. He could know that he has been unconscious whenever his body has been in state F, and also that his body is about to enter state F and remain there for ever.[19] If we equate perpetual coma with annihilation, then this is evidence of one's approaching annihilation. The fact that it is reached by an extension of the notion of coma or interrupted consciousness is important, however. We have no basis for attributing to our man the thought that his body is due to be destroyed and that if he lacks a body he cannot exist at all.

In real life, our basis for believing in our own approaching annihilation is nothing like the basis just described. It does not involve one's past comas, and does involve other conscious beings. My reasons for think-

---

[19] I owe this idea to R. I. G. Hughes.

ing that I shan't last for ever essentially involve my knowing that I inhabit an objective realm containing other conscious beings, having evidence for certain generalizations about how the existence of those beings connects with the states of their bodies, and applying those generalizations to myself. The reason why one needs to invoke other conscious beings, and to theorize about them and oneself together, is fundamentally simple. My beliefs about death (construed as more than mere perpetual coma) must be based upon my experience of death; but the only deaths I can experience are those of others; and if those experiences are to support my belief that I shall die, I must class myself with the 'others' in the relevant respects.

Observe how far I have come from the ground floor of the Cartesian basis. My knowledge that I shall die involves my having knowledge of my own body, and of the bodies and minds of other conscious beings, and it involves my regarding myself as being in relevant ways *just one conscious being amongst many*. Rather than being identical with my world, or the limit of my world, I see myself merely as one member of a populous kind within the world.

These points imply a marginal criticism of Kant's handling of the first paralogism. He writes as though the judgment that I am sempiternal has content, is experience-dividing, involves using a certain concept empirically *in concreto*, even at the level where one has the Cartesian basis with nothing erected upon it. At any rate, he seems not to have noticed how very far from true that is.

5

THE SIMPLICITY OF THE SOUL

§ 27. The soul as simple

The second paralogism is less elusive. Descartes and Leibniz did both say that souls are simple, non-composite, indivisible, without parts; and Kant can plausibly trace this view to facts about the Cartesian basis, and can fairly warn against inflation.

Kant sees 'The soul is simple' as arising as follows. Within the Cartesian basis, the notion of a composite – or of a thing with parts – is the notion of several items which I somehow apprehend or think as a unity by interrelating them in a suitable way. So my basic notion of compositeness is that of several items which I somehow unite; and this pre-requires myself, my intellectually or perceptually uniting self, to combine the items into a whole. So I cannot apply the notion of a composite to myself: 'Although the whole of the thought could be divided and distributed among many subjects, the subjective "I" can never be thus divided and distributed, and it is this "I" that we presuppose in all thinking.'[1] In the paralogism itself, the crucial fact about the soul or thinking 'I' is said to be that it 'can never be regarded as the concurrence of several things acting', and this is just because the soul or thinking 'I' must do any 'regarding' that occurs.

Let us see how the simplicity of the soul figures in the writings of Descartes and Leibniz – but not Spinoza, for he thought that the soul is complex.[2] Descartes sometimes writes as though he based the simplicity thesis on self-observation: 'When I consider the mind, that is, when I consider myself in so far as I am just a thing that thinks, I can distinguish in myself no parts, but know and clearly conceive myself to be a thing single and entire.' That seems a poor basis for confidence that all souls are simple, and one may reasonably guess that Descartes had something better in mind than mere introspection.

Elsewhere, he puts it differently. 'The mind cannot be conceived except as indivisible', Descartes says, because 'we are not able to con-

---

[1] A 354. Next quotation: A 351.
[2] *Ethics* Part II, proposition 15. Next quotation: *Sixth Meditation*, about four-fifths of the way through.

ceive of the half of any mind.'³ The position is now based not upon introspectible simplicity, but upon the unintelligibility of the notion of a half-mind. Notice, incidentally, that nothing analogous to this can be said about bodies, though it can about specific kinds of body. There is not even *prima facie* sense in 'half-body', as there is in 'half-mind' and 'half-chair', say. The source of the difference is clear: for something to count as a mind, there is a certain complex structure which it must have; and similarly to count as a chair; but not, it seems, to count as a body. Now, it may be true that we cannot really make sense of 'half-mind', but this is not a matter I shall explore, although it will be touched upon in § 29 below. There remains a different *prima facie* possibility, namely that a mind should be divided into two whole minds which had been parts of their 'parent' and which were in some way smaller or lesser, though not less complete, than it. Descartes must rule this out too if he is to maintain that minds are not divisible or composite, and I have little doubt that he would want to rule it out, perhaps using a line of thought like that of the second paralogism: the notion of *x*'s being halved is basically that of *my* observing elements *y* and *z* changing their interrelationship in certain ways; and that pre-requires an undivided *me*.

Whether or not Descartes was relying on anything like the second paralogism, Leibniz probably was. He is deeply committed to the view that each soul is *a* substance, and is therefore not an aggregate or a composite. So Leibniz must maintain that souls are simple. He could infer this from the independently grounded doctrines that souls are monads, and that monads are simple; but in fact his reasons run rather in the opposite direction, with the simplicity of the soul being part of the case for identifying souls or minds with monads (which are defined as simple). So Leibniz needs reasons for claiming that souls are simple, and I agree with Parkinson that he seems not to give any.⁴ Yet I think I know why Leibniz was sure that souls are simple: he was led to this by something very like the second paralogism.

My evidence for this involves a background point, namely that it is

³ *Synopsis of the Meditations.* For a remark which ignorantly implies that Descartes did not say this, see J. Bennett, 'The Simplicity of the Soul', *Journal of Philosophy* (1967), p. 651. The concept of a half-mind is interestingly discussed in J. A. Brook, 'Indivisibility, Personal Identity, and the Possibility of Partial Persons', to be published in 1974.

⁴ G. H. R. Parkinson, *Logic and Reality in Leibniz's Metaphysics* (Oxford, 1965), p. 163. That Leibniz is a better source for the second paralogism than Descartes is well argued by Margaret Wilson, 'Leibniz and Materialism', *Canadian Journal of Philosophy* (1973).

not Leibniz's custom when theorizing about substances to proceed in a first-person manner, basing his remarks about substances in general upon what he can say about himself. Arnauld challenged one of Leibniz's views on the ground that it was false of *him*, and he implied that one ought to take oneself as the test case in any question about substances.[5] Leibniz endorses Arnauld's tactic: 'I agree that in order to judge of the concept of an individual substance, it is a good thing to consider the concept I have of myself'; but this is mere politeness, for Leibniz continues his discussion in terms of 'myself and every other individual substance', and gives a reason for thinking that there is not, after all, any profit to be gained from paying special attention to oneself when assessing doctrines about substance.

In one group of passages, though, Leibniz seriously takes a first-person singular slant on substances. In each of them, he is expounding the idea of a substance as simple, as single, as non-composite, as not an aggregate:

I saw that these forms and these souls must be indivisible, just as is our mind...By means of the soul or form there is a true unity corresponding to what is called 'I' in us.[6]

In the first draft of the same work, Leibniz wrote:

When I say *moi*, I refer to a single substance...Setting aside souls and other such principles of unity, we could never find any corporeal mass or portion of matter which would count as a genuine substance.

Then there is this:

Substantial unity requires a being which is complete and indivisible and naturally indestructible,...such as can be found in a soul or substantial form, for example that which one calls *moi*...For the above mentioned *moi*, or what corresponds to it in each individual substance, couldn't be created or destroyed by the assembling or dispersal of parts.

And also this:

Internal experience refutes the Epicurean doctrine [that the soul is material]. This experience is the consciousness within us of this Ego which perceives the things occurring in the body. And since this perception cannot be explained by figures and movements, it...makes us recognize an indivisible substance in ourselves which must itself be the source of its phenomena.

---

5 For Arnauld's remarks, see *Leibniz–Arnauld*, pp. 29–30. For Leibniz's reply, see *ibid.* pp. 49–50.

6 'A New System of the Nature and the Communication of Substances', §§ 4 and 11, in Loemker, pp. 454 and 456. Next three quotations: Gerhardt, Vol. IV, p. 473; *Leibniz–Arnauld*, pp. 94–5; Reply to Bayle, Loemker, p. 578.

Leibniz did not usually work from the Cartesian basis, approaching metaphysical questions with the heuristic solipsism which asks: 'What am I to say, and on the basis of what data?' In particular, he does not use himself as a touchstone for his whole doctrine about substances, e.g. appealing to introspection to support his claim that substances are active. Yet when the simplicity of substances is in question, he makes conspicuous use of the first person singular. Leibniz seems to have thought that the simplicity of the soul is somehow especially evident in one's own case, and I conjecture that he is led in that direction by something like the second paralogism.

§ 28. Mental fission

I have guessed that Descartes would, in defence of his view about simplicity, deny that a soul could split into two complete souls. According to that guess, he would see a problem not just about describing the products of mental fission as 'half-souls', but also about their relation to one another in the composite soul before it was divided. Let us explore this further.

Descartes says: 'If a foot, an arm, or any other part of the body is cut off, I know that my mind is not thereby diminished.'[7] A physical amputation might deprive me of my memory, say, or of my hearing or my ability to spell; but Descartes can concede this, for he is saying that one could not lose a *part* of one's mind, and faculties or abilities such as those I have mentioned are not parts: 'Nor can [the mind's] faculties of willing, sensing, understanding, etc. be spoken of as being its parts; for it is one and the same mind which wills, which senses, which understands.' What would qualify something as a part of my mind, then? Presumably its being able to continue in existence while being lost to *me*. Even if the removal of my foot deprived me of my memory, one might say, that would not be because the memory was retained by my foot.

Of course, a foot is not the sort of thing that can have a memory, but that is not Descartes' point. Let us suppose that my body is halved, and that each half is rapidly regenerated to form a complete human body. Can we intelligibly suppose that half of my mind is inherited by one of these bodies and the other half by the other? Descartes, if I understand him, would say 'No'. Kant also seems to construe Descartes in that way, for it is against the rational psychologist that he says:

7 *Sixth Meditation*, about four-fifths of the way through. Next quotation: *ibid.*; see also *Passions of the Soul* § 47.

Just as we can think all powers and faculties of the soul...as diminished by one half, but in such a way that the substance still remains, so also, without contradiction, we can represent the extinguished half as being preserved, not in the soul, but outside it; and we can likewise hold that since everything which is real in it...has been halved, another separate substance would then come into existence outside it. (416n.)

On this question, I agree with Kant against Descartes.

Here is what can be intelligibly supposed to happen – described from the outside. A person P divides, physically and mentally, into two people P_1 and P_2. That these are two people, and not one with two bodies, becomes increasingly obvious as they go their separate ways, eventually acquiring very different characters. Since P_1 is not identical with P_2, we cannot identify each of them with P. Yet each of them is physically and mentally continuous with P, claiming P's memories and so on, so that each would be identifiable with P if it were not for the rival claims of his opposite number. In this case, it seems best to say that neither off-shoot *is* P, though each is continuous with him: and that strongly suggests that we should say, with Kant, that P's mind has divided into two minds. Why not?

To see the force of the second paralogism, try out the above story with yourself in the role of P. Let your imagination carry you clear through the fission and out the other side. To do this, you must imagine yourself as entering the operating-theatre as P and leaving it as *one* of the off-shoots – waking up in the recovery room and seeing someone *like yourself* in the next bed. There is no other way of imagining the case from the inside, and so from the standpoint of the Cartesian basis, where there is only 'the inside', division of one's mind cannot be intelligibly supposed. That is the strength of the second paralogism.

There is supposed to be a danger that we shall take the paralogism's conclusion to have content which it really lacks, and this threat can be made good in relation to the fission story. Because I have to imagine myself as one of the two products of the fission, there is a danger that I shall think that if the fission did occur then, however symmetrical it looked from the outside, there would have to be an asymmetry in there somewhere. Tempting as this is, it is wrong. What sort of asymmetry could it be? 'One of the off-shoots must know that he is P, while the other must know that *he* is an impostor' – but we obviously have no basis for that. Perhaps, then: 'One of the off-shoots knows that he is P, while the other sincerely but wrongly thinks that he is P' – but that is

86

just empty. To see its emptiness, consider the situation where P_1 and P_2 both say in unison: 'The rational psychologist is right! On the inside one does detect the asymmetry, for I know that I am P and my opposite number is not.' Their both sincerely agreeing with the rational psychologist would show that he is wrong.

I imagine waking up in the recovery room and seeing someone like me in the next bed, but it is arbitrary which bed I put myself into. The danger is that I shall think that I could be identified with one of the two off-shoots because there is an asymmetry, whereas really the appearance of asymmetry arises solely from my having to identify myself with one of the off-shoots. I have to identify myself with one of the off-shoots, not because I am possessed of an unassailable simplicity but only because of the indivisible unity of a representation, which governs only the verb in its relation to a person' (A 355).

§ 29. Mental disunity

Descartes says: 'It is one and the same mind which wills, which senses, which understands.' He is sure not just of the soul's indivisibility but also of its unity with respect to how its various faculties are interrelated at a single time; and this probably encouraged him to think that there could not be a half-soul. However, this kind of unity can also be subjected to pressure. *yet each is treated as a complete soul!*

We need not invent cases this time, for they already exist as a result of brain-bisection, in which direct neural contacts between the two cerebral hemispheres of the human brain are surgically severed. Broadly speaking, sensory intake and behavioural output relating to each side of the body are processed and controlled by the cerebral hemisphere on the opposite side, and speech is controlled wholly by the left hemisphere. In a normal person, any information reaching one hemisphere is immediately neurally transmitted to the other hemisphere as well; and even after brain bisection the patient can usually route sensory information to both hemispheres, e.g. by turning his head, keeping both nostrils open, looking at his hands, and so on. When such manoeuvres are made impossible or irrelevant, however, extraordinary results are obtained. For example:

If a concealed object is placed in the left hand and the person is asked to guess what it is, wrong guesses will elicit an annoyed frown, since the right hemisphere, which receives the tactile information, also hears the answers. If the speaking hemisphere should guess correctly, the result is a smile. A smell fed to the nostril which stimuates the right hemisphere will elicit a verbal denial that the subject smells anything, but if asked to point with the left hand at a corresponding object he will succeed in picking out e.g. a clove of garlic, protesting all the while that he smells absolutely nothing, so how can he possibly point to what he smells.[8]

Quite generally, each hemisphere goes its own way, sensorily and behaviourally; and yet the patient feels normal, and has no sense of lacking unity.

Clearly, he does lack unity. But how deep does that go? In the contrived situation which exposes behaviourally some results of brain-bisection, do we have the workings of a single fragmented mind or two limited minds? In the article from which I have just quoted, Nagel says that this has no right answer, because each possible answer – 'One mind' and 'Two minds' – is open to insuperable objections. I agree with this, but not with Nagel's explanation of it.

Nagel rightly says that brain-bisection is hard to imagine from the inside: it is 'difficult to conceive what it is like to *be* one of these people'.[9] But he gives this fact the wrong sort of force:

> The fundamental problem in trying to understand these cases in mentalistic terms is that we take ourselves as paradigms of psychological unity, and are then unable to project ourselves into their mental lives, either once or twice. But in thus using ourselves as the touchstone of whether another organism can be said to house an individual subject of experience or not, we are subtly ignoring the possibility that our own unity may be nothing absolute, but merely another case of integration, more or less effective, in the control system of a complex organism.

I deny that in 'using ourselves as the touchstone' we are 'subtly ignoring' anything. Suppose that we resolutely face 'the possibility that our own unity may be nothing absolute', and that we go the whole way with Nagel: 'The ultimate account of the unity of what we call a single mind consists of an enumeration of the types of functional integration that typify it.' Keeping all that firmly in mind, we now turn back to the brain-bisected person and ask 'How many minds are involved here?'. Still the answer is that there is no fully correct answer. Nagel implies that we cannot (for short:) count the patient's minds because we cannot think ourselves into his/their mental life, but I contend that the exact converse is true.

Nagel says that 'our conception of ourselves...to a considerable

[8] T. Nagel, 'Brain Bisection and the Unity of Consciousness', *Synthese* (1971), p. 400.
[9] *Ibid.* p. 407. Next two quotations are both from *ibid.* p. 410.

extent constrains our understanding of others.'[10] In the same vein, he speaks of 'assumptions [which] are associated with our conception of ourselves', and says that 'it is just these...that make it impossible to arrive at an interpretation of the cases under discussion in terms of a countable number of minds.' These remarks suggest that our view of ourselves somehow distorts our view of the brain-bisected patient in such a way that we cannot count his minds; but I see no reason to accept the suggestion. Agreed: when I ask how many minds the patient has, I am using a concept of 'a mind' which owes much to my view of myself as having a single mind; and it is because I have this concept of 'a mind', and not some other, that I can find no acceptable way of counting the patient's minds. But that doesn't imply that I am significantly 'constrained' by my conception of myself, or that in asking how that conception applies to the brain-bisected person I am 'subtly ignoring' anything. These charges of Nagel's are no more appropriate here than they would be if I were confronted by a self-sufficient organic configuration (not involving mentality) which I could not acceptably classify either as a single organism or as a colony.

On a related matter: I agree with Nagel that one is prone to an 'illusion' which consists in 'projecting inward to the center of the mind the very subject whose unity we are trying to explain: the individual person with all his complexities'.[11] That seems to be precisely the illusion that Kant says may be engendered by the second paralogism. If I fall prey to it, because I have noticed that 'this representation, "I", does not contain in itself the least manifoldness' and 'for this reason seems to... denote a simple object', I shall be led to deny that my own unity is, in Nagel's words, 'merely another case of integration...in the control system of a complex organism'. This denial will be based upon the typically rational-psychologist mistake of thinking that the notion of 'integration in a control system' requires the thought of myself as doing the integrating.

This 'illusion' bears upon the question 'How many minds does the brain-bisected patient have?' – not by generating the question, nor by rendering it unanswerable, but rather by suggesting that it must have a correct answer. Just as in the fission case there was a temptation to say that either P_1 or P_2 must be identical with P, even if we cannot discover which, so here one is tempted to say that the brain-bisected person must really have one mind or really have two, only we cannot discover

[10] *Ibid.* p. 407. Next quotation: *ibid.*
[11] *Ibid.* p. 410. Next three quotations: A 355; A 381–2; Nagel, *loc. cit.*

which answer is right. The source of this temptation is the illusion, of which Nagel speaks, that I have a peculiarly intimate and secure knowledge of my own unity, so that if I underwent brain-bisection myself I should know for sure how many minds were involved.

I.e. seeing it from the inside - from a purported unity.

§ 30. Simplicity and immateriality

The soul's simplicity is supposed to imply its immateriality: 'The assertion of the simple nature of the soul is of value only in so far as I can thereby distinguish this subject from all matter...This is...the only use for which the above proposition is intended.'[12] Kant also suggests that immateriality would imply immortality, but I don't want to sort out the issues which that claim raises. Our concern is with the inference from simplicity to immateriality.

Descartes makes that move in his clearest argument for his substance-dualist view that nothing can be both thinking and extended. 'Body is by nature always divisible, and the mind is entirely indivisible', Descartes says, and he infers from this that 'the mind or soul of man is entirely different from the body.'[13] In giving primacy to this argument, Kant shows a clearer perception of Descartes' work than Descartes himself had. Descartes places the argument rather inconspicuously in the *Sixth Meditation*, without sufficiently emphasizing its crucial role in support of substance-dualism. (In the Objections to the *Meditations*, indeed, four of the objectors thought that Descartes had tried to defend substance-dualism in the *Second Meditation*, which he had not; and another of them, Hobbes, thought that he had not tried to defend it anywhere.[14]) The 'indivisibility' argument abundantly deserves the spotlight which Kant shines on it. Among other reasons for this, there is the fact that the argument helps us to relate Descartes' thought to Spinoza's. It seems clear that Spinoza's view that something can be both thinking and extended gets strength from his denial that the mind is in any way simple, which in turn is helped by his total indifference to the Cartesian basis.

Kant's treatment of the argument from simplicity to immateriality is basically sound, but there is a twist to it.

The central point is that at the level of the Cartesian basis there is something wrong with even asking whether the soul is material. For at

---

[12] A 356. The relation of immateriality to immortality is impeccably handled by Descartes in the *Synopsis of the Meditations*.

[13] *Sixth Meditation*, about four-fifths of the way through.

[14] Regarding the four, see F. C. Copleston, *History of Philosophy* (London, 1958), Vol. 4, p. 95; regarding Hobbes, see Haldane & Ross, pp. 61, 63.

that level the soul is my soul, my thinking self; and material things are, according to Kant's phenomenalism, logical constructions out of my sensory states; and so there cannot be any question of any soul's *being* a material thing. He says:

> If I understand by soul a thinking being in itself, the question whether or not it is the same in kind as matter – matter not being a thing in itself, but merely a species of representations in us – is by its very terms illegitimate. For it is obvious that a thing in itself is of a different nature from the determinations which constitute only its state. (A 360)

That reflects Kant's assumption that the rational psychologist is treating the soul as a 'thing in itself'. He is assuming that in so far as I know anything about myself this is because of the data I get from inner intuition, data which alone present me with myself as I appear to myself (334). So if I am a rational psychologist, and think that I can know about myself without any appeal to specific data of inner intuition, this commits me (Kant assumes) to thinking that I can know about my soul 'as it is in itself' and not merely 'as it appears through inner intuition'. Since the soul which concerns the psychologist is not an appearance, and since Kant says that no concepts can legitimately be applied to it, it is inevitable that he should conclude that the rational psychologist is concerned with the soul 'as it is in itself'. If that language is ever to be used, this is the place for it.[15] Still, Kant could have avoided it altogether, and yet made his point: 'The question whether or not the soul is the same in kind as matter – matter being a species of representations in us – is by its very terms illegitimate. For it is obvious that any item is of a different nature from the determinations which constitute only its state.'[16]

Kant might have left it at that, but he goes further. He contends that even if we do inflate the conclusion of the second paralogism, and 'allow it full objective validity', it does not show that the soul is immaterial. Since the 'soul' of rational psychology is a thinking being 'in itself', he says, we cannot intelligibly ask about its identity with an 'appearance' such as matter, but only about its identity with the something-in-itself which appears to us as extended matter. Of this unknowable item-in-itself, Kant says:

> I can...very well admit the possibility that it is in itself simple, although owing to the manner in which it affects our senses it produces in us the intuition of the extended and so of the composite. I may further assume that [it] is in itself the

---

[15] For a detailed discussion of the point, see *Bounds of Sense*, pp. 172–3.

[16] The paragraph on A 384–6 is along these lines, though it does use the 'as it is in itself' language.

possessor of thoughts, and that these thoughts can by means of its own inner sense be consciously represented. In this way, what in one relation is entitled corporeal would in another relation be at the same time a thinking being, whose thoughts we cannot intuit, though we can indeed intuit their signs in the [field of] appearance. (A 359)

Kant is not himself taking this possibility seriously. His point is merely that if you try to learn about the soul in the rational psychologist's way, with no appeal to data, you must enter the realm of things as they are in themselves; and then you can suppose anything without fear of refutation.

So we should not take pleasure in Kant's development of the supposition quoted above:

Accordingly, the thesis that only souls... think, would have to be given up; and we should have to fall back on the common expression that men think, that is, that the very same being which, as outer appearance, is extended, is (in itself) internally a subject, and is not composite, but is simple and thinks.

Those words might be used by someone who is envisaging a cogent solution to the problem of other minds – a solution which shows how we can have criteria for the use of a concept of a man, perhaps something like *a person* in Strawson's sense, an item to which we can apply both mentalistic and physicalistic predicates. Kant, however, has no such proposal in mind. He is concerned with a supposed bringing together of mind and body in a context where the 'body' is only the something-in-itself which underlies extended appearances, and the 'mind' is the soul-in-itself which the rational psychologist theorizes about. So far from solving the other minds problem, this could not possibly solve anything; which is exactly Kant's point about it. Incidentally, one real philosopher did espouse this non-solution, for Leibnizian monads are supposed to be 'internally' thinking and 'simple' and also to appear to outer sense as material.

6

THE IDENTITY OF THE SOUL
(Compare #28, 29)

§ 31. The third paralogism: blind alleys

The third paralogism concludes that the soul is 'a person'.[1] Kant normally uses the German word *Person* to connote freedom or moral responsibility, but that is irrelevant to the third paralogism. Its real topic is something to do with the re-identification of the soul at different times. Thus the first premiss says: 'That which is conscious of the numerical identity of itself at different times is to that extent a person.' (The phrase 'to that extent' implies that 'personality', whatever it is, is a matter of degree; but I cannot explain or justify that.) That identity is crucial appears earlier, when Kant sketches the paralogisms and says that the first three assert respectively that the soul 'is substance', that it 'is simple', and that 'as regards the different times in which it exists, it is numerically identical'. In another work, Kant contrasts the morality-oriented sense of *Person* with a different sense in which personality 'is merely the power of being conscious to oneself of the identity of one's existence in different circumstances', which is clearly a pointer towards the third paralogism.

There is plenty of precedent for the assumption that the concept of a person involves knowledge of self-identity. Beck tells me that Wolff defined 'person' as a thing which 'maintains a memory of itself'. Locke said that a person can 'consider itself as itself, the same thinking thing, in different times and places'.[2] Leibniz endorses this, not only in his replies to Locke but elsewhere as well.

The third paralogism remains unexplained. Are we to suppose that the rational psychologist claims to have proved that the soul 'maintains a memory of itself', and that Kant denies his right to claim this? I can make no sense of the paralogism along those lines. I shall later argue that 'person' is irrelevant to the serious content of the third paralogism, and that the latter's conclusion is not properly expressible by anything of

---

[1] A 361. Earlier sketch of the paralogism is on 402. Final quotation in this paragraph is from *Introduction to the Metaphysic of Morals*, in T. K. Abbott (ed.), *Kant's Critique of Practical Reason and Other Works* (London, 1909), p. 279.

[2] *Essay* II. xxvii. 11. For Leibniz's endorsements see *New Essays* II. xxvii. 9–29; *Discourse on Metaphysics* § 34; *Leibniz–Arnauld*, pp. 64, 160–1.

the form 'The soul is....'. (That would partly explain Kant's letting 'person' push its way on-stage: at least it does not push anything else off.) If that is right, we do not have to find a working role for 'person' in our account of the paralogism. Yet that leaves us with difficulties enough, and the English commentaries are unhelpful. Strawson makes the relevant remark that in the paralogisms chapter 'A crucial concept...is that of numerical identity through time, the persistence of an identical thing.'[3] But this absorbs the third paralogism into the general line of thought that is common to the first three. Strawson does not try to sort out the special features of the separate paralogisms.

In trying to understand the third paralogism, the main trap to be avoided, apart from the distraction of 'person', is a formulation in which the paralogism's conclusion is trivial. I have already quoted one instance of this: 'As regards the different times in which it exists, [the soul] is numerically identical.' This does not clearly mean anything. We can force meaning onto it by taking 'it is numerically identical' to mean 'it is numerically identical with itself'; and then the sentence becomes flatly trivial – a routine case of the more general triviality that *anything* is numerically identical with *itself* throughout the time of *its* existence. This has nothing to do with the soul, and arises purely from the connection between the concept of identity and the use of 'it' and 'itself'.

Kant again slithers into triviality here: 'Since we reckon as belonging to our identical self only that of which we are conscious, we must necessarily judge that we are one and the same throughout the whole time of which we are conscious' (A 364). The first part of that looks interesting, but what follows the comma is trivial. I, for one, judge that *everything* is 'one and the same throughout the whole time of' its existence, whether conscious or not. Kant does once concede that the conclusion of the third paralogism is 'analytic' (408), but he surely does not mean it to be as uninterestingly analytic as it is in these trivializing versions, in which it does not analyse or rest upon or illuminate the notions of the soul or of consciousness or of personality.

§ 32. Locating the third paralogism

Setting aside 'person', and the trivializing versions, we are left with this: 'I refer each and all of my successive determinations to the

---

[3] *Bounds of Sense*, p. 162. For more on Strawson's running together of the first three paralogisms, see § 38 below.

numerically identical self...[in such a way that] the personality of the
soul has to be regarded not as inferred but as a completely identical
proposition of self-consciousness in time' (A 362). Let us not be bemused
by the recurrence of 'personality'. I do have certain knowledge about
myself which I can plausibly be said to have 'not as inferred' but in
some more immediate way. Rather than consisting in my knowledge
of some single proposition, it is my knowledge of truths of a certain
kind – namely ones expressible in specific judgments of self-identity,
i.e. ones of the form 'It was I who was F at t'. The third paralogism is a
fumbling attempt to say something about judgments of that kind,
namely the following. In the Cartesian basis I cannot know that someone was F and wonder whether it was I: I recollect my past states *as
mine*, and so judgments of the form 'It was I who was F' cannot be
'inferred', for I cannot have the memory-datum 'Someone was F'
without having it either in the form 'I was F' or in the form 'Someone
else was F'.

So much for the paralogism's basis, but what about its conclusion?
What is the empty or formal truth which we are in danger of thinking
to have content? Really, there isn't one – or not one of the form 'The
soul is...'. Kant speaks of 'that numerical identity of our self which we
infer from identical apperception':[4] the phrase 'identical apperception'
refers to the matter which I have presented as the basis of the paralogism; and 'numerical identity of our self' should point to the paralogism's conclusion, but it gives us no help because it leads only to
triviality. Nor do Kant's warnings against inflation point to anything
coherent and non-trivial which could be the proposition which is not
to be inflated. We must not be led astray, he says, by 'the concept of
personality', or 'the identity of the consciousness of myself at different
times', or the fact that 'in my own consciousness, identity of person is
unfailingly met with'. I can make nothing of these.

Let us forget the paralogism's conclusion, which seems to be a myth
generated by Kant's passion for order and his incompetence at achieving
it. What is serious in the paralogism, I suggest, concerns the danger of
misunderstanding that fact about the Cartesian basis which I take to be
the paralogism's foundation – namely that my recollection of someone's being F must occur as a recollection of my being F or as one of
someone else's being F.

Kant says that 'we can never parade [this] as an extension of our self-
knowledge...and as exhibiting to us from the mere concept of the

----

4 A 365. Next three quotations: *ibid.*; A 363; A 362.

identical self an unbroken continuance of the subject.'⁵ He also says that the paralogism 'in no way proves the numerical identity of my subject'. And then there is this:

> In my own consciousness...identity of person is unfailingly met with. But if I view myself from the standpoint of someone else (as object of his outer intuition), [the picture changes]. Although he admits...the 'I' which accompanies...all representations at all times in *my* consciousness, he will draw no inference from this to the objective permanence of myself.

We now have three accounts of what we are warned not to infer from the paralogism: 'an unbroken continuance of the subject', 'the numerical identity of my subject', and 'the objective permanence of myself' – this last being handled through an equation of '*P* is not objectively valid' with 'An outside observer might not accept *P*'. Three crucial concepts, then: continuance, identity, permanence.

Of these, permanence and continuance can be set aside. 'Permanence' translates *Beharrlichkeit*, by which Kant often means 'sempiternity', but not here. When he speaks of the view 'that everything in the world is *in a flux* and nothing is *permanent* and abiding',⁶ he seems to use 'permanent' to mean only 'fairly durable'; and on the next page he clearly takes a thing's 'permanence' to involve only its lasting long enough to be the subject of across-time identity-statements. So 'permanence' in this present sense is intimately connected with identity, and Kant himself says that of the two concepts identity is the more basic one: 'This permanence...is in no way given prior to [the] numerical identity of our self..., but on the contrary is inferred first from the numerical identity.' Although this remark flirts with the trivializing formulation discussed above, its main thrust is clear: judgments as to things' durability are based upon, rather than the basis for, across-time identity-judgments. As for 'continuance', Kant eventually admits that it is simply irrelevant to the across-time identity of minds or souls: 'The possibility of a continuing consciousness in an abiding subject...is already sufficient for personality. For personality does not itself at once cease because its activity is for a time interrupted.' The only way to make 'continuance' relevant after all is to render it synonymous with that durability, or obedience to across-time identity-statements, which I have just been discussing. Either way, continuance need not concern us as a separate topic. Our sole concern is with identity.

---

⁵ A 365–6. Next two quotations: A 363; A 362–3.
⁶ A 364. Next two quotations are both from A 365.

But what point about identity is Kant trying to make? I think that there may be two, of which I shall discuss one in §§35–7 and the other immediately.

§33. Quasi-memory

Our concern is not with any one judgment about the soul, but rather with every judgment of the form 'It was I who was F at t'. What Kant is saying about such judgments is not that we must be careful not to inflate them, but rather that however confidently we accept them they may be simply false. He says: 'We must necessarily judge that [P]. We cannot, however, claim that this judgment would be valid from the standpoint of an outside observer' (A364). Unfortunately, P is the triviality 'We are one and the same' etc., but still this remark shows that the third paralogism is concerned with *some* (kind of) judgment which we do and even must make and which nevertheless may be false or unacceptable to a well-informed observer. I contend that what is in question here are sincere judgments of the form 'It was I who was F at t'.

We are concerned only with falsehood in the identity-component in such judgments – i.e. with the possibility that not I but someone else was F at t. This would be merely boring if it took the form: I seem to recollect being F at t, but in fact I was not; and it just happens, by co-incidence, that someone else was F at t. That combination of memory-mistake and coincidence has no philosophcal interest and does not engage with Kant's discussion. What we must consider is something different, namely the case where my memory of being F at t is wrong only in respect of the identity of the person whose being-F-at-t is remembered.

That seems *prima facie* to be impossible. In remembering something, I have to remember it 'from the inside' or 'from the outside' – so my memory of a given event comes with the identity of the subject of the event built right into it. I may recall that the picnic was spoiled by illness, while not recalling whether it was I who was ill, but in that case I do not recall the being-ill but only its social consequences. Shoemaker has lucidly stated and explained this point:

When a person remembers a past event there is a correspondence between his present cognitive state and some past cognitive and sensory state of his that existed at the time of the remembered event and consisted in his experiencing the event or otherwise being aware of its occurrence. . . This past cognitive and sensory state is always a past state of the rememberer himself.[7]

To that we need add only this: for almost every value of F, the state I am in when I am aware that someone is F automatically determines whether it is I or someone else who is F.

That seems to make it impossible for my memory to err about the identity-component in judgments of the form 'It was I who was F at t'. Yet Kant, on my present construal of him, is challenging this. He is suggesting that what seems to be my memory of my being F may really be a memory of someone else's being F.

This may be a conflict with the normal meaning of 'remember', so I borrow Shoemaker's term 'quasi-remember'. A genuine memory of being F requires that the rememberer was previously F, whereas a genuine quasi-memory of being F requires only that someone was previously F. In Shoemaker's words:

Someone's having [a quasi-memory] of an event does involve there being a correspondence between his present cognitive state and a past cognitive and sensory state that was [an awareness] of the event, but. . . this correspondence, although otherwise just like that which exists in memory, does not necessarily involve that past state's having been a state of the very same person who subsequently has the [quasi-memory].[8]

So I can quasi-remember an event 'from the inside' although it happened to someone else, or 'from the outside' although it happened to me – as long as someone else was aware of it at the time. All memories are quasi-memories, but perhaps the converse could fail. Kant's claim, I suggest, is that my seeming memories could turn out to be only quasi-memories, their identity-component sometimes being false.

Now, Shoemaker proves that if we don't strengthen the notion of quasi-memory it collapses under its own weight. For one thing, I cannot identify any particular thing involved in a quasi-remembered event. I quasi-remember a viewing of a building just like the Taj Mahal. If I were *remembering*, I could say ' . . . a viewing of the Taj Mahal'; for on this planet, which is the only one I have ever been on, the only building just like that is the Taj Mahal itself. But I may be only quasi-remembering someone else's viewing of another building just like the

[7] S. Shoemaker, 'Persons and their Pasts', *American Philosophical Quarterly* (1970), p. 271.
[8] *Ibid.*

Taj Mahal on a planet in a distant galaxy.[9] Another difficulty concerns the quasi-remembering of processes. I quasi-remember picking up a stone and throwing it, but nobody ever picked up a stone and threw it, for what I quasi-remember is Smith's picking up a stone and Jones's throwing it. Clearly, the example could be cut into still thinner temporal slices. As Shoemaker says, 'The knowledge of the past provided by such a faculty of quasi-memory would be minimal indeed.'

To remedy this defect, Shoemaker adds to the notion of quasi-memory a further element which he thinks is present in the ordinary notion of memory – namely that if I remember being F then my cognitive state has been partly caused by my earlier being F.[10] Borrowing from this, we get the stipulation that if I quasi-remember (someone's) being F then my cognitive state has been partly caused by someone's earlier being F. Given certain limits to what causal chains can be like, e.g. that they must follow spatio-temporally continuous paths, that solves the two difficulties sketched above, and some others.

For memory, not every sort of causal chain will suffice. Suppose I was F at t_1, I told you this at t_2 and then forgot it myself, and then at t_3 you reported that I had been F at t_1 and I believed you. My belief at t_3 was *partly caused* by my being F at t_1, but it need not have been a memory of that earlier state. This is because the belief is not related by the right kind of causal chain to the earlier being-F – the kind which Shoemaker calls 'M-type' for short. Shoemaker subjects quasi-memory to this same constraint: my present cognitive state is a genuine quasi-memory of an earlier episode only if it arose from it through an M-type causal chain.

I shall assume that an M-type causal chain must include, perhaps amongst other elements, a continuous series of events within the confines of a single body. This may be too strong; it is certainly stronger than anything Shoemaker proposes. The extra strength, however, is harmless in my present context.

My present cognitive state, then, is a quasi-memory of someone's being F only if it arose through an M-type causal chain from an earlier being-F; and so that earlier occurrence of being-F must have been associated with my present body, for otherwise the relevant causal chain could not have stayed within the confines of a single body. But if *I have the body* and *quasi-remember* the experiences of the person was F, does it not follow that I *am* the person who was F? In rescuing quasi-

9 *Ibid.* pp. 274–6. Quotation at end of this paragraph: *ibid.* p. 277.
10 This thesis is defended, and I believe was first propounded, in C. B. Martin and M. Deutscher, 'Remembering', *The Philosophical Review* (1966).

memory from debilitating weakness, I seem to have strengthened it to a point where it no longer differs from memory.

But not really, for a series of events could stay 'within the confines of a single body' while that body underwent amoebic fission or fused with other bodies. So we have the following possibility. Someone was F; he then divided into two people, of whom I am one; and I now have a quasi-memory of (his) being F. My present cognitive state has issued from a causal chain which was suitably bodily confined all along its route, and yet I am not the person who was F, for reasons given in §28 above. This would be a quasi-memory which was not a memory.

As well as fission there could be fusion, perhaps. Shoemaker introduces both, under the general description of 'branching' and 'coalescing' of M-type causal chains. I choose to stay with fission.

§ 34. Kant's observer

I have construed Kant as saying that when I make a memory-based judgment of the form 'I was F at t', I may be wrong about *who* was F at t. He is absolutely right: there is nothing incoherent in the idea that something which I take to be a memory is really only a quasi-memory. It must be admitted, though, that Kant himself does not show or even argue that he is right. It has been left to Shoemaker to fill in enough details to create a presumption that the idea contains no lurking inconsistencies.

More important than the assigning of credit, though, is the fact that Kant's contention, true as it is, does not justify anything of the form: 'We must necessarily judge that P, but this judgment might not be valid from the standpoint of an observer.' Granted, I might think that I was remembering (my) being F, and an observer might tell me: 'You are only quasi-remembering being F. There has been a split, and although you are continuous with the person who was F you are not identical with him.' But then I *could* discover this for myself, e.g. by spying on the other person resulting from the split. There is no reason why I should stubbornly insist, in the face of any evidence, that it was I who was F. Kant seems to think otherwise, and that is an error.

Kant is silent about the observer's criteria for my personal identity. In filling this gap with material taken from Shoemaker, I have replaced his 'branching and coalescing M-type causal chains' by the narrower 'fission and fusion of persons'; but my argument does not depend upon this narrowing. As long as the observer has some grounds for his judg-

Another case of zero application!

No!

This leaves out the analytical / subjective aspect Kant feels is crucial here.

ments about my identity, I could have those grounds too and could assess them just as he does. Furthermore, if the 'observer's standpoint' is, as Kant implies, the touchstone of what is 'objectively valid', then I *ought* to handle the evidence as the observer does. So Kant has no reason to say that I 'must necessarily judge' something which an observer could rightly deny. The point could be stated in terms of another of his formulations:

> Can a man be conscious of these changes and still say that he remains the same man (has the same soul)? The question is absurd, since consciousness of such changes is possible only on the supposition that he considers himself in his different states as one and the same subject.[11]

If we cleanse this of its trivializing elements, it says in effect that if I have a quasi-memory of a past state I must consider that state to be mine. But that is just wrong, for if the quasi-memory is not a memory, and the state was therefore not mine, there is no obstacle to my accepting that fact. If on the other hand the only possible quasi-memories are memories, then Kant has not identified any judgment of mine which an observer could rightly deny.

'But quasi-memories would have to be, at least, *prima facie* memories. One could not help taking them to be memories until they were shown not to be.' That may be true, but it is much weaker than the position Kant seems to be taking. Admittedly, he does not explicitly say that I cannot help making and sticking to judgments which an observer might rightly reject, but if that is not his position then he has lost me utterly.

Why does Kant not allow me to amend my judgments of self-identity in the light of evidence which the observer has? Apparently he thinks that my judgments about my identity are insulated from the observer's, each being based upon something which is irrelevant to the other. In his view, my judgments of self-identity are based solely upon the 'unity of my self-consciousness'; and he thinks that this has no implications for any judgment about my identity which an observer might make, as is shown by his remark that the unity of self-consciousness is consistent with 'the dictum that nothing is permanent', meaning that nothing lasts for any length of time. Just after that, Kant says that 'the only permanent appearance which we encounter in the soul is the representation "I"' which, for all we know, may 'be in the same state of flux as the other thoughts which, by means of it, are linked up with

---

[11] *Anthropologie in pragmatischer Hinsicht*, footnote to § 4; quoted in W. H. Walsh, *Reason and Experience* (Oxford, 1947), p. 196. I have changed the wording slightly.

one another' (A 364). This seems to mean that within the soul we find nothing that bears at all upon any objective judgment of permanence or lastingness, and therefore nothing that bears upon any objective judgment of across-time identity.

Exactly!

The 'insulation' view is also involved in a passage where Kant contrasts the 'time [which] is represented in me' with 'the time in which the observer sets me', the latter being 'not the time of my own but of his sensibility' (A 362–3). I don't understand this obscure echo of the doctrine that time is the form of inner sense, but the play with 'my time' and 'his time' seems to credit the observer and myself with different and non-interacting ontological frameworks.

Someone might argue that the 'insulation' view is at least half right: the observer's judgments about my identity must be based upon criteria for personal identity, whereas mine cannot be criterial at all; and so my judgments of self-identity cannot take account of anything upon which his are based. That argument fails, though, for Shoemaker has shown that over a certain limited area there can be criterial judgments about one's own identity. My quasi-memory of (someone's) being F supports, non-criterially, the judgment that either I was F or someone related to me in a certain way was F; but then criteria for personal identity are needed for me to determine which of those alternatives is the right one. So my basis for judgment can include elements from the observer's domain.

But isn't Kant's point about all awareness of memory for identification of the self?

Conversely, also, the observer can avail himself of the basis which is naturally regarded as primarily mine. At any rate, he can avail himself of my *statements* of the form 'I seem to remember being F at t' or 'I quasi-remember being F at t' or the like. These presumably express my *judgments* of that form, and thus reflect that 'unity of self-consciousness' which is my immediate basis for judgments about my own identity. Kant says nothing about overt statements of self-identity, this being part of his general neglect of language and indeed of all questions about physical behaviour. This helps to explain, though not to excuse, his reticence about what criteria for my identity the observer does use.

No!

I have by-passed the closing sentences of Kant's discussion.[12] They say that there is some kind of question about my identity which I cannot answer satisfactorily, because I could not offer data to support any answer without somehow presupposing a certain answer. But why this should be so, and indeed what kind of question Kant has in mind, is opaque to me.

[12] A 366, 'For this concept...desired to know.' See also A 346.

§ 35. Identity and substrata

I now offer a completely different account of the third paralogism – not rivalling the previous one, but picking out a different strand in the tangle of Kant's thought about personal identity. This section is philosophical; exegetical applications come in §§ 36–7 below.

Our concern is with the notion of a *substratum*.

This has been used in attempts to explain property-instantiation, i.e. to explain or analyse statements of the form 'There is something which is *F*'. Some philosophers have thought that they could analyse 'thing which is *F*' in terms of an alleged concept of a 'thing which…', this being an *ingredient* in every concept of the form 'thing which is *F*' and therefore not *identical* with any such concept. Instead of 'thing which', let us say 'substratum', the idea being that whenever any properties are instantiated they somehow inhere in or are borne or supported by an underlying thing-which or substratum.

The notion of substratum is intensely unpopular, for reasons which are not always made clear. Critics sometimes rail at the idea of 'bare particulars' which do not themselves have any properties although they support properties. But supporting a property *is* having it; and so this criticism implies that because the substratum has all the properties it doesn't have any properties, which one writer has diagnosed clinically as 'so idiotic as to be almost incredible' although 'real humans *have* gone in for it.'[13] Underlying the idiocy there is in fact a perfectly legitimate point, but this is not the place to expound it.[14] Anyway, I agree with the majority verdict that the notion of a substratum, as expounded above, does not help to explain what it is for properties to be instantiated.

The pseudo-concept of substratum has also been given a different role which is what primarily concerns us here.[15] This is a role in analysing across-time identity-statements. It has been thought that statements of the form

(1) The thing which is *F* at t_1 is the thing which is *G* at t_2

can be analysed into, or explained as owing their truth to, corresponding statements about the persistence from t_1 through to t_2 of some substratum.

[13] G. E. M. Anscombe, 'Substance', *Proceedings of the Aristotelian Society*, suppl. vol. (1964), p. 71. [14] For an exposition, see *Locke, Berkeley, Hume* § 11.

[15] On the distinctness of the two roles, see C. D. Broad, *The Mind and its Place in Nature* (Cambridge, 1925), pp. 558–62.

Let us try to see what could make such an analysis seem plausible.

I need the intuitive notion of a 'momentary predicate', explained as follows: F is a momentary predicate if no statement of the form 'Fx at t' covertly or implicitly says anything about x's state at any time other than t. Momentary predicates can be applied to things at given instants, just on the evidence those instants contain. That exposition does not make 'momentary predicate' precise. It is not meant to, for I am reconstructing a line of thought which is inherently imprecise.

Now, it is plausible to suppose that if F and G are momentary predicates then no conjunction of the form

(2) $(\exists x)(Fx$ at $t_1)$ & $(\exists x)(Gx$ at $t_2)$

can entail the corresponding statement of the form

(3) $(\exists x)(Fx$ at t_1 & Gx at $t_2)$;

in which case nothing of the form of (2) could entail any across-time identity-statement of the form of

(1) The thing which is F at t_1 is the thing which is G at t_2.

From this it is but a short step to the further thought that since truths like (2) are logically insufficient to establish (1) or (3), the latter must involve a truth of a radically different kind. This is where the notion of a substratum enters the picture. The thought is that however many type-(2) truths you establish, there remains always the further question of whether the thing which is F at t_1 *is* the thing which is G at t_2. This question, which is the residue after *every* type-(2) truth about the nature of things at t_1 and the nature of things at t_2 has been set aside, is a question about a substratum or property-bearer or the like.

This line of thought, though plausible, is mistaken. It may be true that, however many type-(2) facts we have assembled, we can always properly ask the type-(1) question 'But is it the same thing which was F at t_1 and G at t_2?' To answer such a question, however, we can only assemble more type-(2) facts. Please yourself about whether to say that a set of type-(2) statements can after all entail or lead logically to a type-(1) statement. What matters is that our type-(1) statements are just a means for handling certain sets of type-(2) facts; the latter give all possible evidence for the former, and all we need for a complete understanding of type-(1) statements is to see how they relate to the type-(2) statements which are their basis. There is no need to connect them with any statement about a substratum.

'In saying that we must base type-(1) statements on type-(2) evidence,

you forget that we can establish the former by continuous observation.'
No, I don't. The chair I now occupy is the one I occupied five minutes
ago: I have been wakefully aware of its pressure upon me throughout
that time. But now let t_1 and t_2 be instants within that period and
separated from one another by only a microsecond. The question of
whether the chair I was sitting on at t_1 *is* the chair I was sitting on at t_2
makes perfectly good sense, and the right answer could be negative.
How do we rule out a negative answer? Clearly, not by saying that I
continuously observed the chair from t_1 through to t_2, for there is no
content to the notion of continuous observation, of a technologically
unsophisticated sort, through a period of only one microsecond. Our
evidence that it was the same chair is just this: I occupied an F chair at
t_1 and I occupied an F chair one microsecond later, and there is no evidence that it was not the same chair. So continuous observation does
not yield evidence for type-(1) statements of a different kind from
type-(2) truths. All it does is to provide type-(2) truths in which the
time-interval is very short – short enough to make it reasonable to
accept the type-(1) statement unless there is positive evidence against it.
Nor does this notion of positive counter-evidence introduce any
radically new element. In assessing any such evidence – e.g. that one
chair had been whipped out from under me and replaced by another,
without my noticing – we should be involved yet again in assessing
type-(1) statements in the light of corresponding type-(2) statements,
perhaps with the time-intervals even shorter still.

  The notion of a substratum corresponds to the idea of an impossibly
absolutely continuous observation – the idea of knowing for sure that x
really did last from t_1 through to t_2, and not merely that things like x
were to be found at various times throughout that interval. The substratum analysis, aiming to get right down to real, jumpless, across-
time identity, descends to a level where it loses all empirical content.
In refusing to let the identity question be settled by type-(2) information,
the substratum-theorist puts it beyond the reach of any findable
answer.

§ 36. Substrata: two sources

In § 37 I shall argue that Kant uses 'The soul is a person' to mean 'The
soul is an enduring substratum of mental states' or 'Across-time identity-statements about the soul assert the persistence through time of a
substratum'.

How could the notion of a substratum have shouldered its way into this part of the *Critique*? Kant did not accept the substratum analysis for across-time identities generally: he tied the notion of an enduring and re-identifiable outer substance to the having of certain sorts of experience, whereas the substratum analysis implies that experience is irrelevant to across-time identities. But there are two reasons why Kant might have entertained the substratum analysis in connexion with the soul in particular.

The first is as follows. The best way of refuting the substratum analysis is by showing that identity-statements are based upon truths of the form (2) 'Something was F at t_1 and something was G at t_2.' But judgments of self-identity seem not to have such a basis. Within the Cartesian basis I cannot have any type-(2) data except with the corresponding type-(1) judgments built into them, so to speak, so that I can know that some (mental) thing was F at t_1 only by remembering being F at t_1. At any rate, the rational psychologist holds this view; and Kant himself nearly holds it, for although he implies that my judgments of self-identity might be challenged by an observer, he seems to think that I cannot myself offer or accept such a challenge. And so we find him saying early in the *Critique*: 'All possible appearances...belong to the totality of a possible self-consciousness...Numerical identity is inseparable from [this], and is *a priori* certain.'[16] Also, in discussing the third paralogism: 'The personality of the soul has to be regarded not as inferred but as a completely identical proposition of self-consciousness in time.'

So the best way of refuting the substratum analysis seems inapplicable to the identity of the soul. This could encourage Kant to think that the rational psychologist is especially prone to accept the substratum analysis of across-time mental identity.

Secondly, the substratum analysis might have entered the paralogisms chapter through a common mistake – namely that of confusing (a) 'thing in itself' with (b) 'substratum'. From Berkeley onwards, this confusion has been endemic. Many philosophers have conflated the issue about (a) things in themselves as distinct from the sensory states which are their appearances, with the issue about (b) substrata as distinct from the properties which they support. Some of these philosophers use 'idea' to cover both (a) sensory states and (b) properties, so that things-in-themselves and substrata seem alike in being sustainers or supporters of 'ideas'. Also, it is plausible to say that we can know things

---

[16] A 113. Next quotation: A 362.

only (a) through their appearances and (b) through their properties, and these might seem to be two versions of a single claim. The conflation of (a) with (b) has other sources as well.[17]

Now, we know that Kant sees the rational psychologist as regarding the soul as (a) a thing in itself (see §30 above). If Kant were guilty of the confusion I have described, that could encourage him to think of the rational psychologist as one who regards the soul as (b) a substratum. Admittedly, the confusion concerns 'substratum' as property-bearer rather than as guarantor of across-time identity; but the two roles are connected, and there is some explanatory value in the hypothesis that Kant muddled (a) with (b).

Anyway, the hypothesis is true.

Kant's uses of *Substratum* (and sometimes, in B, of *Substrat*) should be noted. Without endorsing what I have called the substratum analysis of property-instantiation, he often uses 'substratum' in distinguishing (b) between things and their properties or determinations: 'The substratum of all that is real...is *substance*; and all that belongs to existence can be thought only as a determination of substance';[18] 'Substances, in the [field of] appearance, are the substrata of all determinations of time.' In other places, however, 'substratum' is used in antithesis not to (b) 'determinations' but to (a) 'appearances', as though the word meant about the same as 'thing in itself'.[19] At least once, both uses of 'substratum' occur in a single paragraph: Kant speaks of (a) 'the relation of the appearances' to a certain 'substratum', just before the remark, quoted above, about (b) 'the substratum of all that is real' in relation to 'determinations'.

The clearest evidence I have for the mix-up, though not with 'substratum', is this passage:

> If I understand by soul a thinking being in itself, the question whether or not it is the same in kind as matter – matter not being a thing in itself, but merely a species of representations in us – is by its very terms illegitimate. For it is obvious that a thing in itself is of a different nature from the determinations which constitute only its state. (A 360)

Kant there moves smoothly and immediately from (a) contrasting 'thing in itself' with 'our representations' to (b) contrasting it with 'the determinations which constitute only its state'.

---

17 For fuller treatments of this topic, seee *Kant's Analytic* § 46; *Locke, Berkeley, Hume*, Ch. III.
18 225. Next quotation: 231.
19 See A 359, 645. Final reference in this paragraph: 225.

In the light of this conflation of Kant's, I submit, we cannot rule out the hypothesis that the rational psychologist, in Kant's picture of him, views the soul not just as a thing in itself but also as a substratum.

§37. Substrata: four consequences

Four aspects of the discussion of the third paralogism are explained by the hypothesis that Kant is fighting the view that the Cartesian basis teaches us that the soul is an enduring substratum.

(1) The hypothesis provides a possible reading of 'person' according to which Kant does after all have a point about the judgment that the soul is a person. He may be using 'person' to mean 'enduring substratum', and questioning whether the soul *is* a person; or he may be allowing that the soul is a 'person', meaning only that it lasts through time and has memory, and warning us not to inflate that into a claim about an enduring substratum. He is nicely poised between the two positions in the remark: 'This identity of the subject...does not... signify the identity of the person, if by that is understood the consciousness of the identity of one's own substance' (408). Either way, Kant is not challenging my judgment that I am the one who was *F* at *t*, but merely warning me against thinking that this judgment (or some fact about my basis for it) implies that I am a substratum of mental properties or determinations.

I am conjecturing that Kant thinks of that inflation, or illegitimate inference, as somehow connected with the term *Person*, and also – I now add – with the portentous phrase 'numerically identical'. When the latter is given an everyday meaning, it turns several of Kant's remarks into trivialities (see §31 above). Kant, however, does not think of the form '*x* is numerically identical with *y*' in terms of such humdrum statements as 'This is the book you lent me' and 'I am the one she insulted', but rather takes it to have heavy metaphysical overtones. They seem to be overtones of the substratum analysis of across-time identity.

(2) In one of his warnings against inflation, Kant says that we must not take the third paralogism 'as exhibiting to us from the mere concept of the identical self an unbroken continuance of the subject' (A366). This could be a pointer to the substratum notion of an absolute, total continuity – a continuity dense enough to fill any possible gap between any pair of instants. For Kant could be saying that although I truly judge that it was I who was *F* at *t*, this does not imply that between

myself-now and myself-at-*t* there stretches a substratum manifesting that special sort of unbroken continuity which lies so deep that there couldn't be empirical evidence for it.

(3) In §§ 32–34 I construed Kant as saying that my judgments of the form 'I was *F* at *t*' might involve a mistake about *who* was *F* at *t*. With Shoemaker's help, I defended that claim; but that defence did not explain what Kant's own reasons were, and there really is a puzzle about this. Perhaps the explanation is that he did not clearly distinguish 'That judgment might be false' from 'The substratum judgment corresponding to that judgment might be false'. Admittedly, that does not explain how an outside observer could be an authority on the matter.

(4) The earlier interpretation created another puzzle as well. Why does Kant say nothing about the standards or criteria according to which our judgments of self-identity might be false? For example, he says: 'We are unable to prove that this "I", a mere thought, may not be in [a] state of flux' (A 364), with no hint as to what the cash-value of this might be. My present hypothesis suggests an explanation: the thing 'we are unable to prove' is not assigned a cash-value because it does not have one; the relevant criteria are not described because there are none. What is being said to be possibly false is not the humdrum judgment that I was *F* at *t*, but rather the uncheckable judgment – embodied in 'person' and 'numerically identical' – that the former judgment is true because of the existence of an enduring substratum. – *where it is to mark a definiteness of identity.*

That line of explanation can be re-applied to explain, as nothing else does, this remarkable passage: (*which comes before (A 361)*)!

If...we postulate substances such that the one communicates to the other representations together with the consciousness of them, we can conceive a whole series of substances of which the first transmits its state together with its consciousness to the second, the second its own state with that of the preceding substance to the third...The last substance would then be conscious of all the states of the previously changed substances, as being its own states...And yet it would not have been one and the same person in all these states.[20]

I contend that this passage is written *ad hominem*. In it, 'substance' means 'substratum-substance', and Kant is saying to the substratum theorist: 'This is the sort of pseudo-problem that you have committed yourself to taking seriously, and that shows that your position is untenable.' On that reading of it, the passage strikingly resembles one in which Locke

[20] A 363–4n. On Kant's argument as an *ad hominem* one, see *Commentary*, p. 462n., and *Bounds of Sense*, p. 168. The two Locke quotations: *Essay* II. xxvii. 11, 13; see 11–29 *passim*, especially 23.

But Bennett does show how difficult it is to understand this passage in anything but a substance/substratum way.

discredits 'substance', meaning 'substratum-substance'. For Locke, 'person' is an empirically usable term, to be contrasted with '(substratum-) substance', but that is a merely verbal difference between him and Kant. The vital similarity is that in each passage the notion of a substratum is shown to be useless. Here is Locke:

> [The question] whether we are the same...*substance* or no..., however reasonable or unreasonable, concerns not *personal* identity at all. The question being what makes the same person; and not whether it be the same identical substance, which always thinks in the same person...For, it being the same consciousness that makes a man be himself to himself, personal identity depends on that only, whether it be annexed solely to one individual substance, or can be continued in a succession of several substances.

Locke's intention there is clearly ironical. He frequently attacks substratum-substance by pretending to take it seriously and showing where it leads. For example:

> If the same thinking substance...be changed, [can it] be the same person? I answer, that cannot be resolved but by those who know what kind of substances they are that do think; and whether the consciousness of past actions can be transferred from one thinking substance to another.

The mocking remark that we must leave it to 'those who know' is echoed later by the suggestion that we leave it to God.

I do not credit Kant with a consciously mocking or ironical intention. But parts of his discussion of the third paralogism have the structure if not the tone of irony. They apply the substratum analysis to judgments of self-identity and show that the latter, on that analysis, cannot be verified or falsified.

To explain Kant's discussion of the third paralogism, we must suppose that he wants to say something about enduring substrata. But that does not cover his remarks about what would be valid from the standpoint of an observer, and so, I am afraid, we also need the interpretation which I presented in §§32–4 above.

The two interpretations might be seen as applications of a single highly general thesis. We could take Kant's discussion of the third paralogism to have the over-all message: 'When you judge "It was I who was *F* at *t*", on the basis purely of what lies within your own consciousness, then your judgment entails nothing about what lies outside your consciousness. For example, you might be tempted to think that you have secured a truth about the endurance of an underlying substratum, or some truth which an observer might acknowledge (e.g.

one about a single human body); but nothing of either of these sorts is guaranteed by anything which is founded solely on the Cartesian basis.' But I doubt if it is really helpful to interrelate the substratum point and the 'observer' point in this manner.

§ 38. Strawson on the paralogisms

Just because Strawson is so considerable a Kantian commentator, I want to explain my reservations about his treatment of the paralogisms chapter.

According to Strawson, Kant's basic insight about the soul is that a certain 'key fact' about the Cartesian basis 'explains three things':

It explains the temptation to permit ourselves the use of the notion of the subject of experience ('I') while thinking exclusively in terms of the inner contents of consciousness...; it explains why that notion, so used, is really quite empty of content; and it explains why it *seems*, therefore, to be the notion of an absolutely simple, identical, immaterial individual.[21]

Those last four words point to the four paralogisms: 'simple' points to the second, 'identical' to the third, 'immaterial' to the second and the fourth, and 'individual' perhaps to the first. That, however, is almost Strawson's only allusion to the separate identities of the paralogisms.

Most of Strawson's account is true and helpful, but two aspects of it raise doubts. One is his emphasis upon the 'key fact' that 'immediate self-ascription of thoughts and experiences involves no application of criteria of subject-identity'.[22] This fact does dominate the third paralogism, though we found it hard to discover *what* its importance is there; and the 'key fact' *may* also somehow underlie the first two paralogisms. But when Strawson makes it central to the paralogisms as a whole, without a great deal of supporting exegetical argument, he throws things out of balance.

His doing so can be explained. In his book *Individuals*, Strawson argues somewhat as follows. Self-consciousness requires the application of criteria for personal identity; these require physical embodiment; and so any knowledge of oneself as a thinking being involves knowledge of oneself as a fully embodied *person* – a being with physical as well as mental attributes. This leads Strawson to conclude that the concept of a thinking subject, a Cartesian 'I' or soul, is an abstraction from the concept of an embodied person, that the latter concept is the more basic

[21] *Bounds of Sense*, p. 166.   [22] *Ibid.*

of the two, and that we ought not to think of a person as composed of a mind and a body, as though these were both independently intelligible.

Strawson sees Kant as arguing for part of this Strawsonian position. That, I submit, explains his over-emphasis on the 'key fact' about 'application of criteria of subject-identity'.[23]

That is not the only harm done by Strawson's attempt to enlist Kant in the service of his theory. Strawson admits candidly that Kant 'makes only a minimal reference to the empirical criteria of subject-identity',[24] i.e. the criteria which involve physical embodiment, and he speaks of Kant's 'neglect of the empirical concept of a subject of experience', i.e. the concept of an embodied person. But this neglected topic, Strawson claims, is a natural supplement to what Kant does say: 'Nothing in Kant's account excludes, and everything in it invites, such supplementation.'

Nearly everything Strawson says about the paralogisms chapter is true as it stands, but its over-all tendency is to minimize the differences between Kant's position and Strawson's. Consider Strawson's allusion, quoted earlier, to 'the temptation to permit ourselves the use of the notion of the subject of experience ("I") while thinking exclusively in terms of the inner contents of consciousness'. According to Strawson's own theory, indeed, one can make judgments of the form 'I am F' only if one is (or has been) embodied. Kant, however, holds no such view, and has no reason to speak, as Strawson does, of 'the *temptation* to permit ourselves...' etc. Kant freely allows that one might be able to make judgments of the form 'I am F' on the basis purely of 'inner contents of consciousness'. Earlier in the *Critique*, I admit, he argues that 'inner experience...is possible only on the assumption of outer experience'; but that argument requires only that one perceive an objective realm, and does not demand embodiment or the thought or memory of embodiment. Anyway, that view of Kant's plays no part in the paralogisms chapter.[25]

The central thrust of that chapter is something of the form: 'The use of "I" in the Cartesian basis seems to entail that P, but really it doesn't.'

[23] See also the reference to Kant in P. F. Strawson, *Individuals* (London, 1959), p. 103.
[24] *Bounds of Sense*, p. 166. Next two quotations: *ibid.* pp. 169 and 170.
[25] A different view is expressed by G. H. Bird, *Kant's Theory of Knowledge* (London, 1962), pp. 177ff. On the strength of the 'outside observer' in the discussion of the third paralogism, Bird takes the paralogisms chapter to be arguing that 'knowledge of others' is 'prior' to 'self-knowledge'; and he links that with Kant's earlier argument which I have mentioned, whose conclusion Bird takes to be that 'our recognition of outer objects is in some way prior to our recognition of inner states.'

On the other hand, Strawson's doctrine has the form: 'One could not have any coherent use of "I" which was not linked to an empirical concept of a subject of experience.' Kant's text does not hint at the slightest suspicion that the 'I' of the Cartesian basis is incoherent unless it is abstracted from a fuller use of 'I' in which it does rest upon criteria and does refer to an empirical subject of experience.

This is not to deny that Strawson can argue for his position by raising difficulties for Kant's. Kant says that no concepts at all can be applied to oneself considered as the omnipresent 'I' which thinks, the limit of one's world in the Cartesian basis. Strawson could say: 'But if I could not apply any concepts to myself, how could I legitimately make use of "I"?' Or, in more Kantian language: 'If when restricted to the Cartesian basis I could not have a *concept* of myself, what is meant by saying that I could nevertheless have a *representation* of myself?' This is a good question, and Strawson has an interesting answer to it. But Kant does not, and it is misleading to say that his discussion in the paralogisms chapter 'invites' us to give Strawson's answer to the question, or even to ask the question in the first place.

As a measure of the gap between Kant's position and Strawson's, consider the fact that Kant's attack on rational psychology, as a pseudo-science which has no data, is accompanied by a warm endorsement of 'empirical psychology', which Kant envisages as 'a kind of physiology of inner sense' and as resting wholly on the data of inner intuition.[26] He says explicitly that if in investigating the soul one were to admit any data whatsoever, 'even pleasure or displeasure', that would 'transform rational psychology into empirical psychology', with which Kant has no quarrel at all. In short, he explicitly sanctions that first-person, not-essentially-embodied knowledge of the mind which Strawson condemns.

[26] 405. Next quotation: 401; see also 405–6 and A 382.

7

INFINITY

§ 39. The antinomies chapter

In Kant's usage, an 'antinomy' is a pair of good-looking arguments for apparently conflicting conclusions. In the chapter on the Dialectic to which I now turn, he offers four antinomies, each purporting to exhibit a conflict which can be resolved only with help from Kantian philosophy. Sometimes Kant suggests that his principles discredit the questions to which the antinomal arguments offer answers,[1] but he also suggests that in the first two antinomies each of the opposing conclusions may be false, while in the third and fourth both conclusions may be true. Indeed, no one account will do. The chapter is in fact a medley, and the several sorts of unity claimed for it are all spurious.

For one thing, the ostensible topic is cosmology, or 'the world-whole' (434); but only the first antinomy, about the age and the size of the world, clearly has such a topic. The second antinomy concerns the infinite divisibility of matter, and is 'cosmological' only in a stretched sense. The third concerns the first event that ever happened, but Kant rapidly moves on from that into a perfectly uncosmological problem about human freedom. The fourth antinomy, about the existence of a 'necessary being', is cosmological enough, but it heavily overlaps the discussion in the theology chapter of the 'cosmological argument' for the existence of God.

Kant's poor selection of material for the antinomies chapter may be partly due to his bad theory, to be discussed in my final chapter, about how all the Dialectic's troubles arise from reason's inherent tendency to error. Although most of the Dialectic's serious content can be grasped without reference to this theory, it does make its presence felt in the antinomies chapter, among other things by providing the setting for Kant's feeble account of why there are exactly these four antinomies (442-3). I do not know whether the theory of reason actually con-

---

[1] 509-10; see also *Prolegomena* §§ 52c, 53. Next two references: 534-5; 559-60. For a good discussion of an uncertainty in Kant's handling of the proposal that in the first two antinomies both Thesis and Antithesis may be false, see J. E. Llewelyn, 'Dialectical and Analytical Opposites', *Kant-Studien* (1964).

strained Kant to select these four, or merely helped him to rationalize a selection he had made on other grounds.

In expounding the alleged fault-line running through the faculty of reason, Kant speaks of 'a natural and inevitable illusion', a 'dialectic' which is 'inseparable from human reason, and which, even after its deceptiveness has been exposed, will...continually entrap [reason] into momentary aberrations ever and again calling for correction'.[2] When cosmological questions are involved, Kant thinks, reason's 'illusions' or difficulties have an inherently antinomal form. Whereas the paralogisms involve 'a purely one-sided illusion', with reason generating 'no illusion which will even in the slightest degree support the opposing assertion', reason's difficulties with cosmological concepts are two-sided. In 'this cosmological field', reason 'soon falls into such contradictions that it is constrained...to desist from pretensions [to knowledge]'. 'We have here', Kant says, 'an entirely natural antithetic.' So the antinomies, rather than being a mere expository device, are supposed to reflect the basic structure of the problems being explored.

I shall reject that view. Not only is the underlying theory of reason false, but also much of the material in the chapter has been distorted by being forced into the antinomal form.

Kant has an associated view which is even more thoroughly false. His chapter-title refers to the 'Antinomy' – not 'Antinomies' – of pure reason. He sees the chapter as having a single basic topic, namely reason's tendency to turn against itself when it tries to think about the world-whole. This alleged 'conflict or antinomy of the laws of pure reason'[3] is a mirage, and like other mirages it can lead one astray. It must be what Gottfried Martin had in mind when he wrote: 'The Kantian antinomies [are] extremely far-reaching. If one can avoid being held up by formal examination of the particular inferences, and can give unhindered attention to the essential problem...etc.' Martin does not identify this 'essential problem' which is to be our excuse for not being 'held up' by details, but it seems to concern antinomies as such – not just Kant's, but also certain logical paradoxes which were discovered in the twentieth century and which have been called 'antinomies'. There is in fact no significant similarity between the two groups of 'antinomies'; or, if there is, we shall not discover it from Martin, since he refuses to be 'held up' by Kant's antinomies, and in his

---

[2] 354-5. Remaining quotations in this paragraph: 433.
[3] 434. Martin quotation: G. Martin, *Kant's Metaphysics and Theory of Science* (trans. P. G. Lucas, Manchester, 1955), p. 62. Logical antinomy: *ibid.* pp. 54-5.

INFINITY

one account of a logical 'antinomy' he gets it wrong. Martin's 'essential problem', like Kant's unitary 'antinomy of the laws of our reason', does not exist. This chapter of Kant's can yield philosophical profit only through those allegedly hindering details which Martin advises us to ignore.

Here is a quick sketch of the chapter's structure. There are nine sections, of which 1, 3, 4, and 5 are less important than the rest. The opening pages and Section 1 use the theory of reason to explain why there are just those four antinomies, and to defend describing the first two as 'mathematical' and the third and fourth as 'dynamical'.[4] I find these labels unhelpful, and shall say no more about them. Section 2 opens with a sketch of the philosophical method which Kant aims to follow in this chapter – the 'method of watching, or rather provoking, a conflict of assertions, not for the purpose of deciding in favour of one or other side, but of investigating whether the object of controversy is not perhaps a deceptive appearance...in regard to which...neither [side] can arrive at any result' (451). The Section then presents the actual antinomies, each pair of arguments being followed by a pair of 'Observations' on them. The two opposing conclusions in each antinomy are called Thesis and Antithesis respectively. Sections 3, 4 and 5 comment broadly on the antinomies: each Thesis represents 'dogmatism' or rationalism, each Antithesis represents empiricism; the antinomies are important; they cannot be evaded through a plea of empirical ignorance; and so on. These sections are interesting and sometimes amusing, but since they are not central, deep, or difficult, I shall not expound them except for the following point. Section 5 says that in each antinomy one side makes something 'too large for our concept' while its rival makes it 'too small'.[5] It becomes perfectly clear later that it is supposed always to be the Antithesis which makes something too large, and the Thesis which makes it too small.[6] This suggests that the chapter has some shape and unity after all. But when he comes to the fourth antinomy Kant has to reverse the roles: in that case the Thesis makes something too large and the Antithesis makes it too small. He seems not to notice this collapse of his scheme. Sections 6, 7 and 8 assemble the materials out of which, Kant says, solutions for the antinomal problems are to be fashioned. In Section 6 he introduces as 'the key' to the desired solution his doctrine called 'transcendental idealism' (see §23 above). We shall see that transcendental idealism is indeed at work here,

4 446–7. See also 110, 199–202, 557–8.   5 514–16; see also 450.
6 556–7. The reversal of the roles: 516.

116

both as a form of phenomenalism and as the more dubious theory that we cannot know things 'as they are in themselves'. Section 7 develops the application of transcendental idealism to the antinomies, and also prepares the way for the introduction, in Section 8, of the notion of a 'regulative principle' – meaning a principle which seems to describe the world but really serves only to guide or regulate scientific inquiry. These three important sections ignore the third and fourth antinomies entirely, and have little to do with the second. Finally, in Section 9 Kant undertakes to solve his antinomal problems, one by one. He has already given most of his solution for the first antinomy and some of it for the second, and these two are treated quite briefly in Section 9. More than half of the section is a discussion of the problem of human freedom, supposedly connected with the third antinomy. It gets so much space at this stage because nothing earlier in the chapter has prepared the way for it.

The first antinomy will be treated in this chapter and the next. The second antinomy will be the topic of Chapter 9, and the third the topic of Chapter 10. The fourth will get one section of Chapter 11. The consideration of each antinomy will involve materials which are scattered through the cosmology chapter, especially the three-quarters of it which comprise Section 2 and Sections 6 to 9.

§ 40. The limits of the world

The first antinomy pits the Thesis that 'The world has a beginning in time, and is also limited as regards space' against the Antithesis that 'The world has no beginning, and no limits in space; it is infinite as regards both time and space'.[7] Let us start with the temporal half of the Thesis – the proposition that the world began.

Kant says that the antinomies occupy 'a dialectical battlefield in which the side permitted to open the attack is invariably victorious' (450), and we find that each antinomal argument, except the one for the fourth antinomy's Thesis, does indeed attack the opposing position. Instead of a direct argument to show that the world did begin, therefore, we are offered an alleged difficulty about the supposition that it did not. It is as follows.

If the world had no beginning then 'up to every given moment an eternity has elapsed'. Kant thinks of this eternity as involving an

[7] 454, 455. The main passages about the first antinomy are 454–61 and 545–51. See also 438–40, 514–15, 523–5, 531–3.

infinite series: for example, if the world never began then at the instant when you started reading this section the completion occurred of a certain infinite series of non-overlapping events, using 'event' to mean a minute's worth of happenings, say. So if the world did not begin, then a certain infinite series has been completed. But, the argument continues: 'The infinity of a series consists in the fact that it can never be completed through successive synthesis. It thus follows that it is impossible for an infinite world-series to have passed away' (454). That, I have to report, completes Kant's argument against the view that the world had no beginning.

Each antinomal argument is supposed to be initially compelling, using 'principles which every dogmatic metaphysics must necessarily recognize',[8] so that each pair of them creates an impasse from which Kantian philosophy affords the only rescue. But the above argument does not compel, for it is open to an objection which is obvious and not particularly Kantian.

Let P be the series of non-overlapping events earlier than the instant when you started reading this section. P is a *discrete* series: that is, each of its members has a next neighbour, and each non-terminal member has two next neighbours. Now, a *discrete series which has two termini must be finite.* We can count along any discrete series, from one member to the next, and if the series has two termini then we can count from one to the other, missing no members and ending up with a finite number. The infinite ascending series of fractions n such that $1/4 \leqslant n \leqslant 1/2$ has two termini, but it is not discrete. There is a way of arranging those same fractions into a discrete series, but then they will not be in ascending order, and the series will have only one terminus. So any infinite discrete series must be open at one end, like

$$0, 1, 2, 3, 4, 5, \ldots$$

or $$\ldots, -5, -4, -3, -2, -1, 0$$

or open at both ends, like

$$\ldots, -5, -4, -3, -2, -1, 0, 1, 2, 3, 4, 5, \ldots$$

That is all the truth there is in the claim that an infinite series 'can never be completed through successive synthesis', in which 'successive synthesis' means something like 'counting' or 'enumerating one by one'.

So Kant's argument exploits a pun. Because the discrete series P is

[8] *Prolegomena*, Appendix.

infinite, it cannot be 'completed' in the sense of having two termini; from which Kant infers that it cannot be 'completed' in the sense of *terminating* or having a terminus at its temporally later end. Kant expresses the argument as though it concerned human activities, so let us follow suit in stating the objection: the argument has not ruled out the possibility that as you started reading this section someone said '*t* minus 0', a minute earlier he said '*t* minus 1', and so on backwards through every event earlier than your section-start, which is to say every member of the infinite discrete series *P*.

Strawson is the only helpful commentator on this argument.[9] After voicing the objection which I have just presented, he follows it up with a hint as to what Kant might be up to:

A temporal process both completed and infinite in duration appears to be impossible only on the assumption that it has a beginning. If...it is urged that we cannot conceive of a process of *surveying* which does not have a beginning, then we must inquire with what relevance and by what right the notion of surveying is introduced into the discussion at all.[10]

I think the notion of surveying has a place in the discussion, and that this helps to explain the text. Still, it won't entirely rescue Kant's argument, for it won't support his clearly implied claim that there is an internal defect in the very notion of a temporally elapsed infinity. Whatever force Kant's argument has depends upon more than just an account of what 'infinity' means or what infinity consists in.

Surveying enters the picture through Kant's transcendental idealism, construed as the relatively weak doctrine that anything I can intelligibly say about the world must be expressible as a statement about what I could in principle discover for myself. This somewhat phenomenalist view explains Kant's view that the notion of an infinitely old world is 'too large for our concept' (514). To attribute to something a certain age, Kant thinks, I must be able to conceive of directly discovering that that is its age – by co-existing with it and counting its birthdays, so to speak. So the thought of an infinitely old world involves that of my

9 Some others are quickly surveyed in J. Bennett, 'The Age and Size of the World', *Synthese* (1971), pp. 128–9. To that gallery I would now add Al-Azm, *Kant's Arguments*, who reduces Kant to a mere scholar: 'The ideas expressed in the Thesis are...straightforward statements of the Newtonian position' (p. 9), the latter 'is based on the firm assumption that every process has a beginning' (p. 17), and so it is 'historically irrelevant' (p. 16) to criticize the Thesis-argument for the obvious lacuna in it. M. S. Gram, 'Kant's First Antinomy', *The Monist* (1967), at pp. 513–18, offers a more interesting *philosophical* defence of the Thesis-argument against the standard criticisms.

10 *Bounds of Sense*, p. 177.

having counted every member of the series P; and Kant, for reasons I shall explain in my next section, cannot stomach the idea of an infinite task's being actually completed.

Now consider the spatial half of the Thesis, which objects to the world's being infinitely large. Kant's argument for this says that infinite size is impossible *because* infinite age is impossible. Although Kant does not say explicitly why that implication holds, I am fairly sure that he is relying on his near-phenomenalism or on the concept-empiricism upon which it rests. Because of this latter doctrine, Kant believes that any thought of a thing's size involves the thought of directly discovering it to be that size. From this he sometimes infers that the concept of size is essentially serial: 'The concept of magnitude...is that determination of a thing whereby we are enabled to think how many times a unit is posited in it. But this how-many-times is based on successive repetition, and therefore on time.'[11] In our present context, however, he concedes that something which could be perceived all at once – 'given in intuition as within certain limits' – need not be thought of serially, but where infinite sizes are in question the concession does not apply. If a thing is infinitely large then its magnitude 'can be thought only through the synthesis of its parts, and the totality of such a quantum only through a synthesis that is brought to completion through repeated addition of unit to unit.' So the thought of an infinitely large world has nested within it the thought of completing an infinite task, namely the surveying or 'synthesizing' of all the members of some infinite series of portions of world; and this latter thought is, in Kant's view, impossible.

Kant does not refuse ever to apply the concept of infinity to the empirical world.[12] On the contrary, he says: 'Since the future is not the condition of our attaining to the present, it is a matter of entire indifference, in our comprehension of the latter, how we may think of future time, whether as coming to an end or as flowing on to infinity.' There, the main point is that we do not have to speculate about the extent of future time as Kant thinks we must about past time, but the passage also implies that we can harmlessly suppose that events will never end.

We can expect trouble, Kant says, only with the idea of an infinite *past* series (439); but since he thinks that a present infinity covertly in-

---

[11] 300. Remaining quotations in this paragraph: 454–6. See also 439–40.
[12] As is suggested by T. D. Weldon, *Kant's Critique of Pure Reason*, 2nd edn (Oxford, 1958), p. 206, and by Kemp Smith, *Commentary*, p. 484. Next quotation: 437; see also the end of the paragraph on 539–40.

volves the thought of a past one, we could say that his view is that the only innocent infinities are future ones. Kant himself does not formulate his position in temporal terms. He says that an infinite series is troublesome if it is 'regressive' rather than 'progressive', proceeding from 'conditioned' to 'condition' rather than vice versa (438–40). He thinks that any temporal account of the line between troublesome and innocent infinities is a mere consequence of the supposedly deeper regressive/progressive distinction and the associated line between 'condition' and 'conditioned': future infinities are innocent because the future is not a 'condition' of the present as the past is. Kant equates x's being a 'condition' of y with x's somehow making y possible (see §84 below): and so he may be right that yesterday is a 'condition' of today although *analytically?* tomorrow is not. But his view that infinite series are troublesome only if they are regressive, i.e. run from conditioned to conditions, depends upon his theory of reason; and I shall show in my final chapter that that theory is not helpful. In the meantime, the temporal way of distinguishing troublesome from innocent infinities can be allowed to stand on its own feet.

§41. Infinite tasks *What kind of t-q is involved here?*

Kant allows the idea of a future infinity, even when construed as a possible infinite future for oneself. He would therefore agree with Dretske that it is only medically impossible that someone should count all the natural numbers.[13] Dretske finds nothing incoherent in the supposition that someone has begun to count the natural-number series 0, 1, 2,..., and will continue at a steady rate without ever stopping, in which case he will count all the natural numbers. He will never have counted them all, but given any natural number he will eventually have counted it. If you dislike saying that our man will count all the natural numbers, say instead that he will count each of them – it makes no real difference. The basic point is that we can envisage beginning on some task and never stopping, just as we can envisage lasting for ever.

Of the idea that someone might have counted from infinity, or might have completed an infinite task, Dretske says 'I'm not sure this makes sense.' He shows that the idea is not formally defective: its logic exactly mirrors that of 'counting to infinity', with 'he will never finish' replaced by 'he never started', and so on. Yet Dretske, like Kant, has doubts.

[13] F. Dretske, 'Counting to Infinity', *Analysis* (1965).

Regarding the case over which he has no doubts, Dretske uses an argument which is not *clearly* distinct from this: 'We can suppose that someone will count to 100, say; and if we can suppose that someone will count to n then we can suppose that he will count to $(n+1)$; so we can suppose that someone will count every natural number.' If that argument were effective, it would remain so under a systematic replacement of 'will count to' by 'has counted from', which would dispose of Dretske's doubts.[14] But the moral is not that counting from infinity is intelligible. Rather, it is that that argument does not show that counting to infinity is intelligible.

Dretske's doubts can perhaps be justified. The notion of having performed a series of operations involves that of remembering performing them, possessing that part of one's past. How much I have done or undergone determines how much of me there is now. (Series of diminishing tasks, an infinite number of which add up to only a finite achievement, are not in question here.) So the idea of having completed an infinite task involves the idea of possessing, *now*, an infinite stock of memories; and it is plausible to suppose that this cannot coherently be entertained. In contrast, the thought that I shall perform an infinite task does not involve the thought that I shall ever be infinitely epistemically endowed.

This difference between infinite past and infinite future arises from two facts in combination. One is a fact about infinity: in any infinite discrete series with a terminus, each member is separated from the terminus by only a finite number of members. For example, there are infinitely many natural numbers, but each of them is finite and is therefore only finitely many 'plus-one' steps above zero. (There will be more on this in §44 below.) So someone starting an infinite task will always have only a finite task behind him and an infinite one ahead, whereas someone completing an infinite task has always had an infinite amount of it behind him and only a finite amount still to be performed. The second explanatory fact concerns an asymmetry in sentient beings, namely that they have more epistemic grasp of their past than of their future, so that someone's having an infinite future does not imply, as would his having an infinite past, that he is infinitely epistemically endowed now. We ought to drop the counting-from-infinity example. Our topic is the Kantian notion of one's grip on the contingencies of one's past experience; and so we should think of tasks or biographies

---

[14] J. D. Wallace, 'The Beginning of the World', *Dialogue* (1967–8), does argue in precisely that way for the possibility that someone should have completed an infinite task.

which are not rule-generated as counting is, so that each episode is a partly brute-fact addition which imposes some extra load on the memory.

If the epistemic asymmetry were reversed for some creature, then for him the entire argument would flip over; but I doubt if that reversal makes sense. Again, there is no difficulty about supposing a creature who lives for ever but whose memories never reach back more than a century, say; but we can ignore this possibility, for we introduced sentient beings in order to ground 'what might be true' in 'what one might directly discover to be true', and so someone with a memory cut-off simply does not serve our purpose.

On certain assumptions, therefore, a past infinity does while a future one does not involve the thought of being infinitely knowledgeable or memory-laden right now. This latter notion seems to me, as presumably to Kant and to Dretske, to be objectionable. I have no proof of this, but at the end of §42 I shall make one move in its defence.

§ 42. The futurizing move

Kant does not explicitly formulate the problem about completed infinite tasks, let alone any solution to it. Yet some things he says seem to be aimed at that problem. In expounding these, I shall use 'infinite' where Kant might use 'non-finite'. His distinction between these is irrelevant just now, for even if it were valid the problem of completed *non-finite* tasks would still remain.

The problem-solving moves to which I have alluded take the following form. Kant takes a statement which threatens to involve the thought of a completed past infinity, applies to it his phenomenalistic spelling-out in terms of 'what I could discover', and thus projects the infinity into the future. For example, the notion of an infinitely large world becomes, under phenomenalist analysis, the notion of a never-ending, non-repetitive series of world-explorations which I might perform in an infinite possible future. Thus:

Nothing is really given us save perception and the empirical advance from this to other possible perceptions...To call an appearance a real thing prior to our perceiving it, either means that in the advance of experience we must meet with such a perception, or it means nothing at all.[15]

Note the word 'advance' (*Fortschritt* and *Fortgang*), which implies that

[15] 521. Next quotation: 523–4; see also 528–9.

the perceptions in question lie in the future, so that they are conceptually harmless however numerous they are. Again:

If...I represent to myself all existing objects...I do not set them in space and time [as being there] prior to experience...To say that they exist prior to all my experience is only to assert that they are to be met with if, starting from perception, I advance to that part of experience to which they belong.

I conjecture that here again *one* thing Kant is doing is to project an infinity into the future, liking it better once he has got it there.

The same move is made even with the notion of an infinitely old world. Kant says that the proposition that the world is infinitely old, when spelled out in terms of what I could discover, transmutes the infinity of *past events* into an infinity of possible *future investigations*:

The real things of past time...are objects for me and real in past time only in so far as I represent to myself (either by the light of history or by the guiding-clues of causes and effects) that a regressive series of possible perceptions in accordance with empirical laws...conducts us to a past time-series as condition of the present time...All events which have taken place in the immense periods that have preceded my own existence mean really nothing but the possibility of extending the chain of experience from the present perception back to the conditions which determine this perception in respect of time. (523)

Kant calls the series 'regressive' because, considered as a series of *topics of investigation*, it moves from times back to earlier times. But considered as a series of *investigations* it takes place in a possible future, and that, I contend, helps to draw the sting from the supposed infinite age of the world.

As I said, Kant does not state the problem in my terms. Here is a possible explanation for this fact. Kant solves his problem by resolutely applying a phenomenalist analysis to statements about troublesome infinities; but what creates the problem in the first place, by making those infinities look troublesome, is the mildly phenomenalist view that any statement about an infinity involves some thought of an infinite 'synthesis' or enumeration. So the problem is solved by moving from half-hearted to whole-hearted phenomenalism. This makes the problem essentially unstable, which may have inhibited Kant from getting clear about it.

With that in mind, and remembering that Kant's phenomenalism is embedded in his so-called 'transcendental idealism', consider his remark that the antinomies yield an 'indirect proof of the transcendental ideality of appearances' (534), by showing that problems which arise when you lack transcendental idealism can be solved when you have it. If this claim were based on the material I have presented so far, and thus on the phenomenalist component in transcendental idealism, it would be quite false; for someone who allowed *no* connexion between 'what there is' and 'what one could in principle discover' would not have the problem in the first place. In §45 below I shall present another way of viewing Kant's 'indirect proof'.

This problem of Kant's assumes that there is a conceptual difficulty about the idea of having an infinite stock of memories. That assumption might be challenged as follows: 'I can easily suppose myself to have an infinite stock of memories, possessed dispositionally – which is how we *do* possess most of our knowledge of all kinds. There is nothing unmanageable about supposing that I am able to give the right answers to infinitely many distinct questions about my past, and it seems reasonable to regard each such ability as (a manifestation of) a memory. So where is the difficulty?' That is all right in itself, but it makes infinite knowledge acceptable by equating it with the infinity of distinct questions which I could correctly answer in a possible future. So the objection does not go against the initial claim that I can coherently connect the thought of infinity with the thought of myself only in the thought of an infinite future. The only difference it makes is in how that claim is to be defended. Instead of saying 'Infinite past involves infinite present, and this is always objectionable, so there is only infinite future', we shall weaken the middle clause to '. . . and this is always objectionable unless construed as a kind of infinite future'. The conclusion will still follow.

My reason for qualifying rather than totally retracting the claim about infinite-present is as follows. Memories can be *episodes* which relate to one's past in something like the way in which sensory states relate to one's present environment. So there is still room for the substantive claim that one cannot make sense of the idea of having an infinite endowment of memories of that kind. If someone said that he could make sense of this, I couldn't argue with him; but I shouldn't believe him.

§43. Infinite number

I now turn to some other aspects of Kant's treatment of the first antinomy – aspects stemming from his inadequate understanding of the concept of infinity.

It was not until fairly late in the nineteenth century that the work of Cantor, Frege and others made the concept of infinity fully manageable. Before then, certain mistakes were endemic, the natural effect of which was to make philosophers uncomfortable with 'infinite' and downright resistant to 'infinite number'. I shall illustrate these mistakes through philosophers who matter to us for other reasons – I am not offering even an outline history of the topic.[16]

The discomfort arose partly from such questions as 'How long is half an infinite line?' and 'If there are infinitely many natural numbers, how many even numbers are there?' If there were finitely many even numbers, then we should have $n = 2m$ for infinite n and finite m, which is impossible. As for the possibility that there are infinitely many even numbers, that would yield $n = 2m$ for infinite n and infinite m, and some philosophers found absurd the idea of one infinity's being greater than another.[17] Descartes did not accept that: 'What ground have we for judging whether one infinite can or cannot be greater than another?', but his own discomfort is evidenced by his adding: 'It would no longer be infinite, were we able to comprehend it.'

Leibniz had the problem too, though he handled it better. He argued that if there are values of n and m such that there are n natural numbers and m even numbers, then we should have to say that $n = m$ because the natural numbers can be paired off with the even numbers without remainder on either side; but this is unacceptable because it would imply that 'the whole is not greater than the part'.[18] This does not assume that one infinite cannot exceed another. Rather, it says that $n = m$ because the n-membered and m-membered sets satisfy a sufficient condition for having the same number of members. Since this *is* a sufficient condition, and is indeed crucial to the post-Cantor understanding of infinity, we must regard Leibniz as being well on the road to the truth.[19]

[16] For more of the history, and other good things, see J. F. Thomson, 'Infinity in Logic and Mathematics', in P. Edwards (ed.), *The Encyclopedia of Philosophy* (New York and London, 1967). Some earlier views of Kant's about the infinity of the world are described by A. O. Lovejoy, *The Great Chain of Being* (New York, 1960), pp. 140–1.

[17] For example Spinoza; see the end of § 13 above. Quotations from Descartes: Letter to Mersenne, C. Adam and P. Tannery (eds.), *Oeuvres de Descartes* (Paris, 1897–1910), Vol. I, p. 147; see also *Principles of Philosophy*, Part I, § 26.

[18] Letter to Malebranche, Gerhardt, Vol. I, p. 338.

[19] He was anticipated by others, e.g. Galileo. For more about this, and for a splendid philosophical discussion, see B. Russell, *Our Knowledge of the External World* (London, 1926), Lectures VI and VII. For further references, see S. C. Kleene, *Mathematical Logic* (New York, 1967), p. 176, n. 121.

But he could not accept this conclusion, and so he evaded it by saying that although there are *infinitely many* natural numbers there is no such thing as an *infinite number* of Fs for any F. He prevents the above problem from arising by denying that there are numbers n and m such that there are n natural numbers and m even numbers.

This was not just an *ad hoc* escape from a difficulty, for Leibniz did have an embryonic theory of number according to which there is indeed no number of natural numbers. His view was that there cannot be a number n such that there are exactly n Fs unless the Fs constitute a 'veritable whole'. For example: 'There is an infinity of things, i.e. there are always more of them than can be assigned. But there is no infinite number, neither of line nor of other infinite quantity, if these are understood as veritable wholes.'[20] The last phrase is not explained, but one can see the general idea. Leibniz does not count the Fs as a veritable whole if the most precise thing we can say about how many Fs there are is

(a) No finite set of Fs includes all the Fs.

He seems to think that if there could be an infinite n, the statement

(b) There are n Fs

would entail and explain (a) but would not be equivalent to it. Precisely because he thinks that we cannot formulate a statement which is stronger than (a) in the required way, Leibniz thinks that there cannot be an infinite number. This use of the notion of a 'whole' occurs frequently in Leibniz's writings: 'There never is an infinite whole in the world, although there are always wholes greater than others to infinity. Even the universe itself could not pass for a whole.'[21] Also: 'The infinite plurality of terms...means [only] that there are more terms than can be designated by a number'; 'I admit no true infinite number, though I confess that the multitude of things surpasses every finite number, or rather every number.'

Locke was of a similar mind about this. He denied that 'endless addibility' yields 'a clear and distinct idea of an actually infinite number', because: '[It consists] only in a power still of increasing the number, be it already as great as it will. So that of what remains to be added (wherein consists the infinity) we have but an obscure, imperfect, and confused idea.'[22] Leibniz endorses this, except for the hint that the trouble concerns 'infinite' rather than just 'infinite number'. Agreeing

---

[20] *New Essays* II. xvii. 1.
[21] *Ibid.* II. xiii. 21; see also Loemker, p. 627. Next two quotations: Letter to Bernoulli, Loemker, p. 514; Letter to Masson, Gerhardt, Vol. VI, p. 629.
[22] *Essay* II. xxix. 16. Next quotation: *New Essays* II. xvii. 8.

that the latter is an absurdity, he adds: 'But this is not because we could not have an idea of the infinite, but because an infinite could not be a true whole.'

This line of thought is older than Leibniz. Aristotle equated 'number' with 'limited plurality' and with 'plurality measurable by one'.[23] He also said that 'infinite' can mean 'what is incapable of being gone through', and inferred that 'number taken in abstraction cannot be infinite, for...that which has number is numerable' and thus capable of being 'gone through'.

A natural accompaniment of the view that number is what is 'measurable by one', or theoretically countable, is the view that any number n must be exact or determinate or hard-edged, so that 'There are n Fs' says exactly how many Fs there are. And that in turn could introduce the Leibnizian notion of a 'whole', for one might naturally suppose that the possibility of saying *exactly* how many Fs there are depends upon the Fs constituting a 'whole' in some strong sense. Kant, whose thought on these matters was intensely Leibnizian, exemplifies this last move when he says that 'infinite whole' could not be defined in terms of 'greatest magnitude', because the latter phrase 'does not represent *how great*' the magnitude is (458–60). My guess is that the unexplained notion of 'how great', or of something exact or 'determinate', has the force of 'just so many and not a single one more or less', this being understood to require a value of n such that $(n+1) > n$. By that standard, indeed, n must be finite.

The standard is no longer acceptable, for we now know that $(n+1) > n$ and $(n.m) > n$ are both false for infinite n. We are separated from Kant and Leibniz by the great nineteenth-century work on the foundations of mathematics. This work has moved us from a situation where Hume could reasonably say that 'the capacity of the mind is limited, and can never attain a full and adequate conception of infinity',[24] and Descartes could say 'It is in the nature of the infinite that I who am finite and limited should be unable to comprehend it', through to a position where Wittgenstein can be entitled to say: 'Our use of the word "infinite"...is *straightforward*...and our idea that its meaning is "transcendent" rests on a misunderstanding.' Work which could produce such a difference as that should not be underestimated.

23 *Metaphysics* 1020a13, 1057a3. Next quotation: *Physics* II, Ch. 4, 204. I owe these references to Michael Beebe.
24 *Treatise*, p. 26. Next two quotations: Descartes, *Third Meditation*, about three-fifths of the way through L. Wittgenstein, *The Blue and Brown Books* (Oxford, 1958), p. 95.

§44. Numbers and natural numbers

The work in question was a general analysis of the concept of number, so that the problems about infinity were solved by doctrine which was developed to for quite other purposes. The first and chief ground-breaker, I believe, was Cantor; but the main materials were first assembled into a coherent philosophical analysis of the concept of number in Frege's great, lucid work *The Foundations of Arithmetic*.[25]

Before dealing with the concept of *number*, as used in 'There is one even prime number' and 'There is no square number between 5 and 8', Frege deals with the concept of *cardinality* – that is, with the use of numerical expressions in 'There is one Pope', 'I have three radios', and 'There are infinitely many molecules' and the like. It is harder in English than in German to keep these apart from one another. To refer colloquially in English to cardinality, one must use the word 'number', in expressions of the form 'The number of Fs'. In German, the word *Anzahl* is a non-technical term meaning 'cardinality', as distinct from *Zahl* which means 'number'. So I might investigate the *Anzahl* of people in the room; but 2 is the only *Zahl* which is both prime and even.

Frege's account of cardinality shows that the statement 'There are infinitely many Fs' is an absolutely satisfactory cardinality-statement, that is, that 'infinitely many' is just as numerical as is 'three' in 'I have three children'. Furthermore, given any cardinality-concept (*Anzahl*), Frege shows how to derive from it a corresponding number (*Zahl*). So we get the result that there is an infinite number, its status as a number being claimed not dogmatically but on the strength of a deep, powerful, general theory of number. For all the details, read Frege.

So there is a number which is the number of the set of natural numbers, say. Its name is conventionally written as $\aleph_0$ (read 'aleph-null'). It is basic to Frege's whole theory that if the members of two sets can be paired off without remainder on either side, then the two sets have the same cardinality. So $\aleph_0$ is the number of the set of natural numbers, of the set of even numbers, of prime numbers, of natural numbers > 7, and so on. So it is false that $(\aleph_0 + m) > \aleph_0$, and that $(\aleph_0 . m) > \aleph_0$; but now that the status of $\aleph_0$ as a number is firmly assured, we can accept

---

[25] G. Frege, *The Foundations of Arithmetic* (trans. J. L. Austin, Oxford, 1950); first published in 1884. See §§ 85–6 of it for an acknowledgment of Cantor. A large step towards the breakthrough of Cantor and Frege is taken in B. Bolzano, *Paradoxes of the Infinite* (trans. D. A. Steele, London, 1950); first published in 1851.

these consequences as genuine results rather than as threatening absurdities.

Among the infinity-problems which beset Cantor's predecessors, was the problem of how 'infinite number' could relate to 'highest number'. Let us see how the Cantor–Frege developments deal with this matter.

For present purposes we can take it that $\aleph_0$ is the highest number. Cantor developed a theory about higher infinite numbers $\aleph_1$, $\aleph_2$, ... etc., but his methods are controversial, and anyway they lie far beyond anything envisaged by any of his predecessors. (Leibniz argued that there could not be a highest number, because any number can be doubled and thus shown not to be the highest. That argument assumes that $(\aleph_0.2) > \aleph_0$; and it is misleading to say, as Rescher does, that it 'has fared better historically' than some other arguments because 'it survives in modified form' as Cantor's argument for infinities greater than $\aleph_0$.[26] The alleged 'modified form' involves a total rejection of the basic assumption of Leibniz's argument.) In taking $\aleph_0$ to be the highest number, I am adopting the position of someone who accepts the Cantor–Frege theory of number, while rejecting Cantor's transfinite arithmetic. Some mathematicians do take precisely this position.

Leibniz says that the idea of a highest number 'implies a contradiction'.[27] So does Kant: 'No multiplicity is the greatest, since one or more units can always be added to it.' That is invalid, and the crucial point to be made in correcting it is that $\aleph_0$ is not a natural number, i.e. not a number which can be reached by 'plus-one' steps starting from zero. Frege's work shows that 'number' is wider than 'natural number'; but earlier thinkers, not surprisingly, thought that a highest number would have to lie enormously far along the series of natural numbers. Descartes, indeed, seems to have tolerated the notion of a highest number, thus misconceived. He says that 'in counting I cannot reach the greatest of all numbers', and from this he infers, with gross invalidity, that 'in enumeration there is something that exceeds my powers', from which he infers further that 'there is always more to be conceived in the greatest number than I can ever conceive.' Although he hesitates to use the term 'infinite', Descartes refers confidently to 'this concept of an indefinite number'. He seems to think that there is an indefinitely or unreachably high *natural* number – one which is unthinkably far along the series from 0 – and even if this is not the highest number it is pro-

---

[26] N. Rescher, 'Leibniz' Conception of Quantity, Number, and Infinity', *Philosophical Review* (1955), p. 112.

[27] Letter to Malebranche, Loemker, p. 211. Next two quotations: Kant, 458; Descartes, Reply to Second Objections, Haldane & Ross, pp. 37–8.

tected, by its own unthinkability, from being shown not to be the highest by the standard add-one ploy.

That is all perfectly wrong. Nothing compels me to admit that there is a natural number which is unthinkable by me, and the nearest we can get to a respectable version of a highest number, or of Descartes' 'indefinitely great number', is by introducing $\aleph_0$. The vital point about $\aleph_0$ is that, rather than having an unthinkably remote location on the natural number series, it is not in that series at all.

That connects with another important point, namely that although there are infinitely many natural numbers, each of them is finite. So in an infinitely large world, nothing need be an infinite distance from anything else. It suffices that although every intra-mundane distance is finite, no such distance is the greatest. We have already met this point in §41 above.

A recent writer gets the point abundantly wrong:

Any object in space, however far distant, is a finite distance only from every other object. But between any object and any other there can then be only a finite number of objects, and therefore, however vast the total number of objects may be, it will still be finite.[28]

The error of this should by now be clear. Granted that there are only finitely many bodies between any two bodies, there may be infinitely many bodies altogether; just as there are only finitely many natural numbers between any two natural numbers, even though there are infinitely many natural numbers altogether. Avoid the thought, 'No natural number is the highest number because each is outranked by $\aleph_0$'. For that, although true, distracts one from the vital thought, 'No natural number is the highest because each is outranked by another natural number.'

Kemp Smith says that the Thesis of the first antinomy is based on the claim that 'we cannot comprehend how, from an infinitude that has no beginning, the present should ever have been reached.'[29] That repeats the mistake I have been discussing. The idea is that if the series of past events stretches back infinitely far, then some events must have occurred an infinitely long time ago; and 'we cannot comprehend' how the event-sequence ever got from an infinitely distant time to the present, this being like a journey from here to an infinitely distant star. If Kant was arguing like that, which I doubt, then he was in error. The mistake, of which Kemp Smith seems unaware, is that of moving from 'past time is infinite' to 'some past times are infinitely remote'.

[28] P. M. Huby, 'Kant or Cantor? That the Universe, if Real, must be Finite in both Space and Time', *Philosophy* (1971), p. 127.　　　[29] *Commentary*, p. 484.

Not only is 'infinite distance' not implied by 'infinitely large world', it is also incoherent in itself. Newton said that 'we are able to understand' the notion of 'an infinite distance',[30] but if he meant that infinite distance is possible, then he was wrong. If two things were infinitely far apart, then the series of non-overlapping miles between them would be infinite and discrete, and yet would have two termini; and that is impossible (see §40 above). Here is another argument for the view that nothing could be in our space yet not relatable to us by an infinite journey. If x is infinitely distant, then we cannot lessen its distance from us, so we cannot define x's direction from us by reference to the journey which would most rapidly bring us closer to it, so we have no content for the notion of x's direction from us, so x does not lie in our space.

§ 45. The weakening move

Sometimes, Kant takes exactly Leibniz's view about infinity and infinite number. That is, he says that any number must be 'determinate', and must be applicable to a certain kind of 'whole', and that there cannot be an infinite number because nothing infinite can manifest the required sort of wholeness or determinateness. 'A determinate yet infinite quantity', he says, 'is self-contradictory' (555). He does allow that an indeterminate quantity can be infinite, but such a quantity would not be equal to any number. This is in the spirit of Leibniz's remark that there is an infinity (an infinite quantity) of things but that there is no infinite number.

In the context of this doctrine, Kant distinguishes sharply between the word *Zahl*, meaning 'number', and the word *Menge*, which I translate by 'quantity'. This is not 'quantity' in the sense of 'stretch' or 'amount', as applied to something which is essentially uncountable (e.g. 'quantity of water'). There is nothing wrong with speaking of the *Menge* of members of a series, for example. The point is just that the notion of *Menge* is supposed to be weaker than that of genuinely numerical how-many-ness: any assemblage has a *Menge* of members, but if the assemblage is not 'determinate' its *Menge* is not equal to any *Zahl*. I cannot find that Kant uses *Anzahl* (cardinality), but he would presumably agree that he uses *Menge* as one might use *Anzahl*, except that the former term – he thinks – avoids the implication that what is involved could be assigned a number.

[30] I. Newton, *Unpublished Scientific Papers* (ed. R. and M. B. Hall, Cambridge, 1962), p. 101.

That Leibnizian doctrine of Kant's comes to the fore only in one part of the discussion of the second antinomy, and Kant's reason for introducing it there is a bad one, as I shall show.[31] Kant's more usual position, which permeates his handling of the first antinomy, is somewhat different. It is the position that an assemblage which is not determinate, or not a genuine 'whole' or 'totality', cannot be infinite at all. In this context, Kant claims to distinguish 'more than finite' from 'infinite', and what he requires for the latter is just that sort of determinateness which his other doctrine requires not for infiniteness but only for measurability by a *Zahl*. The two doctrines, though mutually inconsistent, are alike in general spirit. Each of them implies that something which is not determinate might be more than finite, and each of them also offers a denial about such an item – one saying that its *Menge* could not be equal to any number (though it could be infinite), and the other that its *Menge* could not be infinite at all. Our present concern is with the latter doctrine, according to which something's being more than finite does not entail its being infinite.

Here is one of Kant's ways of making capital out of the supposed gap between 'more than finite' and 'infinite'. It concerns, once more, the phenomenalist component in his transcendental idealism. Kant takes this to imply that any statement about the world's size is equivalent to one about how long one could continue a non-repetitive exploration of the world: 'Only by reference to the magnitude of the empirical regress [i.e. the series of possible explorations] am I in a position to make for myself a concept of the magnitude of the world' (547). So the truth about how long the regress can be is not *a result of*, but *is*, the truth about the world's size.

Now, what is the strongest statement that could be made about the size of any possible 'empirical regress'? Whatever it is, it can never be a statement which treats such a regress as a 'whole' or a 'totality', for the regress must be viewed as lying in the future:

The empirical synthesis . . . is necessarily successive, the members of the series being given only as following upon one another in time; and I have therefore, in this case, no right to assume the absolute *totality* of the synthesis and of the series thereby represented.[32]

---

[31] See § 57 below. The passage is 551–5. In Kemp Smith's translation the Leibnizian doctrine is invisible, because *Menge* and *Zahl* are both regularly translated by 'number'. The only Kantian commentator I have found who handles the distinction between them correctly is M. S. Gram, 'Kant's First Antinomy', *The Monist* (1967), pp. 511–12.

[32] 528–9. Next quotation: 539–40; see also 523–4, 533–4.

From a given pair of parents the descending line of generation may proceed with-out end, and we can quite well regard the line as actually so continuing in the world. For in this case reason never requires an absolute totality of the series, since it does not presuppose that totality as...given, but only as something...that allows of being given, and is added to without end.

Kant infers from this that the strongest intelligible statement about the size of such a regress is that 'No finite amount of it includes it all'. As applied to the size of the world, this would yield the statement that 'Every finite world-exploration leaves some world-exploring undone'; and that, according to Kant's phenomenalism, is equivalent to 'Every finite portion of world leaves out some world'. So this last statement is the strongest thing one can say about the size of the world. That, Kant thinks, saves us from thinking of the world as infinite. Thus:

This cosmic series can...be neither greater nor smaller than the possible empirical regress upon which alone its concept rests. And since this regress can yield neither a determinate infinite nor a determinate finite...it is evident that the magnitude of the world can be taken neither as finite nor as infinite.[33]

The regress consists only in the *determining* of the magnitude, and does not give any *determinate* concept. It does not, therefore, yield any concept of a magnitude which...can be described as infinite...The regress does not proceed to the in-finite, as if the infinite could be given, but only indeterminately far.

All this is what I call 'the weakening move'. Thinking that he has a difficulty about supposing that the world is infinite, Kant seeks to avoid it by adopting only the allegedly weaker supposition that the world is more than finite or that no finite amount of it includes it all.

This whole line of thought is really independent of phenomenalism. Given that Kant sees objections to the world's being finite and to its being infinite, sheer opportunism could lead him to occupy the sup-posedly intermediate position that it is more than finite yet not outright infinite. The formulation 'Every finite amount of world excludes some world' need not have been derived from 'Every finite world-explora-tion would leave some world unexplored'.

Kant would not agree with that, because of a line of thought which is intertwined in his text with the one I have just presented. His 'trans-cendental idealism' includes phenomenalism, and we have seen that he uses phenomenalist formulations of statements about the world's magnitude in an attempt to fend off the notion of infinity. But his transcendental idealism also says that the world is not 'a thing in itself' –

---

[33] 546n. Next quotation: 551; see also 533, 536.

a phrase which Kant sometimes uses incautiously, as in our present context where he says that it is only because the world is *not* a 'thing in itself' that we can say something intermediate in strength between 'The world is finite' and 'The world is downright infinite'. Thus: 'If we regard the two propositions, that the world is infinite in magnitude and that it is finite in magnitude, as contradictory opposites, we are assuming that the world...is a thing in itself.'[34] This is supposed to yield the famous 'indirect proof' of the 'transcendental ideality' of the world:

> If the world is a whole existing in itself, it is either finite or infinite. But both alternatives are false (as shown in the proofs of the antithesis and thesis respectively). It is therefore also false that the world...is a whole existing in itself.

I cannot defend the first sentence of that, any more than any other positive use of the pseudo-concept of a thing in itself.

So Kant links the concept of infinity with that of a thing in itself. Leibniz once said: 'The true infinite exists, strictly speaking, only in the absolute, which is anterior to all composition, and is not formed by the addition of parts';[35] and Kant seems to echo this idea that the province of 'the true infinite' is the realm of unempirical monads or things in themselves.

One of Kant's ways of tying 'infinite' to 'thing in itself' is curious and subtle. He has certain turns of phrase which he apparently uses *both* to distinguish the infinite from the merely non-finite *and* to distinguish things in themselves from appearances. Here, for example:

> [We must not regard the world] as a thing given in and by itself, prior to all regress. We must therefore say that the quantity of parts in a given appearance is in itself neither finite nor infinite. For an appearance is not something existing in itself, and its parts are first given in and through the regress of the decomposing synthesis, a regress which is never given in absolute completeness. (533)

The topic here is divisibility rather than extent, but that does not affect my present point, which is that the statement 'The world is not given prior to all regress' apparently means both (1) that we cannot formulate statements about the world which entail, but are not entailed by, statements about possible experience, and (2) that we cannot formulate any stronger statement about a quantity than that it is non-finite. Of these

---

34 532. Next quotation: 534–5. For a very helpful discussion of the relationship between transcendental idealism and Kant's handling of the antinomies, see S. F. Barker, 'Appearing and Appearances in Kant', *The Monist* (1967), especially pp. 438–41.
35 *New Essays* II. xvii. 1.

two, (1) forbids us to speak of the world as it is in itself, while (2) forbids us to apply to the world that concept of outright infinity which Kant thinks is stronger than mere non-finiteness.

In using phrases like 'prior to all regress', Kant invokes both (1) and (2) without clearly distinguishing them. Both elements are present in almost every sentence of this:

> Of this empirical regress the most that we can ever know is that from every given member of the series of conditions we have always still to advance empirically to a higher and more remote member. The magnitude of the whole of appearances is not thereby determined in any absolute manner; and we cannot therefore say that this regress proceeds to infinity. In doing so we should be anticipating members which the regress has not yet reached, representing their quantity as so great that no empirical synthesis could attain thereto, and so should be determining the magnitude of the world (although only negatively) prior to the regress – which is impossible. (547)

This clearly offers a phenomenalist warning against trying to think of the world in super-sensory terms; but it also warns against trying to use the concept of infinity as Kant understands it; for 'representing their quantity as so great that no empirical synthesis could attain thereto' surely means 'thinking that there are n of them for some uncountably high n'.

Against the background of this supposed link between 'thing in itself' and infinity, we can get into proper focus Kant's denial that the world is a 'whole' or a 'totality'. This denial is sometimes offered as the core of his entire treatment of the first antinomy: 'I can say nothing regarding the whole object of experience, the world of sense';[36] so that the Thesis and Antithesis are 'quarrelling about nothing', having been deceived by a 'transcendental illusion', and Kant hints – without saying outright – that this is the illusion that one can think about the world as a whole.

This alleged solution of the antinomal difficulty arises from putting together the two main strands in this part of Kant's thought. Firstly, the world is an appearance, so it can be thought about only in terms of possible unending empirical procedures ('regresses'), and so it cannot be thought of as a whole or totality:

> [The first antinomy presents] a conflict due to an illusion which arises from our applying to appearances that exist only in our representation...that idea of absolute totality which holds only as a condition of things in themselves.[37]

[36] 548. Next two quoted phrases: 529.
[37] 534. Next quotation: 533. 'Potential infinite': 445.

Secondly, a genuine infinite would have to be a true 'whole':

> Since the world does not exist in itself, independently of the regressive series of my representations, it exists *in itself* neither as an *infinite* whole nor as a *finite* whole. It exists only in the empirical regress of the series of appearances.

And so Kant thinks he can show that the world is not infinite, without having to allow that it is only finite. He fails, of course, because he is wrong about the concept of infinity. His argument rests upon his false assumption that the statement 'Every finite set of Fs excludes some Fs', because it does not represent the Fs as a 'totality', does not involve outright infinity but only more-than-finiteness or 'potential infinity'.

All the Kantian materials presented in this section are fairly bad. In particular, the alleged 'indirect proof' of transcendental idealism requires both (a) the dubious link between 'in itself' and 'whole' etc., and (b) the mistaken view that 'whole' or a relative of it is required for 'infinite' in its proper sense. Still, Kant might have done worse, for he might have used this putative proof of transcendental idealism:

> The antinomic concepts [of finite world and infinite world] have a priori validity but they cannot be applied to things in themselves. Things obviously cannot themselves be both at once, and it is very improbable that they should happen to fall on one side or the other of the alternative.[38]

§ 46. Infinite and indefinite

Kant sometimes speaks of series which are not infinite but only *indefinite*, and he connects this with remarks about *regulative* principles.[39] His remarks in this vein create problems.

The first antinomy is supposed to arise from 'the principle of reason'. We shall see that the exact nature of this 'principle' is rather obscure, but it is convenient to start off with the supposition that it says something to the effect that for certain values of F, every item which is F has a condition. This could lead to our first-antinomy troubles, perhaps, by implying that every event has an earlier event as its 'condition', and that every stretch of world has a larger stretch as its 'condition'; whence it might seem to follow that the world is infinitely old and infinitely large. All this has roots in Kant's theory of reason, which I shall evaluate in Chapter 12 below. My present concern is merely to explain one limited use which he makes of the theory – namely his attempt to solve

---

[38] G. Martin, *Kant's Metaphysics and Theory of Science* (trans. P. G. Lucas, Manchester, 1955), p. 64. [39] 536–51, 589–90.

the first antinomy by claiming that the 'principle of reason' is a 'regulative' one.

For Kant's central treatment of regulativeness – defining what I shall call the *official* sense of the term 'regulative' – we must look to the Appendix to the Dialectic, together with one passing remark and one longer passage in the theology chapter.[40] A principle is 'regulative' in this official sense if it seems to make an assertion about the world but really ought to be construed only as an injunction about how to investigate the world. For example, 'Every event is caused by an event', construed as a regulative principle, advises us to seek causes and never to admit that any given event is uncaused. Part of the case for regarding a given principle as regulative is that if it is construed instead as fact-stating or 'constitutive' it then cannot be decisively established or refuted by empirical evidence. (I shall amplify this sketch in §86 below.)

Now, if the 'principle of reason' is regulative in that sense, then it merely enjoins us to seek conditions for all items of certain sorts, and never to admit defeat. Instead of saying that, given any event, there *is* an earlier one, we shall merely resolve always to push our pre-historical researches back further still, never admitting that we have discovered the first event. Similarly, rather than saying that there *is* always more world to be discovered, we shall merely adopt the policy of always searching assiduously and optimistically for more world.

Kant associates this with the claim that the series of past events, like that of ever-larger stretches of world, is not infinite but indefinite.[41] This should mean that the strongest thing we can say about each series is not that it does not end but just that we should behave as though we knew that it does not end. Kant puts it like that, when he says that with an infinite series 'we necessarily *find* further members of the series', whereas with an indefinite one 'the necessity is that we *enquire* for them'.

This is a radical change of tune. We have seen Kant try to solve his problems by saying that the problematic series are not infinite but are merely non-finite, but now he will not even say that much. All he grants is that we should never act as though we had reached the end of the series.

This new position cannot be Kant's considered view of the matter. For one thing, the first antinomy gives arguments purporting to show that the world *is not* limited in space and time, and Kant never retracts or seriously modifies these arguments. Also, if we cannot know that

---

[40] 670–732, 597, 644–8.   [41] 538–43. Next quotation: 542–3.

the world *is* more than finitely old and large, why must we engage in all the struggles described in the present chapter?

The fact is that when Kant uses the notion of 'regulative principle' in the antinomies chapter, he mainly deserts the official account given in the Appendix. Consider this, for example: 'A continued empirical synthesis, on the side of the conditions, is enjoined or *set as a task*, and...*in this regress* there can be no lack of given conditions.'[42] The first clause uses the language of regulativeness ('set as a task'), but the second clearly implies that the series *is* non-finite, not merely that we ought to work on the assumption that it is. Similarly here:

[The regulative principle] says no more than that, however far we may have attained in the series of empirical conditions, we should never assume an absolute limit, but should subordinate every appearance, as conditioned, to another as its condition, and that we must advance to this condition. This is the *regressus in indefinitum*.

The clause 'we should never assume an absolute limit' evokes the official notion of regulativeness, but the words 'we must advance to this condition' push that notion aside by implying that *there is* always a condition to advance to. This is one of many places in the antinomy chapter where Kant uses 'regulative' and related terms as follows: a proposition is said to be regulative, or to 'set us a task' or the like, meaning simply that *its content can be expressed in statements about possible future experience*. Here is an example:

It is a principle of reason which serves as a *rule*, postulating what we ought to do in the regress, but *not anticipating* what is given *in the object as it is in itself, prior to all regress*. Accordingly I entitle it a *regulative* principle of reason.

The invocation of regulativeness, on that construal of it, does not rival but merely repeats the position I examined in §42 and §45 above.

We still connect 'regulative' with 'indefinite', with the latter attenuated to match. To call a series 'indefinite' now means only that its members lie in the future so that its magnitude is not 'determinate'. Thus, Kant first introduces 'indefinite' when discussing 'what we are to mean by the synthesis of a series, in cases in which the synthesis is never complete';[43] he alludes to 'an indeterminately continued regress (*in indefinitum*)'; he says explicitly that an indefinite regress is 'clearly enough distinguishable from' an infinite one because the former 'determines no magnitude in the object'; and then there is this:

The regress in the series of appearances, as a determination of the magnitude of the world, proceeds *in indefinitum*. This is equivalent to saying that, although the sensible world has no absolute magnitude, the empirical regress...must always advance from every member of the series...to one still more remote.

In the light of remarks like these, Kant's appeal to regulativeness, and his associated claim that the troublesome series are indefinite, can be seen to repeat the lines of thought involved in the weakening move and perhaps the futurizing move. An indefinite series, understood in this way, is one which is more than finite (although, lacking a determinate magnitude, it is not outright infinite). In contrast with that, if the official account of regulativeness is allowed to fix the meaning of 'indefinite', then an indefinite series is one which we ought to treat as non-finite although we cannot know whether it really is so.

There are two sources – which may be interrelated – for Kant's tangled uses of 'regulative' etc. and 'indefinite'.

(1) One is a certain ambiguity, which I have already noted, in the language of regulativeness. We find another example of it when Kant says of the so-called principle of reason: 'It cannot tell us *what the object is*, but only *how the empirical regress is to be carried out*.'[44] This could express the official doctrine about regulativeness, namely, that the principle does not assert anything but merely gives marching orders to the scientific inquirer. In the upshot, however, it turns out to express something quite different. What Kant is saying is that the principle asserts something not about 'the object' *in itself* but only about 'the object' *as it appears*, that is, only about the outcome of certain investigative procedures.

(2) The 'principle of reason' itself contributes to the trouble. I have represented it as saying that every item of such and such a kind has a condition; and that, when taken as 'regulative' in the official sense, says not there there always is a condition but only that we should always behave as though there were. But that was a misrepresentation of the content of the 'principle of reason', adopted temporarily because several aspects of Kant's text seem to point towards it. I now have to confess that what Kant actually offers as 'the principle of reason' is this: 'If the conditioned is given, the entire series of all its conditions is likewise

44 538. Final quotation in this paragraph: 542.

given.'[45] In calling *that* 'regulative', he is presumably not holding back from any claim of the form 'Every *F* item has a condition', but only from one of the form 'If an *F* item is given, then its conditions are all given'. But what on earth does that mean? Understanding 'given' as Kant usually understands it, the 'principle of reason' when taken constitutively would imply that if I perceive a part of the physical world I perceive the whole physical world, or that if I observe an event I observe all earlier events. But it is impossible that he should have thought that the antinomies arise from a tendency to believe anything like *that*. I have no confident suggestions as to what Kant's 'principle of reason' means, though I shall advance a tentative suggestion very near the end of §90.

Along with the difficulty of knowing what the 'principle' means when taken at face value, as fact-stating or constitutive, there is a difficulty about what it comes to when construed regulatively. If the 'principle of reason' ought to be understood merely as giving advice, *what* advice does it give? Kant has no clear answer, and indeed no one answer, to this. His applications of the regulative/constitutive contrast in this area are cloudy and confusing. For example, when he speaks of a certain regress as being 'set as a task', that suggests a contrast between 'Search for conditions' and 'The conditions do exist'; but Kant instead contrasts 'set as a task' with 'already really given', which leaves so much middle ground uncovered that one does not know what is going on.[46] There is a similar unclarity when Kant plays off 'we must find' conditions against 'we must enquire for' conditions, without making clear whether he thinks that there always *are* conditions.[47] Again, when he says that 'we must always enquire for a still higher member of the series, which may or may not become known to us through experience', that is consistent with his thinking that there always is a further member of the series and even with there being, perhaps unknown to us, some reliable way of discovering it. But if that is being allowed, then what is being disallowed? Presumably, the belief that the further members of the series are all 'given' – which brings us back to the original difficulty that we do not know what this means. All this unclarity carries through into the associated language of 'indefinite' as against 'infinite', making it less fit than ever to do any serious work in resolving the antinomies.

By the way, Descartes' contrast between 'infinite' and 'indefinite' wavers in much the same way as Kant's, though without help from the

---

[45] 525; see also second paragraph on 364.   [46] 526, 536.
[47] 542–3. Next quotation: 546.

notion of a regulative principle. Something is indefinite, Descartes says, if 'I do not discern in [it] any end',[48] or if the most we can say of any finite amount of it is that 'it is not impossible for God to have created more'. Yet he calls the material world 'indefinite', although he is prepared to say: 'I think it implies a contradiction that the world should be finite.' He might try to disarm that through humility about his logical capacities, as when he says that the world 'may have some limits that are known by God, though they are incomprehensible by me'.[49] But he is not humble about his belief that *God* has no limits. He insists that he can conscientiously apply 'infinite' to God, though not to anything else, but his reasons are incoherent: 'We have some reason which makes it known' that God is unlimited; 'We understand [God] to be in every part unlimited', and so on. This may reflect mere piety, but I suspect that Descartes is also fumbling with the distinction between non-finiteness and outright infinity, refusing to call the world infinite because he cannot see how to assign to it a non-finite 'determinate magnitude', to use Kant's phrase. Leibniz came to see the situation in that light. Writing at a stage when he had not yet seen any difficulty in the notion of infinite number, he brushed Descartes off with the remark that 'the indefinite of Descartes is not in the thing but in the thinker'.[50] But much later he allowed that there is 'some reason' for Descartes' replacing 'infinite' by 'indefinite' in most contexts, the reason being that 'there never is an infinite whole in the world'.

---

[48] Letter to More, in C. Adam and P. Tannery (eds.), *Oeuvres de Descartes* (Paris, 1897–1910), Vol. V, p. 274. Next two quotations: *Principles of Philosophy*, Part I, §26; Letter to More, Adam and Tannery (eds.), *op. cit.* p. 345.

[49] This quotation and the next have the same source, I believe, but I cannot now locate it. The following quotation is from *Principles of Philosophy*, Part I, §27 (Latin version; the French version is better).

[50] 'The Theory of Abstract Motion', §2, Loemker, p. 139; see also 'Selections from the Paris Notes', Loemker, p. 159. Next quotation: *New Essays* II. xiii. 21. For a fuller treatment of Descartes' views on infinite/indefinite, see A. Koyré, *From the Closed World to the Infinite Universe* (Baltimore, 1957), Ch. 5.

8

LIMITS

§ 47. Leibniz on space

On the Antithesis side of the first antinomy, Kant argues against the world's being merely finite in age and size. The temporal half of this will be discussed in § 51 below. The spatial half depends partly upon a doctrine of Leibniz's about space, which I shall now expound.

Leibniz says that 'Without the things placed in it, one point of space does not absolutely differ in any respect whatsoever from another point of space.'[1] From this he infers that we can distinguish parts of space only because we can say things of the form

$$(1) \quad x \text{ is in location } L,$$

these being the basis for our ways of referring to individual spatial locations. Statements of the form (1) in their turn rest upon ones of the form

$$(2) \quad S(x_1, \ldots, x_n),$$

where S expresses some n-adic spatial relation. By 'the relational theory of space' I mean the theory that (2) underlies (1) which underlies any possible discrimination between spatial locations.

Leibniz is an apparent paradox – a philosopher who banishes relations from his basic account of reality, and who yet invented the relational theory of space. The latter theory is in fact only a stage on the way down. Leibniz thinks that statements of form (2) rest upon ones of the form

$$(3) \quad C(x_1, \ldots, x_k)$$

where C expresses what we should call a causal relation. (Leibniz would deny that it is genuinely causal, but he would agree that it involves some true, highly general, contingent, universal proposition relating events in some objects to events in others – one of a 'few free primary decrees capable of being called laws of the universe and which regulate sequences of things'.[2] It will aid brevity, and do no harm, if I describe such matters as 'causal' rather than as 'expressive of the non-causal but

---

[1] Leibniz III 5, this being shorthand for: *Leibniz–Clarke*, Leibniz's third letter, § 5. This form of shorthand will be used throughout the present chapter.

[2] *Leibniz–Arnauld*, p. 43.

divinely pre-established harmony', which is how Leibniz saw them.) Finally, Leibniz believes that (3) are entailed by monadic facts of the form

$$(4) \quad Fx \ \& \ Gy \ \& \ Hz \ \& \ \ldots$$

In what follows I shall sometimes attend to the move from (2) down to (3), but the further move to (4), though it is vital to Leibniz's strategy for reducing everything to monadic facts, is irrelevant to our present concerns.

Now, let 'OW' name our world, and consider a possible world PW of which it is stipulated that it is exactly like OW in every respect except perhaps ones expressible in statements of form (1) above. In particular, every statement of form (2) which is true in OW is also true in PW, but the door is left open to the possibility that OW differs from PW in having a different over-all location or spatial orientation from OW. Leibniz says that on these data there can be no difference between OW and PW.[3] This certainly follows from the relational theory, but Leibniz tries to recommend the theory by arguing independently for this consequence of it. If OW and PW were distinct possibilities, Leibniz argues, then God's having instantiated OW would show that he had preferred it to PW; but there is no possible basis for a preference either way; and so, Leibniz concludes, OW and PW are not distinct possibilities. This involves the assumption that God could not choose between two alternatives which were equally good, like the ass which starved to death between two equally large and aromatic bales of hay, and one can sympathize with Clarke's protest against this account of the divine psychology. Furthermore, why should we agree that there could not be a basis for preferring OW to PW, unless we are already satisfied that PW is not distinct from OW? This argument about God's dilemma is really just a dramatic version of the simple *assertion* that $PW = OW$.

Leibniz argues better when he uses the notion of possible observation. Although he was not in general very empiricist, he does argue in an empiricist manner on this issue. It would be in the spirit of some of Leibniz's arguments to contend that PW is not distinct from OW because our experience would not have been different if we had inhabited PW rather than OW. Leibniz himself, however, does not argue in quite this way. Rather than comparing OW with PW, he attends to alterations in OW, for example the possibility that it might be drifting

---

[3] Leibniz III 5. Clarke's protest: Clarke III 5, IV 18. Leibniz's reply to it in V 17 is clear and perfectly wrong. The argument at the end of this paragraph comes from an unpublished paper by John Cook.

through space without any internal spatial re-arrangements.[4] He argues plausibly that nothing could count as evidence that such a change was occurring, whence he infers that no sense attaches to the notion of a change-of-place of the entire universe. Clarke objects that if the universe underwent uniform motion and then suddenly stopped, 'the parts would be sensibly shocked'. Leibniz ignores this, as he also ignores Clarke's allusions to some arguments of Newton's, in which phenomena concerning rotation are claimed to be explicable only on the assumption that there is absolute space.[5] This raises issues which are still controversial, and which I have neither the space nor the competence to discuss. Anyway, some work of Shoemaker's which I shall mention again in §51 below can easily be adapted to provide a case which rather clearly *would* give empirical evidence that the world was moving uniformly through space. Rather than denying that there could be such evidence, I think, one should concede that it is possible while maintaining that this is consistent with the rather limited doctrine which I call the relational theory of space. My central purpose, in any case, is not to evaluate Leibniz's theory but to understand some of its implications.

Leibniz does not explain in detail *how* statements of the form (1) are used to distinguish various parts of space, but the following seems to be a tenable view of the matter, and perhaps even a rational reconstruction of the conceptual scheme that we do use for naming locations. We have a three-dimensional coordinate system, each point on which is named by a number-triple, so that $83:17:175$ names the point where $x = 83$, $y = 17$, and $z = 175$. We tie this system to the real world by (a) giving an empirical cash-value, in terms of spatial or underlying causal relations, to distances on the coordinate system, i.e. to differences between number-triples; and (b) by stipulating that a certain point on the coordinate system – say the point $0:0:0$ – is to be identified with some place in the world which is identified in terms of an object occupying it. This anchoring is achieved by a stipulation of the form: '$0:0:0$ is the place where object X is at time t.'[6]

---

4 Leibniz V 29, 52; see also IV 13. Next quotation: Clarke V replying to 52-3.

5 Clarke IV 13; see also Introduction to *Leibniz-Clarke*, pp. xxxiv-xl. For part of the continuing controversy, see J. Earman, 'Who's Afraid of Absolute Space?', *The Australasian Journal of Philosophy* (1970). The work of Shoemaker's is: S. Shoemaker, 'Time without Change', *The Journal of Philosophy* (1969). Its relevance to the present topic was called to my attention by Norman Swartz.

6 Strictly speaking, the anchoring system must be more complex than this, for a reason which Kant was probably the first to notice. See J. Bennett, 'The Difference Between Right and Left', *American Philosophical Quarterly* (1969).

This does not imply that the object X can never change its position. When there is a change of spatial relations amongst two or more objects, the question of which we describe as moving and which (if any) as remaining stationary is to be settled in the interests of economy of description and efficiency of theory,[7] and so we could have grounds for saying that between t and t^* the object X moved away from 0:0:0. That would not affect our anchoring of the system to the world through the stipulation that 0:0:0 is where X was *at t*. It is amusing to note that there is no obstacle in the relational theory as such, though there may be in accepted physics, to our having direct evidence that the entire universe – the totality of all the things in space – had moved *piecemeal* from one location to another.

§ 48. Leibniz on vacuum

Leibniz's relational theory of space rules out much less than is sometimes realized. For our purposes, what primarily matters is that it does not rule out the possibility of vacuum, empty space, unoccupied locations. For its own interest, and its relevance to Kant, I shall devote a section to this matter.

Leibniz did deny that there is any vacuum, but his reasons for this were moral and theological.[8] He rightly did not think that the possibility of vacuum is ruled out by the relational theory of space. Do not be misled by the fact that Leibniz mentions God's choices in connexion with both the denial of vacuum and the relational theory of space. There is no vacuum, Leibniz thinks, because God in his benevolence and wisdom chose to fill it all. The relevance of God to Leibniz's case for the relational theory is quite different. It concerns the possible worlds PW and OW which I introduced early in §47: if PW were distinct from OW, Leibniz argues, then God would have solved an insoluble problem by choosing which to make real; but no one can solve an insoluble problem; so $PW = OW$. Since this asserts the identity of a supposed pair of *possibilities*, it is offered as a logical truth. It is not suggested that God chose to make PW identical with OW.

How does Leibniz's theory cope with the notion of unoccupied locations? Our chief clue is his passing remark that 'Space...is nothing at all without bodies, but the possibility of placing them.'[9] Let us build

---

[7] Leibniz says as much in Leibniz V 47 and 53, and in *Leibniz–Arnauld*, pp. 84–5.
[8] Leibniz IV Postscript and V 30.
[9] Leibniz III 5. In what follows, I also rely partly on Leibniz's definition of 'place' in V 47.

on this. For simplicity's sake, I shall consider space and its contents only at some one time, abstracting from all the complications which movement introduces; so every formula should be understood as implicitly qualified by '...at time t'.

Suppose we have three objects, a, b and c, which are interrelated as the apexes of an equilateral triangle:

$$a \qquad\qquad b$$

$$c$$

The fact that they are thus related is to be analysed into something of the form $C(a, b, c)$ where C expresses a causal relation. If there is an object d equidistant from all three, this is a fact of the form $C^*(d, a, b, c)$ where C^* is a causal relation; and if there is no object related in that way to a, b and c then this is a fact of the form $\sim (\exists x)C^*(x, a, b, c)$. Now for the statement that *there is a location* equidistant from all three objects. Following Leibniz's hint about 'the possibility of placing them', I take this to be analysable into: *It is causally possible that* $(\exists x)C^*(x, a, b, c)$ – by which I mean that the existence of a thus-related object is consistent with the conjunction of all causal laws (as we should call them) together with some set of propositions assigning to each actual object its spatial location at the time in question. These propositions could be the set of causal truths which constitute the analyses of every truth of the form 'x is between y and z on a straight line', where x, y and z are objects.

So any assertion of the existence of a particular bit of vacuum or empty space is equivalent to the assertion that there causally could be but actually is not an object having certain causal relations with specified actual objects. In my example I took three objects at random, and dealt with a location which was identified only in relation to them; but I could with no difficulty have identified it instead by its place on the over-all coordinate system, by causally relating the crucial (possible) object to ones which had already been assigned coordinates.

My example concerned a bit of intra-mundane space, i.e. space within the world, space with objects all around it, but it could as well have dealt with extra-mundane space, i.e. space lying beyond the boundaries of the world. Leibniz thought so too: 'Extramundane space [and other] empty space...differ only as greater and less.'[10]

To see that this is right, consider again the three objects a, b and c, and suppose this time that a and b lie at the extreme edge of the universe and

[10] Leibniz IV 7.

that c lies some distance in from the edge. This implies, among other things, that if the straight line which runs through c and cuts the line a–b at right angles passes through the location of any actual object, the latter is between c and the line a–b. And that statement analyses into something of the form

$$(x)[C(x, a, b, c) \to C^*(x, a, b, c)].$$

To say that there is space beyond the a–b line is to imply among other things that it is causally possible (in the sense I have explained) that

$$(\exists x)[C(x, a, b, c) \ \& \sim C^*(x, a, b, c)],$$

i.e. causally possible that some object lies on the line I described but does not lie between c and a–b. So a good part of the content of the statement that there is only empty space beyond the a–b line – this being the assertion of the existence of some extra-mundane space – is given by the statement that the above existential statement is causally possible but is in fact false.

Incomplete as that is, it shows the kind of way in which the existence of extra-mundane space can be asserted in conformity with the relational theory of space. It seems clear that a mere increase of complexity, with nothing new in principle, could yield a Leibnizian analysis of the statement that the world – the totality of all the objects in space – is entirely surrounded by space. That is really all I need for my Kantian purposes, but for the rest of this section I shall explore the matter further, just for its Leibnizian interest.

It is surprisingly often denied that the relational theory can allow for the existence of extra-mundane space. Al-Azm, for example, says that Leibniz ought to hold that extra-mundane space would have to be absolute space, i.e. that the assertion of its existence could not be analysed in accordance with the relational theory. And he even goes so far as to say that the impossibility of absolute motion of the world is 'precisely' the same as the impossibility of extra-mundane space.[11] Alexander, also, says that Leibniz has a problem about allowing the possibility of any vacuum, extra- or intra-mundane. He says that Broad 'attempts to meet this objection', citing a passage where Broad does no such thing, and where in fact he says that 'there is no close logical connexion between the controversy about Absolute and Relative Space...and these controversies about [vacuum].'

---

[11] *Kant's Arguments*, pp. 23–4. Next two quotations: H. G. Alexander, Introduction to *Leibniz–Clarke*, p. xxviii; C. D. Broad, 'Leibniz's Last Controversy with the Newtonians', in *Ethics and the History of Philosophy* (London, 1952), p. 186.

This misunderstanding started with Clarke, who says that the possibility of 'an empty extra-mundane space' conflicts with Leibniz's view 'that space is nothing but the order of things co-existing'.[12] This may be right, given the literal meaning of 'order of things co-existing'; but the main outlines of Leibniz's theory, in which space is defined in terms of causally possible interrelationships of bodies, clearly allows for the possibility of empty space.

Still, Clarke is right to say that Leibniz is not always clear and firm enough about whether his rejection of vacuum is supposed to follow from the relational theory.

Sometimes we can defend Leibniz. For example, Clarke points out that Leibniz infers from his relational theory that 'There is no space, where there is no matter', which could be taken to rule out vacuum.[13] But it could instead mean only that a world which lacked matter would lack space, i.e. that if there were no matter at all there would be no space. Michael Beebe has pointed out to me that on that interpretation Leibniz is still wrong, for there is a possible world PW answering to this description: PW contains monads which do not constitute an extended realm but which manifest a law-like, God-ordained harmony which allows the addition to PW of monads which would constitute an extended realm. In PW there are no space-occupying things; but the existence of such things in PW is (as we should say) causally possible, and that, according to Leibniz's theory, implies that in PW there is space. Still, Leibniz's mistake is a subtle one, and – the main point – it is not the mistake of denying the possibility of vacuum.

When Leibniz says that the universe couldn't be moving through space all at once (*tout entier*) because 'there is no real space out of the material universe',[14] we might take him to mean that there is no *absolute* extra-mundane space, i.e. none to which the relational theory does not apply. That verges on special pleading, though, and even if we accept it Leibniz's remark is still a clumsy and ill-directed one. Even

[12] Clarke V replying to 26–32. Leibniz's actual phrase in V 29 is 'an order of the existence of things', but 'an order of things' occurs in Leibniz III 4 and IV Postscript.

[13] Leibniz V 62; noted by Clarke, V just before reply to 33–5. Clarke expresses his complaint by saying that Leibniz represents vacuum sometimes as merely contrary to God's goodness yet at other times as 'absolutely impossible in the nature of things'. He evidently assumes that Leibniz would regard anything ruled out by the relational theory as 'absolutely impossible'. Perhaps indeed Leibniz would, but if so he would be wrong. Some unpublished work of Michael Beebe's has convinced me that the relational theory is empirical: there could be a space in which things were, and there could be one in which they were not, locatable without being interrelated.

[14] Leibniz V 29. Next two quotations: V 53; IV 7.

less defensible is his statement that 'I ought not to admit a moveable universe; nor any place out of the material universe', juxtaposing claims which belong on different levels. Nor can I defend him when he alludes to 'the reason which shows that extra-mundane space is imaginary' and which also 'proves that all empty space is an imaginary thing', the context suggesting that the 'reason' in question is the relational theory of space. Rescher endorses this mishap with the comment: 'The impossibility of a void is shown by arguing that a void would be a special case of an absolute space.'[15] That must mean that empty space would have to be absolute space, i.e. that the relational theory cannot allow for the possibility of empty space. That is false, and I contend that Leibniz, despite occasional waverings, knew that it is false.[16]

As evidence of Leibniz's uncertainty about the status of his denial that there is vacuum, Clarke refers to this:

Since space in itself is an ideal thing, like time, space out of the world must needs be imaginary, as the schoolmen themselves have acknowledged. The case is the same with empty space within the world; which I take also to be imaginary.[17]

This passage also illustrates Leibniz's penchant for saying that according to the relational theory space – not necessarily empty space – is 'ideal' and 'imaginary'. He is entitled to express the relational theory by saying that space is 'merely relative',[18] and, meaning the same thing, that space is not 'absolute'. It could be all right for him also to say that space is not an 'absolute reality', if this meant 'only a relative reality'. Leibniz, however, takes it to mean that space is not a reality at all – that it is 'imaginary' rather than 'real'. This is said not just about Newtonian absolute space, but about *space* – and that is puzzling.

One possible explanation is that Leibniz is using 'real' and 'ideal' to mean 'mind-dependent' and 'mind-independent' respectively. In that usage, which Kant also sometimes adopts, 'Space is not real' means only that space is mind-dependent. Leibniz did of course hold that view, regarding the spatial world as merely an appearance to us of an underlying monadic reality (see §15 above), and no doubt he sometimes uses 'not real' and perhaps 'ideal' to express this doctrine. Oddly, he also sometimes uses 'ideal' etc. just to express the limited doctrine that the extended world is relational whereas monadic reality

---

[15] N. Rescher, *The Philosophy of Leibniz* (Englewood Cliffs, N.J., 1967), p. 94.
[16] Thirty years earlier, Leibniz did not know this. See his 'First Truths', Loemker, p. 269.
[17] Leibniz V 33.
[18] Leibniz III 4. Next quotations: III 5 and IV 16; IV 10; IV 14.

is not. This usage is illustrated when he says that a certain relation, 'being neither a substance nor an accident [monadic property], must be a mere ideal thing',[19] and of another that it is 'a merely mental thing whose basis is the modifications of the individuals'. But these usages hardly explain the remarks which have been puzzling us. For one thing, it would be misleading to say 'Space is not real' on the strength of a doctrine which applies no more to space than to the things in space – i.e. the doctrine that 'Matter...is only a pure phenomenon..., as also are space and time.' In any case, the doctrine that the extended world is a relational appearance of a monadic reality is not part of the relational theory and is not deployed against Clarke.

Another possible explanation is suggested by this: 'The parts of... place, considered in themselves, are ideal things; and therefore they perfectly resemble one another like two abstract units. But it is not so with...two spaces filled up.'[20] This uses 'ideal' to mean 'abstract', like a number, rather than 'mental', like an illusion. An empty space is 'ideal' in this sense because it consists only in the *possibility* that something should have certain relational properties; just as Leibniz says about 'time, without things' that it too is 'a mere ideal possibility'. But even if this explains Leibniz's application of 'ideal' to empty space, it hardly explains 'not real' or 'imaginary'. Leibniz evidently did not think his position out with perfect efficiency.

§ 49. Why the world is not finite

To understand Kant's 'proof' that the world cannot be simply finite in size, one must see that he is free to accept Leibniz's relational theory, which says that the individuation of places rests upon (1) statements about spatial locations of objects, which in turn rest upon (2) statements about spatial relations amongst objects. I am not sure about the reduction of (2) to (3) statements about causal relations among objects, and clearly Kant is not in a position to go the whole way down to (4) monadic statements about simple unempirical substances. Kant's transcendental idealism sharply conflicts with that last part of Leibniz's total doctrine, but it does not clash with the relational theory, if the latter is taken to involve only the move down as far as (2). The relational theory says which sort of spatial statement is basic (whatever its further

---

[19] Leibniz V 47. Next two quotations: Letter to Des Bosses, Loemker, p. 609; *Leibniz–Arnauld*, p. 152.
[20] Leibniz V 27. Next quotation: V 55.

analysis might be), whereas transcendental idealism describes the further analysis of the basic sort of spatial statement (whatever sort that might be). The two are compatible because they answer different questions.

Connected with his not going down as far as (4), Kant could not accept Leibniz's picture of the relational theory as (part of) a complete reductive analysis of our entire system of spatial vocabulary. Kant would say that the 'objects' whose interrelationships the theory speaks of must themselves be physical or at least have spatial properties. So there could be no question of his accepting the theory as more than a basing of one part of our total spatial-conceptual scheme (parts-of-space) upon another part of that same scheme (relations-amongst-objects). Some of the discussion of space in the Aesthetic seems to be directed against any larger pretensions which the relational theory might have;[21] but there is the above more modest reading of the theory, and that, I repeat, Kant is perfectly free to accept, as not conflicting with transcendental idealism or indeed with any other substantial part of his philosophy. In the main he does accept it, notably in his defence of the spatial half of the Antithesis of the first antinomy, that is, in arguing that the world cannot be merely finitely large.[22]

The argument assumes that space is infinite, and devotes its energies to trying to show that the world is as large as space, i.e. that there is no extra-mundane space. If there were, Kant says, so that the world was nested in a space larger than itself, then things would 'not only be related *in space* but also related *to space*' (455). And what is wrong with that? One answer is that Kant thinks that the world's being related *to* space is ruled out by the Leibnizian relational theory.

That would be an extremely natural mistake. The relational theory can be expressed in the form: statements about where things are ('related to space') are reducible to statements about how things relate to one another ('in space'), and so there cannot be a fact of the former sort over and above the totality of facts of the latter sort. In an early work, Kant explicitly links in-space/to-space with relational/absolute,

---

[21] 39; see also 331-2. For an excellent statement of the extent of Kant's acceptance of Leibniz's relational theory, see G. Buchdahl, *Metaphysics and the Philosophy of Science* (Oxford, 1969), p. 601; see also *ibid.* pp. 577-8.

[22] Kant's views about space changed through the years. See, with caution, Introduction to *Leibniz–Clarke*, pp. xlv–xlviii, and also *Commentary*, pp. 140-2. For evidence of Kant's acceptance of a relational theory of space, at a time between the publication-dates of A and of B, see his *Metaphysical Foundations*, Ch. 4. R. Palter, 'Absolute Space and Absolute Motion in Kant's Critical Philosophy', *Synthese* (1971), subtly discusses this chapter, and implies that Kant saw the real strengths in Newton's position better than Leibniz did.

when he contrasts 'the relation of one thing in space to the next' with 'the relation of the system of these positions to absolute space'.[23] Using this formulation, we could say that what is wrong with 'The world moves uniformly through space' is that it implies that things change their relation *to* space without changing their relations to one another *in* space. And one might think that the same objection can be brought against the idea of the world's being in – or surrounded by – space. As evidence that Kant does construe the in-space/to-space contrast in that way, consider this half-footnote:

If we attempt to set...space outside all appearances, there arise all sorts of empty determinations of outer intuition, which yet are not possible perceptions. For example, a determination of the relation of the motion (or rest) of the world to infinite empty space is a determination which can never be perceived, and is therefore the predicate of a mere thought-entity. (457n.)

This clearly puts 'The world is surrounded by space' on a par with such arguably vacuous suppositions as the 'uniform motion' one.

That this is a mistake has, I hope, been sufficiently shown in §48 above. Kant, however, adds his own personal touch to the error. He rightly thinks that the relational theory rules out the notion of the world's having a 'determinate position' in space.[24] He says: 'All places are in the universe, and the universe is not, therefore, itself in any place.' If this means that we can give no content to anything of the form 'The universe is in *L* rather than in *L**', then it does indeed follow from the relational theory. Even if the whole universe shifted (this being known by direct observation in the case of a piecemeal shift, or less directly for a Shoemaker-type uniform shift), the relational theory would let us give content to 'where the universe is now' and to 'where the universe was before the shift' only by relating these two locations to one another, and so neither would be what Kant calls a 'determinate position'. So far so good. But Kant errs in supposing that if the world lay within extra-mundane space it must have a determinate position in it. In fact, the world's being surrounded by empty space does not imply that there must be any answer, or even any sense, to the question '*Where* in space is the world?'

Kant knew that the Leibnizians did not take 'There is no absolute space' to entail 'The world cannot be finite', but he wrongly thought that

[23] 'Concerning the Ultimate Foundation of the Differentiation of Regions in Space', first paragraph; in G. B. Kerferd and D. E. Walford (eds.), *Kant: Selected Pre-Critical Writings* (Manchester, 1968), pp. 36–7.

[24] 549n. Next quotation: 530.

they could block this entailment only by making a move condemned by Kantian philosophy. His discussion of the point starts with this:

I am aware that attempts are made to evade this conclusion by arguing that the world could have limits in...space without one's having to admit...absolute space extending beyond the real world; which is impossible. I am completely satisfied with the latter part of this opinion of philosophers of the Leibnizian school.[25]

What is here called 'impossible', by the Leibnizians and by Kant, is not *absolute space* but rather *absolute space beyond the real world*. It is suspicious that Kant does not address himself to absolute space as such, i.e. to the relational theory. It is as though he simply did not distinguish 'absolute space' from 'extra-mundane space'.

In his next paragraph, Kant discusses the Leibnizian claim that a finite world need not be nested in absolute space. Astonishingly, he envisages this as being defended by 'getting rid of time and space', or 'surreptitiously substituting for the sensible world some intelligible world of which we know nothing' (461). In short, Kant sees the Leibnizians as fending off the Antithesis-argument by saying that the real, monadic world is not spatial anyway. It is not surprising that Kant protests at this, but why does he credit the Leibnizians with this implausible move in the first place? Why should they do anything as absurd as using the plea that the world is not really spatial, in defence of the claim that 'the world could have limits *in space* without...' etc.? Furthermore, there are two perfectly good options open to a Leibnizian who thinks that the world is finite. One, of course, is to maintain that there is extra-mundane non-absolute space. The other is to say that the finite world is contained in a skin-tight, finite space. Antipathetic as this would be to Kant, because of his Euclidean predilections, it is still a possible view which he shouldn't have overlooked.

This strange passage about 'philosophers of the Leibnizian school' may be directed towards some episode in Wolff or Baumgarten of which I know nothing. Be that as it may, it is just a philosophical fact that extra-mundane space need not be absolute, and that the world could be *in* space without having a *determinate position in* it; and the failure to grasp this – i.e. to see that a Leibnizian could allow for extra-mundane space, whether or not Wolff did allow for it – must be laid at Kant's door.

[25] 459; Kemp Smith's translation renders this passage unintelligible.

§ 50. Other arguments

The Leibnizian argument which I have described is to be found in the Observation on the Antithesis and in half of a footnote which Kant added to the Antithesis-argument in B. He seems to have two further arguments against the possibility of a finite world in an infinite space. One is in the Antithesis-argument itself, and is partly to be found in the footnote to which I have referred. I shall come to it shortly. The other argument should be got out of the way first. Here is Kant's clearest statement of it:

[If the world had an edge] it would be limited by empty space. Since [the world is an appearance], this limit of the world would have to be given in a possible ex-perience, that is to say, we should require to have a perception of limitation by completely empty space. But such an experience, as entirely empty of content, is impossible.[26]

This occurs in the problem-solving Section 9. It should be Kant's last word on the subject, and thus his deepest and most considered account of what the difficulty is about the world's being smaller than space.

The basic point here is that extra-mundane space cannot 'be given in a possible experience', which echoes Kant's earlier rhetorical question, purporting to be relevant to the first antinomy, 'How can there be any experience of the completely void?'[27] But what exactly is being claimed here? If Kant is saying that there could not be empirical evidence for extra-mundane space, he is just wrong. If on the other hand he is saying only that such space could not be straightforwardly perceived, what he says is true but does not – except on extravagantly empiricist assumptions – justify denying that there could be extra-mundane space. In another work, he seems to imply that he counts something as 'capable of being sensed' just so long as it can be 'indicated by what can be sensed'; but if we hold him to that, construing the latter phrase in the most natural way, then extra-mundane space is 'capable of being sensed' after all.

In any case, there is an internal obstacle to Kant's basing the Antithesis on any claim about the imperceptibility of extra-mundane space. Earlier in the *Critique* he has insisted that no sort of empty space can be

---

[26] 548–9, slightly modified to omit parallel remarks about empty time. Here and elsewhere, Kemp Smith uses 'absolutely' to translate words which are not related to Kant's technical term *absolut* and which are therefore better rendered by 'completely', 'entirely' or the like. On 'absolute', see 380–2.

[27] 515. Next reference: *Metaphysical Foundations*, p. 19.

given in experience: 'The proof of an empty space...can never be derived from experience.'[28] Yet he says explicitly that the Antithesis-argument tells only against extra-mundane space and not against 'empty space within the world'. There seems to be no way in which Kant can develop an argument which is *both* based on the impercepti-bility of extra-mundane space *and* inapplicable to intra-mundane vacuum. In one strange passage he purports to distinguish 'vacuum' generally from the special case of 'a void...outside the world', but only by unwarrantably equating 'outside the world' with 'beyond the field of possible experience'.

There is one point about imperceptibility which does uniquely con-cern extra-mundane space: not that we cannot perceive it, but rather that we cannot perceive it to be extra-mundane. In one place Kant represents the Antithesis of the first antinomy as the position of some-one who 'will never allow...that any limit of his insight into the extent of nature is to be regarded as the widest possible' (497) – that is, presumably, the position of someone who will never admit that there isn't some more world out there somewhere. That position could bear on the first antinomy. It would generate a reply to someone who hoped to avoid the infinity problem by discovering for sure that the world is finite – the reply, namely, 'You haven't a hope'. But if this were the whole story, then the first antinomy would once more collapse into something uninteresting. For what it would leave on the side of the Antithesis is not 'The world is infinite', but only 'For all we can know, the world may be infinite', or perhaps 'The world is infinite' construed as a 'regulative principle' in the official sense.

In any case, let us not forget how different (1) the line of thought about 'empty space cannot be perceived' is from (2) this latest line about 'it may not be extra-mundane after all'. According to (1) there is some difficulty in the idea of the whole world's being surrounded or 'limited' by empty, unperceivable space. But what about the idea of the *known* world's being surrounded by a shell of empty space, with more undiscovered world lying further out still? The line of thought (2) offers this as somehow problem-solving, because the space in ques-tion is not extra-mundane. But it still falls foul of (1), for it involves the idea of something's being limited by a stretch of space which cannot be perceived. It seems clear that the conceptual trouble alleged by (1), whatever it is, is supposed to lie at the boundary between the *known* world and what immediately surrounds it.

[28] 214; see also 260–1, and *Kant's Analytic*, p. 175. Next two quotations: 459–61n.; 281.

What is this conceptual trouble? We still have no satisfactory answer to this. The best answer I can give, though it may bear somewhat on some passages already quoted, is mainly supported by two further bits of the text. One is in the Antithesis-argument itself. Immediately following the contrast between 'related in space' and 'related to space', in which I found a Leibnizian significance, Kant continues with something which looks unLeibnizian:

> Since the world is [something] beyond which there is no object of intuition, and therefore no correlate with which the world stands in relation, the relation of the world to empty space would be a relation of it to no *object*. But such a relation, and consequently the limitation of the world by empty space, is nothing. The world cannot, therefore, be limited in space.[29]

The other passage is the first half of that footnote whose second half was my main source for the Leibnizian argument. The crucial bit of it is this: 'Empirical intuition is not...a composite of appearances and space...The one is not the correlate of the other in a synthesis' (457).

I could make nothing of these baffling remarks until R. I. G. Hughes showed me what they mean. They express a single argument which is quite different from anything I have so far presented. Kant is assuming that if two items are spatially related to one another, they must exist independently of that relation; and one mark of this independence would be that we could intelligibly suppose that they might have been interrelated in some quite different way instead. When he says that the world and space are not 'correlates' of one another 'in a synthesis', he is denying that they are ontologically on a par with one another and just happen to be interrelated in one way rather than another.

Kant has a defensible point here, and it applies to more than just spatial relations. For example, the statement 'He has a nasty temper' monadically describes a man, rather than relating a man to a temper; and this is because the man and the temper are not 'correlates' in a 'synthesis' – a temper could not exist apart from the man and could not be related to him in some other way instead. (There seem to be some relations to which the point does not apply: two items can be related by *non-identity* without its being possible that they should have been related in some other way instead.)

So Kant's premiss is sound, and it clearly applies to the case of the world and extra-mundane space. These are not 'correlates' in a 'syn-

---

[29] 455–7. Kant actually says 'Since the world is an absolute whole...' etc.; but the phrase 'absolute whole' is idle in the argument, and merely incites Kant's later accusation that the argument treats the world as 'a thing given in itself, in its totality' (549n.).

thesis', happening to be related by containment but capable of being related in other ways instead. But this does not imply what Kant infers from it, namely that 'The world is surrounded by extra-mundane space' is *false*. All that follows is that this is not a genuinely relational statement which reports a relation between two ontologically independent objects, the world and outer space. If its falsity followed from Kant's premiss, then by a similar argument we could infer from an account of the ontological status of tempers that 'He has a nasty temper' must always be false.

So I am allowing that it may be true that the world is surrounded by space; and of course that is a relational way of stating it, using a sentence in which two noun-phrases are linked by a verb-phrase. Still, one can grant all that while still denying that that relational formulation is the best or the most fundamental way to express the claim. One might contend, for example, that the situation with regard to the world and space is best expressed by a conjunction of 'The world is finite' with a set of statements of the form

It is causally possible that $(\exists x)C(x, a, b, c, \ldots)$,

each asserting the existence of a portion of extra-mundane space (see §48 above).

There is another defect in Kant's argument. One could adduce Leibniz's relational theory in support of the denial that the world is 'the correlate' of space 'in a synthesis', and indeed one could base that denial simply on common sense. Kant, however, infers it from the claim that the world and space 'are connected in one and the same empirical intuition as matter and form of the intuition'. This clearly invokes his doctrine that space is the 'form' of outer sense, but the invocation is a mistake. If x is 'the form' of something of which y is 'the content', this does indeed yield a powerful reason for denying that x and y are independent 'correlates' etc.; but the outer-sense theory does not imply that if there were extra-mundane space *it* would relate to the world as form to content. Rather, the theory says that the world's *spatiality* is its form, or is conferred upon it by a formal fact about outer sense, and this entails nothing about what the status would be of extra-mundane space if there were any.

Kant must have been anxious to find some basis which is Kantian rather than Leibnizian for the denial that the world could be embedded in extra-mundane space. We have now seen him pursuing that goal in three different ways: with the point about the unperceivability of (limitation by) empty space, with the claim that any given stretch of space might turn out not to be extra-mundane after all, and now with the use of the outer-sense theory to support the denial that the world and extra-mundane space could enter into a genuine, object-relating, spatial relationship.

Let us now turn to the temporal half of the Antithesis.

§51. Why the world did not begin

If the world had begun, Kant argues, then 'there must have been a preceding time in which the world was not, i.e. an empty time.'[30] (He construes 'empty time' as time when nothing exists. It would be better to take it as time when nothing happens, reflecting the fact that time relates to change as space does to matter, as Leibniz knew.) Kant's argument continues like this: 'No coming to be of a thing is possible in an empty time, because no part of such a time possesses, as compared with any other, a distinguishing condition of existence rather than of non-existence.' Typically, Kant does not elucidate the clause following 'because', let alone explain why it implies that there cannot be a first event.

The most natural reading is a causal one: a first event, being the first, could not have had a prior cause and therefore could not occur. This must be wrong, however, for Kant continues: '...and this applies whether the thing is supposed to arise of itself or through some other cause.' Something which 'arises of itself' must be either uncaused or self-caused; it does not have a prior cause; and so Kant's point cannot be that in an empty time there could not be a prior cause of a first event.

Kant may be suggesting that no sense can attach to the notion of *when* pre-mundane time ceased and the world began, this being analogous to his point that the world could not have a 'determinate position' in space. That was Leibniz's own view. He argues that since time is a construct out of temporal relations amongst events, it makes no sense to suppose that the world might have begun earlier than it did, unless this means that there might have been events before the one which was in fact the first.[31] This could be expressed by saying that the world cannot have a determinate position in time, i.e. that there can be no answer to the question 'When did the world begin?', except for an internal one like 'in 4001 B.C.' (analogous to saying where the world is by locating

---

[30] 455. Leibniz reference: Leibniz V 62. Next Kant quotation: *loc. cit.*
[31] Leibniz III 6, V 56.

its edges in relation to Mt Robson, say). I conjecture that Kant is inferring from this that the world cannot have begun. The inference is invalid, though, for it merely assumes without reason that if the world began it must have done so at a 'determinate time' in the non-internal sense.[32]

That argument of Kant's uses Leibnizian materials. He also makes a non-Leibnizian remark about pre-mundane time – a remark which belongs with §50 above rather than with §49. He says that if the world began it 'would be limited by empty time', and that to know about that 'we should require to have a perception of limitation by completely empty time. But such an experience, as entirely empty of content, is impossible. Consequently, an absolute limit of the world is impossible empirically, and is therefore altogether impossible.'[33] This argues that there could not be pre-mundane time because there could not be empirical evidence for its existence. I believe that this is correct.

It is arguable that although there can be empirical evidence for the existence of empty space, there cannot be for the existence of empty time. There are certainly relevant differences between the two. For example, we can put an object in a given place, thus establishing the place's existence, and then remove the object without allowing anything else to replace it; but a period of time cannot be thus filled and then emptied, because periods of time do not last through time as regions of space do. I used to hold the popular view that there could not be evidence for the existence of empty time, but Shoemaker has refuted that.[34] His work, however, shows only how we could have evidence for the existence of intra-mundane empty time. It could be adapted to cover post-mundane time as well, but it offers no promise of our ever being able to describe evidence for the existence of pre-mundane time. I conjecture that this cannot be done, and that the notion of 'time before the first event' should be rejected.

Does this put me on the side of the Antithesis? Not at all. From the impossibility of pre-mundane time I do not infer the impossibility of a first event. Rather, I infer that if there was a first event it occurred at the first time. There ought to be no conceptual difficulty about allowing that there was a first time. Sir Thomas Browne felt none when, presumably relying on the Book of Genesis, he said: 'Time...is but five days older than ourselves, and its horoscope is the same as the world's.'

---

[32] The inference is attributed to Kant, and endorsed as valid, by Al-Azm, *Kant's Arguments*, p. 45.

[33] §49, omitting parallel remarks about empty space. See note 26 above.

[34] S. Shoemaker, 'Time without Change', *The Journal of Philosophy* (1969).

People who think there is a radical incoherence in the idea of a first time never succeed in displaying one. The logic of it is as follows. Let H be some unique historical event, say the death of Berlioz, and let n be the number of years back from H to the first event. Then the phrase 'n years before H' names the first time, and any phrase of the form 'k years before H', for $k > n$, *makes sense* but does not *refer to any time*.

Early in the *Critique*, Kant has what looks like an argument to show that time could not in the strict sense begin: 'Time...remains and does not undergo existence-change [*wechselt nicht*]. For it is that in which... succession or co-existence can alone be represented.'[35] This perhaps establishes that the existence of the first time should not be regarded as an occurrence or a happening, but it surely does not prove that there could not be a first time.

Whether or not because of that argument, Kant firmly rejects the possibility that there was a first time. From the true premiss that 'empty time prior to the world' is a 'non-entity',[36] he immediately infers not that the first event must have occurred at the first time but rather that there cannot have been a first event. Indeed, he says explicitly that a beginning 'is an existence preceded by a time in which the thing is not', and also that 'empty time prior to the world has to be assumed if we are to assume a limit to the world in time.' He does not explain why.

So Kant's Antithesis-argument rests on the invalid inference from (1) 'There cannot be pre-mundane time' to (2) 'There cannot be a first event or a beginning of the world'. It should therefore be rejected.

Let us revert briefly to Leibniz. Kant probably didn't think out his position on the age of the world in relation to Leibniz's views. When he does invoke the latter, it is usually as mechanical by-products of the more considered Leibnizian views about world's size. For instance, after giving a reason why there cannot be extra-mundane space, Kant adds abruptly: 'This is likewise true of time.'[37] He also repeats a kind of accusation we have met before: the Leibnizians think that 'a limit of the world in time' does not require 'absolute time prior to the beginning of the world', but they have secured this position by 'surreptitiously substituting for the sensible world some intelligible world' and by 'getting rid of time'. One can hardly believe that Kant had his mind

---

[35] 224–5; see also 183.

[36] 461. Next two quotations: 455, 461, modified to omit remark about space (see also 13, 47–8)

[37] 461. Next quoted phrases: 450 and 461.

on his work at this point. Leibniz did indeed think that ultimate reality is non-temporal, but it would be excessively peculiar to adduce that in support of the claim that the world could have a limit *in time*! In the correspondence with Clarke, certainly, no such manoeuvre occurs.

Leibniz had theological reasons for thinking that the world began, and he notes that it could still be temporally infinite because it might never end.[38] (He says that a spatially limited world must be finite; but what about a cylinder of finite cross-section and infinite length?) As for whether a beginning of the world would be preceded by pre-mundane time: I can find no evidence as to Leibniz's view about that in his letters to Clarke.

[38] Leibniz V 74. Regarding final sentence in this paragraph: for some related remarks see *New Essays* II. xv. 11.

9

DIVISIBILITY

§ 52. Simple substances

The second antinomy concerns divisibility. It pits the Thesis that every 'composite substance' has indivisible parts against the Antithesis that extended things cannot have indivisible parts. The reference to extension is essential: the divisibility of matter is being inferred from that of space, and Kant's occasional hints that the antinomy concerns the simplicity of the soul are just wrong.[1]

In this section I shall discuss the Thesis-argument, the Antithesis-argument will be the topic of §53, and most of the remainder of the chapter will explore the conflict between them.

Deprived of its useless and confusing *reductio ad absurdum* form, the Thesis-argument goes as follows (462-4). From any composite substance 'remove in thought all composition', that is, think about its raw materials without any thought of how they are assembled to constitute the composite substance. As a crude analogy: one might 'remove in thought all composition' from a house by thinking of its constituent bricks – as a jumble, not as assembled in any particular fashion. But the analogy *is* crude, for a brick also has parts, so that if we had removed in thought *all* composition from a house we would not be thinking of ordinary space-taking bricks. Now, the argument continues, if upon removing in thought all composition from a composite substance we still have something to think about, some elements which are not themselves composed of anything still smaller, then those elements will be simple or non-composite or indivisible, and to that extent the Thesis will be satisfied. To complete the argument, then, Kant has only to rule out the possibility that when we remove in thought all composition from a composite substance there is nothing left for us to think about. In his own words, he has to show that it is always 'possible to remove in thought all composition' from a composite substance.

To this end, Kant argues that it is part of what 'substance' means that where substances are concerned the bricks exist independently of the building-plan: 'Composition, as applied to substances, is only an acci-

---

[1] 471; 494; 496.

dental relation in independence of which they must still persist as self-subsistent beings.' It is obviously true that a substance exists independently of any facts about how it relates to anything else to compose a larger whole, but Kant must mean also that the existence of a substance does not depend upon any putting-together of parts to compose that substance. This stronger, less obvious claim can also be justified, by a line of thought which I presented in § 12 above: because a substance is an item which cannot be handled adjectivally in an adequate account of the world, it cannot be an aggregate and therefore cannot have parts. Kant hints at this basis for the Thesis when he later remarks that 'the concept of substance' is 'meant to be the subject of all compositeness' (553).

If that is Kant's argument, then he is committed to thinking that every substance is non-composite. This would permit him the phrase 'substantial whole that is composite' and 'composite made up of substances', both of which he uses (466), but it condemns his use in the Thesis of the phrase 'composite substance'. The fact that he does use that phrase, and that he doesn't actually say outright that every substance must be non-composite, suggests that he may be trying to get by with a weaker doctrine than that, namely that every instance of compositeness involves a putting-together of substances. But that doesn't just stop short of entailing that *every* substance is non-composite – it doesn't entail that *any* substance is non-composite. For it does not rule out the possibility that every substance is composed of smaller substances (which are composed of still smaller substances which...etc.), just as every fraction is the sum of smaller fractions (which are sums of still smaller fractions which...etc.). On that basis, therefore, the Thesis-argument would fail. The text, however, is not clear enough for us to be sure exactly what Kant is relying on in his argument for the Thesis.

Throughout most of the antinomy chapter after Section 2, Kant writes as though his Thesis-argument had to do not with the concept of substance but rather with that of infinity. To deal properly with that, we must first see what he has to say in defence of the Antithesis.

§ 53. The divisibility of the extended

The Antithesis-argument is also tangled into the form of a *reductio ad absurdum*, but its main thread can safely be straightened out into a direct argument: 'Everything real, which occupies a space, contains in itself a manifold of constituents external to one another, and is therefore composite' (463); and from this, plus the premiss that the world consists of things in space, we immediately get the first clause of the Antithesis, namely, 'No composite thing in the world is made up of simple parts.' The loops and curves of Kant's *reductio* are idle, though one detail should be mentioned, namely the remark: 'A real composite is made up not of accidents (for accidents could not exist outside one another, in the absence of substance) but of substances.' This merely reminds us what sort of compositeness we are concerned with – the question is whether a thing has several parts, not whether it has several qualities or 'accidents'.

(The Antithesis has a second clause, 'There nowhere exists in the world anything simple', to which Kant devotes two more paragraphs of argument and an extra page of 'Observation'.[2] This second-clause material, in which Kant fidgets with the irrelevant idea of the simplicity of the soul, is unprofitable. I shall say no more about it.)

The second antinomy, then, presents a difficulty which I indicated back in §12. On the one hand, no genuine substance can have parts; on the other, everything which stretches through a region of space must have parts; and yet one would like to bring the concept of a substance to bear upon extended things.

One of Kant's ways of dealing with this situation, though not one which looms large in the text, is to disown the Thesis on the grounds that it requires an illegitimate concept of substance. This line of thought first appears in the 'Observation' on the Antithesis, the first long paragraph of which contains two attacks on some un-named 'monadists'.[3] In the course of the second of these attacks, Kant says:

It may be true that when a whole, made up of substances, is thought by the pure understanding alone, we must, prior to all composition of it, have the simple. But this does not hold of [what we find through] empirical intuition in space, [for this] carries with it the necessary characteristic that no part of it is simple...The monadists...seek escape from this difficulty...But we have a concept of bodies only as appearances; and as such they necessarily presuppose space...The argument of the monadists would indeed be valid if bodies were things in themselves.

Kant is saying here that we ought to employ only an empirically usable concept of substance, that this must be applicable to objects given to us through outer sense, and that no such objects can be experienced as 'simple' or non-composite. That last claim is based upon Kant's outer-

[2] 463–5; 471.
[3] 467–9. The first of the two attacks ends about where 467 ends. The next quotation differs slightly from Kemp Smith, in the interests of clarity.

sense theory – that nothing could be given to us as outer or objective unless it were spatially organized, and therefore, by the Antithesis-argument, composite. Thus, later in the paragraph, he insists that the monadists can think that the outer world is composed of simple substances only because they decline 'to treat space as a condition of the possibility of the objects of outer intuition'.

But that merely throws weight behind the Antithesis, and thus serves to tighten the antinomal log-jam. If we are to be extricated from the impasse by a victory for the Antithesis, then we need, in addition to reasons for accepting the Antithesis, a release from any obligation to accept the Thesis. Kant's official view, of course, is that neither side of the antinomy achieves an outright victory, but he does offer some heavy hints that the Thesis ought to be rejected and the palm given to the Antithesis. The long passage last quoted suggests that the Thesis-argument is vitiated by not being sufficiently empirical, being somehow tied to 'pure understanding alone' to the neglect of intuition. This suggestion is carried further in one paragraph of the 'Solution' in Section 9 – a paragraph which, though Kant does not say so, is an outright attack on the Thesis-argument.[4] It repeats the point that the latter, in arguing that outer things can be non-composite, implies that they can be thought of as outer even though one has abstracted from 'the connection in space, whereby they constitute a body'. This echoes again the outer-sense doctrine that everything which is given as outer must be spatially organized; but, again, that does not explain what is wrong with the Thesis-argument's 'proof' that the outer world must be composed of things which are non-composite and so, presumably, not extended. Given a plausible 'proof' that P must be true, it is not enough to counter it with a proof that P cannot be true. One needs also to know what is wrong with the first 'proof'.

Similarly, the last sentence of our paragraph says that we must attend only to the data of intuition, 'in which unconditionedness is never to be met with' – meaning that we could not discover by observation that anything was non-composite. But that, even if true, is of no avail against the Thesis-argument. A proof that there must be simple things is not embarrassed by the claim that we couldn't discover any empirically.

However, the paragraph under discussion does apparently try to

---

[4] 553–4 – the fourth paragraph of the 'Solution'. This solitary paragraph is the only treatment of the second antinomy, after Section 2, which focuses on substance rather than on infinity. It is evidently a clumsy interpolation, for the fifth paragraph of the 'Solution' carries on seamlessly from the third.

discredit the Thesis-argument and not merely to contradict its conclusion. Noting that the argument relies on the view that substances must be non-composite, because 'the concept of substance...is meant to be the subject of all compositeness', Kant comments:

While this is true of a thing in itself..., it does not hold of that which we entitle substance in the [field of] *appearance*. For this latter is not an absolute subject, but only a permanent image of sensibility.

In short, the Thesis-argument needs a rationalistic concept of substance, and fails for an empirical, Kantian one. The latter involves the notion of permanence or sempiternity, and Kant has a bad habit of assuming that the empirical cash-value of that is 'a permanent image' or 'an abiding and continuing intuition' (A350). But that is not important just now. The above passage, in a much deeper way, libels Kant's own dealings with the concept of a substance, the libel residing in the implication that the Kantian concept of substance involves the notion of permanence *but not that of 'absolute subject'*.

We have seen that Kant defines 'substance' as that 'which can be thought only as subject, never as a predicate of something else';[5] and he moves from this, by the two routes I described late in § 19 above, to the conclusion that empirical substances must be 'permanent'. So far from having a concept of substance according to which '*x* is a substance' entails '*x* is permanent' *rather than* '*x* is irreducibly substantival', it is deeply built into Kant's doctrine that the former entailment holds *only because* the latter holds. But then if Kant admits this, his attack on the Thesis-argument collapses. The latter needs only that the concept of substance include that of absolute subject or the like, whatever else it may include; and this is what I have been arguing that Kant has no right to deny. He is entitled to affirm that the empirical concept of substance *also* includes the notion of sempiternity – but what harm does that do to the Thesis-argument?

§ 54. Real divisibility

There is a more profitable line which Kant might have taken. It involves a distinction which is allied to one which he employs for a different purpose, namely the distinction between *conceptual* divisibility and what I shall call *real* divisibility.[6]

---

5 186; see also 149, 288.
6 Kant's allied distinction is in 554–5, which I shall discuss in § 57 below. The distinction I am drawing was mentioned in § 12 above.

Something is 'conceptually divisible' if we have language in which to discriminate sub-regions of it. So anything extended is conceptually divisible, because we can describe its size and shape by a formula placing it on a coordinate system and then, by simple mathematics, construct a new formula which marks off something less than the original object. Or we could use plain English: however small x is, we can intelligibly refer to 'the largest sphere [or, if x is a sphere, the largest cube] contained wholly within x'.

Real divisibility is to be understood as stronger than conceptual divisibility. What the Antithesis establishes is that extended things are all conceptually divisible, and it has no tendency to show that they are really divisible as well. That opens up a possible escape from the antinomal difficulty: if we can say that a substance may be conceptually divisible just so long as it is not really divisible, we shall be able without inconsistency to agree with the Thesis that the extended world is made up of substances, while also agreeing with the Antithesis that everything in the extended world is conceptually divisible.

An excellent case can be made for thus relaxing the conditions for a thing to count as a substance, quite independently of the fact that this would provide a possible solution to the antinomy. The title of 'a substance' was to be denied to any aggregate, because an aggregate can be described in a manner which makes it purely adjectival upon its parts – for instance we can tell the whole truth about a cloud just by stating enough facts about particles of water. But the question of whether something *can* be handled adjectivally, by some desperate conceptual means, hardly seems interesting, and one might guess that in that sense anything *can* be handled adjectivally. What matters, I suggest, is whether it would be profitable or pointful to handle the given thing thing adjectivally, that is, whether a complete description and scientific explanation would require that the thing be handled adjectivally, or – what comes to the same thing – whether it would require that separate reference be made to the thing's parts.

That would still imply that a cloud is not a substance, for the description and explanation of it in terms of its constituent water-particles, far from being a mere conceptual *jeu d'esprit*, is essential to a complete causal explanation of all the facts about the cloud. By way of contrast, consider an unbreakable and homogeneous atom x, which we can conceptually divide into parts b and c. We could replace each statement about where x is by a pair of statements about b and c, but there would be no point in doing this: it is an adjectival handling of x which we should not be led to by an endeavour to be thorough in our descriptions and explanations. So, I would argue, it would not be a reason for denying that x is a substance.

I am contending (a) that a good sense to give to 'really divisible' is that a thing counts as really divisible if and only if it can be conceptually divided into parts which there would be a serious scientific point in distinguishing from one another; and further that (b) something can count as 'a substance', even if it is conceptually divisible, just so long as it is not 'really divisible' in the sense just defined.

To bring real divisibility down to earth somewhat, I offer the conjecture that a thing will be 'really divisible' in my sense if and only if it is either *breakable* or *heterogeneous*, that is, if and only if it has parts which can be spatially separated from one another, or else which are or could become qualitatively different from one another. This is not a new definition of 'really divisible', but rather a consequence, I believe, of the original definition.

It is obvious that if something is breakable or heterogeneous, then it is really divisible; but the converse needs argument. Well, consider an object x which is conceptually divisible into parts b and c but which is not breakable or heterogeneous. What I have to show is that x is not 'really divisible' in my sense, that is, that there could be no serious scientific point in attending separately to its parts b and c. Consider how, given the initial stipulations, b and c can differ from one another. (1) They may differ in size and shape, in ways which follow logically from the formulae which mark them off in the first place. (2) They will always be differently located, as a logical consequence of the demarcating formulae together with statements about how x is located and oriented. (3) They will differ in their spatial relations to other things, as a logical consequence of the demarcating formulae and statements of the locations of x and of other things. Those seem to be the only differences there could be between b and c. If that is right, then there could never be any scientific need to distinguish b from c, for all the facts about them would follow by logic from their demarcating formulae together with facts which could be covered without mention of b and c. I conclude, therefore, that anything which is neither breakable nor heterogeneous is not 'really divisible' in the sense of my definition. If that is wrong, though, I should drop the conjecture and retain the definition, for it is the latter which best justifies the use of the concept of real divisibility in the account of what a substance is.

Leibniz would have been sympathetic to the idea that a substance is a

non-attribute which there is no serious intellectual reason ever to describe in terms of its parts, but he would have denied that this could
make room for extended substances. (1) For some reason, he thinks that
'fluidity' is the 'original' condition of extended things, and that what
has to be explained is always cohesion rather than dissipation;[7] and from
this he would presumably infer that every extended thing is breakable.
(2) Furthermore, even if there were unbreakable 'atoms', Leibniz says,
they would be 'still further composed of parts, for an invincible attach-
ment of one part to another (if we could reasonably conceive or assume
this) would not at all destroy the diversity of these parts'. The 'diversity' referred to is not mere numerical distinctness, but qualitative difference, for Leibniz is here relying on his doctrine of the identity of
indiscernibles.

So Leibniz thinks that every extended thing is both breakable and
heterogeneous, thus falling doubly short of counting as a substance by
the criterion I have been advocating. Perhaps his rationalism is the ultimate source of all this; but even if it is, that does not justify Kant's
charge that a rationalist concept of substance is at the root of the difficulty, and that rationalists err in connecting 'substance' with 'absolute
subject' rather than with 'something permanent'. The line of thought
which I have been developing, and which I think Leibniz would have
rejected, is not that we divorce 'substance' from 'absolute subject', but
merely that we apply the latter phrase in a certain way.

§ 55. Kant against atomism

What was Kant's attitude to the possibility that extended things might
be composed of homogeneous and unbreakable atoms? As a start to
answering that, we must look at a passage which seems to have a quite
different topic. Early in § 53 above I referred to a paragraph in which
Kant launches two attacks on 'the monadists'. One of these, alleging
that the monadists use a rationalistic concept of substance as a basis for
the Thesis, has already been discussed. Now we must look at the other
(467).

The proof of 'the doctrine of the infinite divisibility of matter', Kant
says, is 'purely mathematical', and is 'based upon insight into the con-
stitution of space [as] the formal condition of the possibility of all
matter'. The monadists, however, are accused of supposing that ex-

---

[7] *New Essays* II. xiii. 23; see also xxiii. 23. Next quotation: 'A New System of the Nature
and Communication of Substances', Loemker, p. 456.

tensionless monads – or 'physical points', as Kant calls them – can 'fill space through their mere aggregation'. Kant scoffs at this 'absurdity', calling it a 'futile attempt to reason away...the evident demonstrated truth of mathematics'. It is as though he pictured the monadists as hoping to fill space by heaping extensionless monads together in breath-takingly large quantities, thus flouting the 'evident demonstrated truth' that $(n.o) = o$ for any n, finite or infinite. The chief monadist, Leibniz, was in no danger of taking such a position. He insisted that monads are not themselves in space at all, that you don't get at (the thought of) a monad by (mentally) dividing extended things, and, in a phrase, that monads are 'not parts but foundations' of material things.[8] Of course, the target may be a lesser 'monadist', but would anybody be guilty of such a view as the one just described? I do not think so, nor do I think that Kant can have thought so. What, then, *is* the theory which Kant is trying to set up for attack?

Well, in the *Metaphysical Foundations of Natural Science* Kant attributes to 'the monadists' a position which differs in only one respect from the one he seems to attribute to them in the *Critique*, this difference being enough to hoist the theory from the depths of idiocy up to the level of thorough respectability.[9] Although this better theory was not held by Leibniz, one can believe that some of his would-be followers entertained it. It is the theory that extended things are made up of 'physical points' each of which, though having no size itself, dominates a region of space, prevents anything else from entering that region, and, in Kant's words, 'fills a space by mere repulsive force'. According to this theory, presumably, extended things will be composed of only finitely many unextended components.

This must surely be what Kant wanted to attack in the *Critique*, though that implies that he shouldn't have spoken of physical points as filling space 'through their mere aggregation'. For what is proposed is not that space gets filled by a sheer assembling of these unextended items – which begets the scandalous idea that super-infinite quantities of them would be needed – but rather that it gets 'filled', in a certain sense, by the causal repulsive power which the items exercise.

Leaving exegesis of the *Critique* aside now, let us look at the account of the matter which Kant presents and attacks in the *Metaphysical Foundations*.

[8] Letter to De Volder, Loemker, p. 536. Leibniz is admittedly less cautious in a letter to Arnauld, Loemker, p. 360, and in *Monadology* § 2.

[9] *Metaphysical Foundations*, p. 50. I am indebted to Michael Beebe for bringing this illuminating passage to my attention.

The first thing to be said is that Kant, on his own showing, has mis-described the position under attack. If a thing's causal properties give it a 'repulsive force' throughout a region of space, then it is rightly described as itself extending throughout that region. Kant nearly admits this when he says that each monad would *fill* a region of space by means of its repulsive force; and it is also implicit in his remark, earlier in the *Critique*, that 'We are acquainted with substance in space only through forces which are active in this and that space, either bringing other objects to it... or preventing them penetrating into it' (321). This implies, surely rightly, that at this metaphysical level we cannot distinguish the extent of a thing from the extent of its influence. Yet Kant seems mainly to adopt the picture of a supposed physical point as something which does not itself stretch through a region of space although its influence does.

In the course of presenting a view like the one Kant is here attacking, Strawson combatively distinguishes the size of a thing from the spatial extent of its influence:

> One is no more obliged to suppose that a particle must fill the space which it uniquely occupies than one is obliged to suppose that the unique occupant of a railway carriage must fill the railway carriage – though one might suppose that
> · his repellent aspect was what accounted for his unique occupation of it.[10]

That is true if the carriage just happens to have only one occupant, but a Strawsonian 'point-particle' is 'supposed to exert some causal power throughout the region of space of which it [is] the unique occupant'. If this 'causal power' is the irresistible 'repulsive force' of which Kant speaks, then the analogue would be someone whose occupancy of a railway carriage makes it causally impossible for anything else, however small, to intrude into any part of the carriage. I contend that one *is* obliged to suppose that such an occupant fills the entire carriage. What Strawson's example most strongly suggests, however, is an intermediate position according to which a point-particle makes it difficult but not impossible for other things to enter the territory which it dominates. Perhaps Strawson's view could be saved in that way, but one would need more details before one could evaluate such a middle-strength position.

The 'monadist' theory which Kant presents and attacks in the *Metaphysical Foundations* is not middle-strength, however, and so it ought not to be expressed in terms of a distinction between the extent

[10] *Bounds of Sense*, p. 184.

of an item and the extent of its repulsive influence. Properly expressed, the theory is just classical atomism, which says that extended things can be divided into finitely many extended but physically unbreakable and homogeneous atoms. There is indeed evidence in the *Metaphysical Foundations* that Kant would accept that construal of the 'monadist' theory, but first let us examine his attack on the theory when it is taken at face value.

The attack rests upon this premiss: If a region of space R is dominated by a 'repulsive force' which prevents anything from entering R from the outside, then every sub-region r of R must also be dominated by a force which protects r's borders from invasion. That sounds reasonable in itself; but Kant takes it to imply that the source of the repulsive force dominating r must lie within r itself and must be separable from the sources of such power which dominate other sub-regions. In his own words, each r must contain 'repulsive force to counteract on all sides all remaining parts, and hence to repel them and likewise be repelled by them, i.e. to be moved to a distance from them'.[11] No good reason to accept this is provided.

Kant's view is in clear conflict with the 'monadist' proposal when the latter is taken at face-value. The 'monadist' says that the whole of a region R may be permeated by a repulsive force whose entire source lies within one part of R, so that some sub-regions of R would be affected by a repulsive force whose source lay outside them; which is just what Kant has declared to be impossible.

Kant's position, when properly understood, contradicts classical atomism – that is, it contradicts the 'monadist' position when *it* is properly understood. Kant says, in effect, 'If R is permeated by a repulsive force, then every sub-region r of R contains an independent source of repulsive force.' That, I contend, is equivalent to saying 'If R is full of matter then every sub-region r of R also contains matter which is separable from the rest.' And that precisely denies the atomist claim that there is a limit to how finely portions of matter can be physically divided.

Furthermore, Kant himself draws that conclusion, which suggests that he did after all see the so-called 'monadist' position as equivalent to atomism. He writes:

As far as the mathematical [conceptual] divisibility of space...reaches, thus far does the possible physical division of the substance that fills the space likewise reach. But the mathematical divisibility extends to infinity, and consequently also the physical, i.e. all matter is divisible to infinity and indeed is divisible into parts each of which is itself in turn material substance.[12]

[11] *Metaphysical Foundations*, pp. 49–50.   [12] *Ibid.* p. 50. Next quotation: *ibid.* p. 48.

In Kant's usage, 'physical divisibility' is breakability, for he says: 'The separation of the parts of matter is physical division.' So he is claiming that there are no extended and unbreakable atoms. Given his basic view about how a region of space can be filled – by 'repulsive force' or by matter – he is absolutely right to make this claim. The basic view itself, however, is not adequately supported, and Kant cannot be credited with having refuted atomism.

§ 56. Substance and substances

Kant's considered view, it seems, is that everything extended is not just conceptually but really divisible. He is therefore committed to saying that the extended world is not made up of substances, according to the criteria for 'a substance' which I have proposed. In the *Critique* he does not squarely face up to this fact, because, as we have seen, he dismisses the problem about substance which the second antinomy raises, convicting it on a trumped-up charge of undue rationalism (see § 53 above). Still, there is evidence as to what line he would have taken if he had addressed himself to the question. I shall indicate it in a moment.

In the course of a quarrelsome correspondence with Leibniz, Arnauld raised the question of whether we have to suppose that there are any unbreakable items. Unfortunately, he didn't handle the question very well. For one thing, he wrote as though Leibniz's indivisibility criterion were an arbitrary departure from a more usual account of what a substance is:

[To accept Leibniz's position] one would first have to define 'substance' and 'substantial' in the following terms: *I call 'substance' and 'substantial' that which has a true unity.* But...this definition has not yet been accepted, and...[one is] as entitled to say: *I call 'substance' that which is not modality or state,* and [to] maintain that it is paradoxical to say that there is nothing substantial in a block of marble, since this block of marble is not the state of being of another substance.[13]

This does less than justice to the underlying connexion between 'non-aggregate' and 'non-attribute', a connexion which Leibniz, replying, points to positively if not altogether clearly: 'What constitutes the essence of a being through aggregation is only a state of being of its constituents.' I shall not dwell on that now. What matters more is Arnauld's next move. He concedes that the block of marble, although

---

[13] *Leibniz–Arnauld*, pp. 107–8; italics added for clarity. Next two Arnauld quotations are both from *ibid.* p. 108. Leibniz's replies: *ibid.* p. 121; see also *ibid.* p. 108 n. 2.

not an attribute, is not a substance either – 'not a single substance but many substances mechanically joined together'. That, however, concedes Leibniz's point that a single substance must be indivisible in some appropriate sense. Arnauld goes on to suggest that 'in the whole of corporeal nature there are only...aggregates of substances, because of none of these parts can one say, accurately speaking, that it is a single substance.' Leibniz's reply to this is beyond dispute: 'Being is one thing and beings another; but the plural presupposes the singular, and where there is no being, still less will there be many beings.' Arnauld is indeed clearly wrong in saying that there are no substances but only collections of substances.

Still, Arnauld might evade this counter-attack by shifting his ground and saying that the block of marble is neither a substance nor an aggregate of substances but is nevertheless substantial. This would avoid the damaging 'plural'. Although Arnauld does not properly isolate it from neighbouring questions, his remarks do urgently raise the question of whether we must use the notion of 'a substance' if we are to allow that anything is 'substantial'. My answer to this question will be No.

Leibniz's answer is Yes. Mixed in with his point that aggregates of substances require substances, there is the deeper point that an aggregate 'will have no reality at all if each constituent being is still a being through aggregation', i.e. that if there are no truly simple substances then 'one must acknowledge that no reality can be found in bodies'.[14] When he says that 'what is not truly *one* being is not truly one *being* either', he is using a stressed truism to embody the controversial thesis that if there is to be a genuine reality of any sort (being, *être*), it must either be a single substance or else be composed of them. Later, he says outright that 'only indivisible substances and their different states are absolutely real.' Leibniz's adherence to this doctrine was absolute, for his whole metaphysic rests upon it, but I cannot find that he ever supports it with convincing arguments.

However, one can avoid accepting the view that a reality must consist of substances, if one invokes the distinction between the count-term 'a substance' and the mass-term 'substance'.[15] In the latter use, we do not speak of 'a substance' or of '*n* substances', but rather of quantities or portions or amounts or stretches of substance. Now, even if we agree with the rationalists and Kant and others that one must be able to

[14] All quotations in this paragraph are from *ibid*. pp. 120–1, 153.
[15] The distinction is briefly invoked in § 13 above. For more about it, see W. V. Quine, *Word and Object* (Cambridge, Mass., 1960), §§ 19–20, and also an excellent discussion of Kant's, 212. Final reference in this paragraph: 224.

identify the items which a satisfactory science would fundamentally be about, these items may be not substances but portions or quantities of substance. There might be no basic things, but just basic kinds of stuff. We could still regard substance as sempiternal, as Kant does when he says of 'substance' that 'its quantum in nature is neither increased nor diminished', thus quietly replacing his usual count-term by a mass-term.

That is one of several places where Kant uses 'substance' as a mass-term. The same use occurs in *Metaphysical Foundations of Natural Science*, for example in a passage I quoted, where he says that all matter is divisible into 'parts each of which is itself in turn material substance' – not, be it noted, '*a* material substance'. Passages like these suggest that if Kant had squarely faced the problem posed for him by the second antinomy, he would have resolved it by saying that although there are no (indivisible) extended substances, the physical world is nevertheless made up of one or more kinds of substance.

Since this option was wide open, why did Leibniz so firmly and confidently reject it? I used to think that a possible answer was that he saw that if there are no substances but only infinitely really divisible portions of substance, then there can be no final, basic, comprehensive science; and one would expect Leibniz to think that that is too high a metaphysical price to pay. The argument for thinking that it would have to be paid is as follows. If there are no substances then, however small are the portions of substance we are generalizing over in a given set of scientific laws, there will always be a serious point in generalizing over still smaller portions; from which it seems to follow that no set of scientific laws can be the final and most basic ones. If there were portions of substance which were the smallest it was scientifically profitable to discriminate – the argument concludes – then those portions would be substances.

Steven Savitt has shown me that this is invalid. Suppose that our science works down to a level where it distinguishes portions of substance which, though breakable, are homogeneous. We might be able to generalize about these, *and about every sub-portion of them, however small*, in a single finite set of generalizations which would then be our final, basic science. There needn't be any smallest portions which are generalized over, for we may have laws of the form

$$(x)(n)((Fx \ \& \ x \text{ has a volume of } n \text{ cm}^3) \to Gx)$$

where n ranges over *all* fractions below a certain value.

This option would not be open to Leibniz. Because of his principle of the identity of indiscernibles, he denies that there could be a homogeneous extended thing.[16] So he would have to say that anything which was really divisible was heterogeneous, which seems to imply that if there are only really divisible portions of substance then there couldn't be a basic science – which Leibniz might well regard as a *reductio ad absurdum*. Still, that argument requires the identity of indiscernibles, which is a relatively special feature of Leibniz's philosophy. The argument does not justify or even explain Leibniz's apparent belief that it is rather obvious that reality must consist of substances.

§57. The supposed infinity problem

All through the later sections of the antinomy chapter, except for one stray paragraph which I have already discussed, Kant treats the second antinomy as the source of a problem not about substances but about infinity, as though the Thesis were based upon an objection to things' having *infinitely* many parts. This misrepresents the actual antinomy, and regrettably leads Kant to scamp his discussion of substance. Still, an infinity issue does arise from the antinomy, and we ought to see how Kant handles it. Apart from one passing reference (515), the relevant passages are all in the last three sections.

In Section 7, Kant briefly applies to the second antinomy the 'weakening move', as I call it, which he has developed at more length for the first.[17] His conclusion is: 'The quantity of parts in a given appearance is in itself neither finite nor infinite.' That is what one would expect: how many parts a thing has is measured by the magnitude of the possible series of ever-finer divisions of it; since this series must be viewed as lying in a possible future, it can never be a 'whole', cannot have a magnitude 'in itself'; and so, Kant would naturally think, its magnitude can never be infinite even if it is more than finite.

In Section 8, Kant introduces his infinite/indefinite contrast,[18] and one would expect him to say that extended things are indefinitely but not infinitely divisible. On the contrary, he flatly contradicts Section 7 by opting for 'infinite' against 'indefinite', and he gives a strange reason for doing so: 'The division of a...portion of matter given between certain limits must be said to proceed *in infinitum*. For this matter is

---

16 *Leibniz–Clarke*, Leibniz's fifth letter, § 22.
17 533–4. On 'weakening move', see § 45 above.
18 540–2. On infinite/indefinite, see § 46 above. Next two quotations are both from 541.

given as a whole, and therefore with all its possible parts, in empirical intuition.' Shortly thereafter he says: 'The further members of any continued division are themselves empirically given prior to the continuation of the division. The division, that is to say, goes on *in infinitum*.' This is just a mistake. If these 'further members' are physical or conceptual dividings of a piece of matter, then they are obviously not 'given prior to the continuation of the division'. Perhaps Kant is thinking of a series not of *dividings* but rather of *sets of parts* – a series whose first member is some set of two parts which jointly comprise the whole object, the second a set of three parts, and so on. But are the further members of this series 'given prior to the division'? If so, that is only because the object itself is given prior to the division; but that means that Kant is identifying the object with every set of all its parts – an identification which is also suggested when Kant says that 'this matter is given as a whole, and therefore with all its possible parts, in empirical intuition.' But if the object is identical with each set of its parts, the only 'series' we have is a nonsense-series whose members are: the object, the object, the object,...

Kant must have felt uneasy about this, for one page later he says that although the relevant 'series of conditions' can be continued *in infinitum*, it is not 'given as infinite in the object'. He is clearly trying to claw his way back to the position of Section 7 which he ought never to have deserted.

That struggle continues through the first three paragraphs of the 'Solution' of the antinomy in Section 9.[19] After repeating his bad reason for saying that the divisibility of matter involves a regress *in infinitum*, Kant says:

We are not, however, entitled to say of a whole which is divisible to infinity, that *it is made up of infinitely many parts*. For although all parts are contained in the intuition of the whole, *the whole division* is not so contained, but consists only in the continuous decomposition, that is, in the regress itself, whereby the series first becomes actual...[The series] is a successive infinite and never *whole*.

The same line of thought is expounded at greater length in the *Metaphysical Foundations of Natural Science*, where Kant again emphasizes that a thing which is infinitely divisible need not have an infinite quantity of parts, and need not involve an infinite which is whole or determinate, just so long as it is an appearance and not a 'thing in

[19] 551–3. Next quotation: 552.

itself'.[20] Here, as in the *Critique*, this claim is made in respect of real as well as of conceptual divisibility.

Even if a thing is an appearance, Kant thinks, there is one way in which it may have parts whose existence is not a mere matter of possible futures. This is discussed in the fifth paragraph of the 'Solution' – an obscure passage which I think I now understand (554–5). Kant here distinguishes between (a) 'the subdivision of an appearance, viewed as a mere filling of space' and (b) a thing's having parts which 'are in a definite way separated from one another, so that they constitute a *quantum discretum*'. One might think that this is just the distinction between conceptual and real divisibility, but that would be a misunderstanding of Kant's intent, for under (a) he includes one facet of real divisibility, namely breakability or the capacity for being physically dismembered. The divisibility of type (b) is that in which the thing's parts are distinguishable from one another by some fact about their *actual* condition – presumably the fact that they are actually separated, with gaps between them. (Perhaps (b) also covers the case where the parts, though not separated, are qualitatively different from one another. Kant says 'separated' (*abgesonderten*); but Kemp Smith's rendering as 'distinguished off from one another', although it is inaccurate, may nevertheless convey a part of Kant's thought.) So Kant is distinguishing (a) mere conceptual divisibility, together with the case where some (homogeneous?) thing is breakable but not broken, from (b) the case where the thing's parts are separated from one another – or, perhaps we must add, are qualitatively different from one another.

What Kant mainly says in the fifth paragraph of the 'Solution' is that it is logically impossible for something to be infinitely (b)-divisible, that is, for it to be already 'separated' into infinitely many parts:

In the case of an organized body conceived as articulated in *infinitum* the whole is represented as already divided into parts, and as yielding to us, prior to all regress, a determinate and yet infinite quantity of parts. This, however, is self-contradictory.

Just below that, Kant says: 'To view anything as being a *quantum discretum*, is to take the quantity of units in it as being determined, and therefore as being in every case equal to some number.'[21] So the self-

---

[20] *Metaphysical Foundations*, pp. 52–6. Unfortunately, *Menge* is here sometimes translated by 'number'.

[21] See the opening paragraphs of § 45 above. Kemp Smith translates this as: '...to take the number [*Menge*] of units...as...determined, and therefore as...equal to some number [*Zahl*]'.

contradictory notion to which Kant has referred is that of an infinite number, as distinct from an infinite quantity. His more usual view, as we have seen, is that we cannot even apply 'infinite quantity' to the phenomenal realm. But here, for rather dim reasons, he thinks that he must suspend that view and allow that there may be infinite quantities of parts, just so long as they are indeterminate and thus not equal to any number.

Kant is arguing that the quantity of 'separated' parts of a thing must be determinate, because such parts are 'already' there in advance of anything we might do. One could object that the non-finite array of world-regions is also 'already' there, and yet Kant regarded it as indeterminate because through a phenomenalist analysis he could project it into a possible future (see §42 above). Kant would reply, I suppose, that the series of world-regions is not given, as the parts of a thing are, 'within limits'. I am not sure how to evaluate this, but really it does not matter very much, since the associated assumptions about infinity and number and determinateness are wrong anyway.

What does matter, if Kant's text is to be understood, is that the fifth paragraph of the 'Solution' is not distinguishing conceptual from real divisibility, and is not trying to prove that extended things are only finitely physically divisible. What it is trying to show is that the view that 'the whole is organized to infinity' is 'not a thinkable hypothesis' – and here again we must take 'organized', like 'articulated', to invoke the idea of a thing's having parts which are (heterogeneous or) already separated.[22]

As for how finely a thing may be organized or articulated, Kant rightly says that that is something 'only experience can show'. He also says: 'It is true...that the parts of matter could become articulated in the course of their decomposition *in infinitum*', which I take to mean that there is no limit to how finely one could produce articulation or jointedness in a thing by actually dismembering it.[23]

§ 58. The divisibility of space

It is perhaps worth remarking that something like the distinction between conceptual and real divisibility can be applied to *space*. To give

[22] Kant's words are *organisch* and *gegliedert*, which Kemp Smith translates by 'organic' and 'organised' respectively. The second word has as a root the noun *Glied*, meaning 'limb' or 'member' or 'joint'.

[23] My translation is disputable. Kemp Smith's, however, renders the sentence unintelligible or, at best, contradictory to the rest of the paragraph.

content to this, I offer the suggestion that it might actually be false that space is infinitely really divisible, although its infinite conceptual divisibility is mathematically secure.

This is only to take seriously the commonly held view that geometrical propositions could be empirically refuted – a view which is often applied to the parallel postulate, but less often to 'Space is infinitely divisible'. The latter is indeed sometimes thought not to be empirical, with the suggestion that it just stands to reason that however short a distance n cm is there must be the shorter distance $n/2$ cm. It is true that however small n is, there must be the smaller $n/2$, but does this truth about fractions imply anything about space? We shouldn't expect it to yield truths about atoms of lead, say, claiming that a gram of lead must be made up of 10^{100} portions of lead each weighing 10^{-100} grams; for we know that no portion of lead weighs as little as that. Even if lead differs relevantly from space, e.g. in being a kind of substance, the example should serve as a warning against hastily drawing empirical conclusions from premisses about fractions.

Presumably 'Space is infinitely divisible' should be given empirical content if there is a satisfactory way of doing so. I suggest that we equate 'There are distances as short as n cm' with 'It is causally possible to measure distances as short as n cm'. Then 'Space is infinitely divisible', which is equivalent to 'There are no shortest distances', becomes equivalent to 'There is no causally imposed limit to how finely spatial measurements could be made'. (Technological obstacles are, of course, irrelevant.) In defence of this, I would point out that in many contexts we do equate *what there is* with *what it is causally possible for us to find*. For example, there are no leaden parts of an atom of lead, because our causal theory implies that no such parts could be isolated; there is no relation of absolute simultaneity, because it is causally impossible to establish one. My proposal about the existence of distances applies this same general equivalence.

This would give a thoroughly factual, scientific status to the question of whether space is infinitely divisible or whether, on the contrary, there are atoms of distance. Faced with this suggestion, Kant might have said that we couldn't have evidence that it was causally impossible to measure distances shorter than n cm – that the most we should ever say was that we had not found a way of measuring yet shorter distances (see §§86–7 below). But that would be wrong. There could be evidence that a certain distance – perhaps the diameter of the smallest kind of substance – was the shortest that could be measured. I believe that one of the biggest changes in science in this century has been the development of 'limit-setting' hypotheses: that there is no basis for predicting the path of a certain particle, not just that we have not found one; that nothing could exceed the speed of light, not just that we do not yet know how to speed things up beyond that velocity; that energy is quantized, not just that we haven't managed to isolate or measure intermediate amounts of energy. Scientifically, these may be a very mixed bunch, but they form a philosophical natural kind which is of some interest.

The divisibility of time could be handled analogously. How could time fail to be infinitely divisible? Well, suppose that there cannot be finer temporal measurements than those which measure the distance travelled by an object of known velocity, and suppose also that there are causal limits to how finely distances can be measured. If those suppositions are right, then temporal measurements can be refined indefinitely only if objects can be speeded up indefinitely, and there is evidence that that is causally impossible. That is what lies behind the suggestion that time is discrete, and that an atom of time – a 'chronon' – is the length of time it takes a light-wave to traverse the diameter of an electron.[24] I am not defending this, but merely setting it up as a possibility, against Kant's dogmatic claim that 'There is no time that is the smallest'.

Kant thinks that the infinite divisibility of space is guaranteed by geometry, but his account of geometrical truth as synthetic and a priori is an unhappy one. He tries to present geometry as having limiting implications for the given world without being endangered by it, and that is impossible. In John Wisdom's words: 'No stakes, no winnings.' This criticism does not touch Kant's view that things in space are given through outer sense, nor even his view that outer sense has a special 'form' which it imposes on all its deliverances. In a notably shrill passage, Kant says that these doctrines of his *are* threatened by any challenge to Euclidean geometry:

The idle objections, that objects of the senses may not conform to such rules of construction in space as that of the infinite divisibility of lines or angles, must be given up... Whatever pure mathematics establishes in regard to the synthesis of the form of apprehension is also necessarily valid of the objects apprehended. All objections are only the chicanery of a falsely instructed reason, which, erroneously professing to isolate the objects of the senses from the formal condition of our

[24] G. J. Whitrow, *The Natural Philosophy of Time* (London, 1961), p. 156. Kant's claim is on 254.

sensibility, represents them, in spite of the fact that they are mere appearances, as objects in themselves.[25]

This takes the content of 'pure mathematics' to be fixed beyond any possibility of dispute, choice, or variation. But it is not. We now know that 'pure mathematics' can describe many possible spaces which are not Euclidean, including ones which are not infinitely divisible. So now the question is: which geometry fits the perceived outer world? In Kantian terms, this is to ask *what* the 'form' of outer sense is, i.e. what characteristics are to be found in all outer things because of the way outer sense is. And it could include the question of whether space is infinitely divisible.

A few pages later Kant actually argues for the 'continuity' – meaning infinite divisibility – of space: 'Space and time are *quanta continua*, because no part of them can be given save as enclosed between limits (points or instants), and therefore only in such a fashion that this part is itself again a space or a time' (211). But this argument needs two premisses – not just 'Every part of space is a space', but also 'Every part of space has parts'. For the latter, Kant offers no cogent arguments.

[25] 206–7. For a penetrating exploration of how infinite divisibility relates to the outer-sense doctrine, see C. Parsons, 'Infinity and Kant's Conception of the "Possibility of Experience"', *The Philosophical Review* (1964).

10

FREEDOM

§ 59. The third antinomy

Both sides of the third antinomy assume that whatever happens is caused to happen. The Antithesis says that the only causality is the causality of *nature*, in which an event is caused by something earlier. The Thesis denies this, in the interests of an alleged causality of *freedom*, in which the cause does not ante-date the effect. The Thesis-argument is a genuine *reductio ad absurdum*: it offers no positive doctrine of freedom, but rather presents an alleged difficulty in the Antithesis. I shall now examine this.

The Thesis-argument starts by arguing, quite cogently, that in the causality of nature every cause must be an event or happening. If it were a 'preceding state' which 'had always existed', its effect 'also would have always existed, and would not have only just arisen'.[1] This is important, for it implies that if every event is caused through the causality of nature then every event is caused by an earlier event which is caused by... and so on, without beginning. So no causal-explanatory chain can be completed, or, as Kant says, there can be 'no completeness of the series on the side of the causes'.

What is the difficulty about that? Kant seems poised to raise a problem about infinity, but in fact he does no such thing. The argument concludes thus:

The law of nature is just this, that nothing takes place without a cause sufficiently determined *a priori*. The proposition that no causality is possible save in accordance with laws of nature, when taken in unlimited universality, is therefore self-contradictory; and this cannot, therefore, be regarded as the sole kind of causality.[2]

The whole weight falls on the phrase 'sufficiently determined *a priori*', which Kant, typically, does not explain. Here is Kemp Smith's account of what Kant means:

The vital point of this argument lies in the assertion that the principle of causality calls for a *sufficient* cause for each event, and that such sufficiency is not to be found in natural causes which are themselves derivative or conditioned [or caused].

[1] 472; see also 570.
[2] 474. Next two quotations: *Commentary*, pp. 492–3; A. C. Ewing, *A Short Commentary on Kant's Critique of Pure Reason* (London, 1938), p. 218.

According to this, the Thesis-argument claims that we have not assigned a sufficient cause for an event if we have merely adduced something which in turn needs explanation but is not explained. Ewing also accepts that reading of the argument, and endorses the argument as thus interpreted:

If the cause is viewed as explaining or giving the reason of the effect, then this suggests that there must be something which is its own cause, otherwise causation gives no ultimate explanation or reason at all, just as it would be futile to give a chain of reasons for accepting a proposition if none of them could, any more than the original proposition, be seen to be true in their own right.

This, though plausible, is wrong. It rests on a mistaken conflation of reasons for happening with reasons for believing. It is true that my deriving Q from P gives you no reason to believe Q unless you already believe P, but it is not analogously true that my showing you how e_1 led to e_2 gives you no explanation of e_2 unless you can explain the occurrence of e_1. A justification needs a justified basis, but an explanation does not need an explained basis.

Schopenhauer, who accepted this interpretation of the Thesis-argument, put an accurate finger on the defect in it when he said that 'state A is a sufficient cause of state B' just so long as it has properties which are sufficient to guarantee that B will ensue. 'In this way my demand that it be a *sufficient* cause is entirely satisfied, and that demand has no direct connection with the question how state A itself arrived at actuality.'[3]

Unfortunately, Kant's text only feebly supports the Schopenhauer interpretation. The crucial clause of the Thesis-argument is: '...nothing takes place without a cause sufficiently determined *a priori*.' Kant does not emphasize 'sufficiently' as Kemp Smith does in his *Commentary* and also, in a lapse of editorial restraint, in his translation. More important, the phrase is not 'sufficient cause', as both Schopenhauer and Kemp Smith imply, but rather 'cause [which is] sufficiently determined'. I do not know what that means, but it cannot mean the same as 'sufficient cause' – for the latter points rather to the idea of an *effect* which is sufficiently determined.

The phrase '*a priori*' seems not to carry the Kantian technical sense of 'independently of all experience', but rather the pre-Kantian sense of 'in advance' or 'independently'.[4] So the thought is that the cause must

---

[3] A. Schopenhauer, *The World as Will and Representation* (trans. E. F. J. Payne, New York, 1958), Vol. I, pp. 497–8; quoted in *Commentary*, p. 493n.
[4] I here follow H. Heimsoeth, *Transzendentale Dialektik* (Berlin, 1967), p. 239n.

be sufficiently determined – whatever that means – in advance of, or independently, of its relation with the effect. That also goes against the Schopenhauer reading, according to which the argument turns upon a point not about what the cause must be like independently of the effect, but on the contrary about how the cause must relate to the effect.

I do not have an interpretation of the Thesis-argument of the third antinomy. The literature contains several suggestions other than the Schopenhauer one. (1) Heimsoeth speaks of the demand of the principle of causality that every event have 'sufficiently, and thus completely, determined causality'; but what does that mean?[5] (2) In the Ewing passage I have quoted there is, as well as the Schopenhauer reading, a hint of something else, when Ewing says '. . . otherwise causation gives no ultimate explanation. . .' It is true that if there is only the causality of nature then no causal explanation can be 'ultimate' in the sense of leaving nothing to be explained. But if that were the point of the Thesis-argument, then the latter would be attacking a version of the 'principle of causality' which affirms *both* that there is only the causality of nature *and* that every event has an 'ultimate' explanation. That is such an obvious straw man that Kant cannot have taken it seriously or supposed that the Thesis-arguer would do so. (3) Strawson says circumspectly that the Thesis-argument 'derives what force it has solely from the assumption of a beginning of the world', but I submit that that is misleading. The Thesis-argument does involve the thought of a world-beginning, as Kant makes clear in his 'Observation' upon it; but only because it supposedly uncovers a reason for thinking that the world must have begun, not because of any 'assumption' that the world began. (4) According to Beck, the Thesis-argument 'is largely a repetition of the Aristotelian–Thomistic proof of the impossibility of an infinite series of causes and hence of the necessity of a first cause'. In his account of how this proof is supposed to work, the key phrase is 'a condition that is *a priori* sufficient', which leads right back to the difficulties of the Schopenhauer interpretation. As for the suggestion that the argument is directly concerned with infinity: that gets little support from Kant. He does once indicate that infinity is crucial to the third antinomy, in his laconic metaphor about 'too large' and 'too small'.[6] He makes nothing of this, however, and he later says explicitly that infinity is not the point of the antinomy, and that what matters is not

---

[5] *Ibid.* p. 239. Next two quotations: *Bounds of Sense*, p. 208; *Practical Reason*, p. 184.

[6] 516. Next two quoted phrases: 563–4. The final phrase tends to support Schopenhauer's reading of the Thesis-argument, but I cannot square it with the text of the latter.

'the magnitude of the series of conditions' but rather 'the dynamical relation of the condition to the conditioned'. That means that the crux is not an infinity-problem but rather some issue about the nature of the causal relation.

In Kant's thought, as we have seen, 'infinity' connects closely with 'totality'. The latter notion can be connected with the third antinomy, for in one place Kant writes as though the crucial point in the Thesis-argument were that if there is only natural causality then 'no absolute totality of [causal conditions] can be obtained'.[7] Yet somewhat later he insists that that is not the point of the antinomy after all:

[The Antithesis] would seem to imply the existence of a chain of causes which in the regress to their conditions allows of no *absolute totality*. But that need not trouble us. The point has already been dealt with in the general discussion of the antinomy into which reason falls when in the series of appearances it proceeds to the unconditioned. (571)

I confess defeat: I cannot discover how the Thesis-argument of the third antinomy is supposed to work. We shall see in a moment, however, that this failure is not important.

§ 60. From cosmology to humanity

The Antithesis-argument contends, rather laboriously, that if a given event is not explicable through the causality of nature then we have two successive states of the world of which the latter 'in nowise follows from' the earlier, and this 'renders all unity of experience impossible'. This relies upon Kant's doctrine, which he has defended in the Analytic, that we could not experience a reality which did not completely conform to the causality of nature. Kant is here re-affirming that doctrine and, perhaps wisely, ignoring the Thesis-argument.

The Thesis has said not just that natural causality does not reign supreme, but that there is another kind of causality – that of freedom – in which an event's cause does not precede the event itself. In a second paragraph of Antithesis-argument, Kant says that this is no help. Either the so-called causality of freedom 'abrogates those rules through which

---

[7] 561. Kant's phrase is *absolute Totalität der Bedingungen im Kausalverhältnisse*. I am fairly sure – although my advisers do not enthusiastically support me on this – that Kant means 'absolute totality of conditions [which are] in causal relation [with one another]'. In the third antinomy 'conditions' are causes, and so the phrase means something like 'absolutely complete causal chain'. Kemp Smith's rendering – 'absolute totality of conditions determining causal relation' – is unintelligible to me.

alone a completely coherent experience is possible', or else it does after all involve events' being 'determined in accordance with laws', and in the latter case 'it would not be freedom; it would simply be nature under another name'.

Clearly, Kant is putting all his trust in the Analytic's doctrine that all possible experience – or, in that last curiously weakened formulation, all 'completely coherent experience' – must conform to the causality of nature. The scales are weighted in favour of the Antithesis. It is supported by one of Kant's most deeply-held doctrines, whereas the Thesis-argument is desultory and obscure, and Kant's lack of confidence in it is shown by the fact that he does not allude to it again after its initial statement.

His real concern in this area, however, is less one-sided. His support of the Antithesis has the basis which it seems to have; but his sympathy for the Thesis, judging from his subsequent treatment of the third antinomy, has its roots in a view not about causal sufficiency or the completeness of causal chains or anything of that nature, but rather about human freedom. What really engages Kant's interest in the Thesis is not so much that it 'offers a point of rest to the enquiring understanding in the chain of causes' as that it offers 'a liberation from compulsion'.

Those phrases both occur in the Antithesis-argument, with no comment on the gulf that yawns between them. Throughout the antinomy chapter after Section 2, however, Kant is not juggling two topics at once in his treatments of the third antinomy, for he almost completely ignores the Thesis-argument as stated, concentrating instead on the freedom of 'my thinking self', i.e. on the view that 'the human will is free'.[8] The only exceptions to this are: two brief mentions of 'freedom' with no explicit restriction to the human sphere, the standard too-large/too-small remark, one weak attempt to link the third antinomy with the other three, and a mention and subsequent setting aside of a problem about 'absolute totality'.

Kant does not simply drop the issue with which he began, picking up the problem of human freedom instead. In his 'Observation' on the Thesis, he tries to link the two topics so as to justify his shift from one to the other. The Thesis-argument, he says, has proved that there is causality of freedom in one special case, namely the first event that ever occurred, and since the existence of freedom 'is thereby proved (though not understood)' we are then free to allow that some later

---

[8] 494, 503. The list of 'exceptions': 497 and 509; 516; 533–4; 561 and 571.

events 'within the course of the world' – specifically, human actions – also fall under the causality of freedom (476–8).

One could not be swayed by this even if the Thesis-argument were impeccable. If the concept of freedom solves problems about humans, then why invoke cosmology in its defence? If it cannot satisfactorily solve such problems, how could cosmology rescue it? There is no philosophical justification for leading into human freedom through the Thesis-argument which Kant has given us.

A different link between human freedom and the original antinomy is indicated in a wild passage where Kant implies that in each antinomy the line between Thesis and Antithesis correlates with one between 'practical principles' and theoretical knowledge.[9] This promises to tie the third antinomy in with human freedom, because Kant's interest in freedom is largely practical or moral: 'If our will is not free', he says, '*moral* ideas and principles lose all validity.' However, the alignment of Thesis/Antithesis with practical/theoretical is totally baseless. Kant tries to make it plausible by associating the line with rationalist/empiricist and then illustrating this with Plato/Epicurus, two philosophers who did differ in how devoted they were to moral or practical matters. It would be equally cogent to associate Thesis/Antithesis with Leibniz/ Hume, say, and to describe the antinomy as a clash between German philosophy and Scottish.

In one place Kant asks 'whether I am free in my actions or, like other beings, am led by the hand of nature' (491), implying that *only* humans are free. That is surely nearer to his considered view. Let us now turn our attention solely to human freedom, forgetting Kant's cosmological route into the question. That is what Kant does in his 'Solution' in Section 9, where he spends longer 'solving' the third antinomy than he does on the other three antinomies combined.[10] This is because the preceding sections, just because their main content is cosmological, are irrelevant to the problem of human freedom.

§61. The skeleton of a theory

For reasons which I have not yet presented, Kant thinks that humans exercise something he can fairly call 'the causality of freedom'. The Antithesis, however, re-affirms that whatever happens must fall under

9 500. Next quotation: 496.
10 560–86; see also xxv–xxix. In this section I have mentioned every reference the *Critique* makes to the third antinomy.

the causality of nature which relates events with earlier events. If such causality ever failed, Kant says, we should 'almost entirely' lose 'that connection of appearances determining one another with necessity according to universal laws, which we entitle nature, and with it the criterion of empirical truth' (479). Apart from the uncharacteristic phrase 'almost entirely', this is a position which Kant has defended with vigour and holds to tenaciously. He will not relinquish it even in face of a demand for human freedom.

Instead, he tries to reconcile the existence of a causality of freedom with the universal sway of the causality of nature. This reconciliation rests on the view that every event leads a double life, so to speak. On the one hand, an event is (a) an appearance, an empirical item which is given to the senses and which belongs to the world of time. On the other, it is an appearance of (b) an underlying thing-in-itself, an item which cannot be sensorily given and to which temporal predicates cannot be applied, because time itself is an appearance. Every event in its (a) role is caused by an earlier event (nature), but at least some events in their (b) roles are caused by something other than events and so *a fortiori* by something other than earlier events (freedom).

In this section I want only to introduce Kant's theory of freedom and to explain some of the language it uses. Evaluation will come later.

As we have seen, what a thing is like 'in itself' is to be contrasted with how it 'appears' to us. When Kant allows himself the notion of a thing in itself – as he most generously does in his theory of freedom – he says that although we cannot experience things as they are in themselves, we can have the thought of them. He also contrasts 'phenomena', meaning things which can be experienced, with 'noumena' which can be thought but not experienced. So for our purposes we can treat 'thing-in-itself' and 'noumenon' as interchangeable.

When Kant calls something 'intelligible' he means that it cannot be sensed but can be thought, and so we can safely equate 'intelligible' with 'noumenal'.[11] For example, when he speaks of the 'intelligible cause' of something, he means its cause in the noumenal realm, that is, its cause under the causality of freedom. Analogously, a 'sensible cause' is a cause under the causality of nature.

Kant also speaks of the causality of freedom as 'the causality of reason'. Here is one basis for his doing so:

[Man is] to himself. . .in respect of certain faculties the action of which cannot be ascribed to the receptivity of sensibility, a purely intelligible object. We entitle

[11] See, for example, 566, 568.

these faculties understanding and reason. The latter, in particular, we distinguish in a quite peculiar and especial way from all empirically conditioned powers. (574–5)

This contrast between sensibility and other faculties seems to echo the sensible/intelligible distinction. The point, apparently, is that noumenal causality cannot be experienced but can be thought through understanding and reason, *especially* reason. That is suspicious, though, for it is un-Kantian thus to bracket understanding with reason and then incompletely pull them apart. I think that 'understanding' had no business there in the first place, and that Kant should not have tried to base the phrase 'causality of reason' upon the idea that it is a causality which can be thought but not experienced.

His more considered view is that one needs reason not in order to think about freedom but rather in order to exercise it. The spotlight is – in Kant's words – not upon 'speculative reason, by which we endeavour *to explain* [actions]' but rather upon 'reason in so far as it is itself the cause *producing* them'.[12] This introduces *practical reason*, which is just our one and only faculty of reason in its application to moral or practical problems. The details don't matter now, just the bald fact: Kant believes that practical reason is a source of moral judgments, and he equates an action's arising from a moral judgment issued by reason with its falling under free or intelligible or noumenal causality. He sometimes even regards reason itself as noumenal, as though human actions were the appearances of a noumenal reality which consisted in the (atemporal?) activities of practical reason.

The causality of freedom is also called 'the causality of our will', because whenever it is exercised the will is involved. In Beck's words: 'Will is the faculty of acting according to a conception of *law*, which is...a product or discovery...of reason.'[13] One should not, however, have the three-part picture: *reason* acts on the *will* which produces the empirical *action*; for although Kant 'often confuses the reader by speaking of reason as the determiner of the will', he really 'identifies will with practical reason'. That is why he speaks of reason in terms which seem rather to suit the will, namely as a 'cause' which 'produces' actions. One upshot of the identification of will with practical reason is that Kant treats the will, also, as a noumenal item which lies outside time and beyond the reach of empirical inquiry.

One final technicality must be explained, namely the phrases 'in-

---

[12] 578. On the two uses of reason, see 661, and *Practical Reason*, pp. 47–51.
[13] *Ibid.* p. 38. Next quotation: *ibid.* p. 39.

telligible character' and 'empirical character'.[14] How natural causes act upon something depends upon its empirical character, or what it is empirically like; and so, analogously, how noumenal causes act upon it depends upon its intelligible character, or what it is like 'in itself'. The phrase 'intelligible character' fills an otherwise empty place in the theory of noumenal causality, but it fills it only with words. We cannot even conjecture about anything's intelligible character, for that would involve conjecturally applying concepts to it, and we have no concepts for noumenal items. When Kant admits that 'we can have only a general concept of [the intelligible] character' of someone, he is still claiming too much, but I shan't press that point here as it involves evaluation of the theory.

There is a fundamental uncertainty about the theory: is an instance of the causality of freedom to be thought of as *angular* or as *linear*? If it is angular, then we have

$$\text{appearance of } y$$
$$\uparrow$$
$$\text{noumenal cause } x \rightarrow \text{noumenal effect } y$$

where the horizontal arrow expresses the causality of freedom and the vertical one expresses the 'appearance of' relation. On that account, an event has a noumenal cause only at second hand, by being an appearance of something which has a noumenal cause. If Kant were to distinguish will from practical reason, he might have an angular theory, with some fact about reason in the role of x, and some fact about the will as y.

If the situation is linear, on the other hand, all we have is

$$\text{appearance of } y$$
$$\uparrow$$
$$\text{noumenal item } y$$

with the vertical arrow representing both the 'appearance of' relation and the causality of freedom. In this version, an event's noumenal cause *is* the item of which it is an appearance. This linear version is strongly suggested by an episode when Kant, speaking of empirical events, says: 'They must themselves have grounds which are not appearances. The effects of such an intelligible cause appear...etc.' (565). That seems clearly to cast the same noumenal item in both roles – as the 'ground' of which the event is an appearance, and as the 'intelligible cause' of the event – and so it expresses the linear rather than the angular picture. I shall return to this point later.

[14] See 567. Quotation at end of this paragraph: 569.

§ 62. A reconciliation?

We now have before us the outlines of a theory which offers to reconcile 'freedom' in a certain sense with the universal sway of natural causality – or 'determinism', as I shall now say. The central idea is that of two causes 'referring to one and the same effect'.[15] Of a noumenal cause, Kant says: 'Regarded as the causality of a thing in itself, it is *intelligible* in its *action*; regarded as the causality of an appearance in the world of sense, it is *sensible* in its *effects*.' There is no risk of a clash, because:

> While the effects are to be found in the series of empirical conditions, the intelligible cause, together with its causality, is outside the series. Thus the effect may be regarded as free in respect of its intelligible cause, and at the same time in respect of appearances as resulting from them according to the necessity of nature.

That is the reconciling endeavour in a nutshell: the two sorts of causality cannot conflict because they cannot meet. One is confined to the empirical realm, whereas the other is banned from it.

Let us glance back at the original antinomy. The demand of the Antithesis is met by this reconciling theory. Kant's defence of natural causality, in the Analytic, is restricted to the phenomenal realm, because it argues that something must be causally determined if we are to apprehend it. Apart from that, the very notion of 'causality of nature' involves that of temporal priority, and thus of time, and thus – according to Kant – of appearances. So whatever pressures there are behind the Antithesis meet no obstacle from Kant's reconciling theory.

The situation regarding the Thesis is less clear. It is true that the reconciling theory does *prima facie* satisfy the Thesis itself, for the latter says only that there is a causality of freedom as well as one of nature. The theory also satisfies two formulations which occur in the Thesis-argument – one objecting to the view that 'everything takes place solely in accordance with laws of nature' and one rejecting the view that 'no causality is possible save in accordance with laws of nature'. But the core of the Thesis-argument, although I do not understand it, seems to rest on an objection to the view that everything is caused under the causality of nature, whether or not it is caused in some other way as well. Certainly, that is true of it on the interpretation of Schopenhauer and Kemp Smith and Ewing, as well as on the different interpretation(s)

---

[15] 566. Next two quotations: *ibid.* 565. In the paragraph on 572, and again briefly on 580, Kant implies that intelligible causality produces or mediates natural causality; but this – of which I can make nothing – seems not to be his considered view.

of Beck and Strawson. Furthermore, Kant seems to think that he is illustrating the Thesis when, in the course of his 'Observation' on it, he speaks of the possibility of doing something 'in complete freedom, without being necessarily determined thereto by the influence of natural causes' (478), which surely demands more than the reconciling theory will allow.

So Kant's final theory does not, after all, honour whatever it was that was being urged in the argument for the Thesis of the third antinomy. That is further evidence of that argument's irrelevance to his serious concerns. Whether the reconciling theory achieves his real purpose is, of course, something that cannot be assessed until we know what that purpose is, i.e. what he is saying about human freedom. Still, even without knowing that, we can see that his theory has the abstract form of a reconciliation between determinism and something that might be called freedom.

What a price is paid for the reconciliation! It is of the essence of this theory that freedom pertains to the noumenal world, so that Kant can say: 'The inevitable consequence of obstinately insisting upon the reality of [the empirical world] is to destroy all freedom' (565). In saying that the given world is ideal or is not (transcendentally) real, Kant is not now emphasizing the sense-based nature of all our concepts, but is rather, like Leibniz, claiming that underlying the given world there is something more real. This claim is worse than merely dubious. If Kant is right that thinking involves concepts and that these are tools for the orderly management of intuitions, then the theory of noumenal freedom does not even make sense.

Right at the end of his treatment of freedom, Kant is modest about his theory: 'Our problem was this only: whether freedom and natural necessity can exist without conflict in one and the same action.'[16] In the Introduction to B, he is also careful to set his sights low: 'Though I cannot *know*, I can yet *think* freedom; that is to say, the representation of it is at least not self-contradictory.' This is too modest altogether. The doctrine that there is noumenal freedom could be consistent with itself and with determinism merely by being vacuous. One suspects that if Kant has achieved consistency in his reconciling theory, that is only because one half of it has no real content.

[16] 585. Next quotation: xxviii. G. Bird, *Kant's Theory of Knowledge* (London, 1962), pp. 193-8, denies that Kant's theory of freedom requires that there be noumena. According to Bird, a certain problem about freedom is solved by Kant's minimal claim that the representation of freedom is 'at least not self-contradictory'; but I have not grasped what that problem is. See also Kant, xxix.

In fact, Kant wants far more than the mere absence of self-contradiction. The freedom he postulates has to play certain roles in the description of the human condition. These, we shall find, require that freedom be driven out of its noumenal isolation into the empirical realm where it conflicts after all with determinism.

The roles to which I have referred are two in number. One of them, which dominates most of the commentaries on Kant's theory of freedom, will be my topic in §§63–7 below; the other will occupy §§68–70. No doubt the former was uppermost in Kant's mind; but the latter also shows up in his text, and it is worth considering because it shows Kant's theory of freedom to much better advantage than does the role which is usually assigned to it.

§63. Hume and Schlick

A person is often held accountable for things he does. This can be seen in his being praised, blamed, punished, rewarded, contemned, admired, for things he does. It is sometimes thought that none of these is appropriate in respect of an action which arose purely from natural causes, from which it is inferred that if determinism is true, i.e. if every event has a natural cause, then no one is accountable for any of his actions.

One of the two principal aims of Kant's theory of freedom is to justify moral accountability in the face of this threat from determinism, not by denying determinism but by providing a reconciliation.

It will help to set Kant's endeavour in perspective if we look first at two other reconciling endeavours, namely those of Hume and Schlick. These have a common feature which is not shared by Kant's theory. Each of them tries to reconcile accountability with determinism by drawing the line around accountable actions – ones for which the agent may be blamed etc. – in a manner which implies that someone's being accountable for an action positively requires that the action was naturally caused. For both Hume and Schlick, the question of whether there is accountability in a given case depends upon *what* natural cause the action had. The two theories differ in that Hume tries conservatively to rationalize the traditional notion of accountability and all that goes with it, whereas Schlick is more radical: he is prepared to relinquish accountability as ordinarily understood, rescuing only one part of it, or (on a different view) replacing it by something which resembles it in certain ways.

According to Hume, 'The only proper object of hatred or vengeance

FREEDOM

is a person...endowed with thought and consciousness', so that if an *action* is to be condemned it must be because of its 'relation to the person' who performed it. [17] From this he infers that however bad an action may be, 'the person is not answerable for [it]' unless it 'proceeded from [something] in him that is durable and constant', which is to say that it arose from his 'whole character'. Hume is arguing that judgments of accountability require that actions be causally determined, but he also uses these materials to explain the line we draw between actions for which the agent is accountable and ones for which he is not: 'Men are not blamed for such actions as they perform ignorantly and casually, . . . because the principles of these actions are only momentary, and terminate in them alone.'

Hume's theory mislocates the line we ordinarily draw. We do sometimes hold people accountable for actions performed 'casually' or impulsively, with no deep roots in their character; and on the other hand we do allow that someone's 'whole character', the 'durable and constant' aspects of him, might be so disabling or abnormal that we should not hold him accountable for what he does as a result of it.

That, as it stands, is a matter of detail, but it is arguable that no theory along the lines of Hume's can succeed. Can we regard anyone as a 'proper object of hatred or vengeance' in respect of an action which we consciously and steadily view as having arisen wholly from natural causes? Kant thought not. He was deeply conscious of the tension between determinism and accountability. Faced with Hume's theory, he would have said that someone cannot be a proper object of hatred or vengeance – or for that matter of moral admiration or esteem – because of features of him which he has as a result of purely natural causal processes. His central objection to the line Hume draws would be that it is an empirical line: which side of it an action falls on depends upon empirical features of the action, and therefore (according to Kant as well as Hume) on features which are wholly naturally caused. Whether Kant's own theory does better than Hume's remains to be seen.

A different kind of empirical line is drawn by what I shall call 'the Schlick theory'. The first theory of this kind was presented by Moritz Schlick, I believe, but my concern is less with the details of what he said than with the best theory we can devise along the same general lines. [18]

[17] *An Enquiry Concerning Human Understanding*, Section VIII, § 76 of the Selby-Bigge edition (Oxford, 1902); see also *Treatise*, pp. 410–12.
[18] See M. Schlick, *The Problems of Ethics* (trans. D. Rynin, New York, 1939), Ch. 7, especially § 5.

The Schlick theory stresses the question of how we can alter the like-lihood that a given sort of action will recur, and it makes that question dominant in arriving at judgments using the language of accountability. The idea is that we treat someone as accountable for a given action if, and only if, we think that the chance of his doing it again may be raised or lowered by the sort of 'therapy' which depends upon inducements or threats. I shall call it 'the therapy of moral sanctions', and I take it to include the whole range of rewards and punishments in so far as they can be seen as therapeutic, and to include also various statements and gestures and expressions of feeling, evidences of the withdrawal of love, and so on. All of these, viewed as therapy, have in common that they try to modify future behaviour by introducing new conditionals – 'If I do this, then...' – into the decision-making procedure. They are to be contrasted with brain-surgery, psycho-analysis, aversion therapy, and many other ways of trying to modify behaviour. The procedures I include under 'therapy of moral sanctions' are a rather mixed bag, but we do usually suppose that they have something important in common.

Like Hume's account, the Schlick theory can easily allow that an action for which someone is accountable was causally determined. In-deed, it almost insists on this, for the question of how best to alter the chances of recurrence of similar actions is intimately linked with the question of how the original action was caused. Furthermore, the Schlick theory is more accurate than Hume's in its placing of the line around accountable actions. For example, it deems a person not ac-countable for an action if (a) he would have performed it even if he had decided or chosen not to, or if (b) his decision to perform it arose from some aspect of him which was beyond the reach of moral pressures, e.g. because of mental illness.

The Schlick theory is sometimes accused of infringing the principle – which happens to be a Kantian one – that one should always treat people as ends, never as means. The charge is unfair. According to the theory, how we are to treat someone in respect of a given action is to be settled teleologically, but that does not imply that we should try to make the person conformist or docile or profitable to ourselves at no matter what cost in pain or deprivation or other harm to him. The Schlick theory could allow that the welfare of the agent himself is always the dominant consideration, or even that it is the only con-sideration.

Kant also has a doctrine that we should never settle moral questions

this goes with obligation.

teleologically, deciding how to behave by considering what conduct will lead to what results; and this does clash with the Schlick theory. I doubt that Kant really holds to this strange doctrine, but if he does we shall not join him. If we are to be enlisted against the Schlick theory, it must be on better grounds than that.

It may be objected that when people engage in the language and conduct associated with moral accountability, they do not see themselves as merely applying therapies. The Schlick theorist might accept this, and say that he is merely offering a salvage which explains the intelligible content of our notion of accountability; to which he could add that the belief that moral sanctions are not merely therapeutic is incoherent – part of the dross in common thinking which his theory does not even try to legitimize. He would probably have to admit that that belief, even if it is incoherent, is needed for the effectiveness of such milder therapies as expressions of approval and disapproval, though not for imprisonment or torture or financial reward. It seems likely that the effect upon someone of our condemnation of him for some action will depend upon his taking our words to express 'genuine moral condemnation', rather than thinking that we are using moral language as a 'treatment' which aims to reduce the chance of his acting like that in the future. Still, a Schlick theorist might just accept that result. 'I don't say that moral sanctions are a good or reliable or durable type of therapy', he might say, 'but merely that in so far as they are intelligible at all it is as therapy.'

In giving the Schlick theorist that reply, I am taking his theory as one which jettisons the notion of *objective desert* and all questions about whether it is *right* or *proper* or *fair* for someone to be held accountable for an action. That is why I introduced the Schlick theory as an attempt to rescue only a part of the ordinary notion of accountability, or as an attempt to replace that notion by a different though related one. Its aims in this regard are quite different from Hume's. Hume does comment on the 'influence on the mind' of 'rewards and punishments', but his theory of accountability is not based upon therapeutic considerations – as his reference to the 'proper object of hatred or vengeance' clearly shows.

At this point, Kant's dissent from the Schlick theory would be sharp and total, for he would not consider giving up the notions traditionally associated with accountability, or subjecting them to reductive treatment of the sort proposed by the Schlick theory.

The question arises as to whether the full-blooded traditional notion of accountability, complete with such ancillaries as objective desert, can be rescued without implying that some actions are not completely naturally caused. Let us look at Kant's attempted rescue.

§ 64. Restricting determinism

Kant's phrase 'causality of freedom' embodies his view that freedom is an active source of events:

Freedom ought not...to be conceived only negatively as independence of empirical conditions. The faculty of reason, so regarded, would cease to be a cause of appearances. It must also be described in positive terms, as the power of originating a series of events. (581–2)

This seems to concede that one of the things freedom involves *is* 'independence of empirical conditions', suggesting that an action which is due to freedom is not after all naturally caused. This is by no means the only place where Kant deserts his reconciling theory by implicitly allowing that freedom can interfere with – or at least fill a gap left by – natural causality. Here, for instance:

Sometimes...we find, or at least believe that we find, that the ideas of reason have in actual fact proved their causality in respect of the actions of men, as appearances; and that these actions have taken place, not because they were determined by empirical causes, but because they were determined by grounds of reason. (578)

Notice that Kant does not say 'not *only* because they were determined' etc., but 'not because' etc., implying that those actions do not have empirical causes. He says only that we 'believe that we find' such actions, but he stops short of saying, as he is committed to, that this belief of ours is false.

One can understand Kant's drifting into this betrayal of his official theory about noumenal freedom as co-existing with a phenomenal realm which is entirely governed by natural causality. One source of pressure towards his doing so is just the difficulty, noted earlier, of taking someone to be a 'proper object of hatred' or the like while ✓ viewing his actions as wholly naturally caused. All through his discussion of freedom, even back in the third antinomy itself, Kant tends to confuse (a) 'We have a difficulty if there is only natural causality' with (b) 'We have a difficulty if everything falls under natural causality'. For example, he casually runs them together in the conditional: 'If [a] all causality in the sensible world were mere nature, [b] every event

199

would be determined by another in time' (562). His reconciling theory might help with difficulties of kind (a), if there were any, but the evident difficulty about accountability is of kind (b) – it stems from the hypothesis that natural determinism is true – and so the reconciling theory does not help to solve it. If accountability is threatened by the hypothesis that natural causality has everything in its icy grip, then it does not help to suppose that the causality of freedom *also* has a grip on actions. What is needed is to make natural causality unclutch. And so we find Kant quietly construing freedom as being in competition with natural causality.

That point can be stated more abstractly. Kant wants the so-called causality of freedom to be a 'power of originating a series of events' (582). That requires that freedom leave its mark on the world of events, making a difference to what occurs in that world, and that in turn implies that natural causality cannot entirely determine which events occur. We repeatedly find Kant trying to have it both ways: freedom *affects* the world of events, and yet what happens in that world is just what would have happened if there had been only natural causality. Thus:

> Practical freedom presupposes that although something has not happened, it *ought* to have happened, and that its [prior, natural] cause...is not...so determining that it excludes a causality of our will – a causality which, independently of those natural causes, and even contrary to their force and influence, can produce something that is determined in the time-order in accordance with empirical laws, and which can therefore begin a series of events *entirely of itself.* (562)

The phrase 'contrary to their force and influence' strongly suggests that even when natural causes would impel a man to do something, he might nevertheless be led through noumenal freedom to do something else instead. Then Kant takes it back, saying that what the man does is 'determined in the time-order' etc., meaning that it is after all naturally caused. Freedom, then, is idle.

Kant's dilemma can also be seen in his famous defence of the autonomy of freedom as something which is quite separate from the natural causal order, rather than being a special case within it, like accountability in the theories of Hume and Schlick. Kant is discussing the case of a malicious lie:

> Our blame is based on a law of reason whereby we regard reason as a cause that irrespective of all the...empirical conditions could have determined, and ought to have determined, the agent to act otherwise. This causality of reason we do not regard as a merely co-operating agency, but as complete in itself, even when the

sensuous impulses...are directly opposed to it; the action is ascribed to the agent's intelligible character; in the moment when he utters the lie, the guilt is entirely his. Reason, irrespective of all empirical conditions of the act, is completely free, and the lie is entirely due to its default. (583)

Freedom is said to be 'complete in itself' because we can say that something ought to have happened, whether or not it did. But notice that in the case as Kant presents it, the agent *does* tell the lie, and his doing so is presumably the result of natural causes. Freedom's autonomy has been purchased at the price of its being rendered irrelevant to what actually happens. There seems to be no content left to the notion of a *causality* of freedom. Or do those 'sensuous impulses' which 'are directly opposed' to the telling of the lie include *all* the natural-causal factors? If so, then the lie is not naturally caused; and freedom could be the sole cause of the lie, and thus not be idle after all. On that reading, though, Kant's determinism is betrayed, and there is no reconciliation.

§ 65. When does freedom occur?

There is a still deeper and more abstract way of bringing out the fundamental difficulty confronting Kant's theory. According to the theory, it can be right to hold someone accountable for an action because it somehow involved freedom. Let us hold the theory to just that minimum. We shall not inquire into *how* freedom justifies judgments of accountability, and so we shall say nothing about any threat from determinism, or about the need for freedom to be operative or to have a power to originate events or the like. All we are saying is that there is accountability where, and only where, there is freedom. Add to that something which any viable theory of accountability must surely admit, namely that some events are fit subjects for judgments of accountability and some are not, and that we can sometimes tell which are which. These sparse materials are enough to bring Kant's theory to the ground. The reason is obvious: the noumenal nature of freedom, according to the theory, implies that there can be no empirical evidence as to when freedom is present and when it is not.

Kant sometimes implies the contrary. He says of a certain action that 'we endeavour to discover the motives to which it has been due' and that then 'in the light of these, we proceed to determine how far the action...can be imputed to the offender' (582). But if imputability involves freedom, then the latter cannot be assessed in this way -- or not if Kant's theory of freedom is right. If freedom is noumenal, and if the phenomenal realm is always explicable without reference to freedom, then we cannot have empirical evidence for or against any claim about the presence of freedom in a given case.

In one place, Kant concedes as much:

> The real morality of actions...remains entirely hidden from us. Our imputations can refer only to the empirical character. How much of this character is ascribable to the pure effect of freedom, how much to mere nature...can never be determined; and upon it therefore no perfectly just judgments can be passed. (579n.)

This again allows freedom to encroach onto the territory of natural causality; but even with that license the theory of freedom remains obstinately idle, because we cannot discover where or to what extent the encroachment is taking place. To say that 'perfectly just judgments' cannot be made is to understate the case. In fact, we can have no grounds for believing that any judgment of accountability has any justice at all. For example, on Kant's theory we cannot rule out the hypothesis that freedom is always associated with deep psychosis and is never exercised by those who seem – judging by their empirical character – to be stable, responsible and reflective. Rather than supporting the ordinary notion of moral responsibility, Kant's theory abolishes it.

On the linear version of the theory (see §61 above), in which y's free cause is just the thing-in-itself of which y is an appearance, the problem is even worse. For then every human action, since it is the appearance of something noumenal, must involve freedom – and not just our deliberate actions but also our breathing and the beating of our hearts. This would abundantly justify Beck's remark that Kant's theory 'seems to justify the concept of freedom, if anywhere, then everywhere', so that what it yields is 'not what is meant by freedom in any interesting sense, because it is indiscriminately universal'.[19]

Objection: 'That is unfair, because Kant says that freedom involves *reason*, which is surely not involved in rainfall or heartbeats or the actions of the insane.' That presupposes that we know what 'reason' means in this context, but we do not. Kant sometimes contrasts reason with 'sensuous impulses', implying that reason involves proceeding in an unimpulsive, principled, reflective manner.[20] That cannot be what 'reason' means in Kant's theory of freedom, however. Someone who reflects and weighs principles etc. does so at a certain time, because of natural causes, whereas the province of 'reason' is supposed to escape

---

[19] *Practical Reason*, p. 188. Beck has one reason for this claim which is different from anything I have discussed.　　[20] See, for example, 561–2 and 583.

the clutches of natural causality. The normal manageable use of 'reason', in which it is plausible to say that moral accountability requires reason, is a use which operates *within* the phenomenal realm, and so it cannot bear upon 'reason' in the sense of Kant's theory. Kant tends to write as though all the natural causes that could act upon someone were sensuous impulses. That enables him to glide across from (a) a faculty which is contrasted with 'sensuous impulses' properly so-called, to (b) one which is contrasted with all natural causes, which is a glide from (a) an empirical aspect of the natural man across to (b) something which is empirically inaccessible – and therefore useless.

How far a man exercises 'reason', in the sense of Kant's theory, depends upon his 'intelligible character'; for the theory has it that free causality is a function of intelligible character just as natural causality is of empirical character. The trouble is that 'intelligible character' is also empty, as Kant nearly admits:

The transcendental subject...is empirically unknown to us. This intelligible ground does not have to be considered in empirical enquiries; it concerns only thought in the pure understanding; and although the effects of [it] are to be met with in the appearances, these appearances must nonetheless be capable of complete causal explanation in terms of other appearances in accordance with natural laws.[21]

The meaning of this is not clear, but it does clearly imply that 'intelligible character' has no empirical cash-value, and so, one would think, cannot help us in our intellectual handling of the given. Sometimes, however, Kant shrinks from letting 'intelligible character' be entirely insulated from phenomena, as when he says: 'This intelligible character can never...be immediately known, for nothing can be perceived except in so far as it appears. It would have to be *thought* in conformity with [*gemäß*] the empirical character.' This tries to play safe by saying that we can get at the intelligible character only indirectly, by thinking and not by experience. But in conceding that some ways of thinking about it are more 'in conformity with' the empirical character than others, Kant allows the intelligible character to seep through into the phenomenal realm, thus compromising its status as noumenal. The floodgates are opened here: 'The transcendental cause of their empirical character [is] completely unknown, save in so far as the empirical serves for its sensible sign.' Kant should not allow that any fact about x's empirical character is a 'sign' of some fact about that character's 'transcendental cause', i.e. about x's intelligible character.

[21] 573–4; see also 585. Next two quotations: 568; 574; see also 577.

In short, we are simply given no content for 'intelligible character', and so we have none for 'reason' or for 'freedom'. As Beck says, the presence of Kantian freedom 'is not shown...by appealing to...empirically observed relative independence from outward stimuli and inward impulse through the exercise of intelligent foresight';[22] for anything of that kind is a natural happening, with a natural cause. Strawson puts the defect of Kant's theory in a nutshell when he speaks of our inability to establish 'a point of contact, in the way of identity, between a man as a natural being and himself as a supersensible being'. Kant may say that the natural man is an appearance of the supersensible or noumenal being, but that 'point of contact' is purely formal, a theorem in a vacuous theory. What is needed is a point – or rather a *channel* – of contact through which enough material can flow for statements about the noumenal man to help us to understand, describe, assess or evaluate the natural man. That is what Kant cannot allow.

§ 66. Reactive attitudes

Would Kant avoid all these difficulties if he dropped the determinist hypothesis? No; because the difficulties which seem to be created for accountability by determinism are not significantly lessened if we suppose that determinism is false. This is a familiar enough claim, and I shall not try to justify it here though later I shall explain it.

'If the traditional notions of desert, blameworthiness, etc. cannot be squared with determinism or with indeterminism, then those notions must contain some internal logical defect.' We shall see later that this, though plausible, is not quite right, for the particular way in which accountability quarrels with both determinism and indeterminism leaves open the possibility that there is nothing wrong with accountability itself. Yet I am inclined to think that the cluster of notions conventionally associated with accountability *is* internally defective, and that the most we should seek is a maximal consistent salvage from that cluster.

The Schlick theory purports to give such a salvage, and it is acceptable as far as it goes, but I shall argue in this section that the Schlick theory is radically incomplete. Although the argument will not tend to rescue the whole of the traditional accountability cluster – e.g. the idea of objective desert – I believe that it will illuminate Kant's rescue-attempt. The argument owes all its materials and most of its structures

22 *Practical Reason*, p. 194. Next quotation: *Bounds of Sense*, p. 248.

to a piece of work of Strawson's.[23] Still, some of the details are my own, and I am not even sure that Strawson would agree with them.

The Schlick theory allows only for a teleological or practical view of one's fellow men. When someone does something which I favour or oppose, the Schlick theory has me confronting the agent, scrutinizing him, and considering how to raise or lower the chances of his acting like that again. Strawson speaks of 'the objective attitude', but I prefer to call it the practical or teleological concern. It involves objectivity, because I cannot know how to encourage or discourage similar actions unless I know why that one occurred, and so I must view it objectively and get the facts about it. But its involving the teleological thought, 'What am I to do about this in order to produce the best result?', is in my view the essence of it.

There is a large aspect of interpersonal relations which the Schlick theory ignores; for when someone acts in a way I favour or oppose, my concern with his action, even though not involving any such moral notion as that of desert, may nevertheless be of a radically non-teleological kind. For example, I may *resent* what he did. This says more than merely that I dislike or regret it, but it implies nothing about any practical concern. Resentment, like gratitude, looks back at the action, not forward to possible recurrences.

Resentment is just one example from a whole range of 'natural human reactions to the good or ill will or indifference of others towards us, as displayed in *their* attitudes and actions'.[24] These reactions, which Strawson calls 'reactive attitudes', include 'resentment, gratitude, forgiveness, anger, [and] the sort of love which two adults can sometimes be said to feel...for each other'.

Clearly, a large component in any reactive attitude is a kind of feeling, but beliefs are also involved. For example, if I resent an action of yours I must believe that it manifested a certain indifference or hostility towards me. The link between the feeling and the belief is not merely semantic: resentment is not just a certain feeling accompanied by a certain belief, the two being connected only in that if they were not both present 'resentment' would be the wrong word. If it were, then we could coin the term 'resentment*' defined as 'the sort of feeling that occurs in resentment, without the associated belief', and we could make sense of the idea of feeling resentment* towards the weather or the

23 P. F. Strawson, 'Freedom and Resentment', in P. F. Strawson (ed.), *Studies in the Philosophy of Thought and Action* (Oxford, 1968).

24 *Ibid.* p. 80. Next quotation: *ibid.* p. 79.

behaviour of small babies. No feeling could answer to this account of resentment*. I have no explanation for this non-semantic link between feeling and belief.

As Strawson clearly implies, the principal belief-component in any reactive attitude of x towards y is some belief about some attitude which y has taken towards x – in Strawson's words, an attitude of 'good or ill will or indifference'. It follows that one cannot adopt reactive attitudes towards items which one does not think are capable of goodwill to-wards one. As Strawson points out, it goes further than that. The back-ground to any reactive attitude, at least in a mature person, must be the belief that the object of the attitude is someone with whom one does or could have an adult human relationship on equal terms. So a mature person will wish not to have reactive attitudes towards anyone whom he does not believe to be sane and emotionally healthy and not an infant. For example, if someone's ill-will towards me is a direct product of mental illness, I *could* resent it but I should try not to, because I judge that in such a case I ought not to mind about the person's attitude to me. I may well mind very much about his mental illness, but that 'minding' generates practical concern, not a reactive attitude.

The area within which a mature person will have reactive attitudes, therefore, approximately coincides with the area in which the Schlick theory offers to justify the use of moral-sanctions therapies. But this does not imply that reactive attitudes are therapies.

That leads to the real complaint against the Schlick theory, which is that it represents the accountable/unaccountable line as having to be understood either (a) in terms of an incoherent notion of objective desert, or (b) as dividing actions according to which therapies would be appropriate. In fact, I contend, it is also a line which (c) divides actions according to whether they are *prima facie* suitable targets for reactive attitudes. The Schlick theory, therefore, seriously misrepresents what we are doing when we distinguish accountable from unaccountable actions.

In respect of an action for which the agent is not responsible in some fairly normal sense, a reactive attitude would be wrong: the proposi-tional content of reactive attitudes conflicts with the facts of the case. In no other cases would a reactive attitude be wrong in that way, though it might be wrong or imprudent for other reasons – e.g. my anger towards a given person might be so painful to me that I ought to try always to replace anger towards him by an attitude of objective inquiry into the causes and possible cures of the things he does which I oppose. Within the class of accountable actions, reactive attitudes are always admissible, and the teleological or practical attitude is also always admissible; and which attitude one adopts on a given occasion may be a matter of mood or of personal style. As I have implied, one might have policies for some kinds of case. Indeed, someone who wanted to keep his emotional warmth under stern control might devise a comprehensive policy and then train himself to abide by it, so that the situations where he adopted reactive attitudes were precisely those in which such attitudes seemed to him, in a quiet hour, to be acceptable. (Even this repellent figure must achieve his ends by emotional training. We cannot suppose that he asks himself, each time, 'Will it do more harm than good if on this occasion I allow myself a reactive attitude?', for that question can be raised only by someone who is already in the practical, teleological frame of mind.) However full a policy one had, though, it would be based upon considerations of whether in certain kinds of case reactive attitudes are bad or harmful, not upon whether they fit the facts.

The simplest policy (not the easiest) would be to eschew reactive attitudes altogether. I agree with Strawson that if this were possible – which it probably is not – the results would be intolerable. Yet the policy has been urged. Spinoza held a view which could be expressed in the form: 'Because the facts always permit the teleological, objective attitude, they always forbid reactive attitudes.' Strawson's work, I suggest, enables us to explain Spinoza's mistake.

Strawson speaks of a profound opposition between reactive attitudes and the objective attitude, and I think there is a truth in this. It seems to be impossible for anyone at a single time to view a given action (person) both as a complex natural event (object) whose various aspects fit it into the causal world in a certain way, and as a subject for reactive attitudes.

There are two possible explanations for this. (1) Viewing someone as a natural object involves seeing him as an analysed complex, whereas taking a reactive attitude to him seems to involve seeing him as a unitary whole – though I do not fully understand why this should be so.[25] (2) One's reactive attitudes, I suggest, refer essentially to oneself. A significant difference between my regretting your action and my resenting it is that in the latter case I care that you acted in that way towards *me* – not simply to someone to whom you had certain relationships, but to *me*. Bonnelle Johnson has pointed out to me that this

[25] Here I follow R. E. Hobart, 'Free Will as Involving Determination and Inconceivable Without It', *Mind* (1934), p. 14.

might explain the tension between reactive and objective attitudes. If I resent or am grateful for what you did, I have a picture in which *I* loom very large, as victim or as beneficiary; whereas if my attitude to your action is an objective one, my picture of the situation will not be dominated by myself, except perhaps in the role – which is only accidentally *mine* – of someone to whom you relate in such and such ways.

Anyway, reactive and objective attitudes do conflict psychologically, and that fact has explanatory value. Presumably, Spinoza noticed that a clear view of *x* as a natural object or event would not cohabit in his mind with a reactive attitude towards *x*, and he wrongly thought that this was a propositional conflict; from which he inferred that because everything is a natural object or event, reactive attitudes are infected with falsity. He was helped in this direction by the fact that instead of 'reactive attitudes' he spoke instead of 'freedom' and of 'blame' and the like.

We can also explain, now, the puzzling fact that although the notions of responsibility and of objective desert etc. seem to be in tension with determinism, the pressure is not relieved if we suppose that determinism is false. It seems no more just to blame a man for an action which was due to a random movement of a sub-atomic particle than to blame him for something arising from fully determined circumstances over which he had no control. The original trouble was not really with determinism at all, but rather – I contend – with the objective, analytical frame of mind in which the person is seen piecemeal as a causally complex natural object. The real tension is that between reactive attitudes and the frame of mind in which the question arises as to whether actions are fully determined or not.

Someone who has not seen this, and who is not prepared with Spinoza to jettison everything that goes with reactive attitudes, will argue contrapositively: because reactive attitudes are sometimes permissible (or because there is freedom, or because people sometimes really deserve praise or blame), the objective attitude must sometimes be impermissible. That generates the thought that reactive attitudes etc. are permissible only when the agent or his action is not a purely natural object or event which could be viewed objectively and with a purely teleological concern. That in turn leads to the conclusion that reactive attitudes are appropriate only where there is something non-natural going on, something non-empirical which resists being considered in a purely practical or teleological way. A touch of noumenal freedom, perhaps?

Which brings us back to Kant.

§67. Kant and reactivity

Kant and Strawson both start from the insight that there is something valuable in human relationships additional to any sort of teleological concern, however sensitive. Furthermore, both try to describe the extra element without denying that one *can* truthfully regard any human action as a natural event, with natural causes, which can be subjected to a purely teleological concern. Each of them tries to achieve this by indicating two different ways in which one can relate oneself to a human action.

Furthermore, Strawson could follow Kant in saying that one of the two relationships is that in which 'we are simply *observing*, and... seeking to institute a physiological investigation into the motive causes of his actions'.[26] It is in their accounts of the other relationship – the one which cannot be described in terms of natural causes and the practical or teleological concern – that Kant and Strawson part company. For Strawson, the further element consists in reactive attitudes which are largely matters of *feeling*. Kant, on the other hand, contrasts 'simply observing' with 'consider[ing] these actions in their relation to... reason in so far as it is itself the cause *producing* them'. What he adds to empirical observation is not emotional involvement but rather a kind of non-empirical thinking.

Kant's theory is a failure, and Strawson's judgment on it is just:

> The belief in the supersensible reality is essential to this part of Kant's doctrine... But there will be found few, I think, to regard the ideal of moral justice as an adequate basis for such a belief, or to view the problem of human freedom as demanding, or allowing of, solution with its help.[27]

Reactive attitudes are not mentioned in *The Bounds of Sense*, and Strawson has never explicitly offered his theory about them as a rival to Kant's theory of freedom. I do want to present it in that light.

Kant would protest that reactive attitudes are not important in *morality* except perhaps as something one must take account of and struggle against. This is because he has a doctrine that morality has nothing to do with feelings, and also because he thinks that morality must be expressible in general principles, whereas no general policy could settle every question about whether to adopt reactive attitudes on given occasions.

One might challenge either part of this double position, claiming that morality is rooted in feelings or that it need not be embodied in

---

[26] 578. Next quotation: *ibid.*   [27] *Bounds of Sense*, p. 241.

principles. The better response, though, is just to admit that Strawson's theory is not primarily about any specifically moral notions. Strawson has an interesting theory about moral indignation, which he analyses as a vicarious reactive attitude;[28] but I am not sure what to say about it. It seems to conflict with the essentially egocentric nature of reactive attitudes, to which I alluded in §66, and for that and other reasons I prefer to leave 'vicarious reactive attitudes' out of the position I am sketching. As for the specific notion to which Kant addresses his theory of freedom, namely that of objective desert: Strawson's theory does salvage something from this – perhaps enough to refute the view that 'blame is metaphysical', meaning that the common concept of desert requires the existence of something like noumenal freedom.[29] But I do not think that the main interest of reactive attitudes lies in their role in morality. Furthermore, the salvage is incomplete and, I suggest, uncompletable. The ordinary notion of desert, I contend, does contain something incoherent, something which cannot be honoured by reality; and Kant's theory of freedom fails just because it so resolutely tries to rescue that doomed element in common moral thinking.

Although Kant would, for reasons just implied, deny any significant kinship between his theory and Strawson's, the two do have a certain similarity of aim. Each starts with the insight that in interpersonal relationships there are valuable elements which are not captured by – and are indeed in tension with – any description in terms of empirical observation and understanding, practical concern and caring, trying to act for the best. To make good the lack, Strawson invokes certain kinds of feelings, but Kant could not move in that direction. His hostility to feeling, and, connected with that, his view that what is valuable in human conduct is its relationship to a morality which is principled, non-teleological, and absolutely rooted in some sort of *fact* – all this led him to suppose that since knowledge of the empirical man is not a sufficient basis for the whole story about human relationships, we must introduce knowledge of (or at least thought about) the non-empirical man. Needing to go Strawson's way, he was diverted by his beliefs about the status and nature of morality.

I have compared Kant's theory with Strawson's partly in order to get sympathy for the former, but I do not minimize the extent of its failure. Its location of 'freedom' in the noumenal realm, as well as being deeply objectionable on the general ground that Kant has no proper basis for

[28] Strawson, 'Freedom and Resentment', p. 85.
[29] *Ibid.* pp. 92–5.

saying anything about noumena, also renders the theory irrelevant to our ordinary handling of the notion of responsibility. This is because we do ordinarily draw lines in the light of the empirical facts of the case, whereas no such line could bear upon any question about noumenal freedom. Furthermore, on the linear version of the theory, it positively condemns our normal discriminating procedures, because it entails that everything which we do involves freedom, so that no discriminations on this matter can be correct.

These objections to Kant's theory are familiar enough. What is less often recognized is that the theory can also be seen as addressed to an entirely different problem, and that in this latter role it is much more successful. This will be my topic for the next three sections.

§ 68. Agency

I have assumed throughout that people have *agency*, i.e. the capacity for having practical problems or for deliberating about what to do. The Schlick theory attributes agency to those who make judgments of responsibility, because it depicts them as wondering – and then deciding – how to intervene in certain human situations. The theory also presumes agency in those about whom judgments of responsibility are made, for the core of the theory is that affirmative judgments of accountability are meant to introduce attempts to modify the subject's future exercise of his agency. On any viable theory, one would think, accountability involves agency; and it has been cogently argued that an action for which a person is responsible is essentially one in respect of which the question arose, for that person, of whether to perform it.[30]

Anyway, we do have agency; and our picture of what it involves seems, in ways I shall describe shortly, to be threatened by determinism. Nothing in the theory of reactive attitudes, or in the Schlick theory, even seems to bear upon this new problem. This is evident from the fact that one could exercise agency without ever having, or being subject to, reactive attitudes or judgments of accountability.

I shall argue that Kant's theory of freedom seeks to reconcile

---

[30] D. G. Brown, *Action* (Toronto, 1968), § 4. 5. Brown is not offering a rival to the Schlick theory of responsibility because his target is different. He is concerned with responsibility etc. only in the context of 'the spectator's explanations of human action' (p. 5), and does not discuss its relationship to judgments about desert, blameworthiness and so on. He does relate responsibility to the justifying of actions (p. 116), but not so as to touch the exposed nerve, the point where many people's moral intuitions are offended by determinism.

determinism not just with common intuitions about accountability but also with the usual picture of what agency involves.

What *is* the problem about determinism and agency? It might be thought to be this: 'Determinism seems to imply that our handling of practical problems – our weighing of pros and cons, and our eventual decisions – are mere shadow-boxing, a pretence at affecting a course of events which is really settled by causal considerations over which we have no control.' That is wrong, because the factors which determine how I shall eventually act include my deliberation and decision – the vital point being that I am a part of the natural causal order. Locke came close to saying what needed to be said about this:

Volition or *willing* is an act of the mind directing its thought to the production of any action, and thereby exerting its power to produce it... That which determines the general power of directing, to this or that particular direction, is nothing but the agent itself exercising the power it has that particular way.[31]

Granted that how I act depends upon conditions which obtain before I make my decision, it does not follow that the decision is a mockery or is not truly operative. Analogously, the electric current heats the element, which makes the water boil; and so the electric current suffices, in the circumstances, for the boiling of the water. But of course it makes a difference whether the element heats up or not!

A different threat to agency is this: 'Someone who has a genuine practical problem must regard various alternative courses of action as genuinely open, but if natural determinism is true then all but one of the alternatives is radically closed.' That seems to be Taylor's point when he says: 'One can deliberate whether to do a certain act only if he believes... that it is within his power equally to do it, and to forgo it.'[32] He concludes only that someone who 'knows' that determinism is true cannot deliberate about what to do; but he ought to conclude that someone who believes that determinism is true cannot deliberate, which is clearly false. Still, he might retreat to the safer position that in taking a practical problem seriously one commits oneself to several alternatives' being open; so that if determinism is true then agency is always infected with falsehood, because it implies the openness of something which is really closed. This is not clearly true, however, and its reliance on the metaphors 'open' and 'closed' is unsatisfactory.

[31] *Essay* II. xxi. 28–9; see also Hobart, *op. cit.* pp. 8–11.
[32] R. Taylor, 'Deliberation and Foreknowledge', *American Philosophical Quarterly* (1964), p. 76.

Still, there is a point here. It might be expressed by saying that if determinism is true then someone who knew enough science, and enough about himself, could become unable to exercise agency because he always knew predictively how he was going to act. The assumption here is that if I know predictively that I shall do A, then I cannot wonder whether to do A or decide to do A. That seems to me entirely correct, and I shall not discuss it. It could be objected, all the same, that the above 'threat' to agency is negligible. If there is absolutely no chance of my ever attaining a certain level of knowledge, why should I care about the thought that if I were to attain it that would abolish my agency? Well, I care about it because of what it seems to imply for the agency which I do exercise, namely that my very status as an agent depends upon my ignorance and thus requires me to stand in a bad relation to reality. It also suggests that whenever I approach a practical problem, I should first bring as much self-knowledge as possible to bear, so that the area of ignorance within which my agency is to operate shall be as small and as sharply defined as I can make it. Only then – the suggestion is – should I try to decide what to do.

In fact, though, one does not do this. When wondering what to do, I *may* turn my attention to myself, my limits and capacities and dispositions. But often I proceed without considering such matters. I wonder what to do, decide what to do, and then, perhaps, consider whether after all I have it in me to do it.

Spinoza expounds not only determinism's threat to accountability but also – and in language which is strikingly Kantian – its threat to the common view about agency. Of those who do not see the threat, he says:

They seem indeed to consider man in nature as a kingdom within a kingdom. For they believe that man disturbs rather than follows her order; that he has an absolute power over his own actions; and that he is altogether self-determined.[33]

He also refers scathingly to the popular belief 'that the human mind is not the product of natural causes [and] that it has absolute power of determining itself and of rightly using its reason'. Remarks like these prepare the way for an attack on agency – a recommendation that we relinquish our status as agents or at least see it as a product of ignorance. For example:

A final cause, as it is called, is nothing...but human desire, in so far as this is considered as the principal or primary cause of anything...[A given desire], in so far

[33] *Ethics*, Part III, opening paragraph. Next two quotations: *Tractatus Politicus*, Ch. 2, § 6; *Ethics*, Part IV, Preface.

as it is considered as a final cause, is merely this particular desire, which is really an efficient cause, and is considered as primary, because men are usually ignorant of the causes of their desires.

Spinoza's point is that when I picture myself as deliberating and deciding, wondering what to do and then acting for a reason or 'final cause', really all that occurs is a chain of natural events in a natural organic object. If I knew more, he thinks, I should view the situation in this light myself, seeing my desire as just a stage along the way, and not as in any important sense settling any practical question.

Kant holds the common view of agency, pretty much as Spinoza describes it, and he brings his theory of freedom to the rescue. He thinks that agency involves the noumenal faculty of reason. *That* is why agency can stand on its own feet, so that one is entitled just to consider what to do, rather than first submissively asking what one is causally capable of doing:

Reason does not here follow the order of things as they present themselves in appearance, but frames for itself with perfect spontaneity an order of its own according to ideas, to which it adapts the empirical conditions, and according to which it declares actions to be necessary [sc. morally required], even although they have never taken place, and perhaps never will take place. (576)

It seems clear that one aim of Kant's theory of freedom is to reconcile our assumptions about our agency with the hypothesis that every human action is a causally determined process in a natural object. It should also be clear that the two cannot be reconciled in that way. Kant thinks that what entitles us to frame for ourselves an order of our own is that our (noumenal) reason exercises a sort of causality which (a) operates on the world and (b) is completely independent of natural causality, yet (c) never conflicts with natural causality. That inconsistent triad is no better here than it was in the treatment of accountability. The ways in which Kant's theory of freedom does better with agency than with accountability will appear in §71 below. They do not suffice to rescue it even as a treatment of agency.

§69. Self-prediction

There is a better explanation than Kant's of why we are entitled to frame for ourselves an order of our own. The rival view, that self-observation should come first and occupy as much territory as possible, looks to the limiting case where one knows enough to eschew deliberation altogether and always just to predict what one will do; and it is open to question whether that is even theoretically possible. It relies upon a notion which works quite well in most contexts, namely that of observing an object, gradually learning more about its states and their interconnexions, and thereby moving steadily towards a capacity to predict everything that it does. But if the object in question is oneself – so that the *I* who is to observe and predict is the *I* who is to be observed and made the subject of predictions – the ordinary notion no longer functions in the same way, for now the picture is disturbed by the fact that every discovery one makes automatically alters the state of the object of study.

Ryle has made this point, and infers that there are limits to self-prediction:

A prediction of a deed or a thought is a higher order operation, the performance of which cannot be among the things considered in making the prediction. Yet as the state of mind in which I am just before I do something may make some difference to what I do, it follows that I must overlook at least one of the data relevant to my prediction.[34]

It does not follow that I could never rightly replace deliberation by prediction; for although a change in my state of knowledge or thought 'may make some difference to what I do', there could be cases where I knew that it would not do so. It is therefore wrong to handle this matter in infinite-regress terms: 'To predict what I shall do I must attend to my state, and to my attending, and to my attending to my attending..., etc., so that I can never assemble all the facts which might bear upon my prediction.' There need be no infinite regress; for I might discover that I am *F*, and know that there is a well-established scientific law that whoever is *F* does *A* shortly thereafter (there are no limits to the complexity of what *F* can stand for); and in that case I am entitled to predict that I shall do *A*, and to think that all the facts which I am neglecting are irrelevant to my prediction. But although there can be cases like that, there can also be ones of the other sort, to which Ryle calls attention, where the self-predictor would have to overlook something which was relevant.

That is still not the best way to put it, however. Rather than thinking of someone who is trying to predict what he will do, let us rather ask,

---

[34] G. Ryle, *The Concept of Mind* (London, 1949), p. 197. See also K. R. Popper, 'Indeterminism in Quantum Physics', *British Journal for the Philosophy of Science* (1950), especially pp. 174ff.; and D. M. MacKay, 'On the Logical Indeterminacy of a Free Choice', *Mind* (1960).

of someone who *has* acted, whether and in what circumstances he *could have predicted that action*. Determinism threatens agency mainly by casting an unflattering light on the agency which we do exercise, and that is the angle from which it is best to examine it.

Even if natural determinism is true, the answer to 'Was it in principle possible for x to have predicted his performance of A?' may be No. That much is clearly implied by Ryle, but we need to know more about why it is right. There are in fact two possible justifications for a negative answer, that is, two possible theoretical obstacles to self-prediction.

(1) It could be that the prediction that x would do A required reference to facts about him which he could not have known at the time. This should not be found startling, for there are in fact plenty of truths about anyone which he could not know at the relevant time, namely every truth of the form 'Fx at t' which logically or causally rules out 'x believes or knows or is aware at t that Fx at t'. A trivial example: John is not thinking about giraffes, but as soon as John himself has this in mind, it becomes untrue. Given a rich enough science of the mind and of the brain, we could presumably find values of F such that someone whose brain is F cannot know this, because thinking about anything's being F causally requires having a brain which is not F.

However numerous the facts about x which x could not be aware of at the time, it is a further question how many such facts would be relevant to the prediction of x's actions. For all I know, none would; there seems to be no available evidence either way. So all we have so far extracted from Ryle's approach is an open *possibility* – a reply to anyone who claims that if determinism is true then it follows that all exercises of agency could in principle have been replaced by predictions. That is better than nothing, but in a moment I shall offer to improve on it.

(2) The other possible obstacle to self-prediction is as follows. Suppose that I do A, and that this could have been predicted on the basis that I was F at t, and that it is a scientific law that whoever is F does A shortly thereafter. Now, even if my being F is causally compatible with my *being aware that I am F*, it may not be causally compatible with my *making that prediction* – i.e. noting that I am F *and* thinking of that law *and* confidently concluding that I shall soon do A. This, though still within the ambit of Ryle's remarks, is different from the case where I could not have predicted my doing of A because something in the prediction's basis was unknowable by me.

There is reason to believe that in very many cases of actual action, the second obstacle is present. In support of this, I offer the following argument. In stating it, I shall use 'decide' as a shorthand to cover every sort of exercise of agency – practical deliberation, decisions, choices, and so on.

(a) In many cases, a person acts as he does *because* he decided to act like that – and I here use 'because' with a causal force. This can be disputed, but a good many philosophers accept it, and so an argument built upon it may be worth something. (b) A basis for predicting any such action would have to refer to the agent's deciding, or to events which caused him to decide, or to brain-processes correlated with his deciding. I infer this from (a), on the grounds that a valid prediction must take account of everything which is causally relevant to the predicted event. But something which also seems to be true, and whose falsity would in any case abolish determinism's threat to agency, is the proposition (c) that if someone knows, through a scientifically sound prediction, that he is going to do A, then he cannot decide to A (this being shorthand for 'cannot deliberate or in any other way exercise agency with respect to A').

So there are many cases in which a valid prediction of an action must involve reference to the agent's decision or something causally sufficient for it (b); but the agent's predicting the action is incompatible with his deciding (c); and so the prediction is one which it is not possible even in principle for him to have made.

This is a substantive conclusion, which should not be mistaken for the triviality: 'For me to have predicted A (which in fact I did not predict), things would have to have been different in some ways.' I am not merely spinning out the boring truth that counterfactuals are counterfactual. Because I did not predict the result of our last provincial election, it is true that I could not have predicted it unless things had been different in certain ways. But my predicting it was causally compatible with everything which caused the election to result as it did: we can counterfactualize about my state of knowledge without thereby coming under pressure to counterfactualize about the outcome of the election. In contrast with that, my second-obstacle argument concludes that if an action of mine arose from my deciding, then the supposition that I might have predicted it conflicts causally with certain facts about what caused the action, and thus with facts upon which the prediction would have to have been based. In those cases, I have argued, the attempt to counterfactualize about my predicting leads us to counterfactualize about the action.

Here is a possible rejoinder to my discussion of the two obstacles to self-prediction. 'If some actual actions could not have been predicted by their agents, that itself results from the latter's ignorance. As the relevant kinds of knowledge increase, we shall become increasingly able to predict our own actions and decreasingly able to exercise agency.' I cannot disprove that, but nor can I see any reason to believe it. It depends for its plausibility on something which applies to almost everything except self-prediction. In general, if I have an activity which requires gaps in my knowledge of something, then by filling those gaps I can make that activity impossible for myself – e.g. learning so much about how horses perform that I must forgo the pleasures of guessing on the outcome of horse-races. But where knowledge of myself is in question, the situation changes. It is true that if I have complete self-knowledge I cannot exercise agency. But I cannot destroy my status as an agent merely by learning more and more; I must also become a certain sort of person, namely one whose actions do flow causally from states of himself which he can be aware of and which are causally compatible with his predicting his actions. Would I become such a person if my self-knowledge, and knowledge of the relevant parts of science, approached completeness? I have no idea, and no philosophical arguments help me with the question.

If my second-obstacle argument is wrong, then I have no reason to affirm that the actions I do perform, being the kind of person I now am, are ones which I could not have predicted. But there is no evidence for the contrary view either. The crucial point, which does not rely on the second-obstacle argument, is that the mere possibility of the two obstacles to self-prediction is enough to blunt the edge of determinism's threat to agency, for it suffices to show that determinism does not imply that all our exercises of agency could have been replaced by self-predictions.

§ 70. Kant and agency

The argument of the foregoing section justifies one's confronting practical problems with the question 'What ought I do do?' or 'What am I to do?', without making it subservient to the self-observing, predicting question 'What shall I in fact do?' I have said that Kant also seeks to justify this, and have cited one bit of his text in support of that claim, namely the passage saying that reason 'frames for itself with perfect spontaneity an order of its own' and so on. It is now time to adduce some more evidence.

The best and most Rylean passage, so to speak, is one which occurs only in B:

I cannot determine [i.e. have detailed information about] my existence as that of a self-active being; all that I can do is represent to myself the spontaneity of my thought, that is, of the [act of] determining; and my existence is still determinable only sensibly, that is, as the existence of an appearance. But it is owing to this spontaneity that I entitle myself an *intelligence*.[35]

This concerns the spontaneity of *thought*; but I follow Beck in connecting it with the discussion of freedom of action in the Dialectic. Beck interprets it as claiming 'that we have a direct experience of our own spontaneous activity', and comments: 'Kant never tells us what its epistemic character is, but that it occurs is a fact to which the epistemology of the *Critique of Pure Reason* does scant justice.' I contend that the 'representation' of which Kant speaks is not supposed to involve 'experience' or anything with an 'epistemic character'. What it claims, I suggest, is that I have a use for the term 'I', or a place for myself in my conceptual scheme, which does not involve my being a datum or an observed object, and which is associated with my role as an agent. Kant would go on from there to speak of my knowledge of myself as a noumenon, but one could continue instead with the Rylean account which I gave in §69.

In the Dialectic, Kant does not clearly separate the accountability and agency problems. Early in the discussion he says: 'Practical freedom presupposes that although something has not happened, it *ought* to have happened.'[36] That surely concerns the role of freedom in justifying us in holding someone accountable for not doing something which he ought to have done. Later on, Kant says that freedom is needed if 'ought' is to have meaning, because: 'We cannot say that anything in nature *ought to be* other than what in all these time-relations it actually is. When we have the course of nature alone in view, "*ought*" has no meaning whatsoever.' This is addressed to agency. If there is only the natural realm, it implies, then the whole territory is covered by the facts, already causally determined, about what I shall do – so how can I seriously wonder what to do or what I ought to do? In those two passages, the difference between accountability and agency corresponds to that

---

[35] 158n. Next quotation: *Practical Reason*, pp. 194–5. I am indebted to Beck's work for pointing the way to the 'agency' interpretation of Kant's theory of freedom.

[36] 562. Next quotation: 575. The two paragraphs on 575–6 are the fullest treatment of agency in the Dialectic.

between 'ought to have happened' and 'ought to happen'. I suspect that Kant overlooked it.

In the Preface to B, Kant writes eloquently of the need which 'morality' has for 'freedom as a property of our will'.[37] Is he thinking of morality's demand that people be held accountable for their actions, or of its demand that we take seriously and give a fundamental status to our role as agents? The text does not answer. The two concerns are actually conflated in a passage, already partly quoted, about someone who tells a malicious lie. It is mainly a story about accountability, and a desperately bad one. To start with, in investigating the lie 'we endeavour to discover the motives to which it has been due', and 'in the light of these, we proceed to determine how far the action...can be imputed to the offender.' Yet, at the end, 'in the moment when he utters the lie, the guilt is entirely his', and it is imputable to him 'irrespective of all empirical conditions of the act'. There is a total failure of fit here, and of the two conflicting elements the one which squares with Kant's theory of freedom is not the sensible opening part of the paragraph but rather its wildly absolutist close. Look at how that absolutism is defended:

> Our blame is based on a law of reason whereby we regard reason as a cause that irrespective of all the above-mentioned empirical conditions could have determined, and ought to have determined, the agent to act otherwise. This causality of reason we do not regard as a merely co-operating agency, but as complete in itself, even when the sensuous impulses do not favour but are directly opposed to it.

Taken as the treatment of accountability which Kant thinks it is, this produces a kind of accountability which is, in Beck's phrase, 'indiscriminately universal', for it leads to the conclusion that everyone is entirely accountable for everything he does or undergoes. But if we set aside the opening clause, and replace 'could have and ought to have determined' by something like 'can and ought to determine', the result is a moderately acceptable expression of a view about agency.

Agency is in question when Kant speaks of 'a faculty which is not an object of sensible intuition, but through which [one] can be the cause of appearances';[38] and of 'a faculty which is intelligible only, inasmuch as its determination to action never rests upon empirical conditions, but solely on grounds of understanding'. It is also well to the fore when, just before the quoted remark about the meaning of 'ought' in applica-

[37] xxviii–xxix. The malicious lie: 582–3.   [38] 566. Next two quotations: 573–5.

tion to nature, Kant says: 'That our reason has causality, or that we at least represent it to ourselves as having causality, is evident from the *imperatives* which in all matters of conduct we impose as rules upon our active powers.'

As for how the problem about agency should be solved: the Rylean treatment is along the right lines, I believe, and Kant's theory is not. Still, the two are alike in some significant respects.

For one thing, the Kantian contrast between the exercise of freedom and the role of an observer is preserved in the Rylean account, for the latter turns on the difference between what I may observe and what I can *do*. Of course it does not allow that there is anything noumenal about what I do: all my doings are in principle observable; but for a plain reason they are not all observable, or contemporaneously knowable, by me.

Other aspects of Kant's theory of freedom, also, make sense in the light of the Rylean treatment of agency. For example, Kant says that 'man' is 'to himself a noumenon'. If this is to be even remotely defensible, it must mean not that men in general are noumena to one another, but rather that each man is to himself a noumenon. Although the Rylean treatment makes no use of 'noumenon', it resembles Kant's in giving a weighty and central emphasis to the first-person singular; for it allows that I could be a comprehensively observing predictor of the actions of anybody else, and denies me that role only in relation to my own actions.

Again, Kant insists that the causality of freedom is *effective*, that being part of what makes it a 'causality'. Just after saying that 'reason frames for itself an order of its own' etc., he says: 'And at the same time reason also presupposes that it can have causality in regard to all these actions, since otherwise no empirical effects could be expected from its ideas.'[39] Later, he says that 'freedom' is 'the power of orginating a series of events'. Now, if we see the theory of freedom as an attempt to do what is more successfully done by the Rylean defence of agency against determinism, then we can understand what can be meant by 'having causality' and 'power of originating events' in this context. For when the theory is seen in that light, its subject-matter is ordinary empirical deliberating, and of course that is effective and does 'have causality' – *natural* causality. The exercise of reason, on this construal, is an empirical activity with earlier causes and later effects. Yet it is, for the person concerned, 'independent of empirical conditions' in the sense that he

<hr/>

[39] 576. Next quotation: 581–2.

cannot allow it to defer to empirical self-observation and self-prediction.

Those two points – about the first-person singular, and about the 'power of originating events' – both concern agency. If Kant's theory of freedom is addressed instead to the problem of accountability, it no longer gives special work to the notion of how one is to oneself, and, as we saw earlier, the idea of power or causality becomes idle or mischievous. Those are just two ways in which Kant's theory does better with agency than with accountability. There is also another, which I now explain.

Considered as a theory of accountability, we saw, Kant's theory will not let us draw any usable line around the actions for which the agent is accountable. In drawing such a line, we should have to steer by empirical 'signs', but these ought to be altogether irrelevant to questions about the presence of noumenal freedom. And so Kantian 'freedom' is not genuine freedom because it is indiscriminately universal. Kant himself proclaims the universality: 'Reason is present in all the actions of men at all times and under all circumstances, and is always the same' (584). Construed as an episode in a theory of practical reason, this may escape notice; but since Kant equates the province of reason with that of freedom, he is firmly committed to saying that *freedom* is always present and is 'always the same'. How could anyone propound such a ruinously defective theory of accountability?

Perhaps part of the explanation is that 'indiscriminate universality' is not a defect at all in the theory of *agency*. If someone is worried about the implications for his agency of the determinist hypothesis, the right way to remove the worry – the Rylean treatment, to which Kant's theory may be seen as an approximation – is to say something of a relevantly universal kind. What must be said is that on *any* occasion when agency is exercised, one or other of the two obstacles to self-prediction may be present; and, if my argument of §69 above is right, whenever agency is exercised the second obstacle to self-prediction *is* present. Either way, the problem is dealt with by making a point about all cases of agency. It does not require or admit of any line-drawing solution of the form: 'Some cases of agency are..., whereas others are not.'

§71. Excuses for Kant's theory

Although Kant's theory of freedom is significantly similar to viable treatments of real problems, one about accountability and one about agency, the central stumbling-block remains. How could Kant allow himself this positive doctrinal use of the notion of a noumenon or of an 'intelligible' or 'transcendental' cause? When he writes that freedom 'is a pure transcendental idea', and that it 'contains nothing borrowed from experience, and...refers to an object that cannot be determined or given in any experience' (561), one rubs one's eyes. Has he just forgotten his views about how thought relates to experience?

He has not. Those views are based on something like the following. (1) I cannot make a coherent judgment about something unless I could be epistemically related to it, in the sense of needing to take account of it in my handling of reality; (2) I cannot need to take account of anything which is not given to me as a datum of experience; therefore (3) I can make coherent judgments only about things which could be given to me in experience. Now, one might defend the doctrine of noumenal freedom by challenging premiss (2): one item of which I must take account is *not* given to me as a datum of experience – namely, myself. Although I can treat myself as a datum, observing myself in order to discover facts about my current state, in practical deliberation I typically do not do this: I simply *am* myself, and I *confront* the world in which my practical problem arises. So Kant's theory of concepts does perhaps leave room for the notion of oneself as a noumenon, or at any rate as something not given in experience. In Kant's own words: 'Man ..., who knows all the rest of nature solely through the senses, knows himself also through [self-consciousness]...He is thus to himself, on the one hand phenomenon, and on the other hand...a purely intelligible object' (574–5).

'But Kant has already condemned the use of the notion of oneself as something other than a datum. In the paralogisms chapter he forbids me to make anything special of the place of my whole self in my scheme of things.' Beck has dealt with this objection. He points out that the treatment of the paralogisms tried to show 'the theoretical uselessness'[40] of the notion of oneself as a substance etc., but that in that chapter Kant does not deny, and in one place actually asserts, that in 'practical' thinking I am entitled to use the notions of 'freedom and the [nou-

---

[40] The phrase is Beck's, *Practical Reason*, p. 195, n. 53. Kant 'actually asserts' this on 431–2. Final quotation in this paragraph: 578.

menal] subject that is possessed of freedom'. This is not mere special pleading. One can cogently defend the noumenal aspect of Kant's theory of freedom on the grounds that noumena have been banished only from the realm of the *theoretical*, while freedom is purely *practical*. Kant tries to say this himself, when he invites us to 'consider these actions in their relation to reason', and then explains: 'I do not mean speculative [theoretical] reason, by which we endeavour *to explain* their coming into being, but reason in so far as it is itself the cause *producing* them – [that is,] reason in its *practical* bearing.'

This defence will not rescue Kant's theory of freedom, just because it is a *theory*. Its topic is admittedly *practical* reason; but Kant writes *about* this topic, offering such theoretical judgments as that it is noumenal, active, atemporal, and so on. Rather than moving across from theory to practice, he has merely narrowed his concern from theory generally to theory-of-practice in particular.

In my defence of the noumenal aspect of Kant's theory there was a crucial vagueness. I spoke of having to 'take account of myself' as something other than a datum, but if that meant that I must take account of myself in my judgments about what is the case, then the position being defended was condemned by the paralogisms chapter. So also was Kant's claim that each of us *knows* himself as a noumenon, and his even more vulnerable claim – which I have so far suppressed – that this knowledge rests on an awareness of 'acts and inner determinations which [one] cannot regard as impressions of the senses' (574).

One might think that I am here belabouring Kant for something which he could not possibly have avoided, namely the offering of a theory – a set of judgments about what is the case – regarding freedom. If that is inevitable, so much the worse for Kant's plea that he is entitled to use 'noumenon' in this area because his concerns here are practical and not theoretical. But in fact it is not inevitable. In each of the two areas to which Kant's theory of freedom may be addressed, there is something central which is practical and not theoretical.

Consider first the accountability problem – though of course this is in bad shape anyway, because it lacks that first-person emphasis which is needed to give 'noumenon' a finger-hold. In connexion with accountability, what Kant offers is manifestly theory-of-practice: the agent may be held accountable because of something non-empirical which is the case about him. We confront the natural man and wonder whether we can fairly subject him to blame and so on, and Kant says, in effect, 'Yes, you may, because you are entitled to believe that what he does stems from freedom.' Strawson does better, for he says: 'Yes, you may subject him to blame or something like it, because you are entitled to have certain feelings about him.' The difference between belief (Kant) and feeling (Strawson) is that between being and not being wedded to the theoretical sphere. As Strawson remarks, of philosophers like Schlick and Kant, 'Both seek, in different ways, to over-intellectualize the facts',[41] meaning that both treat the problem as too exclusively one about what is the case – or what we are entitled to believe – regarding the given action.

The threat to agency which Kant's theory of freedom tries to meet, and which is properly met by Ryle's point about self-knowledge and self-prediction, cannot be expressed in any theoretical statement about the human condition. 'How about the statement that agency is possible only within the area of one's ignorance?' But that is not a threat – it is simply true. What is threatened and thus in need of defence is our right to *behave* in a certain way. Specifically, it is our entitlement to square up to our practical problems without subordinating them to whatever we can do in the way of self-observation and self-prediction. Just because what is at issue here is conduct rather than belief, it really does fall on the right of the theoretical/practical dichotomy.

To a certain limited extent, then, we can defend Kant's right to use the notion of a noumenon in his treatment of freedom. The defence, furthermore, can reach down to some relatively detailed aspects of the theory, including one which seems at first sight to be simply intolerable.

Kant speaks of a *causality* of freedom, thus implying that the concept of cause is applicable to something noumenal. Yet he has said elsewhere that it is a concept of the understanding, which can be applied only to empirically given items. I do not defend Kant's use of the notion of a noumenal causality: in the area of accountability 'the causality of freedom' is supposed to have an effect yet not to make any difference, and the upshot is that it does harm or does nothing; and in the area of agency the only causality that is involved has nothing noumenal about it. Still, Kant's use can be defended against the specific charge that the concept of cause applies only to items which are given in intuition. What Kant first introduces as the concept of cause is what corresponds to the ability to use and understand conditional judgments – it might be called the concept of if–then-relatedness. The familiar concept of

---

[41] 'Freedom and Resentment', p. 94.

natural cause is supposed to arise from that original one through *schematism*, a procedure for adding temporality to atemporal concepts.[42] This procedure takes us from the original concept of cause to that of if–then-relatedness-in-time, and Kant optimistically equates that with if–(then–later)-relatedness, which may perhaps be identified with natural causality. Now, when Kant insists that the so-called 'categories' are to be used only empirically, this may apply to them only in their schematized forms. So Kant might have some excuse for the notion of noumenal causality, if he could tie this to the pre-schematism notion of abstract, non-temporal if–then-relatedness. Is there any use within his theory for such a notion?

Yes, there is. Any exercise of agency, and thus perhaps any exercise of freedom, involves acting for reasons, acting because of such and such considerations; and this introduces an if–then-connectedness which is not a case of natural causality. Just as predictions and causal explanations involve a movement of the mind from something earlier (cause) to something later (effect), so in practical deliberation the mind moves from reasons to practical judgments about what to do. This is an if–then matter, but not a move from the earlier to the later.[43]

Notice that noumenal causality, on this defence of it, is not 'causality' in any ordinary sense – e.g. not in any sense which involves something like power or effectiveness.

The least swallowable part of Kant's whole theory of freedom is the claim that the causality of freedom is not in time. This follows from Kant's doctrine that time is an appearance, and anyway the theory of freedom needs it: it is because the noumenal cause of an event is not in time, and thus is not itself an event, that it escapes the causality of nature. Kant is unembarrassed:

Inasmuch as it is *noumenon*, nothing *happens* in it; there can be no change requiring dynamical determination in time, and therefore no causal dependence upon appearances...No action begins *in* this active being itself; but we may yet quite correctly say that the active being *of itself* begins its effects in the sensible world.[44]

That is indefensible. Something in which 'nothing happens' cannot be 'active' or 'begin' a train of events. Still, there is an underlying point which may be valid, and which Kant sometimes puts less tendentiously, as when he says that 'Pure [practical] reason...is not subject to the form of time', that 'There is...no time-sequence' in the causality of

---

[42] For more on schematism, see § 19 above, and *Kant's Analytic* § 37.
[43] See, especially, the first half of the paragraph on 575–6.
[44] 569. Next three quotations: 579; 581; 584.

reason, and that 'Although difference of time makes a fundamental difference to appearances in their relations to one another...it can make no difference to the relation in which the action stands to reason.' I conjecture that Kant is thinking about agency. He tends to assume that serious practical deliberation always concerns what one morally ought to do, and he has the further doctrine that what makes an action right is never any fact about the particular circumstances in which it is performed. So the claim that temporal considerations 'can make no difference to the relation in which the action stands to reason', and so on, could be making the point that according to Kant's doctrine of moral relevance someone who is properly considering how to act will not be considering any facts of the form '...at t'. The doctrine of moral relevance is false. But it at least gives content to the view that 'reason' is atemporal, and gives it a more respectable status than that of desperate lemma which Kant retains because it is implied by the noumenal nature of freedom and required to protect freedom from natural determinism.

11

GOD

§ 72. The Kant–Frege view

After psychology and cosmology, Kant has a final chapter on theology. This treats three traditional arguments for God's existence, starting with the so-called *ontological argument*, which goes somewhat as follows.

If the word 'God' means, in part, 'being which is omnipotent, benevolent, omniscient...', then anyone who says 'God is not omnipotent' either contradicts himself or is not using 'God' with its normal meaning. Now, 'God' means, in part, 'being which is *existent*, omnipotent, benevolent...' That implies that anyone who says 'God is not existent' either contradicts himself or is not using 'God' in its normal meaning; whence it follows that 'God is existent', normally understood, is guaranteed as true just by the meaning of its subject-term.

Kant rejects this argument because, he says, 'existent' has no right to occur in a list of terms purporting to express what an item must be like in order to qualify for a certain label. Existent things are not things of a kind; existence is not a state or quality or process; 'existent' is not a predicate. '"Exist"...is a verb, but it does not describe something that things do all the time, like breathing, only quieter – ticking over, as it were, in a metaphysical sort of way.'[1]

Kant puts this by saying that 'existent' is not a 'real predicate' or a 'determining predicate'. It and its cognates can behave like predicates in a sentence, he admits, as when we say 'Unicorns don't exist', which may seem to report something that unicorns don't do. But that only qualifies it as a grammatical or 'logical' predicate:

Anything...can...serve as a logical predicate; the subject can even be predicated of itself...But a *determining* predicate is a predicate which is added to the concept of the subject and enlarges it...'*Being*' is obviously not a real predicate; that is, it is not a concept of something which could be added to the concept of a thing. (626)

Recall that a thing's 'determinations' are its properties or qualities. To 'determine' something is to discover or report detail about it.

This general view about the concept of existence was adumbrated,

---

[1] J. L. Austin, *Sense and Sensibilia* (Oxford, 1962), p. 68n.

against Descartes, by Gassendi. Descartes argues that 'God' means
'...existent...' because it means 'being with all perfections' and
existence is a perfection:

> Existence can no more be separated from the essence of God than can its having
> three angles equal to two right angles be separated from the essence of a triangle...;
> and so it is just as impossible to conceive a God (that is, a supremely perfect being)
> who lacks existence (that is to say, who lacks a certain perfection), as to conceive
> of a mountain which has no valley.[2]

Gassendi denies that existence is a perfection or indeed a property or
quality of any sort:

> Existence is a perfection neither in God nor in anything else; it is rather that in the
> absence of which there is no perfection. For that which does not exist has neither
> perfection nor imperfection, and that which exists and has various perfections does
> not have its existence as a particular perfection...but as that by means of which
> the thing itself equally with its perfections is in existence.

Descartes' reply to this is unsatisfactory:

> I do not see to what class of reality you wish to assign existence, nor do I see why
> it may not be said to be a property..., taking 'property' to cover any attribute
> or anything which can be predicated of a thing.

This amounts to saying that 'existent' must be a determining predicate
because it is a logical or grammatical predicate.

One piece of evidence for the Kantian view is given by Moore.[3] He
contrasts (a) 'Tame tigers exist' with (b) 'Tame tigers growl'. One
might think that each of these reports something that tame tigers do, but
there is a deep-lying dissimilarity which Moore displays by considering
the question 'All of them or only some of them?' Asked of (b), this
makes perfect sense: perhaps every tame tiger growls, perhaps some do
and others do not. But the question cannot be applied to (a): we cannot
suppose that perhaps some tame tigers exist while others do not.

Kant rests a good deal on a different line of argument.[4] He says that
we entertain a possibility by considering some concept built out of
determining predicates, and that to ask whether the possibility is
realized is to ask whether that concept applies to any object. If 'existing'
were a determining predicate, Kant argues, then a bare affirmative

---

[2] *Fifth Meditation*, about one third of the way through. Next two quotations: Fifth Objections to the Meditations, Haldane & Ross, p. 186; Descartes' reply, *ibid.* p. 228.
[3] G. E. Moore, *Philosophical Papers* (London, 1959), pp. 117–20.
[4] The paragraph on 626–7, and start of the following paragraph. Quotation below is from 628.

answer to the question could never be given. Suppose the question is 'Are there any tigers?' The answer that there are tigers means that some existing things are tigers; and that, if 'existing' is a determining predicate, asserts that something instantiates not merely the concept *tiger* but the richer concept *existing tiger*. An affirmative answer to our question is always over-informative, as though 'Are there tigers?' had to be answered by 'Yes, there are striped tigers' or 'Yes, there are fat tigers'. In Kant's words:

> By whatever and by however many predicates we may think a thing – even if we completely determine it – we do not make the least addition to the thing when we further declare that this thing *is*. Otherwise, it would not be exactly the same thing that exists, but something more than we had thought in the concept; and we could not, therefore, say that the exact object of my concept exists.

This argument is resistible. An opponent could reply that just as the answer 'Yes, there are tigers' means 'Yes, there are existent tigers', so the question 'Are there tigers?' means 'Are there existent tigers?'; in which case the answer does not say more than was asked.

it is there an existent body

The quoted passage also suggests that if 'existent' were a determining predicate then we could not entertain some concept and find that precisely *it* was instantiated: if instantiation involved existence, 'it would not be exactly the same thing that exists, but something more than we had thought in the concept.' But what exists is *always* 'more than we had thought in the concept'! Whatever one 'thinks in a concept' must be abstract, omitting answers to at least some questions of detail, and so a reality corresponding to any such thought will always have some features with regard to which the thought was, as it were, silent. Kant implies that we might 'completely determine' a thing, but that is impossible. Anyway, if we could do so, i.e. could think the totality of a thing's determining predicates, perhaps that *would* involve us automatically in thinking of it as existing. In assuming the contrary, Kant is simply begging the question in favour of his view that 'existent' is not a determining predicate. So this argument of Kant's is, in two distinct ways, a complete failure.[5]

but not in respect of its existence

Yet I share the widespread belief that this discussion of Kant's contains something which is important and may be true. We should see him as presenting, in the garb of bad arguments, a considerable thesis or

[5] I here follow J. Shaffer, 'Existence, Predication, and the Ontological Argument', *Mind* (1962), reprinted in T. Penelhum and J. J. MacIntosh (eds.), *The First Critique* (Belmont, Calif., 1969).

hypothesis about the logic of existence. It is at once an answer to Descartes' 'I do not see to what class of reality you wish to assign existence', and an amplification of Gassendi's sketchy remark that existence 'is that in the absence of which there is no perfection'.

Gassendi did well to avoid saying more than he knew. Lacking a positive theory about the concept of existence, he nevertheless saw clearly that an acceptable theory must not imply that existence is a property. Descartes' contemporary Clerselier, who translated the Objections to the *Meditations* and Descartes' Replies to them, must have found the sketchiness of Gassendi's treatment of existence intolerable. For he turned Gassendi's Latin 'It is that in the absence of which...' into his own French 'It is *a form or an act* in the absence of which...'! That is no good at all, of course, but some positive theory was needed, and more than a century later Kant provided it.

According to Kant, every existence-statement says about a concept that it is instantiated, rather than saying about an object that it exists. This is an important precursor of the view of Frege that any legitimate existential statement must be built out of propositional atoms of the form 'There is an *F*', where *F* stands for a determining predicate.[6] According to this Kant–Frege view, the real form of 'Tigers exist' is not like that of 'Tigers growl', but rather like that of 'There are tigers', or 'The concept of tigerhood is instantiated'. Granted that Kant's arguments fall far short of proving this hypothesis, they do at least illustrate and elucidate it; and the hypothesis itself is a philosophical contribution which deserves attention and which may even be true.

The Fregean view about existence can be applied to philosophical problems, as follows. Suppose that a purported existence-statement *S* is somehow problematical. (1) If *S* remains problematical when it is quantified, i.e. translated into the form '...there is an *F*...', then this is a problem which the Fregean view does not solve. (2) If the problem disappears when *S* is quantified, then it has been solved by the Fregean view. (3) If *S* cannot be quantified, then the 'problem' it posed was illusory.

[6] 'Existential propositions are ones which can be expressed in German with *es gibt* [in English with "there is" or "there are"]. This expression is not followed immediately by a name in the singular or by a word with the definite article, but always by a concept-word [determining predicate] without a definite article. In such existential propositions something is said about a concept.' G. Frege, *Nachgelassene Schriften* (ed. H. Hermes *et al.*, Hamburg, 1969), Vol. I, p. 274. I am indebted to Howard Jackson for showing me this passage. For a remark by Frege about the ontological argument, see P. T. Geach and M. Black (eds.), *Translations from the Philosophical Writings of Gottlob Frege* (Oxford, 1952), p. 38n.

Because of (3), the ontological argument can be dissolved. It is based on a definition of the form: 'x is God' means 'x is omniscient and x is omnipotent and x is existent and x is benevolent and...', and there is no way that the component 'x is existent' can be quantified, i.e. expressed in the Fregean form '...there is an F...'.

There are difficulties in this position. For example, the statement 'I exist' seems to be legitimate and yet not quantifiable. There is also the problem, discussed in §21 above, that one cannot report an absolute existence-change in quantified form. In this chapter, however, I adopt the Kant–Frege view as a working hypothesis. The only live controversy I shall enter concerns its powers, not its truth.[7]

§73. Existence and necessary existence

Norman Malcolm has distinguished two ontological arguments, one of which he says is valid and does prove the existence of God.[8] The argument whose invalidity Malcolm concedes is the one I have been discussing. It is invalid, he says, 'because it rests on the false doctrine that existence is a perfection'; and he endorses Kant's handling of this matter, while rightly saying that Kant's position has not yet been conclusively established. The second argument involves a definiens which includes not just 'existent' but 'necessarily existent'. That, Malcolm thinks, makes it safe from Kant's criticisms yet still adequate to prove the desired conclusion.

Malcolm is right to this extent: there is a form of argument which can be used to support the view that 'existent' is not a determining predicate, though it gives no support at all to the view that 'necessarily existent' is not a determining predicate. We have some ways of using 'existent' which can be rapidly and easily quantified: 'Tigers are existent' becomes 'There are tigers'. If we try to use the word as a determining predicate, by giving it a role in which it purports to mark off things of a kind, it always turns out to be vacuous. If I ask you to bring me a beer, and then add '...a cold one', that could make the request harder to comply with; but if I add '...an existent one', your task is not made harder, because an existent beer is just a beer. But it is not obvious that necessarily existent things are not things of a kind. If I ask

[7] For further discussion see W. C. Kneale, 'Is Existence a Predicate?' in H. Feigl and W. Sellars (eds.), *Readings in Philosophical Analysis* (New York, 1949), and W. P. Alston, 'The Ontological Argument Revisited', *The Philosophical Review* (1960).

[8] N. Malcolm, 'Anselm's Ontological Arguments', *The Philosophical Review* (1960). The remark about Kant's position is on p. 44.

you to bring me a beer, and add '...a necessarily existent one, please', you cannot now comply just by bringing me any old beer. The addition has made my order more difficult, and perhaps impossible, to fill. In short, 'existent' behaves vacuously when we pretend that it is a determining predicate, but 'necessarily existent' does not.

Malcolm even claims that necessary existence is a perfection, a property which it is good to have;[9] whereas the view that existence is a perfection involves such absurdities as that 'my future house...will be a better house if it exists than if it does not.'

He also argues convincingly that there is a theological–linguistic tradition in which 'necessarily existent' is part of what 'God' means.[10] One reason for this connects with the preceding point: necessary existence is (analytically) a perfection, and God (analytically) has every perfection. There is also another reason: it does not 'make sense' to ask when God began, or whether God will cease to exist, or what causes God to exist – and such questions can fail to make sense only if God's existence is a logical truth, i.e. only if God has necessary existence. We shall see later that these two reasons clash.

Malcolm also hits back at two other lines of argument used by Kant.

Kant contends that, for any predicate *F*, from the necessity that God is *F* it follows only that *if* there is a God he is *F*:

If, in an identical proposition, I reject the predicate while retaining the subject, contradiction results...But if we reject subject and predicate alike, there is no contradiction; for nothing is then left that can be contradicted. To posit a triangle, and yet to reject its three angles, is self-contradictory; but there is no contradiction in rejecting the triangle together with its three angles. The same holds true of the concept of an absolutely necessary being. If its existence is rejected, we reject the thing itself with all its predicates; and no question of contradiction can then arise. (622–3)

This implies that Malcolm's argument proves, at most, that if God exists then God necessarily exists.

Malcolm denies that his conclusion ought to be weakened in this way.[11] If Kant were right, Malcolm's premises would be consistent with 'God does not exist'. That would make them consistent with 'It is not necessary that God exists', and thus with 'God does not necessarily exist'. But one of Malcolm's premises is, precisely, that it is analytic

9 *Ibid.* pp. 46–7. Next quotation: *ibid.* p. 43.
10 References for this paragraph are all *ibid.* pp. 47–50.
11 *Ibid.* pp. 56–8.

that God *does* necessarily exist. So, Malcolm argues, Kant must be wrong.

This argument assumes that 'God exists necessarily' entails 'It is necessary that God exists', and this move is controversial. I have no quarrel with it if *logical* necessity is involved, as indeed it seems to be when Malcolm says that because God necessarily exists certain questions do not 'make sense'. As against this, however, when he says that necessary existence is a 'perfection', he seems to invoke causal rather than logical necessity, equating necessary existence with indestructibility. On that construal of Malcolm's position, the above argument of his collapses, for 'God is indestructible' is obviously not equivalent to 'It is necessary that God exists', in any sense of 'necessary' which is strong enough to license the further inference to 'God exists'.[12] On the causal construal, then, Malcolm ought to admit that all he has established is the conditional proposition that if there is a God then he is indestructible. So let us now set aside the causal reading of Malcolm's original argument. He needs to construe 'necessarily existent' in terms of logical necessity, for that is implied by his point about certain questions' not making sense, and – far more important – it is required if his conclusion is not to be reduced to a mere conditional.

Kant also attacks the ontological argument on the ground that 'All existential propositions are synthetic.'[13] That, if true, condemns Malcolm's conclusion that it is analytically necessary that God exists. But Kant gives no clear reasons for this claim of his, and Malcolm refuses to defer to it. Malcolm also considers the related, contemporary view that all existential propositions are contingent and so cannot be proved by a priori argument, and he rightly says that this popular dogma is without visible support.

§ 74. Why Malcolm's argument fails

Consider the form 'necessarily *F*', with the adverb being taken to express logical or a priori necessity and thus to express analytic necessity – according to my view and also to Malcolm's.[14] If something is neces-

---

[12] This point is well made by T. K. Swing, *Kant's Transcendental Logic* (New Haven, 1969), pp. 307–9.

[13] 626. Malcolm's refusal to defer: *op. cit.* pp. 52–3. Final sentence of this paragraph: *ibid.* pp. 53–6; see also *Locke, Berkeley, Hume* § 59.

[14] Malcolm, *op. cit.* p. 55: 'I am inclined to hold the . . . view that logically necessary truth "merely reflects our use of words".' Next quotation: *Essay* III. vi. 4; see also the rest of I–13.

sarily *F*, it must be *F* by definition – the term standing for *F* must occur in its definiens. This implies that an object cannot be, in itself, necessarily *F*; because that would require that a certain expression occur in the object's definition, and objects don't have definitions. Cannibals are necessarily carnivores, but we cannot say of any cannibal that *he* is necessarily carnivorous – only that *qua* cannibal he is necessarily carnivorous. The classic source for this point is in Locke, who speaks of necessary properties as 'essences', and says this about them:

yes

> *Essence*, in the ordinary use of the word, relates to sorts, and...is considered in particular beings no further than as they are ranked into sorts...Take but away the abstract ideas by which we sort individuals, and rank them under common names, and then the thought of anything essential to any of them instantly vanishes.

Kant makes the same point, in very condensed form, when he says: 'The absolute necessity of the judgment is only a conditioned necessity of the thing' (621). From this point of Locke's and Kant's, it follows that nothing of the form 'necessarily *F*' belongs in a definiens. A definiens sets a test that an object must pass if the definiendum is to fit it, but for no value of *F* could we test an object to discover whether *it* was necessarily *F*. If an object is *F*, then there will be some *G* and *H* such that *qua G* the object is necessarily *F* whereas *qua H* it is only contingently *F*.

That, I submit, destroys Malcolm's argument. But there is another point which also is fatal. In expressing it, I shall waive the first difficulty, and shall talk freely about objects as being *F*-by-definition and so on.

Malcolm stresses certain facts about the Christian theological tradition. In that tradition it has been widely accepted that something couldn't count as 'God' if we could intelligibly ask about it 'Did it ever not exist?' or 'Will it ever not exist?' or 'Under what conditions would it not have existed?' or 'Because of what other facts does it exist?' or the like. The semantics of the tradition do not allow such questions to arise about God, properly so-called: anyone who asks them shows that he has not grasped the *concept* of God. A being in respect of which these questions cannot be asked must be necessarily existent, it seems.

The phrase 'necessarily existent' needs to be explained: we cannot simply say that it has whatever meaning would turn those questions into logical solecisms. Someone who thinks an expression can do that kind of service owes us a positive account of its meaning which explains how it can do what he claims for it. Thus Kant:

In all ages men have spoken of an *absolutely necessary* being... There is, of course, no difficulty in giving a verbal definition of the concept, namely, that it is something the non-existence of which is impossible. But this yields no insight into the conditions which make it necessary to regard the non-existence of a thing as utterly unthinkable. It is precisely these conditions that we desire to know, in order that we may determine whether or not, in resorting to this concept, we are thinking anything at all. (620–1)

What sort of positive account can be given? Well, if we look for guidance to easier cases, we find that where a question of the form 'Are Fs G?' is clearly improper or unraisable or self-answering, this is because the meaning of F somehow includes that of G. If that points to how 'necessarily existent' has its question-blocking role, we get this: 'To say that something is necessarily existent is to say that its definition analytically involves existence.' A necessarily existent thing, then, apparently has to be a thing which is existent by definition; but Malcolm has agreed that 'existent' is not a determining predicate, so that it cannot legitimately occur in a definiens. I claim, in short, that because 'existent' ought not to occur in a definiens, 'necessarily existent' ought not to occur anywhere.

That argument is Kant's. He considers not the concept of a most perfect being but rather that of a most real thing, an *ens realissimum*. He sees this as a traditional vehicle for the notion of necessary existence, and one which might be thought to escape his central attack:

Notwithstanding all these general considerations..., we may be challenged with a case which is brought forward as proof that in actual fact... there is one concept, and indeed only one, in reference to which the not-being or rejection of its object is in itself contradictory, namely, the concept of the *ens realissimum*... My answer is as follows. There is already a contradiction in introducing the concept of existence – no matter under what title it may be disguised – into the concept of a thing which we profess to be thinking solely in reference to its possibility. (624–5)

That is the core of my second argument against Malcolm: in claiming that God is necessarily existent he is 'introducing the concept of existence', in disguise, 'into the concept of a thing'.

To escape this argument, Malcolm must give a positive account of 'necessarily existent' such that (1) it does not mean anything like 'existent by definition', yet (2) God's being necessarily existent suffices both to block the forbidden questions and to entail that necessarily God exists. These two conditions cannot be satisfied by a single sense of 'necessarily existent'.

236

Malcolm may well be right when he says this:

What Anselm has proved is that the notion of contingent existence or of contingent nonexistence cannot have any application to God. His existence must either be logically necessary or logically impossible. The only intelligible way of rejecting Anselm's claim that God's existence is necessary is to maintain that the concept of God, as a being a greater than which cannot be conceived [and thus as necessarily existing], is self-contradictory or nonsensical.[15]

I have tried to show that the concept of God, on the Anselm–Malcolm account of it, is logically defective; and so I contend that in that sense God's existence *is* self-contradictory or nonsensical. If that convicts a whole theological–linguistic tradition of talking nonsense, so be it. It can be argued that I must be wrong about this. The standards for what makes sense are set by actual meanings, and these are determined by actual uses. From this, some philosophers infer that there could not be a logical mistake made by a whole community. To reply to this line of argument would take me too far afield now.

Just to get it clear: I have argued, firstly, that there is no F such that 'necessarily F' can properly occur in a definiens, and, secondly, that 'necessarily existent' cannot properly occur anywhere at all.

§75. Aquinas's third way

Kant turns next to the so-called cosmological argument for God's existence, versions of which go back at least to Aristotle. One famous version is Aquinas's so-called 'third way' of proving the existence of God; and, although Kant did not directly consider this, I think it will be useful background for us to do so.

Here is the main part of Aquinas's third way:

We find in nature things that are possible to be and [possible] not to be, since they are found to be generated, and to be corrupted...But it is impossible for these always to exist, for if something can not-be, then at some time it is not. Therefore, if everything can not-be, then at one time there was nothing in existence. Now if this were true, even now there would be nothing in existence, because that which does not exist begins to exist only through something already existing. [But there is something now in existence.] Therefore not all beings are merely possible, but there must exist something the existence of which is necessary.[16]

The argument is as follows. If (1) everything exists contingently then

---

15 Malcolm, *op. cit.* p. 49. The last point in this paragraph is discussed in J. Bennett, 'On Being Forced to a Conclusion', *Proceedings of the Aristotelian Society*, suppl. vol. (1961).

16 Reprinted in D. R. Burrill (ed.), *The Cosmological Arguments* (New York, 1967), p. 54.

(2) everything was once non-existent; if (2), then (3) there was a time when nothing existed; if (3), then (4) nothing exists now; but something does exist now, and so (3) is false, so (2) is false, so (1) is false.

I shall discuss the moves from (1) to (2), and from (2) to (3). If everything down to (4) is all right, then the rest of the argument goes through. As for the move from (3) to (4): one can understand someone's thinking that in a state of affairs in which nothing existed, no reality could get going, and I shall not challenge that now (see §51 above).

The move from (1) to (2) relies on the view that if anything exists contingently (or 'can not-be'), then it once did not exist. We are concerned with causal rather than logical modalities here: a 'thing whose existence is necessary' in Aquinas's sense is one which causally cannot be originated or annihilated. (The two seem always to be taken together. Kant once said: 'The inner necessity of persisting is inseparably bound up with the necessity of always having existed',[17] but I don't see why.) So something whose existence is contingent in Aquinas's sense is something which is causally capable of having once not existed. But why does Aquinas assume that every such thing once did not exist? Kant, in an early work, mentions 'that well-known commonplace in certain schools: *Whatever exists contingently, at some time did not exist.*' Kant suggests that the 'commonplace' may be based on the idea that to know that something could be non-existent one must know that it once did not exist. Clearly that would not help Aquinas, for he argues *from* things' contingency *to* their having once not existed.

There is an argument which might support Aquinas on this point. Consider the principle: 'If x's non-existence is causally possible, then the larger n is the less probable it is that x is in existence for n years.' I don't know how to base this on a respectable theory of probability, but it is plausible, and it may help to explain Aquinas's position. The principle implies that the probability of any contingently-existing thing's lasting through an infinite amount of time has a value lower than any assignable fraction, and thus a value $= 0$. Now, it is obvious how to apply this to future time: the larger n is, the greater are the chances of x's being annihilated before n years are over, and there is (virtually) no chance that x will last for ever. The same line of thought applies equally to the past:[18] the greater n is, the less probable it is that x

---

[17] 229. The next quotation is from Kant's Inaugural Dissertation, §29; in G. B. Kerferd and D. E. Walford (eds.), *Kant: Selected Pre-Critical Writings* (Manchester, 1968), pp. 88–9.

[18] That the argument can re-use the same principle, rather than having to adduce a distinct though similar one, was shown to me by Bonnelle Johnson.

has lasted for *n* years; and so the probability of its having always existed is zero. Anyway, that is the best I can do for Aquinas's move from (1) to (2); and the best may be good enough.

The move from (2) to (3) is much worse. All that Aquinas should mean by (2) is that each thing which now exists was once non-existent; but that does not imply that (3) there was a time when *nothing* existed. At most it implies that there was a time when *no now-existent thing* existed, which is compatible with there having been in existence at that time other things which now do not exist. In moving from (2) to (3), Aquinas overlooks the possibility that although there are always things in existence, each thing which ever exists is originated and then annihilated.

Geach speaks of Aquinas's 'lumping together of things' in which he 'pass[es] from particular things to the world as a whole'.[19] But his account of it is too kind to the move from (2) to (3). He reports, with evident sympathy, Aquinas's willingness to speak of the world as a whole, and to ask about it some of the questions that we can ask about parts of it – e.g., 'What caused it to exist?' I am sympathetic to this too, but what is now in question is not just tolerating certain propositions about the whole world, but inferring them from corresponding propositions about each part of the world. That inference is simply not valid. It moves from

$$(x)(\exists t)(x \text{ is contingent} \rightarrow x \text{ did not exist at } t)$$

to $\qquad (\exists t)(x)(x \text{ is contingent} \rightarrow x \text{ did not exist at } t),$

which is no better than moving from 'Everybody has a father' to 'Someone is everybody's father'.

In Geach's reconstruction of the argument, this move disappears. Geach departs from Aquinas's actual order, moving from 'Each thing is contingent' to 'The world is contingent' and from that to 'There was a time when the world did not exist'. This is really no better. The move from '*x* is contingent' to 'At one time *x* did not exist' is plausible only if *x* is an object which exists now, or a collection of objects all of which exist now. But Geach's 'the world' is not such an object or collection. It comprises every non-divine object which ever did or does or will exist, so that a time when 'the world' does not exist must be a time when no non-divine object exists. The contingency of an item of this

---

[19] P. T. Geach, 'Commentary on Aquinas', in D. R. Burrill (ed.), *op. cit.* pp. 64, 66. My main point in this paragraph is efficiently made by Leibniz, *New Essays* IV. x. 6.

kind does not imply or even suggest that there was a time when the item did not exist.

Let us say that the world contains a *stretch* of at least k years if there is some pair of non-divine objects of which one came into existence at least k years before the other did. Aquinas's argument sets no limit to how long a stretch the whole world can contain. His argument therefore allows that for every n the world contains a stretch which is longer than n years, and so it allows the possibility that although every individual thing is contingent there never was a time when nothing existed.

Or consider again the principle that if x is contingent then the probability that x lasts for n years is small in proportion as n is large. If x contains a stretch of k years, then the principle is obviously false for values of $n < k$. And so if we cannot set a limit to how large a stretch x may contain, we cannot tell where, if anywhere, the applicability of the principle begins. So the principle is powerless when x is 'the world'.

§ 76. The fourth antinomy

A version of the cosmological argument appears as the Thesis-argument of Kant's fourth antinomy. This argument has a very different structure from Aquinas's. The crucial point is that Kant here associates an item's being contingent with its being 'conditioned', i.e. its presupposing something which somehow explains its existence. Kant has a theory, which I shall expound in my last chapter, that our faculty of reason makes us postulate an unconditioned source or basis for everything conditioned. Given this theory, plus the association of 'contingent' with 'conditioned', and thus of 'necessary' with 'unconditioned', we have at least the skeleton of an argument for the conclusion that 'There belongs to the world...a being that is absolutely necessary' (480). Here is the argument in Kant's words:

Every conditioned...presupposes, in respect of its existence, a complete series of conditions up to the totally unconditioned, which alone is absolutely necessary. So something absolutely necessary must exist, since alteration exists as a consequence of it.

Kant's concept of a condition/conditioned relationship is extremely general. He would say that x is a condition of y if they are both portions of matter and x surrounds y or has it as a part (first antinomy), or if y has x as a part (second antinomy), or if they are both times and x precedes y (first), or if y is an event and x causes it (third), or if y is contingent and somehow depends upon x (fourth). Kant's general theory about reason's 'demand' for 'the unconditioned' is not helpful, as I shall show in my last chapter. It fails not only to yield a valid Thesis-argument, but even to shed light on why anyone – a rationalist, say – should think that the Thesis-argument is valid. If we are to make progress, we must descend from these dizzying heights to the less abstract level of the notions of the necessary and the contingent. However, if we want coherent material at that level, we really must look to the 'cosmological argument' which is given in the theology chapter; for the fourth antinomy offers little more than confusion.

There are two main sources of trouble in it.

The first source of difficulty is that the arguments for the Thesis and the Antithesis both address themselves to the contingency of *alterations*, and consider whether any alteration is necessary. Although we are not told what a necessary alteration would be, what seems to emerge is virtually a re-run of the third antinomy. That is, the question is taken to be whether the series of causes must or can somehow terminate in something which is not caused by something still earlier in the series, with the Antithesis-argument saying that an affirmative answer to this 'conflicts with the dynamical law of the determination of all appearances in time'. (There is also some play with the question of whether the whole series might be 'necessary' if no individual member of it is necessary, but I shall by-pass that.) Seen in this light, the fourth antinomy adds nothing useful to the third, and does not significantly anticipate the cosmological argument in the next chapter.

Yet later on Kant says: 'We are concerned here, not with unconditioned causality, but with the unconditioned existence of substance itself';[20] and he clearly implies that, whereas the third antinomy treats of how a 'state' arises from its 'cause', the fourth concerns an alleged dependence of 'the contingent existence of substance' on 'necessary existence'. We must conclude that the subject has been radically changed.

Kant may be trying to link the two themes when he says that whatever is 'alterable' is 'conditioned in its existence' (587). That could give the concept of alteration some role in the argument: because there are alterations, there are alterable things, and their existence must be contingent ('conditioned'); from which one might argue somehow to the existence of items whose existence is necessary. But this would not

[20] 587. Next quotation: 588.

restore the fourth antinomy, which is all about necessary and contingent *alterations*.

Anyway, Kant ought not to say that everything which is alterable is contingent in its existence. The fourth antinomy always involves causal rather than logical necessity, and so 'contingent in its existence' here means 'causally capable of being annihilated'. But Kant holds as a fundamental item of doctrine that alterable items are substances, whose most notable feature is that they cannot undergo existence-changes of either sort. This commits him to saying that *nothing* which is alterable is contingent in its existence! This point is clearly made in Strawson's definitive treatment of the fourth antinomy.[21] Strawson also finds a way to reconcile what he regards as the salvageable portions of the 'substances are permanent' doctrine with the 'the alterable is contingent' form of the fourth antinomy. Kant also notices the difficulty, it seems, and argues that substance in space – which he identifies with matter – can after all be annihilated. His discussion leaves one unsure whether this is a retreat from his official doctrine of substance, or whether instead he is merely talking about the *logical* possibility that matter should go out of existence.

That the fourth antinomy *is* concerned with causal rather than logical modalities is clear enough, for Kant argues at length that the Thesis-argument cannot 'carry us to the existence of a necessary being ...conceived in purely intelligible terms' (488), that is, a logically necessary being. Incidentally, his argument for this is invalid. It assumes that 'we cannot argue from empirical contingency to intelligible contingency', i.e. from '*x* is causally possible' to '*x* is logically possible'; whereas really there is nothing wrong with that move. The move from 'causally necessary' to 'logically necessary' is impermissible, of course, and that may be what led Kant astray here. He knew better, as 301–2 shows.

The second major source of confusion in the fourth antinomy is the occurrence in the Thesis-argument of a substantial passage arguing that the necessary item in question 'belongs to the sensible world' or is 'contained in the world itself'.[22] The argument for this is reminiscent of Hume's *Dialogues Concerning Natural Religion*: if you start a causal argument in the framework of natural, empirically discoverable causes and effects, then you must stay in that framework and not switch over to some other sort of cause–effect relationship on the way. This is a curious

[21] *Bounds of Sense*, pp. 215–19. 'Kant notices the difficulty': see the paragraph on 645–7.
[22] The passage starts late on 480. Final reference in this paragraph is to 481–3.

argument to put into the mouth of a proponent of the Thesis! What is more, this material stands directly opposite a paragraph in which the Antithesis-argument *also* tries to rule out the possibility that 'an absolutely necessary cause of the world exists outside the world'.

Kant had two reasons for making the Thesis-arguer insist that the necessary being is 'contained in the world'. One was his desire that the antinomy should 'be cosmological, and [therefore] relate to empirical laws'.[23] He thinks that cosmology carries one beyond the bounds of possible experience only quantitatively, by requiring thoughts of impossibly large procedures of kinds which, in smaller doses, are familiar and manageable. The other reason is that he needs to distinguish the fourth antinomy's Thesis-argument from the cosmological argument in the theology chapter. As one commentator points out, the argument in the theology chapter argues for 'a theological unconditioned which is definitely not a part of the phenomenal world', whereas both sides of the fourth antinomy 'stress again and again that the necessary being under consideration, if it exists, is a part of the phenomenal world'. That is just what Kant wanted us to say, but let us remember that the fourth antinomy can have that distinguishing feature only because its Thesis is contrived and implausible.

Altogether, Kant fails in the fourth antinomy to produce a satisfactory antinomal crunch. The failure becomes conspicuous when he offers his 'solution' in Section 9. 'Both of the conflicting propositions may be true', he says there, 'if taken in different connections';[24] and he cashes this with the proposal that there may be a necessary being but that it 'must be thought as entirely outside the series of the sensible world, and as purely intelligible'. With this supposedly reconciling suggestion, Kant manages to contradict both the Thesis and the Antithesis!

§ 77. The cosmological argument

The cosmological argument in the theology chapter is more coherent. It goes like this:

If we admit something as existing..., we must also admit that there is something which exists *necessarily*. For the contingent exists only under the condition of some other contingent existence as its cause, and from this again we must infer yet another cause, until we are brought to a cause which is not contingent, and which is therefore unconditionally necessary. (612)

[23] 485; see also 447–8. Next quotation: Al-Azm, *Kant's Arguments*, p. 113.
[24] 588. Next quotation: 589; see also *Prolegomena* § 53, last paragraph.

Sketchy as this is, we can separate it from Aquinas's argument from contingency to former non-existence. The basic idea here is that if something's existence is contingent, then it must have been caused to exist by something which, if it is contingent, must in its turn have been caused to exist by something else, and so on. Kant has the cosmological arguer say '...and so on until we are brought to a cause which is not contingent', but why should he not say instead '...and so on *ad infinitum*'? If the series of dependences-for-existence goes back to infinity, each contingent existence can be assigned a cause without our ever having to allow that anything exists necessarily.

Kant has two explanations of why the cosmological arguer rejects this move. According to one of them, the cosmological arguer is assuming that an infinite regress of causes is impossible: 'The series of subordinate causes [must end] with an absolutely necessary cause, without which it would have no completeness.'[25] This supposed demand for 'completeness' owes more to Kant's peculiar theory of reason than to anything in the thought of his predecessors, and Kant's reference to it is a lapse. (It occurs in a footnote which describes the cosmological argument as 'too well known to require detailed statement'. This is as infuriating as his reference to 'the fact that once we assume something to exist we cannot avoid inferring that something exists necessarily', which he describes as 'this quite natural (although not therefore certain) inference'.) I hope that Kant did not hold the considered view that the cosmological argument is based upon a rejection of infinite regresses of causes.

He has another and better account of how the argument is supposed to go. According to this, the cosmological arguer allows that the causal–explanatory regress may be infinite, so that each member of it can be explained by reference to some earlier member of it; but he contends that that would still not explain why the world contained that series rather than some other. This is altogether different from the previous account. Instead of a demand for a *complete* explanation of certain facts, we are now confronted with the demand for an explanation which cannot even begin, let alone be completed, if we are restricted to homogeneous members of an infinite causal regress. In Leibniz's words, we cannot 'advance the slightest towards establishing a reason' for the whole series by giving reasons for some of its members in terms of others.[26]

The line of thought which demands that we explain the whole

25 633n. Kant's other infuriating reference: 643.
26 'On the Radical Origination of Things', Loemker, p. 486.

series, as distinct from explaining each of its members, is more clearly expressed by Kant when he is talking not about the cosmological argument but about the third argument in his trio. Still, the crucial thought is the same:

Nothing has of itself come into the condition in which we find it to exist, but always points to something else as its cause, while this in turn commits us to a repetition of the same enquiry...Over and above this infinite chain of contingencies, we [must] assume something to support it – something which is original and independently self-subsistent.[27]

This pivots on the distinction between explaining the whole series and explaining every member of the series. Something of the same kind may be expressed when Kant says that the cosmological argument involves 'the inference to a first cause, from the impossibility of an infinite series of causes, given one upon another in the sensible world'. Just what that means depends upon the curious phrase 'given one upon another' (*übereinander gegebener*). I cannot explore that now, except to remark that Kemp Smith masks the difficulty by translating the phrase as 'given one *after* another'. That leads him to think that the argument rests 'on the...assumption that an infinite series of empirical causes is impossible'. I am fairly sure that he is wrong about this.

Of Kant's two accounts, the one demanding an explanation for the series as a whole is better than the one demanding an end to the series, because the former is truer to the thought of actual proponents of the cosmological argument. Consider Aquinas, for example. Several of his 'ways' include infinity-rejecting moves. One of these occurs in his 'third way' – not when he argues that something exists necessarily, but rather in a further argument, which I have not so far presented, for his final conclusion that something is inherently or unaidedly imperishable (necessarily existent). Although a thing can owe the necessity of its existence to something else, he says, 'It is impossible to go on to infinity in necessary things which have their necessity caused by another, [and so there must be] some being having of itself its own necessity, and not receiving it from another.'[28] That seems to deny there could be such an infinite regress; but Thomist scholars agree that that was not Aquinas's position, and that his point was rather that even if the series did go to

27 650. Next two quotations: 637–8; *Commentary*, p. 533.
28 Quoted in D. R. Burrill (ed.), *op. cit.* pp. 54–5. Next quotation: P. T. Geach, 'Commentary on Aquinas', *ibid.* pp. 67–8. For a somewhat different account, see F. C. Copleston, *Aquinas* (Penguin Books, 1955), pp. 117–19.

infinity it would necessarily leave something unexplained. Here is what Geach says:

A series of only-derivatively-imperishable things may be 'lumped together', and thus considered will form a system which is in its turn only-derivatively-imperishable; that, then, from which the system derives its imperishable character cannot form part of the system, and cannot occur in the series at any point, [and so must lie] outside the series.

The argument is not valid. Even if we grant that the series 'may be "lumped together"' to constitute a single system about which certain questions can be meaningfully asked, such questions need not have answers. In Geach's terminology, even if every member of a series is only derivatively imperishable, it does not follow that the series as a whole is only derivatively imperishable. Or, to put the point in terms of demands for explanations, it is true that the entire series cannot be explained purely by reference to members of the series, but then perhaps there *is* no explanation for the whole series.

There are hints of that line of criticism in Kant's text, but I shall not dig them out. Most of them are enclosed in a different line of attack which Kant pursues vigorously. The cosmological argument, he says, rests on 'the transcendental principle whereby from the contingent we infer a cause', but: 'This principle is applicable only in the sensible world; outside that world it has no meaning whatsoever...But in the cosmological proof it is precisely in order to enable us to advance beyond the sensible world that it is employed.'[29] The latter claim is justified by the cosmological argument's demand for an explanation not just of each item in the series of things but also of the entire lumped-together series. Certainly Aquinas understood the argument in that way, as did Leibniz: 'The reasons for the world...lie in something extramundane, different from the chain of states or series of things whose aggregate constitutes the world.' Construed in any other way, the argument could hardly pretend to explain the whole world.

The cosmological argument misuses a certain principle because it misuses a certain concept. Kant's basic complaint, it seems reasonable to suppose, is against an abuse of the concept of cause, which he regards as being, like all concepts, a tool for the handling of intuitions. But he need not insist upon his views about the concept of cause and principles employing it, for really the ball is at the other end of the court, and it is

[29] 637; see also 663. Next quotation: Leibniz, 'On the Radical Origination of Things', Loemker, p. 487.

for the cosmological arguer to explain what meaning, criteria and evidence are involved in *his* causal claims. Consider this candid statement of Aquinas's position:

For Aquinas one is involved in a contradiction if one affirms...'there are things which come into being and pass away' and...at the same time denies...'there is an absolutely necessary being'...But the contradiction can be made apparent only by means of metaphysical analysis. And the entailment in question is fundamentally an ontological or causal entailment...Aquinas...was asserting a unique relation between finite things and the transfinite transcendent cause on which they depend.[30]

Kant need not deny that there is this unique, quasi-causal, sub-logical relationship between the creator and creation. All he needs is the aggressive interrogative. The cosmological arguer, he says, 'cannot refuse to meet my demand that he should at least give a satisfactory account of how, and by what kind of inner illumination, he believes himself capable of soaring so far above all possible experience, on the wings of mere ideas'. This is a reasonable request for an account of the epistemology of 'ontological entailment', or of how to go about the relevant kind of 'metaphysical analysis' and what standards to apply in deciding whether one is doing it rightly or wrongly. The answering silence, these past two hundred years, is suggestive.

The main issues discussed in this section could as well have been raised in the context of the third antinomy as of the fourth or the cosmological argument. Kant tries to stop the slide back into an issue about the causes of alterations, but not very powerfully (589). The fact is that when he seriously connects the cosmological argument with the notion of necessary *existence*, it is in a totally different context, to which I now turn.

§ 78. The second step

Kant's handling of the cosmological argument, considered as an attempt to show that something exists necessarily, is rather off-hand. This is because his main target is a move which the cosmological arguer is supposed to make *after* concluding that there is a necessary being. This alleged further move is described in Section 3 of the theology chapter and again in Section 5.[31] Having concluded that there is a necessary

---

[30] F. C. Copleston, *op. cit.* pp. 114–15. Next quotation: 666; see also 649–50.
[31] 613–16 and the paragraph on 633–4. Next quotation: 613. My §§ 78–80 are indebted to P. Remnant, 'Kant and the Cosmological Argument', *The Australasian Journal of*

being, Kant's cosmological arguer next considers what this being can be like. This is not mere curiosity for detail. Rather it is the question as to what a necessary being *could* be like – a demand for 'a concept that squares with so supreme a mode of existence as that of unconditioned necessity – . . . that concept which is in no respect incompatible with absolute necessity'.

We now meet the concept of an *ens realissimum*, or most real being. This was Leibniz's foundation for the ontological argument. He argued that the ontological argument's concept of God is not logically defective, as follows. The concept of God is that of an *ens realissimum*, that is, of a being which has every positive property; but the only logical defect a concept or proposition can have (Leibniz holds) is contradictoriness, in which something is conjoined with its negation; and so the concept of God, which contains nothing negative, must be logically impeccable.[32] This 'proof' is no good. There are logical defects other than self-contradiction, for example the inclusion of 'existent' in a definiens, and anyway the distinction between 'positive' and 'negative' properties is unstable, unclear and language-dependent. Our present concern, however, is with a different use of the putative concept of an *ens realissimum*.

Kant's cosmological arguer, having reached the lemma that there is a necessary being, takes a second step to the conclusion that the necessary being is an *ens realissimum*.

The argument for this second step relies upon a plain fact about the concept of an *ens realissimum*, namely that it is a saturated concept: for any monadic predicate F, the truth-value of 'An *ens realissimum* is F' is settled, one way or another, just by the definition of '*ens realissimum*'. There can therefore be no contingent truths about an *ens realissimum* (referred to as such). It follows that every question of the form 'Why is it [not] the case that an *ens realissimum* is F?' can be answered on conceptual grounds, a fact which Kant expresses by speaking of a concept which 'contains the "Because" for every "Why"'.[33] That is what is supposed to qualify the concept of an *ens realissimum* for the role of concept of a necessarily existing being, as we see from Kant's presentation of the second step:

The proof then proceeds as follows: The necessary being can be determined in one way only, that is, by one out of each possible pair of opposed predicates. It must

Philosophy (1959), reprinted in T. Penelhum and J.J. MacIntosh (eds.), *The First Critique* (Belmont, Calif., 1969), and even more to discussions I have had with Remnant.

32 See Leibniz, *Monadology* § 45, and Kant 329–30, 630.

33 613. Next quotation: 633–4.

therefore be *completely* determined through its own concept. Now there is only one possible concept which completely determines a thing *a priori*, namely, the concept of the *ens realissimum*. The concept of the most real being is therefore the only one through which a necessary being can be thought. In other words, a supreme being necessarily exists.

We are not told why the cosmological arguer thinks that a necessarily existing thing must 'be completely determined through its own concept', but we do not have to discuss that, for in fact what is here said about a necessarily existing being is trivially true of everything. For example, you are completely determined by a certain concept. No one can spell it out in detail, because it includes everything which ever was, is, or will be true of you, complete with dates; but there unquestionably is such a concept. Similarly, it is true of you, as of each other actual thing, that you 'can be determined in one way only, that is, by one out of each possible pair of opposed predicates'.

Connected with that misfire in the argument there is another, namely that the concept of an *ens realissimum* is not the only saturated concept. There are indefinitely many others, each differing from that of an *ens realissimum* only in replacing one or more of its 'positive' predicates by their complements or negations. These concepts would not admit of a Leibnizian consistency-proof, but many of them are consistent for all that – e.g. the one which fits you. Early in the theology chapter, Kant himself acknowledges this (601).

When Kant first presented the cosmological arguer's second step, in Section 3 of the theology chapter, he was guarded about it. He credited the cosmological arguer only with thinking that the concept of an *ens realissimum* is 'that which best squares with the concept of an unconditionally necessary being'.[34] While presenting this sympathetically, Kant admitted that the former concept 'may not be completely adequate to' the latter, and that there may be other legitimate candidates for the role of necessary being. A page or two later he repeated the second point emphatically, saying that 'we are entirely free to hold that any limited beings whatsoever [i.e. ones other than *entia realissima*] may also be unconditionally necessary'.

Yet in Section 5 we are offered the quoted 'proof' that a necessarily existing being must be an *ens realissimum*. The earlier cautions and reservations are not mentioned, and – what is worse – we are not given needed help. We can see unaided that the 'proof' is a failure; but Kant

---

[34] 614. Next two quotations: *ibid.* 616. The core of this early, guarded version of the 'second step' occupies the paragraph on 614–15.

ought to explain why anyone should ever think that it is a success, that is, to explain how the second-step argument is supposed to work by the thinkers who are supposed to employ it.

(In the very first paragraph of Section 3 of his chapter, Kant has tacked on a final sentence which implies an incautious view of the 'second step'. He speaks of our need for an explanatory 'ground' which stays firm because it 'rests upon the immovable rock of the absolutely necessary', and then he continues:

This latter support is itself in turn without support, if there be any empty space beyond and under it, and if it does not itself so fill all things as to leave no room for any further question – unless, that is to say, it be infinite in its reality. (612)

When we replace this by its literal cash-value, it loses its persuasiveness along with its metaphorical charm. There are two sorts of 'further questions' which Kant could have in mind. (1) There is the form of question 'Why does there exist an F?'; but that is answered in advance if F involves the concept of a being whose existence is absolutely necessary, whether or not 'infinite reality' is involved. (2) There is the form of question 'What other features does an F have?'; but every such question is forestalled just so long as the concept of F is saturated – i.e. completely describes its instances – whether or not it is the concept of an *ens realissimum*. Either way, then, Kant has failed to indicate a coherent route from 'absolutely necessary' to 'most real'. To see that the sentence is a late and ill-considered interpolation, observe how the neighbouring sentences relate to one another, and consider also the oddity of the demand for 'support' for an 'immovable rock'.)

However, let us waive all those doubts and difficulties. Suppose that the cosmological arguer has, somehow, taken his second step to the conclusion that the necessarily existing being is an *ens realissimum*. Having got him as far as this, Kant goes into action with a fresh attack.

§ 79. Kant's attack

If the necessary being is an *ens realissimum*, Kant says, then every *ens realissimum* must be a necessary being. This is because the concept of an *ens realissimum* is a saturated one, which implies that whatever is true of any instance of it must be true of every instance of it, because it must be a logical consequence of the concept itself. This argument, incidentally, need not involve the concept of an *ens realissimum* or that of a necessary being. For any saturated concept C and any monadic concept F, if some instance of *F* is an instance of *C* then every instance of *C* must be an instance of *F*.

This argument of Kant's is perfectly correct.[35] But what makes it an objection to the cosmological arguer's second step? There are two possible answers to this. Each occurs in Kant's text, and each is wrong.

The extreme answer, as I shall call it, is that the second step actually uses the ontological argument. Kant says that 'The so-called cosmological proof really owes any cogency which it may have to the ontological proof from mere concepts',[36] apparently implying that the cosmological arguer gets from 'necessary being' to '*ens realissimum*' by means of the ontological argument. Later, he even describes the cosmological argument as 'only a disguised ontological proof'.

This, however, is not borne out by Kant's own account of the cosmological arguer's second step. The only place where Kant treats his opponent as arguing firmly that the necessary being is an *ens realissimum* is in the second-step argument which I quoted in its entirety in my preceding section ('The proof then proceeds...'). By no stretch of the imagination can that be identified with the ontological argument.

Kant leads up to the extreme answer by saying that when the cosmological arguer brings the concept of a necessary being under the concept of an *ens realissimum*, he is 'presupposing that the concept of absolute necessity of existence can be inferred from the concept of the highest reality', and that, he says, 'is the proposition maintained by the ontological proof'.[37] But that proposition is not 'presupposed' by the second step. It may be true that the second step commits the cosmological arguer to the proposition in question, and even commits him to allowing that the ontological argument is valid, but that is not to say that in taking the step he is relying upon or 'presupposing' the ontological argument.

Kant's moderate answer to the question 'What is wrong with the second step?' is the one I have just suggested, namely that the second step commits the cosmological arguer to endorsing the ontological argument as valid. This seems to be Kant's more considered view of the matter. He states it fairly explicitly when he says that if I am entitled to argue that a necessary being is an *ens realissimum*, then 'I must...be able also to reverse the inference, and to say: Anything to which this concept (of supreme reality) applies is absolutely necessary. [That would

---

35 As is argued by Remnant, *op. cit.*, against such critics as J. J. C. Smart, 'The Existence of God', reprinted in D. R. Burrill (ed.), *op. cit.* pp. 266–7.

36 635. Next quotation: 657; see also 653.   37 635, words slightly re-arranged.

commit me to] admitting the ontological proof' (639). This does not have the form 'In using argument C one covertly uses O', but rather 'If one uses C one should admit that O is valid'.

This moderate position is still strong enough to imply that the cosmological argument's second step is invalid because the ontological argument is invalid. It also supports another point which is important to Kant. His cosmological arguer boasts that his argument 'begins with experience, and is not wholly *a priori*' as the ontological argument is, since it has the empirical premiss that something exists.[38] Kant retorts that 'the appeal to experience is quite superfluous', for if the second step is valid then the whole conclusion could have been reached a priori. 'If... we can determine the possibility of a necessary being, we likewise establish its existence. For what we are then saying is this: that of all possible beings there is one which carries with it absolute necessity, that is, that this being exists with absolute necessity.' The wording here wavers between the extreme position and the moderate one, but all Kant needs is the moderate view that if the second step is valid then so is the ontological argument. That, with no suggestion that the second step uses the ontological argument, would suffice to render 'superfluous' the thin contingent premiss of the cosmological argument.

So much for the powers of the moderate view, but is the view correct? It is not. A cosmological arguer, even if he has taken the second step, can reject the ontological argument as downright invalid. He can say: 'The concept of an *ens realissimum* includes that of necessary existence, but all that follows from this conceptual fact is that *if* there is an *ens realissimum* then it exists necessarily.' That is, he can use Kant's own conditionalizing move, which deprives the ontological argument of its existential conclusion. Kant has insisted that the conditionalizing move is correct, so how can he justly refuse to allow the cosmological arguer to make it?

The conditionalizing move, it may be remembered, was rejected by Malcolm when he argued that 'God necessarily exists' entails 'Necessarily God exists' which entails 'God exists', which is the required existential conclusion. I have conceded that this may be valid if the necessity in question is logical rather than causal, but it seems to me quite implausible to suppose that Kant also has developed doubts about the conditionalizing move and is therefore declining to let the cosmological arguer use it.

I conclude that Kant has altogether failed in his attempt to show that

---

[38] 633. Next two quotations: 635; 636.

the cosmological arguer who takes the second step thereby commits himself to the validity of the ontological argument. His own basic materials, however, enable us to construct a more powerful criticism of the cosmological argument than any which he actually offers.

§ 80. The radical criticism

Although Kant's initial dealings with the cosmological argument construe it causally, as though a necessarily existing being were just an imperishable one, he does eventually work around to asserting that the necessity in question must be not causal but logical. This accords with the fact that Kant's sources for the cosmological argument are Leibnizian rather than Thomist; and anyway, Kant says, nothing but logical necessity will suffice for the cosmological argument. 'Reason recognises that only as completely necessary which follows of necessity from its concept.'[39] 'Absolute necessity is a necessity that is to be found in thought alone.' 'If. . . the absolute necessity of a thing were to be known, this would have to be *a priori* from concepts, and never by positing it as a cause relative to an existence given in experience.'

But that immediately yields a powerful criticism of the cosmological argument, namely that its conclusion uses the concept of a being which exists of logical necessity, a being whose existence is guaranteed by a definition or by a fact about a concept, or, in Leibniz's unashamed words, 'a being to whose essence belongs existence'.[40] If Kant's criticisms of the ontological argument are right, then this concept is logically cankered, and so the cosmological argument collapses.

This radical criticism, as I shall call it, is part of what I attacked Malcolm with, after conceding his right to reject the conditionalizing move. It was not addressed to the workings of his argument, but just to its tolerating the notion of logically necessary existence. It therefore holds equally against the cosmological arguer. Furthermore, it applies to him just because he says that there is a logically necessarily existing being: it

[39] 640. Next two quotations: 645; 662.
[40] 'On the Radical Origination of Things', Loemker, p. 487; see also Leibniz, 'Critical Thoughts on the Principles of Descartes', Loemker, p. 386. For a fuller presentation of this line of criticism, see Smart, *op. cit.* pp. 267–9. W. H. Baumer, 'Kant on Cosmological Arguments', *The Monist* (1967), rejects this criticism because the cosmological argument need not, 'as Kant well knew' (p. 530), invoke *logical* necessity. Yet Baumer implicitly denies the cosmological arguer's right to block the ontological argument by making the conditionalizing move, for he says roundly – in agreement with Kant's own attack – that 'any cosmological argument involves an ontological one as an essential part' (p. 528).

does not matter how he reaches that lemma, or whether he goes on beyond it. So this criticism is more radical than Kant's, since he attacks only the second step leading to the final conclusion that the necessarily existing being is an *ens realissimum*.

Early in his section on the cosmological argument, Kant seems poised to launch into the radical criticism. He says that the cosmological argument leads to the belief that there is a necessarily existing being, and that 'since this necessity must be unconditioned and certain *a priori*, reason [is] forced to seek a concept which [will] satisfy, if possible, such a demand, and enable us to know an existence in a completely *a priori* manner' (631). But then, rather than saying that the cosmological argument's conclusion is tainted with the bad logic of the ontological argument, Kant goes on to emphasize the superiority of the cosmological argument over the ontological. The radical attack never gets started.

Nor does it occur anywhere else in the treatment of the cosmological argument, although the discussion of the ontological argument contains it, almost intact, when Kant remarks about the concept of an *ens realissimum*: 'There is already a contradiction in introducing the concept of existence – no matter under what title it may be disguised – into the concept of a thing which we profess to be thinking solely in reference to its possibility' (625).

Peter Remnant, who has helped me to a clearer view of the text in this area, suggests that Kant may have written his Section 5 attack on the cosmological argument before developing the Kant–Frege line on the ontological argument which we find in Section 4. That would explain three striking facts. (1) The radical criticism of the cosmological argument is nearer the surface when the ontological argument is being discussed, in Section 4, than in Section 5 where it belongs. (2) The discussion of the cosmological argument gives no hint as to *what* is wrong with the ontological argument, and indeed hardly suggests that anything is wrong with it. (3) Although in Section 4 Kant claims to disarm the ontological argument by weakening its conclusion to a mere conditional with no existential import, in Section 5 he allows no such resource to the cosmological arguer who is threatened with having to admit that the ontological argument is valid.

Consider also the general tone and texture of Section 5. The cosmological arguer's supposed commitment to accepting the ontological argument is used in the spirit of 'Your appeal to experience is superfluous', rather than 'You are committed to endorsing an argument which is really invalid'. This whole discussion seems to be addressed to an audience who are cool towards the ontological argument without having any firm doctrine about why it is unacceptable. When one reads the section with Remnant's hypothesis in mind, everything falls into place.

§ 81. The argument from design

There is only one other way of trying to prove God's existence, Kant says. As well as the ontological argument from zero contingent premisses, and the cosmological from the premiss that something exists, there is also the 'physico-theological argument' which starts from relatively detailed facts about what the given world is like. What Kant has in mind here is the sort of thing more commonly known as 'the argument from design'. It goes like this:

In the world we everywhere find clear signs of an order in accordance with a determinate purpose...This purposive order is quite alien to the things of the world, and belongs to them only contingently...There exists, therefore, a sublime and wise cause (or more than one), which must be the cause of the world... The unity of this cause may be inferred from the unity of the reciprocal relations existing between the parts of the world.[41]

That sketch omits something which looms large in most versions of this famous argument, though Kant does just mention it later. It is the supposed 'analogy between certain natural products and [artefacts such as] houses, ships, watches'. This raises complex and slippery matters which have a literature all of their own. Kant, however, passes it off with the remark that 'we need not here criticise [the argument] too strictly' on this count.

Even if that analogy is allowed, what can be made of it? The physico-theological argument exploits the analogy by applying to the whole world principles which are found to hold true of certain species of things within the world: ships and watches don't just happen, without the intervention of (mundane) intelligence; and so things like ships and watches cannot just happen, without the intervention of (presumably supramundane) intelligence. This is wide open to attack, especially with Kantian weapons, yet Kant contents himself with the tepid remark that

---

[41] 653. Next two quotations are both 654. The classic discussion of the analogy with artefacts is Hume's *Dialogues Concerning Natural Religion*; for more recent discussions, see A. Plantinga, *God and Other Minds* (Ithaca, 1967), Ch. 4, and R. J Richman, 'Plantinga, God, and (yet) other Minds', *The Australasian Journal of Philosophy* (1972), especially pp. 41–3.

the argument involves 'a mode of reasoning which could not perhaps withstand a searching transcendental criticism'.[42] He also implies that the argument is imperfect when he says that its proponents should not claim 'apodeictic certainty' for their conclusion, and that their 'language' should 'be toned down to the more moderate and humble requirements of a belief adequate to quieten our doubts, though not to command unconditional submission'. We are not told why.

Kant wants to shelter the design argument because he approves of our viewing the world as the work of a superhuman designer.[43] But the indulgent laxity of his handling of the argument has another source as well, namely his wish to press an attack which does not bear on the argument's internal workings. Even if the argument were impeccable, he says, it would not establish the existence of a creator, let alone of an *ens realissimum*:

> The utmost, therefore, that the argument can prove is an *architect* of the world who is always very much hampered by the adaptability of the material in which he works, not a *creator* of the world to whose idea everything is subject. This, however, is altogether inadequate to the lofty purpose which we have before our eyes, namely, the proof of an all-sufficient primordial being.[44]

So the argument from design, Kant says, must fall back on the cosmological argument, which, he adds inaccurately, 'is only a disguised ontological proof'. Kant envisages proponents of the argument from design as boasting that their argument starts from details about how the world is, rather than from the thin premiss that something exists or from no contingent premisses at all. But they have 'no ground for being so contemptuous' of the cosmological and ontological arguments, for eventually the argument from design rests on the other two.

This has no force against someone who uses the argument from design only to establish that the world has a superhuman architect whose power, benevolence and wisdom are shown forth in his works. Kant admits as much: 'The physico-theological argument can indeed lead us to the point of admiring the greatness, wisdom, power, etc., of the Author of the world' (657), but he assumes that no one would be interested in the argument unless it fulfilled the 'lofty purpose' of proving the existence of 'an all-sufficient primordial being'. This is surely false.

[42] 654. Next quotation: 652–3.
[43] See the two paragraphs on 650–2, and § 86 below.
[44] 655. Remaining quotations in this paragraph: 657.

Kant often fails even to distinguish the cosmological argument from the design argument. For example:

Everywhere we see a chain of effects and causes, of ends and means, a regularity in origination and dissolution. Nothing has of itself come into the condition in which we find it to exist, but always points to something else as its cause, while this in turn commits us to repetition of the same enquiry. The whole universe must thus sink into the abyss of nothingness, unless, over and above this infinite chain of contingencies, we assume something to support it – something which is original and independently self-subsistent, and which as the cause of the origin of the universe secures also at the same time its continuance. (650)

The argument from design is vaguely suggested by the phrase 'ends and means' and perhaps also by 'regularity', and it is indicated by the final clause. For the rest, however, the passage points directly towards the cosmological argument. The reference to 'the condition in which we find' things may be meant to suggest an argument which starts from detailed facts about the world, but the significant point is that almost nothing is said about *what* the condition is in which we find things.

This is further evidence that Kant did not wish to apply his mind to the argument from design in itself. Ironically, this section, which ostensibly treats of the argument from design, subjects the cosmological argument to valid internal criticisms which were handled cursorily in the preceding section because there Kant was distracted by his desire to link the cosmological argument with the ontological!

Kant's general passion for order and system makes it unsurprising that he should be entranced by the prospect of bringing down the three theological arguments by a dominoes effect. Also, his theory of reason gives him grounds for wanting to make the concept of an *ens realissimum* – and thus perhaps the ontological argument – fundamental to all theology.

12

REASON

§ 82. Inferences of reason

I have so far avoided Kant's theory about how *reason* generates the problems which are treated in the Dialectic. This theory, which is expounded in the Introduction, Book I and the Appendix to the Dialectic, is a bad one, and the Dialectic's main content is independent of it. Still, the theory of reason is sometimes invoked in discussions of specific problems; and it is also supposed to generate the architectonic – the over-all shape – of the material in Book II, explaining why the proper concerns of the Dialectic are exhausted by psychology, cosmology and theology. This architectonic is a clumsy attempt to rationalize a set of problems which reflect not the structure of reason but the preoccupations of German academic philosophers at the time when Kant was writing. Where the theory has an effect, it is by tempting Kant into a brutal and insensitive forcing of his material into unnatural shapes, and never by genuinely illuminating it. Still, the theory must be attended to.

What sort of faculty does Kant think reason to be? His main explanation, given in two sub-sections of the Introduction, is that reason is a faculty of making logical deductions.[1] The understanding can also be used deductively, Kant says, but only with one premiss at a time, whereas reason's deductive task is the drawing of conclusions from pairs of premisses. He puts it like this:

If the inferred judgment is already so contained in the earlier judgment that it may be derived from it without the mediation of a third representation, the inference is called immediate... – I should prefer to entitle it inference of the understanding. But if besides the knowledge contained in the primary proposition still another judgment is needed to yield the conclusion, it is to be entitled an inference of the reason.

That is ambiguous. It is supposed to distinguish (a) arguments with one premiss from (b) arguments with two, but it could easily be taken instead to distinguish (a′) arguments in which the conclusion follows immediately from the premiss(es) from (b′) arguments in which the conclusion can be derived from the premiss(es) only with the aid of an

---

[1] 359–66. Next quotation: 360.

intermediate lemma. Kant's central concern is with (a)/(b), but his use of 'mediation' and 'immediate' strongly suggests (a')/(b'). So indeed does the language of 'understanding' and 'reason': knowing the 'immediate' consequences of a proposition is part of understanding it, but an awareness of its more remote entailments requires not merely understanding but also deductive capacity of a more sustained kind – reason, in short. Perhaps Kant tended to conflate the two distinctions.

Note that the distinction between (a') and (b') is person-relative. It cannot be a logical fact that R can be deduced from P only by moving from P to Q and thence to R. If the lemma Q is needed, that is because it is needed *by someone* – someone who cannot see that P entails R except by being brought to see that P entails Q and that Q entails R. As for the distinction between (a) and (b): that is really non-existent, because any inference from a pair of premisses is logically equivalent to an inference from a single conjunctive premiss. There is of course nothing wrong with Kant's being interested in certain arguments which are conventionally expressed in a two-premiss form. But he has tried to give a deep characterization of them, because he wants to assign them to the faculty of reason while letting other deductions be performed by the understanding. This, as we shall see, is not Kant's only trouble in trying to isolate the putative faculty of reason.

Kant's word for 'inference of reason' is *Vernunftschluß*, which can also bear the narrower meaning of 'syllogism'. His usual examples are syllogisms, properly so-called – arguments in which a subject–predicate (S–P) conclusion is inferred from a 'major premiss' which connects P with a 'middle term' M, and a 'minor premiss' which connects S with M. For example, 'All men are mortal, Caius is a man, therefore Caius is mortal'. Here is Kant's account of how such an argument is conducted:

In every inference of reason I first think a *rule* (the major premiss) through the *understanding*. Secondly, I subsume a known item [*ein Erkenntnis*] under the condition of the rule by means of the faculty of judgement (the minor premiss). Finally, by a *a priori* use of reason I determine my known item through the predicate of the rule (the conclusion).[2]

Applying this to the example I gave: the major premiss is the 'rule' or universal proposition that all men are mortal, and the term 'man' is

---

[2] 360–1; see also the paragraph on 378, and 386–7. *Erkenntnis* (feminine) means 'knowledge'; it sometimes means that also in Kant's non-standard neuter use, but I am conjecturing that the latter here means 'thing which is known' or 'known item'. Kemp Smith seems to think so too, but his translation of the passage is unsatisfactory in other ways.

what Kant calls the 'condition' in this; in the minor premiss I apply 'man' to an item which I know about, namely Caius; and then by an a priori use of my reason I draw a conclusion in which I 'determine' Caius 'through the predicate of' the major premiss, i.e. I describe him as mortal.

This account seriously lacks generality. It is supposed to cover every *Vernunftschluß* – not just every syllogism, properly so-called, but also certain hypothetical and disjunctive arguments to which, in fact, the very terminology of 'major premiss' and 'predicate' etc. is inapplicable. Nor does the account even fit all genuine syllogisms. There is the trivial point that in many syllogisms the part of the major premiss which re-appears in the conclusion is its predicate- and not its subject-term. Also, and more seriously, there is trouble in Kant's assigning the minor premiss to the 'faculty of judgment'. This invokes his intermittent doctrine that whereas the understanding deals in universal propositions or 'rules', the judgment is the faculty for knowing particular or singular truths (171–4); and so Kant is here implying that in syllogisms the minor premiss is never a universal proposition. This is false. For example, 'All men are mortal; all philosophers are men; so all philosophers are mortal'.

The details of Kant's account of how syllogisms work do not matter. All that concerns us is the vague idea that in an inference of reason something is brought into an explanatory relationship with something else, and this is described as the former's being assigned a *condition*. We shall meet 'conditions' again later.

§83. Ascending reason

We have encountered the 'descending' function of reason, in which conclusions are drawn from premisses. Far more important to us is its 'ascending' function, in which, given a true proposition, we search for other truths from which it could be inferred – moving upwards from conclusion to possible premisses.

If I already accept proposition *P* as true, why should I bother to look for premisses from which I could infer it? Not so as to establish *P*, obviously. Kant's answer is that by finding suitable premisses from which *P* follows, I unite *P* with other truths in a wider intellectual structure:

If...the conclusion is set as a problem – to see whether it does not follow from judgments already given... – I look in the understanding for the assertion of this conclusion, to discover whether it is not there found to stand under certain conditions according to a universal rule. If I find such a condition,...then the conclusion is deduced from the rule, *which is also valid for other objects of knowledge*. From this we see that in inference reason endeavours to reduce the varied and manifold knowledge obtained through the understanding to the smallest number of principles (universal conditions) and thereby to achieve in it the highest possible unity.[3]

This activity of uniting and interlinking is very different from that of deductively inferring from pairs of premises. Kant speaks of 'inferences' which 'proceed from experience upwards to its conditions', but the ascending use of reason is really not inferential at all.

The two functions of reason collaborate, Kant notes, in the hypothetico-deductive method: I try to unite my knowledge by ascending to premises which I do not know to be true but which I entertain as 'problematic', so that then I must test them in ways which involve a descending use of reason (674–5). But this activity, which involves all the resources of experimental and theoretical science, should not be called the 'hypothetical employment of *reason*'. The ascending part is in no way inferential; and although the testing procedure does involve inference, it also includes experiments which presumably do not engage 'reason' in any sense of the term which Kant has introduced.

However, we must accept Kant's usage. From now on, when I use 'reason' without qualification, I shall be referring to the so-called ascending use of reason. We must let this stand on its own feet, forgetting its supposed link with reason's descending or deductive role. Kant himself once refers to ascending and descending reason as distinct 'faculties', and says that 'the nature of' the former 'is not to be understood from [the] definition' of the latter (355–6). And in the *Prolegomena*, he makes 'reason' central to the Dialectic, yet says nothing at all about its descending use.

As well as (ascending) reason, we have another faculty for uniting items of knowledge, namely (theorizing) understanding. 'All our knowledge starts with the senses, proceeds thence to understanding, and ends with reason.'[4] Trying to separate understanding from reason, Kant says that the former unifies our data by applying concepts to them in 'rules' or judgments, and reason unifies our judgments by interrelating them in ever-larger systems of 'principles'. Understanding, he says, 'deals at first hand with the senses', whereas 'reason...has no immediate relation to [objects], but only to the understanding.' Also: 'Understanding...secures the unity of appearances by means of rules, and reason...secures the unity of the rules of understanding under principles.'

---

[3] 361. Next quotation: 366.   [4] 355. Next two quotations: 363; 359; see also 672.

The 'rules' spoken of here are universal truths about the given world, though probably the material to be unified by reason should include also those non-universal propositions which Kant sometimes assigns to the faculty of judgment. As for the 'principles' which reason generates, as the understanding generates 'rules': we know that they are higher and more general than 'rules', but there is no determinate place where 'rules' stop and 'principles' start; and so there is no determinate border between understanding and reason. I earlier criticized the supposed line between the (descending) inferences of understanding and those of (descending) reason, and now I argue that there is no proper line, either, between the (ascending) activity of the understanding in bringing intuition under 'rules' and the (ascending) activity of reason in bringing those 'rules' under wider generalizations called 'principles'.

So far as I can discover, the nearest Kant comes to telling us what 'principles' are, though with no mention of the faculty of 'reason', is when he explains why he does not count as 'principles' those supposedly synthetic and a priori propositions which express the special status of the categories. He says that because the latter propositions concern the conditions of 'possible experience', they are not 'based on concepts'; and for that reason they are not 'properly, without qualification, to be entitled "principles"', this title being reserved for 'synthetic modes of knowledge derived [solely] from concepts' (357–8). On this account, though, Kant should deny that there are any principles at all, for he holds that synthetic truths are all either empirical or else of that special categorial sort which he has just declared not to be principles. In a nutshell, it is a matter of deep doctrine with him that there are no 'synthetic modes of knowledge derived from concepts'. In the rest of his work, the only non-analytic propositional items which are entirely divorced from experience are certain pseudo-principles which reason generates when it malfunctions in a certain way. But we are now trying to understand 'principles' as they figure in Kant's account of ascending reason when it is behaving properly.

There is also another way in which Kant tends to abolish ordinary ascending reason. He has a theory, to be expounded in §85 below, that reason is never content until it has achieved the highest possible level of theory; but sometimes he bends this a little, and writes as though reason's sole function were to insist upon completeness in the ascending endeavours of *the understanding*. Thus, he speaks of 'principles' as determining 'how understanding is to be employed in dealing with experience in its totality'.[5] He says that reason provides 'a canon' for the 'extended and consistent employment' of the understanding. He says of a part of reason's output that it 'serves as a rule for the understanding'. And also this: 'Pure reason leaves everything to the understanding...Reason concerns itself exclusively with absolute totality in the employment of the concepts of the understanding.' Remarks like these virtually imply that reason has no ascending function at all, but only a static function as a goal-setter or overseer for the understanding. Kant's considered view, however, is that reason's goal-setting role is an outgrowth from a more ordinary ascending or hypothesis-hunting activity of reason, and so he ought not to assign all theorizing ascents to the understanding.

If understanding and reason do both have ascending roles, we still have not found a line between them. The clearest line I can devise is one according to which the understanding applies only to the raw data of sensibility, while reason is involved in any further theorizing, any imposition of further intellectual control upon items which are already in some degree conceptualized. But that could not have been acceptable to Kant. Whereas some of his remarks give the understanding too much to do, this latest account gives it far too little. It implies that even in a low-level generalization over such already-conceptualized items as fire and heat, blood and pain, what is involved must be reason and not understanding. At no time does Kant restrict the domain of ascending understanding as severely as that.

The demarcation problem remains, and seems to have no solution. I believe that Kant had no moderately clear view about the putative faculty of reason. We shall probably get closest to his usual working picture if we assign to the understanding the sorts of conceptualizing which are needed for survival in the real world – cavemen's theorizing, as it were – and associate reason with intellectuals' theorizing, i.e. the deliberate and explicit search for relatively high-level explanatory theory in order to give one's corpus of belief more unity than the man in the street needs for his mundane practical purposes. That bases the understanding/reason line on a difference of degree rather than a sharp difference of kind; and that, although Kant could hardly have welcomed it, is indeed the best way to view the matter. From now on, I shall take it that the faculty of (ascending) reason is the faculty for theorizing which is *at least fairly high-level*. This shades off gradually into the low-

---

[5] 378. Next three quotations: 385; 673; 382–3. For an enriched but unclear account of reason's function, see 676.

9-2

level theorizing which is the work of the understanding, but if we keep the level high enough we can avoid border-disputes.[6] This modest proposal hardly squares with Kant's remark that 'without reason [there can be] no coherent employment of the understanding [and thus] no sufficient criterion of empirical truth', but I think that in any case that should be dismissed as extravagant.

Just as the Analytic contends that we must unite our intuitions into judgments of the understanding, so the Dialectic claims that we must unite our judgments into larger theoretical structures. Why must we? Kant has no answer analogous to his claim in the Analytic that if our intuitions are not brought under the understanding we cannot be self-conscious.[7] He says that there is a 'principle of reason' which 'calls upon us' always to pursue further intellectual unification, but its status is not made clear. I think that his more considered view is that we cannot help trying to unify our knowledge: 'Human reason is by nature architectonic. That is to say, it regards all our knowledge as belonging to a possible system.' This may well be true, not about human reason but about at least some human beings – the rationally inquiring ones whose 'craving for generality' Wittgenstein deplored. Kant also sees that craving as likely to lead to trouble, in a way I shall discuss shortly; but, unlike Wittgenstein, he regards the craving for generality in itself as a valuable aspect of the human condition.

§ 84. Conditions

Kant speaks of reason's search for 'conditions', that is, for explanations or groundings or wider and deeper theoretical settings for items of knowledge. Causes are conditions. If I know that Gx, my search for conditions of this fact may lead me to the facts that Fx and that it is a causal law that whatever is F is also G, this yielding a causal explanation of the fact that Gx. But there are conditions other than causes. Any stretch of the physical world has a surrounding stretch as a 'condition' of it, any lump of matter has smaller parts as 'conditions' of it, and so on. Whenever Kant speaks of something as being conditioned or having a condition, the situation is one where something of the form

$$(x)(Fx \to (\exists y)\, yRx)$$

[6] On this matter I am substantially in agreement with T. K. Swing, *Kant's Transcendental Logic* (New Haven, 1969), pp. 241f. Next quotation: 679.

[7] See § 10 above. Next two quotations: 677; 502. 'Craving for generality': L. Wittgenstein, *The Blue and Brown Books* (Oxford, 1958), pp. 17–18.

is true. For example, every event is caused, everything extended is surrounded by something, every period of time is preceded by something. Furthermore, Kant is mainly interested in cases where

$$(x)(Fx \rightarrow (\exists y)(Fy \ \& \ yRx))$$

– every event is caused by an event, everything extended is surrounded by something extended, and so on. But Kant is not restricted to such cases by the meaning of 'condition'. For example, the third antinomy asks whether the regressing series of conditions (causes) of a given event might contain a condition which was not itself an event.

We can speak of x as being R-conditioned by y, or as an R-condition of z, for some specific conditioning relation R. Kant regularly speaks of things as 'conditions' or as 'conditioned', without qualification; but that usage can be allowed for too, because 'x is conditioned' can mean 'there is some R such that x is R-conditioned by something', and Kant himself says in effect that 'x is unconditioned' means 'there is no R such that x is R-conditioned' (382–3).

What sorts of relations make something a 'condition' of something else? For example, why does Kant think that today is a condition of tomorrow but not of yesterday? The formulae above do not yield the answer to this, because Kant thinks that they hold true, if F = 'is a time', both for R = 'is later than' and for R = 'is earlier than'.[8] The only answer we get from him is what we extract from stray phrases suggesting that a given time is 'made possible' by earlier times but not by later ones, or that past times, unlike future ones, are 'conditions of [the] possibility' of the present. These phrases suggest that in general y is a condition of x only if y somehow makes x possible. This allows causes and earlier times and physical parts as conditions, while disqualifying later times, but it does not clearly support Kant's view that any stretch of the world has a surrounding stretch as a condition. Also, on this account of it the concept of a condition is no longer rooted in the structure of deductive arguments. The differences between how today relates to yesterday and how it relates to tomorrow have no place in the abstract theory of syllogisms. However, since we have already left descending reason behind, we need not hesitate to drop syllogisms as well. The account of 'conditions' in terms of what 'makes possible' a given item is, in any case, the best I can do for Kant on this question.

Now, suppose that P is a proposition reporting some fact for which

[8] 394. Next two quoted phrases: 437; 551. See also 439.

I seek 'conditions' of some kind. If I find them, they will be embodied in further propositions, say Q and S, which provide a grounding or explanation or theoretical setting for P, or perhaps which explain what makes P possible. If Q or S is also 'conditioned' in the same way, it will launch reason off on a further ascent. Reason, Kant says, will be dissatisfied until all its conditioned subject-matter is traced back to something unconditioned: 'The principle peculiar to reason...in its logical employment is: to find for the conditioned knowledge obtained through the understanding the unconditioned whereby its unity is brought to completion' (364).

In cases fitting the second of my two formulae, everything which is F has an R-condition which is F and therefore has an R-condition which...etc.; and so we can never meet anything which is not R-conditioned. But Kant does not say that in such cases reason is doomed to failure. Rather he redescribes reason as trying to discover or at least intellectually envisage 'the whole series of conditions',[9] because this series is, for some obscure reason, supposed to be unconditioned. I think it would be best to accept this part of Kant's doctrine as merely an attempt to keep reason striving ever upwards while not making its task look obviously hopeless.

Reason can ascend, generating a series in which each member is conditioned by the next, or it can descend through a series in which each member is a condition of the next. According to Kant, 'the *ascending* series...must stand in a different relation to the faculty of reason from that of the *descending* series',[10] because he thinks that reason's basic aspirations or urges all tend upwards rather than downwards. 'The transcendental concept of reason is directed always solely towards absolute totality in the synthesis of conditions, and never terminates save in what is completely...unconditioned.' The drive towards the unconditioned obviously has to proceed upwards. If there were a corresponding target which drew one downwards, it would have to be the notion of a conditioned item which is not a condition of anything further; and, in Kant's theory, reason has no interest in any such target. His attempts to explain this are unfortunate. One of them is not even coherent. Another, which says that every downward step 'is carried through by the understanding itself', lets understanding usurp the whole descending function of reason.

[9] 364; 379; 380.
[10] 388. Next quotation: 382. The incoherent attempt: 388–9. Final quotation in this paragraph: 394.

§85. The source of dialectical error

Let us leave reason pursuing the unconditioned, and turn to a different theme. The two will soon converge.

According to Kant, the problems treated in the Dialectic arise not from mere carelessness or lack of acuity, but from a 'dialectic', which is a positive propensity for error:

> There exists...a natural and unavoidable dialectic of pure reason – not one in which a bungler might entangle himself through lack of knowledge, or one which some sophist has artificially invented to confuse thinking people, but one... which, even after its deceptiveness has been exposed, will not cease to play tricks with reason and continually entrap it into momentary aberrations ever and again calling for correction.[11]

What is this positive source of error? The Dialectic opens with a flimsy attempt to show that *all* error 'is brought about solely by the unobserved influence of sensibility on the understanding'; but this conflicts with everything else Kant says on the subject, unless we re-interpret it intolerably.

Another account: The Dialectic's problems arise not from the casual misuse of concepts when one 'does not pay sufficient attention' to the proper boundaries of the understanding, but rather from 'actual principles which incite us to tear down all those boundary-fences and to seize possession of an entirely new domain which recognizes no limits of demarcation'.[12] These malign 'actual principles' are said to be 'transcendent', as distinct from 'transcendental'. In fact, Kant has no transcendent principles to offer us. Each time he purports to do so, he weakens the meaning of 'transcendent', sometimes muddying the waters in other ways as well. I now leave 'transcendent principles' permanently behind.

In Kant's dominant account of the source of error, the trouble is caused not by anarchistic 'principles' but by 'a natural illusion' – an inherent feature of our minds which tempts us to error 'even after it has been detected'.[13] (Kant compares this with the kind of sensory situation which, he thinks, is inherently delusive even though it need not cause actual error. That formulation is objectionable, but one sees what he means.) The root of the trouble, more specifically, is the fact 'that there are fundamental rules and maxims for the employment of our

---

[11] 354–5. Next quotation: 350.
[12] 352. Purported transcendent principles: 365; 383; 447–8; 484; 593; 873–4.
[13] 353. Next quotation: *ibid.*; see also 85–6 and the rhetorical questions on 365–6.

reason..., and that these have all the appearance of being objective principles.' These 'maxims' are guides or injunctions – marching orders for the faculty of reason – but they appear to be 'objective' principles which state facts about the world. If we take them to be 'objective' in this sense, we are succumbing to the illusion and falling into dialectical error. Such errors can be avoided, but we cannot make the illusion 'actually disappear' because it is 'natural and inevitable', like the bent appearance of a straight stick half immersed in water.[14] Kant says that the illusion 'rests on subjective principles, and foists them upon us as objective'. In this context, the subjective/objective distinction is not concerned with inner/outer. It is in fact virtually the practical/theoretical distinction – the line between something which tells scientists how to behave and something which reports facts about reality. This use of 'subjective' is seriously misleading.

The 'maxims' of which Kant speaks are supposed to be orders or advice to the faculty of reason 'in its logical employment'. The latter phrase covers descending reason,[15] but what concerns us is that it also covers ascending reason, and that the basic 'maxim' is something we have already met, namely the injunction always to seek conditions for anything which is conditioned. In its 'real' or 'transcendental' use, on the other hand, reason figures as 'the source of certain concepts and principles', and boldly offers claims about the nature of reality. In its logical use, reason organizes and orders and unifies items of knowledge gained through sensibility and understanding, but in its transcendental use it claims to add to our knowledge. These purported additions are the spurious 'objective principles' which result from failing to grasp the imperative nature of the maxims which should guide reason in its logical employment.

So transcendental reason, as such, is a source of error. It consists in the misuse of reason, powered by a misunderstanding of the maxims which should guide reasons's legitimate endeavours. This is the 'pure reason' of which Kant is offering a 'critique'. It is 'pure' in that it involves nothing empirical, but it does not stand in contrast with any empirical or non-pure use of reason. The proper contrast is with the 'logical' use of reason, in which it unifies knowledge already gained through other faculties rather than trying to add to our knowledge through its own labours.

Some more terminology must be introduced. Just as kinds of judg-

---

[14] 354. Next quotation: *ibid.*
[15] See 394. The basic 'maxim': 364. The 'source of certain concepts' etc.: 355.

ment correspond to concepts of the understanding, so kinds of inference correspond to *concepts of reason* – which Kant also calls *ideas*. He associates ideas with certain basic forms of inference, comparing them not with concepts of the understanding generally but only with the privileged dozen, the categories:

The mere logical form of our knowledge contains original pure *a priori* concepts [of the understanding], which represent objects prior to all experience...Similarly ...the form of inferences...contains the origin of special *a priori* concepts, which we may call pure concepts of reason, or transcendental ideas, and which will determine according to principles how understanding is to be employed in dealing with experience in its totality.[16]

Kant distinguishes three forms of inference – categorical, hypothetical and disjunctive – and implies that there is an 'idea' corresponding to each.[17] Sometimes he allows other ideas which do not clearly relate to inference-forms, and he also speaks of 'the idea' associated with the whole ascending use of reason:

[The] unity of reason always presupposes an idea, namely, that of the form of a whole of knowledge...This idea...postulates a complete unity in the knowledge obtained by the understanding, by which this knowledge is to be...a system connected according to necessary laws...This idea is [not] a concept of the object, but only of the thoroughgoing unity of such concepts.

The 'ideas' mentioned earlier might relate to 'the idea' which Kant speaks of here as special to general, like *dog* and *cat* in relation to *animal*. Kant does not say.

Kant often speaks of the 'illusion' that ideas are objective or are 'concepts of objects':

I understand by 'idea' a necessary concept of reason to which no corresponding object can by given in sense-experience. Thus the pure concepts of reason...are *transcendental ideas*...They view all knowledge gained in experience as being determined through an absolute totality of conditions. They are not arbitrarily invented; they are imposed by the very nature of reason itself...No object adequate to the transcendental idea can ever be found within experience.[18]

This suggests that ideas have error built into them, but that is not Kant's considered view. 'The ideas of pure reason', he says, 'can never be dialectical [error-inducing] in themselves.' Also: 'The ideas of pure reason ...become dialectical only through heedlessness and misapprehension.' Really, his view about the illusion regarding ideas is analogous to, and

---

[16] 377–8; wording slightly modified for clarity.
[17] 699–700. Next quotation: 673.
[18] 383–4. Next three quotations: 697; 708; 672.

perhaps only a rewording of, his view about the illusion that certain maxims are objective principles. Specifically, ideas of reason are all right as guides to inquiry, but we must not think that there are objects corresponding to them:

[Ideas of reason] have an excellent, and indeed indispensably necessary, regulative employment, namely, that of directing the understanding towards a certain goal upon which the routes marked out by all its rules converge, as upon their point of intersection. This point is indeed a mere idea, a *focus imaginarius*, from which, since it lies quite outside the bounds of possible experience, the concepts of the understanding do not in reality proceed; none the less it serves to give to these concepts the greatest unity combined with the greatest extension. Hence arises the illusion that the lines have their source in a real object lying outside the field of empirically possible knowledge – just as objects reflected in a mirror are seen as behind it.

This memorable metaphor needs to be cashed in a literal description of a dialectical, illusion-induced, maxim-misunderstanding error. I shall pursue that in §88 below, but first some more text must be introduced.

§86. Regulative principles

One of Kant's descriptions of dialectical 'illusion' is this: there are *regulative* principles which seem to be *constitutive*. This wording of his doctrine of illusion introduces a part of the text which I have quoted from but have not yet discussed, namely the Appendix to the Dialectic.

Kant twice uses 'regulative' and 'constitutive' in the Analytic with meanings which I do not understand.[19] Nor do I follow his attempt to relate those meanings to the ones which now concern us. I shall now ignore the Analytic's uses of 'regulative' and 'constitutive'.

In the Dialectic these terms do not occur until Section 8 of the Antinomies chapter, but they embody the contrast between maxims and objective principles, which permeates the Introduction and Book I. Why does that contrast appear so long before the labels 'regulative' and 'constitutive' are introduced? Presumably because Kant constructed the *Critique* partly by hastily assembling materials written over many years: some of his discussion of dialectical illusion must have been written before he thought of using the 'regulative' terminology in this way, and he didn't bother to insert 'regulative' etc. anywhere in those pages. Anyway, the situation does not reflect any subtle nuances in his thought.

[19] 222–3; 296. Next reference: 692.

In this section, I shall try to sort out the Appendix.

A 'regulative' principle seems to be one which is neither provable nor disprovable,[20] but is a useful guide to scientific inquiry. Combining the second and third points, Kant says that regulative principles 'contribute to the extension of empirical knowledge, without ever being in a position to run counter to it'. Combining the first and third, he says that the regulative principles are defensible only as 'heuristic principles' which can be 'employed with great advantage in the elaboration of experience'.

The principles Kant calls 'regulative' are usually what Watkins has called 'all-and-some principles',[21] that is, ones of the form

$$(x)(Fx \to (\exists y) \ldots).$$

That, it may be noted, is a form shared by the formulae which I used in §84 above as partly expressing the notion of a condition. This overlap is not a coincidence.

If a principle of the above form is not spatio-temporally restricted, then the universal quantifier makes conclusive proof impossible, and the existential quantifier prevents conclusive disproof. For example, the determinist principle

$$(x)(x \text{ is an event} \to (\exists y)(y \text{ is an event } \& \ y \text{ caused } x))$$

cannot be proved, because this would require us to find a cause for every event; and it cannot be disproved, because this would require us to show, for some event, that no other event was suitably connected to it by any causal law – and logical space contains too many possible causal laws.

So it is only because of the size of the task that regulative principles cannot be proved or disproved. We can therefore have a sense of direction with respect to such a principle, moving towards verifying it or towards falsifying it – for example by causally explaining a given event, or by seeking and not finding its cause. That explains how regulative principles can serve as maxims: they advise us never to despair of going further in the verifying direction. For example, the determinist principle embodies the advice always to seek causes and never to admit that any event is uncaused. Each regulative principle sets before us the unattainable goal of complete verification, this being a 'maximum' of

[20] 675 and 716. Next two quotations: 699; 691.
[21] J. W. N. Watkins, 'Between Analytic and Empirical', *Philosophy* (1957); 'Confirmable and Influential Metaphysics', *Mind* (1958).

something quite familiar, a maximum which 'reason follows...ever more closely without reaching [it]'.[22] It is important to remember, though Kant sometimes forgets, that regulative principles transcend possible experience only quantitatively and not qualitatively.

If each of the Dialectic's three main compartments involves a kind of illusion, and every illusion stems from a regulative principle's seeming to be objective, then one would expect Kant to offer three (kinds of) regulative principles, one each for psychology, cosmology and theology. So he does. Suggesting that a regulative principle advises us to view the world *as if* we knew the principle to be objectively true, he applies this successively to each chapter of the Dialectic:

In conformity with these ideas as principles we shall, *first*, in psychology connect all the appearances of our mind, *as if* the mind were a simple substance. *Secondly*, in cosmology, we must follow up the conditions of appearances, in an enquiry which is to be regarded as never allowing of completion, just *as if* the series of appearances were in itself endless. *Thirdly*, in the domain of theology, we must view everything that can belong to the context of possible experience *as if* the sensible world itself had a single, highest and all-sufficient ground beyond itself, namely, a self-subsistent, original, creative reason.[23]

Really, there is no regulative principle which bears on the paralogisms. Consider 'The soul is a simple substance'. Granted, it is not an objective truth; but to make it out to be a regulative principle, Kant has to say that 'advantage can result' from acting 'as if' it were objectively true.[24] This, in fact, has no content. 'The soul is a simple substance' does not generate any advice, good or bad, because the obstacle to allowing it as objectively true is not quantitative. Kant's notion of a 'maximum' is idle here, and so there is no sense of direction which could give content to the notion of acting *as if* the soul were a simple substance.

This is not to deny that the paralogisms rest upon an intellectual illusion, fairly so-called. My concept of myself has a role in my conceptual scheme which *seems* to – though really it does not – show that I am a simple substance. But there the comparison with regulative principles ends. Kant tries to round it out by describing 'all *illusion*', in words tailored to fit the paralogisms, as consisting 'in treating the *subjective* condition of thinking as being knowledge of the *object*'.[25] This exploits

[22] 693, 691.
[23] 700, quoted with many omissions but with no other changes.
[24] 711–12; see the whole paragraph on 710–12. For a desperate attempt by Kant to extract advice from rational psychology, see 421.
[25] A 396. Regarding the final point in this paragraph, see 362–3.

an unclarity. The 'subjective condition of our thinking' which is relevant to the paralogisms is a necessity of thought, stemming from the role of 'I' in the Cartesian basis; whereas the so-called 'subjective condition of thinking' involved in regulative principles is not a necessity but merely a desideratum – a scientific procedure which is safe and may be helpful.

The application of the theory of dialectical illusion to the field of cosmology needs extended discussion. I shall take it up in §90 below.

Kant writes at length about the supposedly regulative status of some theological statement or other.[26] This looks as bad as the psychological application: what prevents us from discovering whether God exists is not the mere size of the task – a 'maximum' of something we can manage in smaller doses – and so we cannot have a sense of direction which would give content to the notion of acting 'as if' God existed. Kant tries to link 'God exists' with a pair of scientific regulative principles.

(1) The first of these is the teleological principle, that every feature of a healthy organism is somehow conducive to its survival (or, apparently, in a footnote on 715, that every feature of the universe brings 'advantage' to something). This could be seen as enjoining us always to seek teleological explanations of phenomena and never to despair of finding them, but Kant does not justify calling this *good* advice. The link between teleology and theology is also fragile. It involves sliding from the teleological notion of 'the purposive unity' of things which are 'connected according to teleological laws', across to the theological notion of the 'wise purposes' of a 'supreme intelligence' which is the 'cause of the universe'.[27] Kant rings many changes on this theme, but I shall ignore them all.

(2) He also links God's existence with what I shall call the *principle of unity* (Kant says 'maxim of unity' and 'principle of genera'). This says in effect that the perfect, complete science would be crowned by a single law from which, together with definitions and structural descriptions, all other laws would follow. The single law would express the 'single...absolutely fundamental power' of the members of the 'one single highest and universal genus'.[28] One can see why Kant would approve of the advice generated by this principle, namely to seek unceasingly for further unity in one's knowledge; for that is the driving

26 713–30; see also 644–8, 700–1, 706.
27 These phrases are all from 714–15; see also 726–9.
28 These two phrases are on 677 and 687 respectively.

force of ascending reason. But the link with theology is tenuous. It depends upon associating 'The world can be described in a sharply pyramidal science' with 'The world is the work of a single, single-minded architect or creator'.[29] Sometimes Kant yokes teleology with unity in phrases like 'systematic and purposive ordering of the world' and 'systematic and purposive unity'. But the issues they raise are separate from one another as well as from theology.

Kant also presents another trio of supposedly regulative principles of which the most interesting are the principles of *homogeneity* and *variety*, according to which any two objects are alike in some scientifically significant respect and unlike in some other. The former of these points towards the principle of unity. Kant's discussion of them (676–91) is lively and penetrating, but it does not mesh with the rest of the Dialectic, and reads as though it were composed at a different time for another purpose.

§ 87. Are there any regulative principles?

We should look harder at the claim that regulative principles cannot be either proved or disproved. One may confirm a universal statement or disconfirm an existential one without ransacking the whole of reality, item by item, or the whole of logical space, possibility by possibility. This is because the statement may be supported by, or in conflict with, a well-tested scientific theory.

For example, one might confirm the principle of unity by actually finding a sharply pyramidal and utterly comprehensive science, thus identifying 'the single highest and universal genus' etc. Or one might, by comparing mutilated organisms with unmutilated ones, show that a given organ was not conducive to health or survival. Again, there are positive grounds for saying that there is no qualitative difference between two electrons.

It may be said that (dis)confirming is not the same as (dis)proving, and that Kant's claim is only that regulative principles cannot be (dis)proved – i.e. absolutely conclusively (dis)confirmed. But the fact that a given principle cannot be (dis)proved, in that sense, does not imply that it should be regarded only as a piece of scientific advice and not as an objective statement; and so that defence of Kant fails to save his position.

Kant might weaken his position in a different way. He could say that

---

[29] See 721–3. Next two quoted phrases: 726; 727.

a principle is to count as regulative *now* if, as well as being salutary in the required way, it is not (dis)confirmed by any scientific theory which *now* merits respect as being well tested and not yet refuted. That account, in which a principle's status as regulative could be a temporary one, would not have been acceptable to Kant. Still, it ought to be acceptable to us. The principle of unity, for instance, might be seen as regulative *now*. The time may come when any well-informed person should accept the principle as true, or when everyone will reject it as false; but at this stage in the development of science it may embody some good advice – 'Always try to increase the unity of science'. Another example might be the 'principle of connexity', which says that every physical property is law-connected with some other physical property.[30] This does good work when adopted as a regulative principle, but no one can say that it cannot ever be strongly (dis)-confirmed.

A principle which was guaranteed to be permanently regulative would have to be necessarily incapable of (dis)confirmation. That privilege might belong to a principle which was somehow presupposed by scientific endeavour as such, so that its confirmation would be question-begging and its disconfirmation self-refuting. I doubt if there are any such principles. Certainly, the determinist principle is not one, for there is now strong evidence that it is false.

In further considering the Appendix to the Dialectic, we shall have simply to forget the doubts which I have raised in this section.

§ 88. Regulative and constitutive

The antonym of 'regulative' is 'constitutive'. So Kant's doctrine about dialectical error can be expressed thus: There are regulative principles which appear to be constitutive, and error results if we allow ourselves to be deceived by this illusion. In the Appendix, however, Kant's attitude to this matter is extremely unstable.

He sometimes says that regulative principles ought to be accepted also as constitutive, i.e. as not mere vehicles for advice but also as statements of fact. For example, of the supposedly regulative idea of God,

---

[30] G. Schlesinger, *Method in the Physical Sciences* (London, 1963), Ch. 3. The relevance of Kantian regulative principles to the contemporary philosophical scene is contended for by S. G. French, 'Kant's Constitutive-Regulative Distinction', *The Monist* (1967). But French can make his case only by construing 'regulative' very thinly, taking it to cover anything which is heuristically helpful and not plainly true or false, with no restriction to principles which transcend experience quantitatively.

he says: 'I shall not only be entitled, but shall also be constrained, to realise this idea, that is, to posit for it a real object.'[31] The oddity of this is hardly lessened by Kant's adding that the posited object is only 'a something which I do not at all know in itself'. We should bury this, along with everything else Kant says about God in the Appendix. Sometimes, though, he says the same thing about other regulative ideas or principles, as when he remarks of one of them that if we are to be assured that it will not cause us 'to follow a path which is perhaps quite contrary to that prescribed by nature itself', then we must know that it is 'in accordance... with nature' when construed as constitutive. This deserts the view that a regulative principle embodies good, *safe* advice, and it abolishes the doctrine about the source of dialectical error.

Perhaps we can explain this strange departure of Kant's from his basic position. He thinks that regulative principles, construed as advice, urge us always to seek further unity in our corpus of knowledge; so they reflect reason's supposedly relentless drive towards the unconditioned; so they amount to more than mere *advice*. Kant may be trying to say this when he becomes diverted into the claim I am trying to explain. That is, observing that regulative principles are not mild imperatives, or maxims of prudence which we may ignore if we wish, he drifts into saying that they are not imperatives at all but indicatives which describe the world. That would explain a passage where he denies that the principle of unity is 'merely an economical contrivance whereby reason seeks to save itself... trouble':

Such a selfish purpose can very easily be distinguished from the [reputable] idea [of a unified science]. For in conformity with the idea everyone presupposes that this unity of reason accords with nature itself, and that reason... does not here beg but command.[32]

If this is not the slide which I have described, then it is something even worse.

(I should mention a strange paragraph which purports to show the objective or constitutive truth of 'the law of genera', which is what I have earlier called the principle of homogeneity:

If among the appearances which present themselves to us, there were so great a variety that even the acutest human understanding could never by comparison of them detect the slightest similarity, the [regulative] law of genera would have no sort of standing; and the understanding itself would be non-existent and therefore no experience would be possible.[33]

[31] 705. Next quotation: 688–9.   [32] 681; see also the paragraph on 678–9.
[33] 681–2, with many omissions; see also the two paragraphs on 684–5.

But the law of genera says that any two things are similar in some non-trivial respect, whereas Kant is here defending only the modest truth that some things must resemble some other things.)

Sometimes Kant says only that we *may* accept some regulative principles as constitutive:

> There is nothing whatsoever to hinder us from *assuming* these ideas to be also objective...The psychological and theological ideas contain no antinomy, and involve no contradiction. How, then, can anyone dispute their objective reality [i.e. the existence of objects corresponding to them]? He who denies their possibility must do so with just as little knowledge as we can have in affirming it. (701)

This again betrays the doctrine of dialectical error, for it implies that no harm can come of the 'illusion', if indeed it is an illusion. I neither know nor care why Kant said this. He explicitly restricts this permissive view to the areas of psychology and theology, where the notion of a regulative principle is a non-starter anyway.

A third position which Kant sometimes takes does respect the view that dialectical error arises from mistaking regulative principles for constitutive ones. It is the position that we can, but ought not to, use regulative principles constitutively. In this vein, he speaks of 'errors which arise from our using the idea of a supreme being...constitutively, and not regulatively only',[34] and proceeds to catalogue the vices which, he says, are nourished by the constitutive use of regulative principles. I cannot find that he ever tells a believable tale about what goes wrong when a regulative principle is used constitutively. Presumably that is because he does not even have a coherent account of what it is to misuse a regulative principle in that way. If some intellectual diabolist said 'I want to use a regulative principle constitutively, and hang the consequences; tell me how to go about it', Kant has no answer.

Kant's best view is not that the constitutive use of regulative principles is mandatory, permissible, or impermissible, but that it is impossible. This is the view that if a principle is incapable of being (dis)confirmed, as Kant thinks that regulative principles are, then *there is no difference* between accepting the advice it embodies and believing that it is true as a matter of fact. Thus, for example, acting as though there were always more world than one had found is the same as believing that the world is non-finite, but acting as though it will rain tomorrow is not the same as believing that it will rain tomorrow. On this account, then,

---

[34] 717. The list of vices: 717–22.

a regulative principle is one which cannot be construed as having more than an imperative content.

This still leaves room for a mistake about regulative principles, which Kant might claim to be the source of dialectical error. It is not the mistake of misusing a regulative principle, but rather that of thinking that some regulative principle is a constitutive one, and thus thinking that one's entitlement to accept it rests upon knowledge of the world rather than upon the principle's embodying sound, safe advice. This is a philosophical rather than a scientific error, which explains why Kant is implausible when he tries to represent it as involving scientific vices of various sorts.

Here is Kant's fourth and best view:

Transcendental ideas never allow of any constitutive employment. When regarded in that mistaken manner, and therefore as supplying concepts of certain objects, they are but pseudo-rational, merely dialectical concepts. On the other hand, they have an excellent, and indeed indispensably necessary, regulative employment.[35]

We misapprehend the meaning of this idea if we regard it as the assertion or even as the assumption of a real thing, to which we may proceed to ascribe the ground of the systematic order of the world...The idea is posited only as being the point of view from which alone that unity, which is so essential to reason and so beneficial to the understanding, can be further extended.

As the second passage indicates, the point is epistemological: we must not think that regulative principles are constitutive, because, as Kant says elsewhere, we must not believe that what entitles us to accept them is our 'insight' into reality rather than 'the speculative interest of reason'.

Now, the regulative principle which most interests Kant is the one which supposedly guides ascending reason in all its endeavours, ordering it always to seek for the conditions of anything which is conditioned. Let us try to warn ourselves, in the manner of Kant's fourth and best view, against succumbing to 'illusion' in connexion with this.

[35] 672. Next quotation: 709; see also 676, 814–15. Final quotation in this paragraph: 704. Kemp Smith's translation tends to suppress this fourth view about regulative principles. On 694 Kant is translated as allowing that regulative principles could, though wrongly, be 'employed as objective principles', which suggests the third view that the constitutive use of a regulative principle is possible but wrong. The word 'employed', however, has no warrant in the German. On the same page, Kant says that one might *view* or *regard* a regulative principle as constitutive, which points unambiguously to the fourth view; but Kemp Smith renders this as '*treat* as constitutive', which could mean 'use as constitutive', thus expressing the third view rather than the fourth. The phrase 'treated as constitutive' also occurs objectionably on 716 and 730.

What is the danger? Perhaps it is the danger that we shall think that what entitles us to insist upon seeking conditions is that we are assured that items of the kinds in question – events, parts of the physical world etc. – always do actually have conditions. But if that is where reason's 'illusion' leads, then its sole function is to engender confidence in the Antithesis of each antinomy; and so Kant should 'solve' the antinomal problems by advising us to drop each Antithesis because we have no firm support for it. In fact, as I showed in §46, his actual treatments of the antinomies are nothing like that and so we cannot countenance this version of the error which is engendered by the 'illusion' inherent in reason.

Another possible account of the threatening error is this: We are in danger of thinking that the sought-for conditions can always be found. But why should that be regarded as an error? What intellectual malpractice can it produce or encourage? It would indeed be bad for us to think that the conditions can always be found quickly, or easily, or by anyone, but Kant rightly does not suggest that *that* mistake is encouraged by an inevitable illusion associated with the 'principle of reason'.

What Kant does say about the error which tempts us in this connexion is distressingly obscure:

The [regulative] principle peculiar to reason...in its logical employment is: – to find for the conditioned knowledge obtained through the understanding the unconditioned whereby its unity is brought to completion. But this logical maxim can become a [constitutive] principle of *pure reason* only through our assuming that if the conditioned is given, the whole series of conditions, subordinated to one another – a series which is therefore itself unconditioned – is likewise given, that is, is contained in the object and its connection.[36]

He simply does not tell us what he means by 'the whole series' being 'given' or 'contained in the object and its connection', and so we are never allowed to understand what the mistake is which we are apt to fall into through an illusion inherent in 'the principle peculiar to reason'. Kant was in enough trouble when he took the mistake to have the form 'thinking that regulative principle *R* is constitutive'. Now he is describing it as having the form 'being led by *R* to accept constitutive principle *C*', and this increases his difficulties; for now he has to say what *C* is, and all he can give us is the mysterious 'If the conditioned is

[36] 364; see also 389 and 526.

given, so are all its conditions'. As I showed in §46 above, when Kant tries to put this account to work he succeeds only in making vacuous, and therefore idle, the whole notion of regulativeness. What happens is that certain principles of the form $(x)(Fx \rightarrow (\exists y)(Fy \ \& \ yRx))$ are said to be only regulative, or are said only to 'set us a task'; this seems to deny our right to say that associated with any F item there actually *is* an endless series of its R-conditions; but really it denies only that if we are 'given' an F item we are thereby 'given' the series of its R-conditions. But *that* had no part in generating the infinity-problems which Kant purports to be solving. It is something we had no inclination to assert in the first place, and indeed – to repeat the point – it is not even clearly intelligible.

Kant also speaks of 'the principle, that the series of conditions... extends to the unconditioned' (365). If this is a rewording of the principle I have been discussing, then it takes us no further. On the face of it, though, it seems to be the different principle that every series of conditions *terminates* in something unconditioned. But how could that arise from a misunderstanding of the injunction always to seek the conditions for anything conditioned? Furthermore, it relates to the antinomies in a most peculiar way; for instead of being the source of each antinomal impasse, the principle is surely at most the source of the Thesis in each antinomy – i.e. of the view that the relevant series terminates. Since Kant's sympathies are generally with the Antithesis, at least in the first two antinomies, he might well be inclined to blame reason's malfunction – its succumbing to intellectual 'illusion' – for the lines of thought behind the Theses; but his official theory, clearly, is that the 'illusion' generates the whole antinomal clash and not just one side of it.

I cannot find any viable candidate for the role of the constitutive principle which may be mistaken for the regulative principle that one should always seek the conditions etc.

§ 89. The architectonic of the Dialectic

I can now deal briskly with the relation of Kant's theory of reason to the over-all shape of Book II of the Dialectic.

An inference of reason may be categorical, hypothetical, or disjunctive, depending upon whether its 'major premiss' is subject–predicate, conditional, or disjunctive. Kant regards this as a fundamental three-part division of the functions of reason, ascending as well as descending.

He further claims that this corresponds to a division of metaphysics into its three branches – psychology, cosmology, theology:

[I must show] how reason, simply by the synthetic employment of that very function of which it makes use in categorical inferences, is necessarily brought to the concept of the absolute unity of the *thinking subject*, how the logical procedure used in hypothetical inferences leads to the idea of the completely unconditioned *in a series* of given conditions, and finally how the mere form of the disjunctive inference must necessarily involve the highest concept of reason, that of a *being of all beings.*[37]

This is an ambitious programme. Kant's execution of two-thirds of it is dismal.

A tenuous link between the subject–predicate form and the soul can be excogitated from the first paralogism's remarks about the soul as 'the absolute subject' of all one's judgments. I showed in §24 that those remarks are fatally flawed, but even if we accept them uncritically they are much too weak for Kant's present purposes. He is committed to saying that when reason ascends in the categorical manner – presumably seeking, for some proposition, premisses from which it follows through a categorical inference – it is 'necessarily brought' to the idea of the soul as a simple substance which has 'personality' and so on. He does not even try to demonstrate this.

At the start of the psychology chapter, where the job should be done, Kant instead quietly shifts his ground. Ignoring the use of reason in ordinary categorical inferences, and the associated ascending activities, he plunges straight into the topic of 'dialectical inferences', that is, ones which involve error induced by 'illusion'. These are brought under Kant's two classifications, as categorical etc. and as psychological etc., and in this context the link between the subject–predicate form and the soul is not altogether implausible. At least, we can recognize the actual paralogisms in it: 'In the first kind of [dialectical] inference I conclude from the transcendental concept of the subject, which contains nothing manifold, the absolute unity of this subject itself, of which, however, . . . I possess no concept whatsoever.'[38] But Kant has *jumped* to the topic of dialectical inferences, and simply shirked the task – to which his theory of reason commits him – of explaining how all this grows, through a natural illusion, out of the ordinary, non-dialectical uses of reason. Later on, he speaks of a mere 'correspondence' between the paralogisms

[37] 392–3; see also 432–3.
[38] 397–8. Next reference: 432. For a final attempt by Kant to connect rational psychology with the theory of reason, see 710–12.

and ordinary categorical inferences, which virtually admits that in this part of the Dialectic the theory of reason has no explanatory value.

The theory's bearing upon cosmology needs a fuller discussion, which I postpone until my next section.

That there should be an integral connexion between God and disjunction is, Kant admits, 'a thought which, at first sight, seems utterly paradoxical' (393). Section 2 of the theology chapter is a pertinacious attempt to base theology on disjunction, apparently calling on several distinct theories which I shall not try to disentangle.[39] The main argument goes as follows. Kant understands disjunction as exclusive – 'P or Q but not both' – and so he associates it with the notion of complementary pairs of predicates, such as 'red' and 'not red', 'wise' and 'not wise'. In any such pair, Kant thinks, one member is positive and one negative, and the former is the senior partner: to understand 'not wise' one must understand 'wise', but not vice versa. Now, any individual thing is describable by one member from each such pair of predicates; so the thought of an individual thing carries with it the thought of the set of all such predicate-pairs; and, because the positive member is always somehow senior or dominant, that leads to the idea of something which falls under every positive predicate, that is, to the idea of an *ens realissimum*! This is an unconvincing tale. Also, it concerns the notion of the complete description or determination of an individual thing, and has little enough to do with disjunctive propositions – for certainly there are plenty of disjunctions which do not involve complementary pairs of predicates. As for disjunctive *inferences*: they are altogether irrelevant, and Kant's attempt to bring them into the story only makes things worse (604–5). Let us drop the whole sorry topic.

Kant smuggled into B a quite different attempt to make the Dialectic's choice of subject-matter look natural, if not inevitable. It is the famous remark: 'Metaphysics has as the proper object of its enquiries three ideas only: *God, freedom,* and *immortality*.'[40] This implies that the paralogisms are about nothing but immortality, and the antinomies about nothing but freedom; and in any case it has nothing to do with reason.

The theory of reason, as well as failing to show how dialectical difficulties about psychology and theology arise, also fails to illuminate those difficulties once they have arisen. For one thing, the theory emphasizes an 'illusion' concerning the status of maxims or regulative

---

[39] 599–611. The main argument: the three paragraphs on 603–4.
[40] 395n. see also xxix–xxx.

principles, and we have seen that the latter are not seriously relevant to anything in the psychology or theology chapters.

Also, consider the notion of *series*. On the one hand, this seems to have no significant role in the paralogisms or in two of the three theological arguments, and accordingly we find Kant using 'series' to mark off cosmology from the other two dialectical areas.[41] On the other hand, it is natural to think of reason's whole (ascending) task as having to do with the ascent of series of conditions, and in conformity with this thought we also find Kant associating 'series' with dialectical error generally.[42] He is evidently undecided about the place of 'series' in the whole dialectical scheme.

I conjecture that Kant developed his theory of dialectical error at a time when he envisaged using it to explain only the cosmological materials of the antinomy chapter, and that he later decided to apply it also to psychology and theology, without considering whether the stretch would tear the fabric. That would explain the inconsistent handling of 'series', which I have just noted, and also the claim that every idea of reason is 'the concept of a maximum' – which clearly fits cosmology far better than it does psychology or theology.[43] The conjecture could also explain Kant's sometimes saying that all dialectical error has an antinomal form, with reason being 'involved in unavoidable self-conflict',[44] yet at other times saying explicitly – as one might expect him to, given the way he has organized Book II of the Dialectic – that the antinomal form of trouble is restricted to cosmology.[45] It is the former of these accounts which, if my conjecture is right, belongs to his earlier position in which dialectical error is equated with the antinomies; so I must not hide the fact that it occurs also in material written for the second edition of the *Critique*. But I think that this, rather than refuting my conjecture, merely shows that Kant remained in thrall to the picture with which he began. After all, he had no coherent alternative to it. Although his later position is that his theory of reason covers psychology and theology as well, we have seen that he does almost nothing to make this believable.

The finer structure of Book II can be dealt with summarily. Kant claims to have categorial bases for the fourfold treatment of the soul and for the fourfold division of cosmology.[46] He also says that 'There

---

[41] 379; 391; 392; 398; 436; 441; 442.

[42] 364; 387-9; 393-4; 671.   [43] 384; see also 596 and 693.

[44] xix n.; see also xx, 22-3, A xii.   [45] 433; 701.

[46] 402 (cf. A 404) and 438-43. Next quotation: 618.

are only three possible ways of arguing for the existence of God by means of speculative reason', but he does not say why.

§90. Reason and cosmology

That was all negative: Kant's theory of dialectical error does not even approximately fit his work on psychology and theology. In the case of the problems raised in the antinomies, the situation is better, for there is at least a *prima facie* fit between the theory and the material which is supposed to fall under it. The problems can be presented as antinomies, they do involve series, they do involve concepts of maxima, and they can be connected with the notion of 'ascending' pursuits of various sorts of theoretical completeness; and these are features which every dialectical area is supposed to possess. Furthermore, the cosmology chapter is supposed to involve the conditional form in a special way, and so indeed it does. Each antinomy involves a series in which every member is related by a conditional to an earlier member – '*If t* is a time, then there is a time t^* which is earlier than t', and so on. This is admittedly weak, but it is better than the link between psychology and the subject–predicate form, let alone that between theology and disjunction.

However, although the theory of reason fits the antinomies chapter, it does not help us to understand it or to find solutions to the problems it raises. I shall try to justify this claim.

To take hold of one end of the thread, consider how regulative principles bear upon the antinomies.[47] In discussing this matter, I shall concentrate on the spatial half of the first antinomy. The discussion is easily extendable to the temporal half, and, less easily, to the second antinomy as well. Despite Kant's claim to be generalizing over 'all cosmical concepts', we must leave the third and fourth antinomies aside.

If the spatial half of the first antinomy rests on a regulative principle, it is presumably the principle 'Every finite amount of world excludes some world'. If this is regulative, then it amounts only to the advice 'Always assume that there is more world than you have so far discovered.' That sometimes seems to be Kant's view of it: 'However far we may have advanced in the ascending series, we must always enquire

---

[47] The main passages are two paragraphs on 443–5, two on 509–12, two on 525–7, two on 536–8, and three paragraphs starting near the end of 545. Next quoted phrase: 514; see also 533–4.

for a still higher member of the series, which may or may not become known to us through experience.'[48] But, as I pointed out in §46 above, if Kant really thinks that the most that can be said for the world's non-finiteness is that we ought never to be sure that we have discovered the whole world, then the spatial half of the first antinomy dissolves far more rapidly and completely than he ever allows. Also, it would follow that the Antithesis-argument, which undertakes to prove that the world cannot be finite, is downright invalid, yet Kant never alludes to any defect in it.

As I tried to show in §46, Kant does not really think that the antinomies do involve principles which are 'regulative' in the official sense expounded in the Appendix. When the language of regulativeness occurs in the antinomies chapter, it has changed its meaning. Kant is not here using phrases like 'set as a task' to distinguish (regulative) advice from (constitutive) statements. Rather, he is using them to convey his phenomenalist view about the basic meaning of any objective statement. He is not saying: 'Don't regard P as a statement of fact, but only as a bit of advice', but rather: 'Understand that P – which is a statement of fact about the phenomenal realm – is equivalent to something of the form "If you do such and such you will discover so and so".' It is this phenomenalistic conditional which Kant is expressing – unhappily, I admit – in terms of something's being 'set as a task'.

Sometimes Kant uses the form 'x is set as a task' both to embody his phenomenalism and at the same time to make a contrast with 'x is already given'. Thus: 'If the conditioned as well as its condition are things in themselves, then upon the former being given, the regress to the latter is not only *set as a task*, but therewith already really *given*.'[49] We have already met this kind of talk. It reflects Kant's view that the maxim 'Search for the conditions of anything conditioned' can be mistaken for the objective principle 'If something conditioned is given, then the whole series of all its conditions is given'. Kant says explicitly that this is the source of all the antinomies: 'The whole antinomy of pure reason rests upon the dialectical argument: If the conditioned is given, the entire series of all its conditions is likewise given; objects of the senses are given as conditioned; therefore, etc.' I still contend that no clear sense attaches to this.

There is another way in which the theory of reason may be brought to bear upon the antinomies. I mentioned earlier that Kant sometimes

---

[48] 546; see also 362–3; 536–7; 547–8.
[49] 526. Next quotation: 525.

expresses the warning that a given principle is regulative, not constitutive, by saying that a given concept is an idea of reason, not an objective concept which could be instantiated in experience. He often emphasizes that one could not encounter an instance of an idea: 'The absolute whole of all appearances...*is only an idea*...We can never represent it in image';[50] 'Just because they are only ideas they have...no relation to any object that could be given as coinciding with them'; 'These ideas are one and all transcendent...[They] carry the synthesis to a degree which transcends all possible experience.' What bearing can such remarks have upon the problems Kant is considering?

On the face of it, they side with the Antithesis: if we could not experience the whole world, that is presumably because it is non-finite in extent; and similarly, perhaps, with past time. Kant might reply that he is not taking sides, for in one place he says that the point is only that one could not *know* that one had experienced the whole world (510–11), which is consistent with the world's actually being finite.

If Kant is not taking sides in the antinomal conflict, is he helping to resolve it? If so, it must be through the following type of doctrine: 'Because nothing could count as knowing that one had experienced the whole of x, the very concept of the whole of x is illegitimate, and so no question about the nature of the whole of x makes sense.' Applied to the first antinomy, that would imply that both sides are incoherent because both purport to say something about the whole extended world, and this is an item which one could not know that one had encountered in experience.

I see no reason to accept that argument for the unintelligibility of 'the whole world'. The proponent of the Thesis could defend himself against it, and his opponent could do so even more easily: 'My claim is that, given any finite portion of world, there is some portion of world outside it. Now show me how in that I have used the concept of an illegitimate totality.'

Also, if it were straightforwardly true that 'Kant claimed that all talk about the Universe as a whole was improper',[51] the first antinomy would be reduced to rubble, and no room would be left for the complex dismantlings presented in Chapters 7 and 8 above. I do not think that that was his position.

Whenever Kant says something intelligible about 'totalities' or the

[50] 384. Next two quotations: 393; 447.
[51] R. G. Swinburne, 'The Beginning of the Universe', *Proceedings of the Aristotelian Society*, suppl. vol. (1966), p. 127.

like, it turns out to be a variant on themes discussed in Chapter 7 above. In a nutshell, what he rejects is not 'all talk about the Universe as a whole', but only talk of that kind which is not understood, phenomenalistically, as talk about possible sequences of future experiences.[52] In Kant's own words, what is under attack is 'that idea of absolute totality which holds only as a condition of things in themselves', i.e. the idea of the universe as something whose present existence consists in more than some facts about an endless series of future possible discoveries. Here again: 'The members of the series [are] given only as following upon one another in time; and I have therefore, in this case, no right to assume the absolute *totality* of the synthesis and of the series thereby represented.' This is that 'futurizing move' which I discussed in §42 above. The notion of a 'totality' – as linked with that of an 'idea' of reason which cannot be realized in anything empirically given – does not add anything to it.

The futurizing move connects with the 'weakening move' – that is, the description of the world's size in the form 'Every finite amount of it leaves some out', which seemed to Kant to fall short of saying that the world is outright infinite (see §45 above). That same line of thought underlies some of his remarks about 'totalities'. For example, he says of a certain series that it is 'never given in entire completeness, either as finite or as infinite', and implies that cosmological series generally 'can never be regarded as being in themselves in their totality either finite or infinite' (533–4). To understand this, we must grasp Kant's difficulties with the concept of infinity, which I discussed in Chapter 7. It is not helpful to introduce the notion of an 'idea' of reason or its kindred.

Admittedly, in one place Kant says that 'the absolute whole of all appearances' is 'a *problem* to which there is no solution', because 'we can never represent it in image' (384). That seems to apply to 'the whole world' on either construal of the phrase, i.e. whether it is taken rationalistically or in a more phenomentalisic manner; and so the remark conflicts with my exegesis. But too many passages go the other way for weight to be given to this one isolated remark.

Also possibly conflicting with my interpretation, there is Kant's account of reason's 'illusion' as consisting in the view that 'the whole series of conditions is given'. I remain sceptical about whether this really means anything; but I should now point out that it could mean '...given as a legitimate subject of thought and discourse', and on that

---

52 On this point I agree with G. H. Bird, *ibid.* pp. 148–9, against Swinburne. Next two quotations: 534; 528–9.

interpretation Kant would be identifying the 'illusion' with the view that we can talk sense about the whole world, the whole of past time, and so on. The fact remains, though, that this does not square with most of the text. And, in any case, it is at least as reasonable to suppose that the notion of the whole series being 'given' is to be understood in terms of 'given prior to all regress'; and on *that* reading, Kant is identifying the illusion with the view that we can talk *non-phenomenalistic* sense about the whole world, the whole of past time, etc.

I conclude that no fresh light is thrown on the antinomies by the notion of an idea of reason. This notion introduces 'not a concept of an object', 'could not be encountered in experience', 'not a true totality', and so on; but Kant's uses of these are, at best, rewordings of those views about phenomenalism and infinity which I discussed back in Chapter 7 without help from 'reason', 'regulative principles', and the rest. That completes my case for saying that the theory of reason, although it fits the antinomies chapter better than the other two, still does not significantly help with that chapter's philosophical content.

INDEX

SUBJECTS

antinomies, 4f., §39, 280–3, §90
  first, chs. 7–8
  second, ch. 9
  third, ch. 10, 241
  fourth, §76

brain-bisection, §29

categories, 24, §10, 35, 54, 187, 226, 262, 283
causation, §7, §20, §59, 190–3, §64, 221f., 225f., 242f., 246f.
character, intelligible/sensible, 190f., 203
concepts, §6, §8, 28, 70f.
conditions, 121, §46, 187n., 240f., 259f., §84, 278–80
cosmology, see antinomies

deliberation, see freedom (agency)
divisibility
  of matter, 41–6, 83, §30, §53, §55, §57
  of space, 13, 170f., §58
  of time, 58, 182
  real, 41–3, §54, 172–4, 180

empiricism, 3, §9, 36, §§16–17, 119f., 124f., 144f., §42, §45, 223f., 286–8
ens realissimum, 236, §§78–80, 256f., 282
existence, §21, §§72–4, §80

freedom, 282
  accountability, §§63–7
  agency, §§68–70
  cosmology, 4f., 159, §§59–60, 241

God, 5, 42, 60n., 110, 273–7, 282–4
  cosmological argument, 114, §§75–80, 256f.
  design argument, §81
  ontological argument, §§72–4, 248, §§79–80, 256

ideas
  Kantian, 268–70, 282, 286–8
  non-Kantian, §§4–5, §11
illusion, §85, 272f., §§88–9, 287f., see reason (theoretical)

infinity, 44, ch. 7, 162, 164, §57, 186f., 244f., 287

memory, 34f., §33, 122f., 125
Menge/Zahl, 132f.
monads, see Leibniz (substance)
morality, 209f., 219f., see also freedom (accountability)

noumena, 190, see things in themselves
number, §§43–4, 132

paralogisms, 4, §§22–3, §38, 223f., 272–3, 277, 281–3
  first, ch. 4
  second, 78, ch. 5, 272
  third, ch. 6
  fourth, 71–2

reactive attitudes, §§66–7
reason
  practical, 190–2, 202–4, 214, 220–2, 224
  theoretical, 2–4, 6f., 114–16, 136, §46, 191, 240, 244, ch. 12
regulative principles, 117, §46, 156, 268, §§86–8, 284–6
representations, 18, 113, 219

schematism, 58f., 225–6
self-consciousness, 30, 32–4, 66–9, 74, 101f., 264
soul
  identity, 86f., ch. 6
  sempiternity, §§25–6
  simplicity, ch. 5, 165, 272
space
  divisibility, §53, 170f., §58
  empty, §§48–50, 160
  outer sense, 54, 158, 166, 182f.
  relational theory, §§47–9
substance
  indivisibility, §§12–14, §§52–4
  mass-term, 43, §56
  sempiternity, §§19–21, 167, 242
  substratum, §§35–7
synthetic a priori, 6f., 182, 262

289

things in themselves, §§17–18, 62, 91f.,
107, 134–7, 167, §§61–2, §65, 221,
§71
time
beginning, §51
divisibility, 58, 104f., 182

empty, 159f.
inner sense, 54, 102, 193, 226f.
transcendental idealism, *see* empiricism *and*
things in themselves

understanding, 1, §6, 191, 258f., 261–4, 266

NAMES

Al-Azm, S. J., 5f., 119n., 148, 160n., 243
Alexander, H. G., 148, 152n.
Alston, W. P., 232n.
Anscombe, G. E. M., 103
Aquinas, T., 186, §75, 244–7, 253
Aristotle, 128, 186, 237
Arnauld, A., 84, 174f.
Austin, J. L., 228
Ayers, M. R., 19n.

Barker, S. F., 135n.
Baumer, W. H., 253n.
Baumgarten, A. G., 5, 154
Beck, L. W., 3n., 5, 16, 55, 93, 186, 191,
194, 202, 204, 219f., 223f.
Beebe, M. D., notes on 128, 149, 171
Bennett, J., 8, 37, 68; notes on 28, 83, 103,
107, 119, 145, 156, 226, 234, 237
Berkeley, G., 10f., 13, 19n., 24–6, 60, 106
Bird, G. H., notes on 112, 194, 287
Bolzano, B., 129n.
Broad, C. D., 103n., 148
Brook, J. A., 83n.
Brown, D. G., 211
Browne, T., 160
Buchdahl, G., 152n.

Cantor, G., 126, 129f.
Clarke, S., 144f., 149–51
Clerselier, 231
Cook, J., 144n.
Copleston, F. C., 247; notes on 3, 90, 245

Descartes, R., 5, 19n., 29n., 60, 66
existence, 229, 231
ideas, §§4–5
infinity, 126, 128, 130f., 141f.
self-consciousness, 32–4
soul, 72, 75–7, 82f., 85–7, 90
substance, §13
Deutscher, M., 99n.
Dretske, F., §41

Earman, J., 145n.

Edwards, P., 79n.
Ewing, A. C., 185f., 193

Flew, A., 11n.
Frege, G., 24, §21, 126, 129f., §72
French, S. G., 275n.

Gassendi, P., 33f., 229, 231
Geach, P. T., 239f., 246
Goethe, J. W. von, 79
Gram, M. S., 119n., 133n.

Hare, R. M., 23n.
Heimsoeth, H., 185f.
Hobart, R. E., 207n., 212n.
Hobbes, T., 90
Huby, P. M., 131
Hughes, R. I. G., 80n., 157
Hume, D., 5, 19n., 33, 55, 128, 242, 255
accountability, §63
cause, 20–2
ideas, 11, 13, 15f., 28

Ishiguro, H., 47n.

Jackson, H., 231n.
Johnson, B., 207f., 238n.

Kant, I.
*Metaphysical Foundations of Natural
Science*, 62, 152n., 155, §55, 176, 178f.
Prolegomena, 7, 62, 78n., 114n., 118,
261
other works, 3n., 55, 93, 101, 152f.,
238
Kemp Smith, N.
Commentary, 131, 184f., 193, 245; notes
on 1, 109, 120, 152
translation, 179, 185, 245; notes on 133,
154, 155, 165, 179, 180, 187, 259, 278
Kenny, A., 33n., 60, 68
Kleene, S. C., 126n.
Kneale, W. C., 42n., 232n.
Koyré, A., 142n.

Leibniz, G. W., 5f., 19n., 55, 61-3, 93, 239n., 248
  cosmological argument, 244, 246, 253
  ideas, 11f., 16, 29
  infinity, 126-8, 130, 135, 142
  innateness, §11
  rationalism, 29, §§16-17, 92, 194
  relations, §15, 143, 150f.
  self-consciousness, 32-3
  soul, §27
  space, §§47-50, 162
  substance, §14, 57, §27, 169-71, §56
  time, §51
  windowless monads, 51, 61f.
Llewelyn, J. E., 114n.
Locke, J., 19n., 33-5, 51, 60f., 93, 212, 235
  ideas, 10-13, 15f., 28f.
  infinity, 127
  innateness, §11
  substratum, 109f.
Lovejoy, A. O., 126n.

MacKay, D. M., 215n.
Malcolm, N., §§73-4, 252f.
Martin, C. B., 99n.
Martin, G., 115f., 137
Mendelssohn, M., 5, 57f.
Moore, G. E., 229

Nagel, T., §29
Newton, I., 132, 145, 152n.

Palter, R., 152n.
Parkinson, G. H. R., 83
Parsons, C., 183n.
Plantinga, A., 255n.
Popper, K. R., 215n.

Quine, W. V., 175n.

Remnant, P., 247n., 251n., 254f.
Rescher, N., 130, 150; notes on 46, 47, 51
Richman, R. J., 255n.

Russell, B., 33, 46n., 126n.
Ryle, G., 24n., §§69-70, 225

Savile, A., 37n.
Savitt, S., 176
Schlesinger, G., 275
Schlick, M., §63, 204-6, 225
Schopenhauer, A., 185f., 193
Sellars, W., 30f.
Shaffer, J., 230n.
Shoemaker, S., §§33-4, 109, 145, 153, 160
Smart, J. J. C., 251n., 253n.
Spinoza, B., 19n., 28f., 43f., 82, 90, 126n., 207f., 213f.
Strawson, P. F.
  Bounds of Sense, 31f., 68n., 91n., 94, 109n., §38, 119, 172, 186, 194, 204, 209, 242
  Freedom and Resentment, §§66-7, 225, 242
  Individuals, 68, 92, 111f.
Swartz, N., 145n.
Swinburne, R. G., 286, 287n.
Swing, T. K., 234n., 264n.

Taylor, R., 212
Thomson, J. F., 126n.

Wallace, J. D., 122n.
Walsh, W. H., 3n.
Watkins, J. W. N., 271
Watling, J. L., 43n.
Watson, R. A., 60n.
Weldon, T. D., 5n., 120n.
Whitrow, G. J., 182
Wilson, M., 83n.
Wisdom, J., 182
Wittgenstein, L., 68f., 128, 264
Wolff, C., 6, 93, 154
Wolff, R. P., 20f.

Yost, R. M., Jr., 12

Ziff, P., 23n.